# A History of the World Economy

# A History of the World Economy

## International Economic Relations since 1850

James Foreman-Peck

*Lecturer in Economics, University of Newcastle upon Tyne*

**BARNES & NOBLE BOOKS**
TOTOWA, NEW JERSEY

*First published in the USA 1983 by*
BARNES & NOBLE BOOKS
81 ADAMS DRIVE
TOTOWA, NEW JERSEY, 07512

© James Foreman-Peck, 1983

**Library of Congress Cataloging in Publication Data**

Foreman-Peck, James.
  A history of the world economy.
  1. Economic history—20th century.    2. Economic
  history—1750-1918.    3. International economic
  relations—History. I. Title.
  HC54.F565  1983  333'.09    82-24295
  ISBN 0-389-20337-8

Printed in Great Britain

# Contents

# Tables

# Figures and Maps

# Preface

International economic history frequently impinges on contemporary discussions of policy. Developing countries still pursue policies intended to minimise their dependence on manufactures from abroad because they believe international trade in the past has retarded their economic growth. Policy-makers in Britain generally until recently favoured free trade often on the unexamined assumption that in her nineteenth-century heyday Britain was well served by it. The interwar period stands as a reminder to all statesmen of the perils of competitive exchange rate depreciations and trade quotas. A return to a gold standard still holds a fascination for some. Yet despite the conscious and unconscious lessons drawn from the history of international economic relations there have been few attempts to synthesise the great volume of research undertaken in the last ten or fifteen years. This makes the area difficult for the student and may also lead to misdirections of research effort through a loss of perspective.

In trying to remedy this deficiency the reasons for its persistence became clear to me. Covering the whole period for almost one-and-a-half centuries involves a highly selective approach, as well as a compression of material. Too much compression involves excessive abstraction and history becomes a type of timeless, and possibly vacuous, theory. So I have tried to include concrete details – for example that Hungary and Czechosolvakia exchanged eggs for coal in 1932, to give some substance to the notion of bilateral trading – while excluding certain topics, such as the causes of the Great Depression in the United States, which do not *directly* bear on the economic relations between nations. Too little compression and selection overwhelms the reader with a mass of facts. The selection required means that this book is *a* history of the world economy not *the* history, which would be an impossible task. The book is not directly concerned with the process of economic growth and development within nations, but only considers growth in so far as it is caused by, or affects, international economic relations. Admittedly this is a difficult course to follow, with many alternative

xi

routes. So is the task I have set myself of writing about economic, not political, relations. Trade flows, commercial and exchange rate policies, foreign investment and international migration, all have political consequences which often give them their main significance, and are equally likely to have political causes of great interest. Although I try to take these into account, the central focus is on the actions traditionally described as economic.

The book attempts to link together international economic theory with history in the hope that both will gain. Furthermore, I wanted to do this in a non-technical way because, although technique is useful, I have found for many students, theoretical ideas become lost amidst what they see primarily as exercises in geometry or algebra. The ideas become discredited in having any relevance to social life, purely because of the way they are so often presented. The greater number of the theoretical concepts are outlined in the first three chapters, though some, such as the technology-gap and product cycle theories of trade, are deferred to later chapters where they are more relevant to the historical material. The repetition of these concepts in different historical contexts will become a way of fixing the ideas, I hope, as well as a way of testing the limits of their applicability.

The book's starting date was determined by the approximate beginning of the period that best corresponds with the central theoretical constructs of international economics. After a chapter that attempts to set the scene, two chapters cover the third quarter of the nineteenth century, one dealing with the history relevant to the pure theory of international trade, the other with that covered by the monetary theory. This division is followed for each of the other three eras into which the history is organised. The final chapter attempts a historical perspective on the international economy in the light of theories of distributive justice and the demands for a new international economic order of the 1970s.

In a book covering such a vast amount of ground it is possible to say confidently that experts in each of the fields covered are likely to find the treatments of their specialisms unsatisfactory. They would have found it more inadequate but for the numerous comments and suggestions of colleagues on draft chapters. I am very grateful to John Armstrong (Ealing College of Higher Education), Dudley Baines (London School of Economics), Steve Broadberry (University College, Cardiff), Forrest Capie (City University), Michael Collins (University of Leeds), Keith Cuthbertson (National Institute of Economic and Social Research), Lorraine Foreman-Peck (University of Newcastle upon Tyne),

Peter Lindert (University of California, Davis), Leslie Pressnell (University of Kent, Canterbury), John Redmond (University of Birmingham), David Rowe and Patrick Salmon (University of Newcastle upon Tyne) and Tom Ulen (University of Illinois, Urbana-Champaign), who all kindly read one or more draft chapters, but are not responsible for the remaining blemishes and omissions. Peter Lindert deserves special thanks for his stamina in reading more than anybody else. G. Austen, T. Balderston and D.E. Moggridge generously made available manuscripts which at the time had not been published. My students in Economic History II at the University of Newcastle upon Tyne also served by providing an audience for the book while it was being written.

# 1  International Economic Relations in the Middle of the Nineteenth Century

By the middle of the nineteenth century, Western Europe and its overseas offshoots, the United States especially, had achieved an unprecedented technological level that was affecting the whole world. Writing in 1847, Marx and Engels noted that the social class created by the new methods of production

by the rapid improvement of all instruments of production, by the immensely facilitated means of communication, draws all, even the most barbarian, nations into civilisation. The cheap prices of its commodities are the heavy artillery with which it batters down all Chinese walls, with which it forces the barbarians' intensely obstinate hatred of foreigners to capitulate.[1]

The history of international economic relations since 1850 is largely an account of the problems, the solutions, the benefits and costs created by this upsurge of economic activity. Destroying traditional industries and creating new, the new technology, machinery and chemistry in industry and agriculture, increased specialisation in production between nations and thereby boosted trade flows. Better communications, steam-ships, railways, the electric telegraph, stimulated the international movement of capital, labour and technology. Bursts of investment in the new techniques were associated with periodic crises which had repercussions on exports or imports. The need to pay for foreign goods by income earned abroad therefore required some adjustment of the economy in the face of these crises. These three themes, trade, factor mobility and balance of payment adjustment form the core of international economic relations. This and subsequent chapters trace out the ideas, institutions and economic conditions that encouraged the expanding

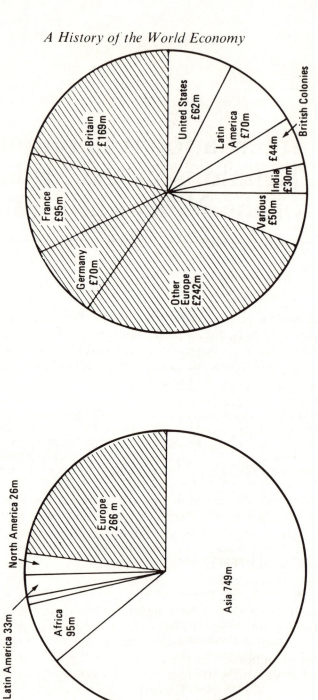

WORLD TRADE IN 1850
(MULHALL'S ESTIMATE), £m

Britain
£169m

United States
£62m

Latin
America
£70m

British Colonies

India
£30m

£44m

Various
£50m

France
£95m

Germany
£70m

Other
Europe
£242m

World Trade £832m

WORLD POPULATION IN 1850
(CARR SAUNDERS' ESTIMATE)

North America 26m

Latin America 33m

Africa
95m

Europe
266 m

Asia 749m

World Population 1171m

**Figure 1.1** World population and trade in 1850

international division of labour, and also explore the political and economic effects.

Viewed from Western Europe, Europe dominated world trade and income, but not world population (see Figure 1). Europe accounted for less than one-quarter of the world's population, but for almost 70 per cent of world trade at the mid-century.[2] One 'guesstimate' gives North-Western Europe almost one-third of world income earned by little over one-tenth of the people on the earth.[3] Within Europe, Britain, with one-third of total fixed steam power installed in the world's factories, achieved the highest national income per head and disproportionately engaged in international trade. Perhaps one-fifth of this trade by European measurements originated in, was destined for, or passed through Britain even though those islands were occupied by less than 2 per cent of the world's population in the middle of the nineteenth century. French trade, although the second largest national total, was little more than half of British trade.

This chapter attempts to set the scene in the 1850s by describing the political changes wrought by international trade at the time and earlier, explaining why these changes came about and showing the consequences. Then the chapter analyses the costs and benefits of trade and their distribution between countries. After considering contemporary doctrines of the gains from economic freedom, the focus shifts to colonialism and the slave and guano trades to bring out general conditions for there to be mutual benefits from trade. Moving on from commodities to countries, economic relations between Britain, India and the United States are described in detail, exploring the different patterns of specialisation and methods of finance of imports, whose political repercussions have already been shown.

## The political impact of mid-Victorian trade

The European and especially British rise to dominate the international economy went hand-in-hand with the extension of political control or influence. The exact nature of the relationship is controversial, some maintaining political action caused economic pre-eminence, and others, the view that will be argued here, that economic relations stimulated political influence. Even so, not all European political acquisitions of this period were primarily by-products of international trade. The rise of the nineteenth-century French empire in particular was fundamentally more politically motivated than was the British. Algeria was annexed in 1830 initially because the Restoration monarchy wanted a spectacular political success.[4] The Indo-Chinese colonies grew from a minor crisis over missionaries in the early 1860s partly as a result of Napoleon III's expansionary intentions. But British acquisitions and exercise of influence abroad were much more a consequence, direct or indirect, of commercial activity.

International economic relations could cause political changes where there was no ultimate source of authority for the consistent enforcement of rights. There was the same need as in domestic trade for the maintenance of law and order if economic relations were to take place on any scale. Gallagher and Robinson asserted that, to meet this need, mid-nineteenth-century British merchants preferred informal control, which allowed much less taxation and interference than if a formal empire had been imposed.[5] But if informal control was impossible, then direct British rule was imposed without hesitation to secure trade. Between 1841 and 1851 New Zealand, the Gold Coast, Labuan, Natal, the Punjab, Sind and Hong Kong were occupied or annexed. In the twenty years after the mid-century Berar, Oudh, Lower Burma, Kowloon, Lagos, the hinterland of Sierra Leone, Basutoland, Griqualand, Transvaal, Queensland and British Columbia were subject to the same process.

Despite the length of this list, empire-building had not begun in the middle of the nineteenth century. The thirteen British North American colonies had been founded and lost by then. Indeed they were engaged in commercial expansion overseas of their own. Most of the Indian sub-continent had fallen under British rule by 1818 as an indirect consequence of trade with Europe and because of wars between the French and British trading companies, on orders from their respective home countries at times of European hostilities. The impact of Europe on India is both the most striking example of the 'imperialism of trade' and in many respects the archetype of a large proportion of later nineteenth-century European acquisitions. Hence the process by which India came under British rule is worth elaborating briefly.

During the eighteenth century the old Moghul Empire at Delhi collapsed, opening the way both for a Hindu revival and for many adventurers who won their thrones by force.[6] In order to obtain security and the stable conditions which were necessary for their trade to make a profit, the British East India Company, and sometimes its servants independently, engaged in intrigue with native princes (each of the three Company stations at Bombay, Madras and Calcutta separately ran its own foreign policies). The Company therefore was drawn into war and the government of Indian provinces.

The continued British success in the eighteenth-century wars with such a vast and ancient civilisation is more problematic than that the wars should have been fought. Sea power, built up over centuries of long-distance trade, was a necessary, but not sufficient condition for eventually land battles had to be won. Superior weapons cannot explain the British victories because military technology was quite easily imported from Europe. Under Ranjit Singh (died 1839), the Sikhs did just this, building up a regular army that included Europeans among the officer corp and using French and Italian generals to train the troops. The Sikh infantry were equally effective as any available to the British in India, and the Sikh artillery was superior. Yet the Sikhs were defeated, and the Punjab annexed by Dalhousie on his own initiative in 1849, because of the lack of an orderly succession and the absence of civil discipline after Singh's death. The British ultimately won India because of the habitual loyalty of their military and civil officers and because, being interested primarily in trade, they did not usually threaten the social and religious objectives of Indian society – as had the Portuguese.

The Indian mutiny and revolt of 1857 shows how far this last generalisation is true. The use of pig and cow fat in Enfield rifle cartridges (that had to be bitten) succeeded in violating the beliefs of both Muslim and Hindu troops. The progressive annexation of territory, of which the latest had been Oudh, reduced the area in which the old ruling class could exercise their prerogatives and benefit from political office. Yet a full-scale revolt did not occur, otherwise the British could not have survived. Brutally suppressed by the Moghuls, the Sikhs had nothing to gain from a restoration of the Moghul empire. By and large the Hindus also preferred to be ruled by the British than by the Muslims, and similarly the Muslims preferred the British to the Hindus.

A relatively equitable and efficient public administration was however costly, as suggested by the continuing concern with the finances of the British East India Company until it was discredited by the Mutiny. The British profits from the Indian trade were barely adequate. Annexations of additional territories were therefore not regarded favourably by a government that would not receive the profits but would bear the costs. Where there was a more or less effective central government, the 'imperialism of trade' led to concessions rather than acquisitions.

Mid-century European trade with China followed this route. The Chinese were unwilling to have full diplomatic relations with the European 'barbarians' even though they allowed some commercial relations. Consequently any incident involving foreign nationals could easily explode into a war in which superior European military technology and organisation would be brought to bear.

Indian opium exports were the proximate cause of British military and naval intervention in China from 1839 to 1842. China had banned opium smoking in 1729, and in 1800 imports of opium were forbidden altogether.[7] By the early 1830s the Indian trade with Canton therefore depended on the ability of British merchants to smuggle opium, which was usually no great problem until 1839, when the law was enforced. The Chinese government allowed foreigners only to trade in Canton, which was too far from the main markets in Central China. There was strong pressure from Lancashire manufacturers, shipowners and advocates of international free trade to negotiate better conditions for British trade in China, as was being done by commercial treaties with the states of Europe and America in this period. In 1839 the Chinese insisted that someone should be handed over to be executed for the murder of a Chinese at Kowloon. The Chinese also ordered foreign ships which had left Canton to avoid confiscation of their opium, and taken refuge at (Portuguese) Macao, and then Hong Kong, either to return to Canton or to leave Chinese waters. When these demands were ignored Chinese war junks fired on two British naval vessels, who retaliated sinking four junks. The resulting fighting ended with the Treaty of Nanking of 1842, which specified the payment of an indemnity, the opening of five ports to British traders, and the ceding of Hong Kong in perpetuity. The trade concessions were extended to the United States and France in 1844.

In 1856 the boarding of an allegedly British registered ship at Canton and the removal of several of her crew began a second war in which Anglo-French forces captured Canton and eventually occupied Peking. The new treaty opened eleven additional treaty ports and the Yangtse river to foreign trade, permitted permanent diplomatic missions at Peking, allowed Europeans to travel throughout China and conceded full toleration of Christianity.

The political impact of western trade on Japan stands at the opposite end of the spectrum from India, leaving China as an intermediate case. Japan had a strong sense of political unity and military discipline. It was therefore able to absorb rapidly what the West had to offer and, before the century was out, had itself embarked on a policy of colonial acquisition. But the opening of Japan differed only from China in that Japanese seclusion had been more total and that the process began later.

The settlement of the west coast of the United States, largely because of Californian gold, brought American ships to the Western

Pacific. American whalers frequently found their way into Japanese waters and hoped to get rights to dock. For a time the Shogun (the hereditary commander-in-chief and virtual ruler until 1868) was able to evade the demands from the United States government for permission to trade or to shelter. But when the Americans sent Commodore Perry for a second time into Suraga Bay in 1854, and when he refused to leave without an agreement which meant in effect the end of Japan's seclusion, the Japanese government had to acquiesce.[8]

This intervention triggered a political turning-point in the Meiji Restoration of 1868 which speeded up a nationalistic drive to modernisation. As part of the agreement extracted from Japan in 1857 her tariffs on imports were not to exceed 5 per cent for forty years from 1858.

Even humanitarian motives (or according to another view, 'moral imperialism') could combine with trade to become a cause of the extension of European control, as did the British attempt to abolish the international trade in African slaves. Kosoko, the ruler of Lagos, refused to co-operate with the British Consul by ending the shipment of slaves.[9] The British navy therefore bombarded the town in 1851 and installed in power Kosoko's more pliant rival, Akitoye. The ending of the external slave trade greatly reduced the revenue available to the rulers of Lagos, and low export duties on the nascent palm oil trade were not an adequate compensation. This trade was not being fostered adequately by the dependent rulers after 1851, because of their unwillingness to confer alienable property rights in the land of Lagos. Their revenues therefore remained lower than before, and foreign and domestic merchants agitated for reform. Concern about the presence of French warships and a possible pre-emptive French annexation, together with a desire to find alternative sources of cotton supply to the United States, encouraged the British in 1861 to persuade Akitoye's son and successor to cede his territory in exchange for a pension to compensate him for his lost palm oil trade revenues. Here European economic interests became increasingly important after the first humanitarian interventions, as they were in the coercion of the governments of China, India and Japan.

## The gains from trade and their distribution

The extension of European political influence clearly allowed a greater volume of trade because of the minimal tariff policies imposed. According to the prevailing liberal ethic, the countries opened up to trade benefitted, as well as the instigators of economic relations. Governments that declined to let their people participate were, in liberal eyes, tyrannical and unrepresentative. The whole world, liberals thought, would gain from being able to buy in the cheapest market and sell in the dearest. Not only would people become better-off in a material sense, but according to advocates such as Cobden and J.S. Mill, the intellectual and moral gains from trade were even greater. The diffusion of new ideas and opportunities, and the interlocking of national interests, were among the greatest benefits of increasing international trade, making war obsolete, they thought.[10]

By the middle of the nineteenth century, in those countries where the beliefs in the advantages of international trade were most strongly held, governments enforced well-defined property rights and laws for exchanging them. Under these conditions, and as long as the distribution of income and wealth within the country was acceptable, there was considerable justification for the belief of freetraders and economic liberals that allowing people to buy and sell freely would maximise national income and welfare. Liberals defined welfare as the sum of the personal fulfilments of individual agents.[11] Liberals generally assumed that if people were allowed to do what they wanted, especially in the area of buying and selling, then they would naturally make themselves as well off as possible. Individual maximisation constrained only by other peoples' fulfilment and the scarcity of resources, was then necessarily the way of maximising society's well-being.

In international relations these doctrines justified the forcible opening of foreign countries to trade and the dependence of Indian exports on the opium trade with China. In his *Essay on Liberty*, Mill who had worked for the British East India Company for thirty-five years, becoming chief administrator in 1856, explicitly referred to the Chinese ban on the importation of Indian opium. This he wrote was objectionable, not as an infringement upon the liberty of the producer or seller, for that was legitimate, but upon the liberty of the Chinese buyer.

He who lets the world, or his own portion of it, choose his plan of life for him has no need of any other faculty than the ape-like one of imitation.... It is possible that he might be guided in some good path and kept out of harm's way.... But what will be his comparative worth as a human being? It really is of importance, not only what men do, but also what manner of men they are that do it.[12]

The weaker economies of Western Europe and the United States did not embrace the free-trade ethic of liberalism as wholeheartedly as did Britain. The ideas of Friedrich List, the German nationalist economist, who died in 1849, attracted a considerable following. List agreed with the liberals that liberty was a fundamental cause of industrial progress, maintaining for instance that national success in navigation was directly proportional to the initiative and courage fostered by national conditions.[13] But List believed in the primacy of the nation over the individual. Protection against foreign competition was necessary for the industrial education of the nation, to integrate new ideas, rights, duties and institutions into national life. Germany, List asserted in 1846, deprived of an energetic commercial policy to restrict international specialisation, unlike the United States, became 'like a colony' in the face of the superior productive power of Britain.

## Colonialism, tariffs and the gains from trade

India actually was a colony and unable to pursue an independent tariff policy. Under British political control during the first half of the nineteenth century, there was a revolutionary change in the composition of Indian trade that would probably not have been allowed to occur had the Indian government been independent. Imports of cotton goods from Britain increased massively to become the largest single category of imports, while cotton piece goods, formerly a major export, dwindled into insignificance.[14] As a result, according to Marx, the plains of India were covered with the bleached bones of starved hand-loom weavers.[15] Morris has denied that the village communities were impoverished by the influx of Lancashire cottons. The primary reliance upon agriculture enabled the extensive manufacturing population of the countryside to continue spinning and weaving during the hot dry season of the agricultural year. The British goods were in any case unable to rival the quality of the muslins of Bengal.[16]

Against Morris, Desai argued from an econometric model that employment of hand-loom weavers can only have failed to decrease if the weavers achieved an impossibly large increases in productivity.[17] The real issue however is not so much what happened to the numbers of hand-loom weavers because of increasing international trade, but what happened to *former* hand-loom weavers. Some probably increased their specialisation in agriculture, supplying exports of opium, raw cotton and rice. Others may have found employment working-up imported cotton twist and yarn to make more satisfactory cloth than the old hand-loom textiles, (the first

Indian cotton mill opened in Bombay in 1851). An independent and probably protectionist Indian tariff policy (similar to that of the United States described in Chapter 2) would have reduced the incentive to introduce the new mechanised textile industry and, by keeping workers in low productivity hand-loom weaving, may well have lowered Indian production and consumption below what was actually achieved.

India was the most important market for the British cotton textile exporters, but Lancashire never supplied more than a fraction of the Indian consumption of coarse cloth and during the second half of the nineteenth century India took little more than one-fifth of the total value of the exports of the industry.[18] Thus it would be wrong to attribute British pre-eminence in the cotton industry to her access to the colonial Indian market. Although the volume and composition of trade would have been different without British political supremacy, such a change would not have made the British much worse off.

China was not a western colony, but a low import tariff had been imposed, similar to that of India. As in India also the gains in China to the instigators of the expansion of trade beyond the western world were disproportionately small compared with the political consequences. Free-traders expected that China would provide a massive market. Sheffield cutlery imports, they thought, would be greeted avidly as far superior to chopsticks, and consignments of pianos would be welcomed as means of increasing the marriageability of girls, as they were in Victorian England.[19] To the surprise of many British manufacturers, the Chinese preferred their traditional ways and for many years unsold cutlery, bent into a variety of ornamental shapes, was to be seen on display in Chinese shops. But if the gains to the West from the opening up of trade with China were small, the costs to the West had not been very great either, in contrast to the Indian trade, because no formal empire had been declared.

As to the gains to the Chinese and the Indians, perhaps the most significant imports that they took from the West were ideas. The massive Taiping Rebellion (1851–64) was inspired by Christian doctrines and, unlike the rulers of China, the rebels welcomed foreign influences. The rulers of China were however sufficiently capable of ensuring their own survival to enlist the military aid of western governments in eventually putting down the rebellion after 20–30 million people had been killed.[20] The British occupation of India transplanted western ideas of nationalism and liberalism and, by providing a communications network, helped to weld the sub-continent into a nation that had not previously existed.

## Violence and the gains from trade

Subsequently, influential historians and politicians have seen the debate about tariff policy or the spread of western ideas as being of marginal importance. The beneficial impact of trade, they assert, was entirely one-sided. International economic relations allowed the rise of Western Europe to its powerful nineteenth-century position by despoiling and correspondingly reducing the income of the rest of the world. Physical violence, confiscation and theft in Asia, Africa and America by the superior European military and political organisations caused divergent paths of economic development in the four centuries before 1850. Successful wars, it has been maintained, excluded other countries from lucrative markets, and allowed the accumulation of capital from profits.[21] The employment of this capital in world markets conferred a monopoly which, allegedly, was used to exploit foreign consumers by the charging of high prices, and to exploit foreign producers by buying at low prices. Chilean economic development in the nineteenth century for instance, Gunder Frank believes, was distorted by the industrial monopoly of Great Britain. This monopoly furthered Britain's development under free trade, but forced Chile to specialise in the production of primary products unconducive to economic development.[22]

The harmful effects of trade on lower income economies can be most cogently argued for the slave trade. The international trade in slaves had been declared illegal by the British in 1807, but despite the employment of ships on the African coasts to intercept slave ships, payments to foreign powers for putting down slave trading, and other expenditures amounting to £29 million between 1808 and 1865, the trade continued because its profitability was assured by the strength of western demand for slave-produced goods, in particular cotton, sugar, and coffee.[23] Klein has argued that in all continental America except the United States slavery was on the decline by the nineteenth century because of liberal ideas, the decline of plantation agriculture and the chaos of war. This did not however prevent Brazil, from the nominal abolition of the trade until 1850, and Cuba, until the 1860s, importing the largest number of slaves annually in their histories.[24] Certainly the slave trade was less than it would have been in the absence of suppression policies. Leveen calculated that slave exports from Africa would have been 820 000 more without such policies, which is 54 per cent of the nearly 1.5 million slaves who were actually imported to Cuba and Brazil between 1821 and 1865.[25]

The United States had also prohibited the trade in 1807, and by

1821 the institution of slavery had been ended north of the Mason–Dixon line, although the legality of slavery in the newly-admitted states to the Union remained a bone of contention until the Civil War. Slaves continued to be smuggled into the cotton growing, slave-based economies of the Southern states and, as the price of slaves rose in the two decades before the Civil War, slave smuggling increased.[26] Probably not less than 250 000 slaves were brought in from abroad between 1800 and 1860.

The trade was especially macabre because not only did it deprive the 'slave exports' of their freedom, but because little care was taken to keep them alive in transit, in view of their cheapness in Africa, and so large numbers perished. In 1840 it was estimated that of 1000 typical victims of the slave trade, one-half died in the seizure, march and detention in Africa. Of the 500 who were embarked one-quarter died at sea, and of the remaining 375 landed, one-fifth would be expected to be dead at the end of the first year.[27]

The costs to the African economies were first, those of a country experiencing massive emigration, the use of resources to support and educate young people without a corresponding return on that investment during the productive years; and secondly, and probably much more important, a lack of security that impeded economic development because of slave raiding parties. Some states, such as Dahomey, the African Sparta, based a large part of their economies on military activity to obtain slaves. The city states of Yorubaland, frequently warring with each other, sold off their captives as a lucrative byproduct. By contrast, the feudal kingdom of Buganda away from the slave trading zones, experienced a substantial growth of commodity production and trade.[28]

As a result of the slavery to which the expansion of trade had given such a boost, the ultimate consumers of goods embodying slave-produced materials paid less than would have been required in a world where all exchanges were voluntary. These consumers throughout the world exploited the slaves, whereas those actually involved in the slave trade and slave plantations are properly described as thieves, and J.S. Mill, among others, recognised at the time. Even after the slaves had been freed, the tropical products they supplied were still artificially cheap, because the ex-slaves usually had few alternative sources of employment, and the majority probably would not have chosen to migrate voluntarily from Africa to work at the market wages in the plantations. Hence the substitution of resources induced by slavery to some extent also persisted after abolition. The cotton produced by free labour in India and the Middle East was less profitable and was therefore produced in smaller quantities, even after the American Civil War, than would have been the case if the slaves had never been transporated across the Atlantic. Indirectly because of the slave trade India and the Middle East had their opportunities to gain from international trade reduced.

Despite the gains to some, slavery was impermissible in liberal ideology, and in English Common Law after the Somerset Case of 1772. The French Revolution abolished slavery, although Napoleon brought it back. Even strong vested interests failed to prevent abolition in the British West Indies in 1834. Significantly by the 1870s the only major area of slave trading was between East Africa and the Arabian peninsula, under the control of Arabs who remained untouched by the doctrines of liberalism.[29]

If the slave trade was fundamental to the rise of Western Europe, then the success of the abolitionists is truly remarkable. In fact the gains from the trade seem to have been too small a proportion of British investment or income to account for British economic pre-eminence, and if this was true of Britain it was even more true of Western Europe. The higher price of British imports relative to the price of exports that would have occurred in a world in which slavery had never been transplanted across the Atlantic, when multiplied by the share of foreign trade in British national income, cannot yield a large figure as Britain's gains from slavery, on any plausible assumption.[30]

In the wider context of all extra-European trade, O'Brien similarly concludes the magnitudes were just not big enough for slavery to have greatly affected the national incomes of the beneficiaries. In 1800 total extra-European trade was in value only around 4 per cent of the aggregate GNP of Western Europe. The maximum likely impact of such trade for Britain was only 15 per cent of gross investment during the industrial revolution.[31]

## Competition and the gains from trade

The slave trade was in any case atypical of international trade in the 1850s. International economic relations in the main were conducted within the framework assumed by nineteenth-century liberals, and there were therefore gains to both parties despite continuous friction about the proper distribution of these gains. In Latin America European manufacturers did not co-operate to maintain prices merely because so many of them had a common nationality. Instead, they competed and prevented large profits from emerging (although exclusive contracts and concessions were contentious in shipping).[32] The guano trade is a case in point. Birds' droppings had no value without international trade, and were a crucial source of Peruvian government revenue in the 1850s. Peru owed this money to the British agricultural demand for natural fertilisers and to the enterprise of Antony Gibbs & Sons, who, according to the City of London rhyme, also became rich from 'selling the turds of foreign birds'.[33] The division of the gains from this trade between the contractor and the owner of the resource was a matter of controversy both at the time and later.

The gains to the contractor from the Peruvian birds' droppings, or guano trade, came from commissions on the costs of arranging the shipping of the guano on behalf of the guano owners, the Peruvian government, and from a commission on the total value of guano sales. The controversy centred on whether Gibbs, the contractor, charged too much. Levin has suggested that the guano trader had a clear interest in raising costs, and thereby increasing his commission on them.[34] He also asserted that the contractor had an incentive, provided by commissions on the total value of guano sales, to sell guano at prices lower than the Peruvian government, the owner of a wasting resource, judged appropriate. The government thus suffered losses, both from the failure to hold down costs and from excessively low prices. Mathew points out that there was no general tendency for prices to be reduced and the inelasticity of guano supply removed any likelihood that Gibbs could increase their commission by reducing them. Successive Peruvian governments did well out of the trade, taking an average of 65 per cent of gross sales proceeds from the Gibbs contracts. Most of the remainder went to the shippers.[35] Gibbs were however guilty of claiming unearned commissions, of the excessive centralisation through London of British and European imports, and of the heavy exporting of 1860–1 just before their contract was to expire for the last time. They certainly made ample profits, but although they undertook virtually all the practical managerial responsibilities of the trade, their commission was still only a fraction of the royalties taken by the government. The government was in fact usually prepared to defend Gibbs against their attackers because of the usefulness of the company in providing loans on the security of future guano exports. The government exercised considerable control over contract terms and pricing, and when domestic agitation against Gibbs proved too strong the contract was not renewed.

Competition between merchants prevented persistent monopoly profits in most spheres of international trade and guano was no exception. Before Gibbs had entered the guano trade in 1842, the

Peruvian government had drawn up contracts with a Peruvian capitalist and with a group backed by a Liverpool firm. Those that needed finance and the associated services under competition had to pay a price sufficient to prevent it being used in the next most profitable use, while those with access to the funds had to charge a price low enough to prevent the customer going to a competitor. The Peruvian government could not themselves provide the services similar to those of Gibbs, and did not think they could buy them cheaper elsewhere. That the government probably did not use the proceeds from the trade wisely cannot be blamed on the British merchants, or on international economic relations generally.

One instance does not of course prove the general point, that the distribution of the gains from trade were fair although the observation of widespread competition between traders gives added force to it. Had trade been monopolistic then nineteenth-century British merchants should have accumulated massive fortunes. Rubinstein's study of the very wealthy in Britain shows that until about 1880 more than half of all the really wealthy men in Britain were landowners and, during the first half of the nineteenth century, the non-landed wealthholders were a virtually insignificant percentage of the entire wealthy class.[36] It is true that non-landed fortunes were earned disproportionately in commerce and finance – by merchants, bankers, shipowners, merchant bankers, and stock and insurance agents and brokers, rather than in manufacturing or industry. But this wealth belonged mainly to merchant bankers and came almost exclusively from the organisation of foreign or government loans. Henry Gibbs (1819–1907), of guano fame, only became a half-millionaire, and that in the course of a long and successful career in merchant banking after he had given up guano. Any exploitation of monopoly positions in international trade by the largest trading nation cannot therefore have been substantial at the mid-century. Hence, apart from the slave trade, and possibly some caveats stemming from imposed tariff policies, a conclusion that both parties usually gained and the distributions were fair seems warranted.

We turn now from the conditions influencing the gains from trade and their distribution to the pattern of trade.

## Economic relations between Britain, India and the United States

The statements of international transactions of three very different but closely connected economies of the mid-century, Great Britain, the United States and India, both provide a snapshot of a major portion of international economic relations of the time, and show the different ways in which economies participated in the burgeoning of world trade. The majority of the North American colonies had thrown off the restrictions imposed upon their trade, industry and agriculture by Britain in the previous century. Yet it was precisely these former colonies, now as the rapidly expanding and independent United States of America, which constituted the most important trading partner of Great Britain, and the most important destination for British emigrants and international investment. Although the merchandise trade of the United States was in the middle of the nineteenth century only about one-third of that of Britain, Britain was reciprocally America's largest trading partner. Second only to the United States in importance to British trade was India, which despite a population eight times as large as Britain's, conducted merchandise (including bullion) trade of only one-sixth the size. Nevertheless the international economic relations of India offer a valuable contrast to those of the other two countries. India was a poor country in terms both of natural resources and the standard of living of the people relative to those of Western Europe or the New World. The United States was rich in natural resources and had a small population who were well-off compared with the rest of the world. Great Britain was one of the most densely populated countries yet was relatively industrialised and rich.

Contemporaries could most easily judge these international differences from the statistics of exports and imports which were among the most reliable national data available and had been collected for many years. These statistics however did not give a complete description of how a nation solved the problem of what to buy abroad and how to pay for it, as does a modern balance of payments statement. Historical research has constructed complete statements for some countries (although many of the figures are subject to wide margins of errors), so that the solutions adopted to the international economic problem are now better understood. First, contemporary statistics did not measure trade in 'invisibles' – services such as shipping, insurance and tourism. Secondly, they did not measure other means of paying for foreign goods, such as the selling of national assets to foreigners, gifts, or other transfers of money across national boundaries, which did not involve a corresponding current exchange of goods or services.

The calculation of some of these items, in particular foreign investment, has often used the principle that 'the balance of payments must balance'. This is merely a statement that if something has been bought from abroad and thereby entered as a debit (a minus) in the balance of payments statement, then the money must have been available to complete the transaction. The means by which this money was obtained appears in the statement as a credit (a plus). In this sense the balance of payments is an 'identity', a relationship that is true by definition; any discrepancy between the debits and credits must be the result of errors of measurement.

Foreign investment has proved one of the more difficult international transactions to estimate directly in the nineteenth century, and so in some cases all the other components of the balance of payments, debits and credits are first computed. Then, since the balance of payments must balance, the difference between the two sums, the 'residual', is attributed to foreign investment. If the discrepancy is negative, foreigners have been investing in the country and providing the foreign currency to buy more imports than would otherwise have been possible. A positive difference is taken to mean the domestic economy has been investing abroad and exports have been higher or imports lower than in the absence of such investment.

Although the balance of payments must balance, it does not have to be in equilibrium. An equilibrium exists if the international transactions that residents can undertake correspond with those they would like to carry out under the prevailing circumstances; in particular, given their limited incomes, productive capacity and prices. A state of disequilibrium occurs in the balance of payments if unplanned credits of debits are accumulated in the course of the year. Unplanned transactions which take place solely to settle the balance and not because of trading or investment opportunities, or reasons of foreign policy or altruism, are defined as 'accommodating'; while planned transactions are called 'autonomous'. Hence a measure of the imbalance or disequilibrium in a balance of payments is the size of accommodating components.

In practice it is difficult to determine under which heading to classify certain transactions. The 'residual method' cannot distinguish between short- and long-term investment, but the distinction is important for assessing whether a balance of payments is in equilibrium, and thus whether adjustment is needed in the domestic economy, because some short-term investments are unplanned. One result of the incomplete balance of payments statistics available to the nineteenth century is that the nature and timing of the adjustment that had to be made to a balance of payments disequilibrium differed from adjustment in the second half of the twentieth century, because the information available to judge whether a disequilibrium existed was so much more inadequate. The classification of precious metal flows is particularly problematic in the nineteenth century because

most of these were probably autonomous rather than accommodating. Gold and silver were the ultimate means of settling imbalances of exports and imports between countries (accommodating
transactions) but gold was also an important export commodity for
the United States, and together with silver was a major import
commodity for India where there was a strong demand for jewellery,
coinage and hoarding (autonomous transactions). The size of the
autonomous precious metal transactions probably eased the adjustment to balance of payments disequilibria, because the proportionate
changes required by accommodating transactions were reduced.

## The British balance of payments

The balance of British merchandise trade in 1858 (Table 1.1) shows
a very substantial excess of imports over exports, amounting to 15
per cent of total imports. But this balance was more than covered
by 'invisibles', by earnings from shipping, insurance and interest on
foreign investments. The largest single import was raw cotton and
the largest single export was cotton manufactures. Thus Britain's
impact on the international economy owed much to her supremacy
in the cotton textile industry in 1858. The countries of origin of
imports reveal the geographical pattern of this impact, with one-fifth
of total British imports coming from the United States, the world's
largest producer of raw cotton, supplying the world's largest
manufacturer of cotton textiles. Even so the cotton industry
employed only about 4 per cent of the British labour force and
generated roughly 7 per cent of national income.[37] India was the
second most important supplier of British imports, sending tea, raw
cotton, rice, indigo and sugar; sugar and tea by now being crucial
parts of the British diet were also major imports.

The repeal of the Corn Laws in 1846 had allowed imports of corn
by the 1850s to become second in importance only to raw cotton.
France in 1858 was the largest supplier of wheat, with the United
States (exporting wheat flour), Prussia and Russia, close behind.
Partly for this reason, France provided 8 per cent of British imports,
the third largest share, followed by Russia and, because of the tea
trade, by China. The third largest import commodity by value was
sugar, supplied by the British West Indies and also to some extent
by Cuba and Brazil. India was Britain's largest market in 1858
although this position was usually taken by the United States. The
United States had been forced into second place by the slump of
1857, while Indian demand was beginning to recover from the ending
of the Mutiny early in 1858. Britain's role as provider of the capital

goods and intermediate products that she had innovated account for the second most important category of exports, iron and steel; one-third of this category consisted of railway products. Essentially Britain exported manufactured and semi-manufactured goods, whether they were made of cotton, wool, flax, iron or steel, and imported raw materials and food, with some high quality consumer goods.

Bearing in mind that the entries in Table 1.1 show the most important traded goods and trading partners, the general impression is of a very diversified foreign trade structure; there was no great dependence on any one commodity or country, except the United States as a source of imports, and on cotton exports which accounted for 30 per cent of exports. In this respect British trade differed from that of the contemporary United States and India, and from the trade of poor countries in the twentieth century. The size of the re-export trade also distinguished British trade from the trade of the rest of the world. Here raw cotton dominated all other commodities, amounting to 17.6 per cent of the value of exports between 1854 and 1859.

Australia,[38] the third largest export market, was the main source of the massive gold inflows from the new mines of 1851 which, together with raw wool exports, provided the revenue to buy British goods. More gold went to France than came in from Australia in 1858. The value of this gold was $2\frac{1}{2}$ times the visible trade deficit (the excess of visible imports over exports) with France, and equal to five-sixths of the total exports of gold bullion and specie.

The other components of the British balance of payments in 1858 can be estimated with much less accuracy, but there are nevertheless large sums of money involved. The largest items are those earnings which Britain received by virtue of her naval supremacy and her high level of financial development. Imlah calculated the net income from foreign trade and services as 5 per cent of the value of imports and exports.[39] The intermediation of Gibbs in the guano trade is one instance of these service earnings. Insurance earnings were a less important contributor to the British balance of payments than foreign trade services, but nevertheless Imlah's estimate for 1858 show this balance to be more than double the value of machinery exports.

Shipping earnings in 1858 were apparently very sizeable, being second only to exports of cotton manufactures as a source of foreign exchange. As with earnings from foreign trade, British ownership of international shipping frequently was a bone of contention, especially in Latin America.

**Table 1.1** *The British balance of payments in 1858*

| Imports by country of origin (%) | | Merchandise imports (£m) | | Merchandise exports (£m) | | Exports by country of destination (%) | |
|---|---|---|---|---|---|---|---|
| USA | 20.8 | Raw cotton | 30.107 | Re-exports | 23.174 | India | 12.4 |
| India | 9.0 | Corn | 20.152 | Cotton Mfrs | 33.422 | USA | 11.3 |
| France | 8.0 | Raw sugar | 12.322 | Cotton Yarn | 9.579 | Australia | 8.3 |
| Russia | 7.0 | Wool | 8.970 | Iron & Steel | 11.197 | Hanse Towns | 8.3 |
| China | 4.0 | Raw silk | 5.661 | Wool & Worsted Mfrs | 9.777 | Others | 59.7 |
| Others | 51.2 | Tea | 5.207 | Linen | 4.124 | | |
| | | Timber | 3.187 | Machinery | 3.600 | | |
| | | Flax | 3.020 | Others | 41.943 | | |
| | | Others | 75.958 | Total | 139.783 | | |
| | | Total | 164.584 | | | | |

*Balance of merchandise trade — 24.801*

| | | | |
|---|---|---|---|
| Gold | 22.493 | Gold | 12.567 |
| Silver | 6.700 | Silver | 7.061 |

*Balance of bullion and specie Flow — 9.865*

| | |
|---|---|
| Balance of ship sales | + 1.0 |
| Balance of foreign trade & services | + 15.2 |
| Balance of insurance etc | + 7.6 |
| Balance of shipping credits | + 24.2 |
| Balance of emigrants' funds | − 1.0 |
| Balance of tourism | − 5.8 |
| Balance of interest and dividends | + 15.9 |
| Balance of foreign investment | − 22.4 |

*Source:* A. Imlah, *Economic Elements in the Pax Britannica* (1958), *Abstract of UK Statistics.*

The 114 000 Britons who emigrated in 1858, almost 60 000 of them bound off or for the United States, probably contributed a small negative item to the balance of payments because of the excess of the money they took with them over remittances to Britain from relatives and friends abroad.

Income from interests and dividends in Table 1.1 was calculated assuming capital losses balanced capital gains, and the net return on investment overseas was 5 per cent. The measure of the stock of British overseas investment is derived by accumulating the balancing item, the measure of foreign investments, from the balance of payments calculations for each year since 1815, by using the principle that the balance of payments must balance. The resulting interest and dividend figure of £15.9 million is consistent with estimates derived from other sources, and is considerably less than the new foreign investment estimate.[40] The foreign investment figure derived from Imlah's balance is £22.4 million, of which the bulk in normal years during the 1850s went to India and the United States. This method of calculating British foreign investment cannot be expected to give accurate results for individual years which may be dominated by short-term influences such as the business cycle. For example, the depression in the United States already mentioned discouraged further foreign investment in 1858. The United States balance of payments, to be considered next, shows a net outflow of investment of $23 million in the year 30 June 1857 to 30 June 1858, although the following fiscal year the outflow was reversed, with net foreign investment of $29 million taking place.[41] British investment in India, as will be argued below, probably amounted to little more than £5.5 million in 1858. Therefore, taking into account both India and the United States, it would seem likely that the British foreign investment figure of £22.4 million in that year is an overestimate.

## The balance of payments of the United States

The depression of 1858 was particularly severe in the United States, as indicated by the outflow of capital in that year. The balance of payments for 1855 (fiscal year ending 30 June) is analysed because more detailed figures are available for that year and because it was a more typical year in the sense that there was net foreign investment in the United States.

The goods of first importance in American trade were close counterparts of those in British trade. Raw cotton accounted for 45 per cent of United States exports and most of this went to the mills of Lancashire (Table 1.2). Britain took 42 per cent of United States merchandise exports which, apart from raw cotton, included leaf tobacco, meat products and wheat flour as the most important items in 1855. Mirroring Britain's international specialisation, the United States exported food and raw materials and imported manufactured goods: iron and steel, cotton manufactures and wool products. Import duties raised the cost of imports by $54 million or 23 per cent of imports for immediate consumption. The duties also offered an incentive to undervalue or under-report imports: North believes the official values need to be increased by 4 per cent as a consequence.[42] Even without the import duties, the United States was running a deficit on the balance of trade. Cuba, the third most important source of imports, suggests an exception to the generalisation that the United States imported manufactured goods. Like Britain, the United States demanded tropical products, especially sugar, although the sources of supply were often different.

The flows of goods are the most easily identified transactions; the others are more a matter of conjecture. It is, however, certain that the balance of trade deficit was permitted by gold exports and the inflows of foreign capital in normal years. United States gold exports, originating mainly in the Californian discoveries of 1848, largely went initially to Britain. In 1857 for example Hughes estimates this was true of 60 per cent of United States gold exports.[43] These gold exports were partially covering the merchandise trade balance; net gold exports were $54 million and the trade balance was $65 million in 1855.

The size of foreign investment in the United States in 1855 ($15 million) is computed as a residual, as in Imlah's estimates, on the assumption that the balance of payments must balance, and hence includes errors and omissions from the other components of the balance. Immigration to the United States, mainly from the Britain and Germany, amounted to 201 000 and this is thought to have given a net benefit to the accounts shown under the heading net private unilateral transfers. Immigrants brought funds with them and paid fares to United States' shipping companies to a greater extent than earlier immigrants in the United States remitted money back to friends and relatives in Europe. The credit from immigrant funds increased with the number of non-Irish who were generally much better off than the Irish. The debit from immigrant funds is the converse; the Irish appear to have remitted the most money on a per head basis, almost exclusively for passage money to bring people out of Ireland. It took approximately three years for an Irish labourer in the United States to save sufficient money to pay the

**Table 1.2**  *The balance of payments of the United States in 1855 (financial year)*

| Country of origin (%) | | Merchandise imports ($m) | | Merchandise exports ($m) | | Country of destination (%) | |
|---|---|---|---|---|---|---|---|
| UK | 41.1 | Iron & steel mfrs | 29 | Raw cotton | 88 | UK | 42 |
| France | 12.4 | Wool mfrs | 28 | Meat products | 16 | British North America | 28 |
| Cuba | 7.0 | Cotton mfrs and semi-mfrs | 18 | Leaf tobacco | 15 | France | 13 |
| | | | | Wheat and wheat flour | 12 | | |
| Others | 39.5 | Others | 183 | Others | 62 | Others | 17 |
| | | (Total finished manufactures | 129) | (Total crude materials | 109) | | |
| | | Total merchandise | 258(268)$^a$ | Total merchandise | 193 | | |

*Balance of Merchandise Trade* $-39$ ($-49$)$^a$

Re-exports 26

| | Imports | Exports |
|---|---|---|
| Gold | 1 | 55 |
| Silver | 3 | 1 |

*Balance of bullion and specie flow* $+52$

| | |
|---|---|
| Balance of ship sales | $+3$ |
| Balance of transport | $+14$ |
| Balance of foreign travel | $-21$ |
| Balance of interest and dividends | $-22$ |
| Balance of private unilateral transfer | $+10$ |
| Balance of government unilateral transfers | $-2$ |
| Balance of foreign investment | $+15$ |

*Source*: D.C. North, 'The US balance of payments 1790–1860', *Studies in Income and Wealth*, vol. 24, Princeton University Press (1960); and *Historical Statistics of the United States: Colonial Times to 1970*, US Department of Commerce (1975).
$^a$North's adjusted figure allowing for undervaluation. These figures are used for the calculation of the balance of foreign investment.

passenger fare, and the remittance values correlate closely with the numbers of immigrants from Britain three years earlier. The government unilateral transfer is part of the payment for the Gadsden purchase (the acquisition of Southern Arizona and New Mexico from Mexico in 1853).

Foreign investment had its costs to the balance of payments as well as its benefits. The payment of interest and dividends on foreign capital in the United States (net of payments to United States capital abroad) required a larger sum in 1855 than was invested in the country. These payments were mainly the result of loans to states in contrast to the imports of capital during the 1850s, which were usually investments in railways. As in the British case, Americans travelling abroad spent more than foreigners in the United States, and the net negative figure was only partly counterbalanced by receipts from shipping. For with the rise of the iron steam-ship, the American mercantile marine was beginning to lose her supremacy formerly based upon the relatively abundant supplies of timber on the Atlantic coast.

## The Indian balance of payments

Information concerning a country's international economic relations are typically less reliable, or less likely to exist, the lower that country's level of economic development or income per head. Yet the major part of the world consisted of relatively low income nations or areas in the 1850s and the two largest countries in terms of population, India and China, were also probably among the poorest. Indian statistics, though notoriously unreliable, are perhaps the most complete of all the poor countries in the middle of the nineteenth century, and India, with a population of 197 million according to the official abstract, was an important force in international economic relations.

India's main trading partners were Britain and China. Britain apparently provided more imports by value than total Indian merchandise imports, suggesting that not only the cotton products, railway materials, and arms, shown in Table 1.3, came from Britain, but also gold. Indian merchandise exports to China were almost as important as those to Britain and corresponded closely to the value of opium exported. The positive balance of merchandise trade was more than balanced by a massive inflow of precious metals, which exceeded half the value of exports. The 'drain' of bullion to India had been a much remarked upon phenomenon at least from Roman times, and is explained by the peasants' desire for hoarding. Some import of precious metals, probably between 30 and 60 million rupees every year was necessary merely to maintain the value of the currency against wear and loss, but during the late 1850s and 1860s these volumes were greatly exceeded.[44] Tooke attributed it to an increase in the desire in the West for Asian goods.[45] He also emphasized the investment in the construction of Indian railways of the time. Although only 332 miles were in operation in 1858, already £23.5 million had been spent on the construction of the system.[46] Jenks estimated £5.5 million (R 55 million) was invested in 1858, virtually all by British savers.[47] Some of this demand for rupees by the British must have been offset by an increased demand for imports of railway material into India, but less than one-fifth of Jenks' figure in 1858 was so balanced according to Table 1.3. The major portion of the money was spent on labour. Hence payment for the investments in India were largely made in precious metals.

The invisible current account items are perhaps the most controversial elements in the study of the Indian balance of payments. Chaudhuri estimated that between 1814 and 1858 India had to export capital amounting to between £5 and £6 million a year, and it was the payment for this transfer that required India to export more than was imported.[48] India's economic structure consequently became 'biased excessively' towards export industries. In 1858 (as was true for most of the remaining years of the nineteenth century) Table 1.3 makes clear that Indians balance of trade surplus cannot be understood solely or mainly in terms of the invisible current account transactions, because the bullion inflow exceeded this surplus.[49] The largest single element of the transfer from India to the Britain was the Home Charges, the payment of pensions to former Indian civil servants and army officers retired to Great Britain, savings of British officials remitted home, and India Offices expenses in Britain. These Chaudhuri estimated at £3.5 million, on average. In addition there was a private export of capital of around £1 million and occasional debt repayments for the Indian government.

In 1858 the government debt was held mainly in India with the consequence that most interest payments were paid to Indian residents; £60.7 million was held in India compared with £8.7 million in the Britain. Interest payments to British holders of the debt amounted to £0.16 million, or R 1.6 million, compared with £2.2 million to holders of debt in India. Though debt payments were low, total Indian government expenditure in Britain amounted to £6.1 million. As far as the balance of payments is concerned some

**Table 1.3**  The Indian balance of payments in 1858

| Country of origin (%) | Merchandise imports (Rm) | | Merchandise exports (Rm) | | Country of destination (%) |
|---|---|---|---|---|---|
| UK 57 | Cotton goods | 47.8 | Opium | 92.1 | UK 38 |
| China 11 | Military equipment | 10.3 | Cotton | 43.0 | China 33 |
|  | Railway material |  | Rice | 34.5 | France 5 |
|  | Cotton twist & yarn | 9.4 |  |  |  |
| Others 32 | Iron | 4.9 | Other | 106.0 | Others 24 |
|  | Others | 69.6 | Total | 274.6 |  |
|  | Total | 151.9 |  |  |  |

*Balance of Merchandise Trade + 122.7*

| | | | | |
|---|---|---|---|---|
| Gold and silver (by sea) | 158.1 | Gold and silver (by sea) | 8.2 | |

Balance of Bullion and Specie Flow − 149.9
Balance of interest and dividends[a] ...
(Interest payment on Indian debt held in UK) − 1.6
(Indian govt expenditure in the UK − 61.0)
Balance of unilateral government transfers, private
unilateral transfers and 'invisibles' trade[a] + 26.2
Balance of foreign investment[a] + 55

*Source: Official Abstract of British India.*
[a] Converted from sterling back to rupees at the official rate of 1R = £0.1. The balance of interest and dividends, of unilateral transfers and invisibles, and of foreign investment are highly conjectural.

of this money is already recorded in the merchandise account as military equipment. Mukerjee has shown that this second 'drain' of funds from India, mainly the Home Charges, was an extremely small proportion of national income (about 0.33 per cent in 1872) and the 'unnecessary' component of these charges, 13 per cent of the total, was even smaller, so that it would be hard to blame any substantial distortion of Indian economic structure on this flow.[50]

Although there are other invisible items, such as the repatriation of profits on foreign investment, the remittance of private European savings and payments for banking services, the evidence of the trade and precious metal balances is that payments on these invisible balances must have been in India's favour; there was no obvious net capital transfer from India to Britain in 1858. Once the railways had been built and interest and dividends had to be paid then the balance of payments would revert back to the position of the pre-railway age. This is borne out by Indian government purchases of sterling in London which were only 13 million rupees in 1857–8, and zero in the following three years. By 1871–2 these sterling purchases had reached 100 million rupees.[51]

## Summary and conclusions

The technological upsurge in lands inhabited primarily by Western Europeans or their descendents disproportionately concentrated world trade, income and political power in the 1850s. The political impact of the West on Asia and Africa was a result of the rising western economic activity, and the political pre-eminence of the West, as it had been earlier, was due to the lesser political and social cohesiveness of other societies at the time of the contact with the West. This meant that the transfer of western technology embodied in goods was either not possible or not sufficient to maintain real independence for many of these societies. Japan is the exception that proves the rule.

Trade expanded partly because European and American political influence ensured low tariffs. Liberals at the time put forward good reasons why all trading nations should benefit from such a policy. In western economies less advanced than Britain these arguments were less wholeheartedly embraced. Formal colonies such as India, and other countries such as China and Japan, had low tariff policies imposed upon them. The foreign trade structure of India was thereby radically changed. This change has frequently been represented as harmful, yet it provided a stimulus to the more productive use of labour and to the development of an advanced technology cotton textile industry that eventually was competitively to exclude British products even under British rule. The tariff policy was not central to European exports judging by the small importance of Asian trade with Europe.

The slave trade, continuing in 1850, despite suppression policies, offers the major foil to nineteenth-century optimism about the gains from trade. Apart from the brutal deaths and deprivations of freedom involved, the African economies suffered because of the drain of prime human capital and because the lack of security and actual destruction caused by slave raiding parties hampered economic development. What statistics there are, when properly analysed, do not confirm the view that Africa's loss was the cause of Europe's economic supremacy, that the capital for European industrial growth was substantially supplied by the profits of the slave trade or other acts of theft perpetrated against the rest of the world.

Economic relations between Latin America and the western world were stormy, but because Latin America had developed institutions and organisations capable of coping with trade on a large scale and because competition rather than monopoly was the rule, generally the mutual benefits expected by the contemporary liberals were achieved. An analysis of the guano trade provided an instance of these mutual gains, and the absence of British million-naires from nineteenth-century foreign trade suggests that competition was prevalent.

The impact of the resource endowments of Britain, India and the United States on the pattern of their economic relations shows some possibly surprising similarities. Both the US and India exported primary products, imported manufactures, and showed concentrated foreign trade structures despite the higher standard of living in North America. Both countries at the mid-century were importers of capital from Britain and both accordingly had to pay dividends and interest abroad. How much capital they imported has to be inferred from the balance of payments identity. India in addition had to pay sums relating to administrative expenses, although these were small in relation to the volume of Indian trade. Britain, unlike the other two countries that were her most important trading partners, earned large foreign balances from managing, financing and shipping foreign trade. This pre-eminence originated in the British naval supremacy and greater commitment to trade because of her popula-tion density and island location. Precious metals were the ultimate means of settling imbalances in the economic relations between states, but the balance of payments of Britain, India and the United

States imply that the bulk of the bullion movements from the US to Britain, and from Britain to France and thence to India, were undertaken as autonomous, rather than as accommodating transactions.

## Notes

1. K. Marx and F. Engels, *Manifesto of the Communist Party*, Moscow: Progress Publishers, first published 1848 (1893), p. 47.
2. The trade figures are in M.G. Mulhall, *The Dictionary of Statistics*, London: Routledge (1899). The population estimates for 1845 given in that source, of 245 m for Europe and 1009 m for the world are probably too low. A.M. Carr–Saunder, *World Population: Past Growth and Present Trends*, Oxford: Clarendon Press (1936), p. 42 gives a European population of 266 million and a world total of 1171 million for 1850.
3. L.J. Zimmerman, 'The distribution of world income 1860–1960', in *Essays on Unbalanced Growth*, E. de Vries (ed.), S. Gravenage: Mouton & Co. (1962) gives the 'guesstimate' for 1860. European incomes are presented for 1860 in P. Bairoch, 'Europe's gross national product 1800–1975', *Journal of European Economic History*, **5** (1976), pp. 273–340.
4. D.K. Fieldhouse, *The Colonial Empires: A Comparative Survey from the Eighteenth Century*, London: Macmillan, 2nd edn (1982), esp. pp. 304–5.
5. J. Gallagher and R. Robinson, 'The imperialism of free trade 1815–1914', *Economic History Review*, 2nd series, **6** (1953).
6. P. Spear, *The Oxford History of Modern India 1740–1975*, Delhi: Oxford University Press, 2nd edn (1978). R.C. Majumdar, H.C. Raychaudhuri and K. Datta, *An Advanced History of India*, London: Macmillan (1958).
7. K. Bourne, *The Foreign Policy of Victorian England*, London: Oxford University Press (1970), pp. 44–5, 81–3. D.K. Fieldhouse, *Economics and Empire 1830–1914*, London: Weidenfeld & Nicolson (1973), pp. 210–23. F. Wakeman, 'The Canton trade and the Opium War', and J.K. Fairbank, 'The creation of the treaty system', both in *Cambridge Economic History of China*, vol. 10, part 2 (1980). D. Hurd, *The Arrow War: an Anglo-Chinese Confusion 1856–1860*, London: Collins, (1967). J.Y. Wong, 'The Arrow Incident: are-appraisal', *Modern Asian Studies*, **8** (1974), pp. 373–89.
8. G.C. Allen, *A Short Economic History of Modern Japan*, London: Macmillan, 4th edn (1981), pp. 22–3. W.G. Beasley, *Selected Documents on Japanese Foreign Policy 1853–68*, London: Oxford University Press (1955), p. 99 gives the text of the American President's letter to the Japanese Emperor.
9. A.G. Hopkins, 'Property rights and empire building: Britain's annexation of Lagos', *Journal of Economic History*, **40** (1980), pp. 777–98.

R.S. Smith, *The Lagos Consulate 1851–1861*, Berkeley: University of California Press (1979).

10. J.S. Mill, *Principles of Political Economy*, vol. 2 Book 3 (first published 1848) London: Longman, 7th edn (1871), pp. 122–3. P.J. Cain, *Economic Foundations of British Overseas Expansion 1815–1914*, London: Macmillan (1980). Cain believes this element has been overstated because of the idealistic views of Cobden, the most prominent member of the Anti-Corn Law League. See also P.J. Cain, 'Capitalism, war and internationalism in the thought of Richard Cobden', *British Journal of Internation Studies*, **5** (1979), pp. 112–30. C.P. Kindleberger, 'The rise of free trade in Western Europe 1820–1875', *Journal of Economic History*, **35** (1975), pp. 20–55. Kindleberger concluded that both ideology and self-interest convinced the English that cosmopolitan as well as national interests would be served by free trade.

11. The mid-Victorian use of the term liberal is not to be confused with the present-day meaning in the United States, closely related to 'radical'. Although in the eighteenth century the word had meant 'open-minded' or 'unorthodox', the association of freedom with the opportunity to express such ideas transformed liberalism by the middle of the nineteenth century into a doctrine of certain kinds of freedom. R. Williams, *Keywords: A Vocabulary of Culture and Society*, New York: Oxford University Press (1976).

12. J.S. Mill, *Utilitarianism, On Liberty, and Considerations on Representative Government*, H.B. Acton (ed.), London: Dent (1972), pp. 151, 117.

13. F. List, *National System of Political Economy*, Philadelphia: J.B. Lippincott & Co. (1856), esp. pp. 181, 183. Translated by G.A. Matile, Preliminary Essay by S. Colwell.

14. K.N. Chaudhuri (ed.), *The Economic Development of India under the East India Company 1814–1858*, Cambridge: Cambridge University Press (1971), Introduction. A. Maddison, *Class Structure and Economic Growth, India and Pakistan since the Moghuls*, London: Allen & Unwin (1971).

15. Cited in W.J. Macpherson, 'Economic development in India under the British Crown 1858–1947', in A.J. Youngson (ed.), *Economic Development in the Long Run*, London: Allen & Unwin (1972).

16. M.D. Morris, 'Towards a Reinterpretation of nineteenth-century Indian economic history,' *Journal of Economic History*, **23** (1963), pp. 612–13. M.D. Morris, 'Trends and tendencies in Indian economic history', *Indian Economic and Social History Review*, **5** (1968), pp. 377–84.

17. M. Desai, 'Demand for cotton textiles in nineteenth-century India', *Indian Economic and Social History Review*, **8** (1971), pp. 337–61.

18. D.A. Farnie, *The English Cotton Industry and the World Market 1815–1896*. London: Oxford University Press (1979), pp. 79, 119.

19. G.C. Allen and A. Donnithorne, *Western Enterprise in Far Eastern Economic Development*, London: Allen & Unwin (1954), pp. 17–18

20. H. Hookham, *A Short History of China*, New York: New American Library (1972), pp. 277–86.
21. M. Barrett Brown, *The Economics of Imperialism*, London: Penguin (1974), ch. 4. I. Wallerstein, *The Capitalist World Economy*, Cambridge: Cambridge University Press (1979).
22. A. Gunder Frank, *Capitalism and Underdevelopment in Latin America: Historical Studies of Chile and Brazil*, New York and London: Monthly Review Press (1967), p. 37.
23. R.B. Sheridan, 'Sweet malefactor: the social costs of slavery and sugar in Jamaica and Cuba 1804–54', *Economic History Review*, 2nd series, **29**, (1976), pp. 236–57.
24. H.S. Klein, *The Middle Passage: Comparative Studies in the Atlantic Slave Trade*, Princeton: Princeton University Press, (1978) p. 18.
25. E. Phillip Leveen, 'A quantitative analysis of the impact of British suppression policies on the volume of the nineteenth-century African slave trade', in S.L. Engerman and E.D. Genovese (eds), *Race and Slavery in the Western Hemisphere*, Princeton: Princeton University Press (1975).
26. D.P. Mannix and M. Cowley, *Black Cargoes: A History of the Atlantic Slave Trade*, London: Penguin (1976), Ch. 12.
27. F. Buxton, *The African Slave Trade: Its Remedy* (1840), pp. 199–202.
28. W. Rodney, *How Europe Underdeveloped Africa*, London: Bogle L'Ouverture (1972), Ch. 4.
29. R.W. Beachey, *The Slave Trade of Eastern Africa*, L.R. Collings, (1976). Slave imports to the Middle East in the 1870s may have averaged 6000–8000 a year. Two-thirds of the population of Zanzibar and Pemba were slaves in 1858.
30. R.P. Thomas and D.N. McCloskey use this method to calculate the total British gains from *all* foreign trade and obtain fairly small numbers. R. Floud and D.N. McCloskey (eds), *The Economic History of Britain Since 1700*, Cambridge: Cambridge University Press (1981). For an alternative view see E. Williams, *Capitalism and Slavery*, London: Deutsch (1964).
31. P.K. O'Brien, 'European economic development: the contribution of the periphery', *Economic History Review*, 2nd series, **35** (1982) pp. 1–18.
32. On shipping, for example, S.G. Sturmey, *British Shipping and World Competition*, London: University of London: Athlone Press (1962); and R. Greenhill, 'Shipping 1850–1914', in D.C.M. Platt (ed.), *Business Imperialism 1860–1930*, Oxford: Clarendon Press (1977). On the prevalence of competition, see Platt's introduction pp. 6–7.
33. A. Sampson, *The Money Lenders: Bankers and a World in Turmoil*, New York: Viking (1982), p. 108.
34. J.V. Levin, *The Export Economies*, Cambridge, Mass: Harvard University Press (1960), pp. 68–71.
35. W.M. Mathew, 'Antony Gibbs & Sons, the guano trade and the Peruvian Government 1842–61', in D.C.M. Platt (ed.) op. cit. The poor

condition of the labourers extracting the guano casts doubt on whether their share in the guano from the trade was fair; although the labour was nominally free.

36. W.D. Rubinstein, *Men of Property: The Very Wealthy in Britain Since the Industrial Revolution*, London: Croom Helm (1981).
37. Farnie, op. cit., p. 24.
38. Germany was in fact a more important market for Britain than Australia but she was still a collection of independent states.
39. A. Imlah, *Economic Elements in the Pax Britannica: Studies in British Foreign Trade in the Nineteenth Century*, Cambridge, Mass: Harvard University Press (1958).
40. L.H. Jenks, *The Migration of British Capital to 1875*, London: Nelson (1971).
41. US Department of Commerce, *Historical Statistics of the United States: Colonial Times to 1970* (1975).
42. D.C. North, 'The US balance of payments 1790–1860', *Studies in Income and Wealth*, vol. 24, Princeton: Princeton University Press (1960).
43. J.R.T. Hughes, *Fluctuations in Trade, Industry and Finance 1850–1860*. Oxford: Oxford University Press (1960), p. 13.
44. D. Barbour, *The Theory of Bimetallism*, London: Cassell (1887), ch. 20.
45. T. Tooke, Appendix 23 to *A History of Prices*, in Chaudhuri (ed.), op. cit.
46. *Official Abstract of British India 1858 to 1867* (1869).
47. Jenks, op. cit., p. 219.
48. Chaudhuri (ed.), op. cit., pp. 35–6. See also A. Gunder Frank, 'Multilateral merchandise trade imbalances and uneven economic development', *Journal of European Economic History*, **5** (1976).
49. A.G. Latham, 'Merchandise trade imbalances and uneven economic development in India and China', *Journal of European Economic History*, 7 (1978), pp. 33–60.
50. T. Mukerjee, 'Theory of economic drain: impact of British rule on the Indian economy, 1840–1900', in K.E. Boulding and T. Mukerjee (eds), *Economic Imperialism: A Book of Readings*, Ann Arbor: University of Michigan Press (1972).
51. Barbour, op. cit., p. 108.

# 2 Economic Growth and Free Trade

The years between the European revolutions of 1848 and the depression of 1873 offer almost a laboratory experiment for testing theories of international markets. Within a month revolution had spread from France to Germany, Austria, Hungary and Italy. Yet a year and a half later, all but one of the overthrown regimes had been restored. The only apparently lasting result had been the abolition of serfdom in the Hapsburg empire. Nevertheless, the rulers of Europe and elsewhere during the third quarter of the nineteenth century recognised that traditional policies had to be changed, and turned with varying degrees of enthusiasm and success to liberalising their economies. The following sections first examine the main influences on the pattern of international trade and go on to test some of the implications of the trade theories, explaining the discrepancies between prediction and reality in these years. Finally the chapter looks at the reasons for the differing extents to which governments allowed free play to international market forces, and the consequences of these policies.

## Transport costs and the pattern of trade

Among the greatest technological changes of the period encouraged by liberal economic policies was the application of steam to land and sea transport. For most of history, the great cost of moving any considerable distance meant that only goods with a high market value in relation to their bulk were traded internationally, or indeed inter-regionally. Silk, spices and precious metals fulfilled this requirement, but being luxuries, far too expensive for the majority of the population in even the richest countries, trade in such commodities never assumed much economic importance. The extension of the railway network altered this position, not only by reducing land transport costs, but more importantly allowing relatively cheap

33

**Table 2.1**   *Length of railway open (km) 1850–75*

| | United States | Great Britain | Germany | France | Canada | Italy | India | Russia |
|---|---|---|---|---|---|---|---|---|
| 1850 | 14430 | 9797 | 5856 | 2915 | 2262 | 620 | 530* | 501 |
| 1875 | 118550 | 23365 | 27970 | 19357 | 6930 | 8018 | 10430 | 19029 |
| % increase | 720 | 138 | 378 | 564 | 206 | 1193 | 1868 | 3698 |

Source:  *Historical Statistics of the United States* (1975); B.R. Mitchell, *Abstract of European Historical Statistics (1975)*; *Statistical Abstract of British India.*
* = 1858

transport over routes where it had been virtually impossible to offer any before. By 1869 the Union Pacific railway, climbing to 8600 feet, had linked the east and west coasts of the United States. As Table 2.1 shows, in many countries the length of railway track in operation increased tenfold in these years, although with the exception of the United States, the economies with the smallest systems tended to grow the fastest.

The US railway system by 1875 was greater than the combined networks of Britain, France, Germany, Italy and Russia. The rapid development of the mid-west of the United States distracted the international flows of capital and people from Canada whose railways accordingly showed the smallest proportionate growth of all the countries except Britain in Table 2.1. Although Germany showed a less spectacular growth rate than the other continental European powers, because she started from a larger base, the size of the German railway system was greater than that of Great Britain by 1875, providing a foundation for the challenge to Britain's manufacturing supremacy that was to emerge after that date.

The importance of the railway system for integrating the different regions of a country was early recognised by the military. The Belgian railway system, one of the earliest completed, and subsequently the densest in terms of length per head of the population, was originally planned with military considerations in mind. The enormous impact on economic development originally ascribed to railways, has been reassessed by many 'social savings' studies. These studies usually attempt to calculate the costs of shipping the freight and passengers by the next best alternative means: by posting coach for passengers and canals for freight. The social saving is then the difference between this and the actual cost. Fogel, who initiated the research programme, recently concluded that only in economies where water was so scarce that canals were not a viable alternative was the social saving from railways large. A study of the impact of railways on the Mexican economy found a social saving of 30 per cent of national income, for example.[1] The reliability of individual calculations on which Fogel's conclusion is based has often been questioned. Hawke estimated the social saving from railways in England and Wales in 1865 was between 7 and 11 per cent of national income, yet a test of the sensitivity of this result to different assumptions, such as the inclusion of the value of time saved travelling, concluded the true social saving could be anywhere between 2 and 25 per cent.[2]

The British and the American railway systems were built to make profits, and consequently if the market was working to allocate resources efficiently, the true social saving figure had to be positive. In India the railway builders were given a guaranteed rate of return out of the tax receipts on the funds invested in the construction, so that even if the market was efficient, a negative social saving figure was possible. The widespread allegation that funds were used inefficiently, and that payments to British investors constituted a great burden on the Indian economy, imply a negative figure. Certainly it is possible that the construction of a system of canals with the dual function of irrigation and transport would have yielded a higher benefit–cost ratio, because the government-financed irrigation projects invariably achieved an adequate rate of return.[3] Canals however would not have achieved the security objectives for which the railway system was designed.

In continental Europe the railway system boosted international trade directly by reducing the costs of moving goods across frontiers, but for Britain, the United States and India their effect was indirect by reducing the costs of moving goods to or from the ports. The transport of goods by sea was subject to a revolution similar to land transport. Shipping benefitted from the more or less continuous improvement that occurred in the fuel consumption of marine engines throughout the second half of the nineteenth century. Steam could provide lower transport costs than sail on short routes while the coal consumption of marine engines was still quite high, but could not successfully compete with sailing ships for bulk cargoes on long routes. The steamship had to carry its own fuel and thus the longer the voyage, the greater was the proportion of the ship's capacity that had to be devoted to carrying coal, rather than cargo. Throughout the nineteenth century Britain was the world's primary coal source, consequently steamship costs increased with distance from Britain. By 1855 almost all the cargo entering Britain in the 'home trade' (from Brest to the mouth of the Elbe) was carried in steamships, although the large export trade in coal from the north–east coast was still carried out under sail in wooden colliers which returned in ballast. Nearly one-third of the Mediterranean trade was also carried by steam at this date. At the same time steam was extending into the grain trades of the Baltic and the Black Sea, although the Baltic timber trade remained largely the preserve of sailing ships.[4]

Technological change in sailing ships was almost exhausted and as a result freight rates showed no tendency to fall on the long-distance routes that they continued to operate. North's index of US export freight rates shows a rise of 26 per cent in the period 1850/5 to 1870/5.[5] These were years of rising prices generally, but the freight factor of wheat (the proportion of wheat price accounted for by freight) also showed an increase on the Atlantic route of 31 per cent over the same period. On the shorter Baltic route to the UK where steam was becoming competitive, the wheat freight factor in contrast fell by 17 per cent. Sailing ships had by this time attained such a level of development that the clipper *Thermopylae*, built for the China tea run, was reputed to be able to sail at 7 knots in a breeze so light that a candle could remain alight on deck. The opening of the Suez Canal in 1869 radically shortened distances from Europe to the East. The distance between Liverpool and Bombay was halved, and the route to China was also reduced. The Canal was unsuitable for sailing ships, primarily because of unsatisfactory wind conditions in the Red Sea, with the consequence that steamship, but not sailing ship, routes were reduced. Hence the tea clippers, unable to compete in the China trade, moved to the Australian wool trade, the distance for which had not been affected by the Canal. More importantly for international trade, the Canal allowed a marked reduction in transport costs on the India and China runs.

The volume and distribution of European trade responded to this reduction of transport costs. Domestically-produced European exports grew much faster than the growth rate of income, during the 1860s.[6] The European average rate was 5.2 per cent per annum and this was pulled down by the comparatively slow growth of British exports at 3.8 per cent per annum. During the decade of the 1870s the European average trade growth fell to 3.1 per cent per annum but remained well above income growth. The greater part of this expansion of trade was trade between European countries, which in 1850 had accounted for two-thirds of European exports. During the free trade era, the trend towards geographical diversification was broken, with a decline in the share of Third

World countries in European trade from a little over one-fifth. The decline is attributable to the greater distances involved in this trade, which therefore could not benefit from the reduced transport costs of the steamship.

## The Ricardian theory of comparative advantage

Though falling costs of freight may explain much of the increased volume and distribution of international trade, it does not explain why various countries specialised in supplying their particular goods and services to the international market, and thus the distribution of the gains from trade. According to Ricardo's (1772–1823) theory of trade the explanation is to be sought in comparative advantage.[7] If the cost of manufactured goods in terms of food in one economy is lower than in another economy, then the first has a comparative advantage in manufactured goods and the second has a comparative advantage in food. The cost of one type of product in terms of the other is the reduction of, say, food output necessitated by transferring resources to increase the production of manufactured goods, holding constant the level of resource utilisation. The principle of comparative advantage explains the pattern of trade in a market economy because it is profitable to export the product in which the economy has a comparative advantage, and to import the other commodity. The gains to be had from trade stem from the specialisation of each country in the production of the goods in which it has a comparative advantage, the export of this goods allowing imports and greater consumption than in the absence of international trade. These benefits accrue even if one economy is more efficient in the production of both goods than the other. In this case there is a wage differential between the two economies to compensate.

Although mainly an agricultural economy, the United States in 1860 employed $1\frac{1}{4}$ million in manufacturing industries. The census of that year provides a detailed statistical account of industry which can be used to illustrate Ricardo's theory. Table 2.2 shows productivity per worker in manufacturing in flour and meal was greater than in all other industries; the United States had a comparative advantage in flour milling relative to other industries, and consistent with Ricardo's theory, this was the largest manufactured export category. Of the other main categories traded, the greater net import of cotton goods than of iron manufactures is consistent with the productivity ranking, but the greater net import of woollen goods relative to cotton is inconsistent. Lumber and forest products were a major export, and productivity in this industry was high by comparison with other industries (the average was $670 value added per worker).

Discrepancies between the prediction of the theory and the data of Table 2.2 arise from the neglect by the theory of distance from potential markets and the costs of moving various products. The weight of bricks in relation to their value made unprofitable imports of these products on a large scale despite the low productivity of the domestic brick industry. A second reason for discrepancies is the emphasis solely on supply, to the exclusion of demand considerations. A strong domestic relative to foreign demand can eliminate exports and draw in imports, even though the economy could export profitably according to supply conditions alone. The inconsistency between the trading patterns and productivities of

**Table 2.2** *Comparative advantage in United States manufactures, 1860*

| | Value added per worker, 000 $ | US Trade will $ (net exports + net imports −) |
|---|---|---|
| Flour | 1.45 | + 15.4 |
| Leather | 1.00 | − 4.3 |
| Printing & publishing | 0.90 | − 0.8 |
| Machinery | 0.81 | 0 |
| Lumber (sawed) | 0.70 | + 5.14[a] |
| Iron | 0.68 | − 16.35 |
| cast | 0.78 | |
| forged, rolled, wrought | 0.66 | |
| pig | 0.54 | |
| Furniture | 0.64 | + 1.03 |
| Carriages | 0.64 | + 0.82 |
| Woollen goods | 0.62 | − 38.3 |
| Blacksmithing | 0.52 | |
| Cotton goods | 0.47 | − 21.62 |
| Tobacco & snuff | 0.47 | − 1.41 |
| Boots and shoes | 0.40 | + 0.6 |
| Brick | 0.40 | + 0.15[b] |
| Men's clothing | 0.32 | − 1.577[c] |
| Silk manufactures | na | − 32.07 |

*Sources: Commerce and Navigation of the United States, Year Ending June 30, (1860); United States Census 1860, vol. 3.*
*Notes:* [a]Boards, planks, staves, etc. Forest product exports were $13.7m
[b]Brick, lime and cement [c]'Wearing apparel' exports; 'Clothing' imports

leather manufactures, printing and publishing, and machinery are most likely explicable in these terms. For machinery, as suggested below, an additional limitation on export possibilities was the unsuitability abroad of machinery built for American conditions. A third restriction on the empirical validity of the theory is tariffs in the domestic economy and abroad offsetting comparative advantage. Between 1857 and the Civil War, American tariffs were lower than at any other time in the nineteenth century, and Table 2.2 shows the 24 per cent tariff on woollen goods did not prevent these being the largest single category of manufactured imports.

The Ricardian theory does not explain why comparative advantages should exist. Much of eighteenth-century trade was based on products that needed climates different from those of the importing country, such as sugar, tobacco, tea and raw cotton, or as in Ricardo's classic example, wine. Even the great nineteenth-century export industry, cotton textiles, depended to a considerable extent upon climate for locational advantage. The influence of Lancashire's natural humidity was estimated as the economic equivalent of a protective tariff of 10 per cent because cotton fibres became more pliable, less brittle and easier to process as humidity increased. The abundant supply of river water was essential to the industries whose demands absorbed up to half of the water used in Manchester and Oldham, and the finishing industries required enormous quantities of soft lime-free water that would neither waste soap nor resist dye.[8]

Another source of comparative advantage is technology differences between nations. The most influential view of European economic development in these years places great emphasis on these differences.[9] Britain, according to this account, exported her new technology which was slowly absorbed by European industry. The question then arises as to why new technologies should spread so slowly over an area in which men and machines were free to move across national boundaries by the middle of the century.

One reason is that the technology adapted to one country's factor endowments may not have been appropriate to the relative resource costs of another country. The abundant timber of the United States made it uneconomical to adopt coal-fired steam engines on the British model, while the fast flowing waters of Switzerland allowed the Swiss textile industry to use water-powered machinery as efficiently as the British textile mills used steam power. Another reason could be that once old methods of production had been adopted, it was not profitable to invest in new techniques until either the old equipment was so worn out it had to be scrapped, or the variable costs of generating a given sales revenue with the old technique exceeded the total costs of earning the same money with the new methods of production. A third explanation might be given in terms of the size of the market. The new techniques might require that there be a larger number of higher income customers within an economic distance of the manufacturer in order for profits to be made. If this were so, the improvement of transport facilities was a prerequisite for the profitability of the other innovations. In the case of Germany, perhaps the establishment of a free-trade area, the Zollverein, beginning in 1834 reduced the economic distance between buyer and seller. A fourth reason why a technological lead may persist is the elapse of time necessary for the discovery and exploitation in the 'follower' economics of the natural resources on which the new technology is based. Until the middle of the nineteenth century the coal and iron ore deposits of the Ruhr were unknown. Then between 1851 and 1857 twenty-seven coke-blast furnaces were built, more than had existed in the entire Zollverein at the earlier date. Output of pig iron in the Dortmund district increased over thirty-five times in the two decades after 1851. If this interpretation is correct then an economy's comparative advantage can be changed not only by imported technology stimulating capital accumulation, but also by the new technology inducing the discovery of natural resources by raising their value.

Consistent with the technological diffusion theory, British contractors were heavily engaged in the construction of the French railway system as Napoleon III pursued a vigorous policy to develop the French economy.[10] At the same time British engineers, navvies and operatives were working in Piedmont, Switzerland, Austria, Spain and, after the Crimean War (1854–6), in Russia and Turkey. In Denmark and Scandinavia, Morton Peto had virtually a monopoly of railway construction in various projects designed to improve the supply of Swedish iron and Danish butter to the English market. Associated with the activity of British contractors in Europe and elsewhere was a marked increase in exports of capital goods from Great Britain. The countries that were investing most heavily in their transport systems increased their purchases by the greatest amounts. Exports of iron and steel from Britain doubled in volume during the years 1850–3.

In contrast to the means of diffusing advanced technology in the twentieth century, the multinational company, enterprise in railways was generally cosmopolitan. For example, a network of railways in the Papal States was conceded in 1857 to a Paris banker, Mires, who sold stock mainly in clerical circles in France and Italy. (Mires was arrested in 1861 for stock manipulation.) The rails however were bought from Newcastle, the engines from Paris, the wheels from Belgium, and the carriages were manufactured for the contractor in Italy. This wide distribution of purchases must in part have been due to the comparative lack of restrictions on international trade in the 1850s in contrast to the twentieth century. Nevertheless, doubt must be cast on the diffusion model if the techniques of production were already so widely spread. Technology differences seem a less plausible reason therefore for the emergence of comparative advantages.

## The Hecksher–Ohlin theory of comparative advantage

An alternative theory of trade traces the sources of comparative advantage to the relative scarcities of the factors of production in different countries. This theory, due to Hecksher and Ohlin (HO), and published in the years between the two world wars, is of considerable interest in explaining much of intra–European trade which cannot be ascribed to climatic factors.[11] Certainly the Ricardian theory would explain such trade if there were differences in production technology between countries, but the persistence of the differences themselves would then require explanation, as already argued. The simple HO theory in contrast assumes the same technology is available to all countries. As a logical construction, the HO theory is more limited than the Ricardian theory because the predictions are not unambiguous. According to this theory, trade takes place between nations because the factors of production do not move across national boundaries very much and so cannot be used in the most appropriate proportions to maximise productivity. The relative scarcity of productive inputs differs from region to region and from country to country. In the absence of trade these different relative scarcities lead to different relative prices within the countries even though countries are assumed to have access to the same production technologies; wheat was cheaper in the United States compared with cotton textiles, than in Britain. Wheat was cheaper because land was so abundant in the United States relative to labour, in comparison with Britain, and because wheat is a product which needs a substantial land input. Similar considerations apply to the production of wool in Australia to a greater extent. Cotton textiles in contrast required little land but relatively large amounts of labour in their manufacture, both in the factory and indirectly, in the construction of the equipment used in the production process.

The implication of the theory is that a nation will export products intensive in the relatively abundant factor of production. In the above example, the United States therefore gained from exporting wheat to Britain, who gained from exporting cotton textiles to the US. Unfortunately once there are more than two countries and two traded goods in the international economy, this implication is not always valid; it is not necessarily true that a traded good will be exported if its relative price exceeds its pre-trade relative price.[12] Furthermore, the notion of factor intensity, central to the HO theory, is ambiguous, once it is recognised that there is a choice of techniques using different proportions of factors to make a product, and when large changes in relative factor prices occur. Then factor intensity reversals may occur; cases in which it is impossible to say which country has a comparative advantage in the production of a good. A case in point might be trade between Britain and India in cotton textiles which could have been made either with labour-intensive techniques (hand-loom weaving) or capital intensive techniques (factory methods). Then possibly at British factor prices, textile production was more capital-intensive than other products while the opposite was true in India. Knowing that Britain had a comparative advantage in capital-intensive produced textiles and India a comparative advantage in labour-intensive textiles is insufficient to explain why one country exported textiles and the other imported them in a trading equilibrium.

Nevertheless the HO theory does suggest certain hypotheses about trade in the period 1850 to 1875. In particular, the theory suggests that the reduction of transport costs opened up vast regions, virtually unpopulated, to the international market, and that the pattern of international specialisation adjusted to take account of this effective increase in the supply of land. Where land was cheap, more was used per worker and the output of agricultural commodities per worker tended to be higher. Land was more likely to be cheaper the lower the population density, although of course the quality and accessibility of land differed between countries. Table 2.3 suggests that the HO theory did correspond with the facts for Britain, the United States and India. The US and India had lower ratios of labour to land than Britain and therefore, as shown in Chapter 1, exported land-intensive, agricultural products (wheat in Table 2.3) to Britain, which exported in return labour-intensive manufactured products.

To the abundance of land in the United States has been attributed not only a comparative advantage in agriculture but also a comparative advantage in (labour-saving) machinery.[13] Because there was no scarcity of land, the productivity of labour in agriculture was

**Table 2.3** *Population densities and wheat exports*

|  | Population densities c. 1860 (person per sq mile) | % of world wheat exports 1854–8 ( − = imports) |
|---|---|---|
| United States | 9 | 24.9 |
| Canada | 9 | 6.4 |
| Russia (in Europe excl. Poland) | 31 | 12.0 |
| India | 117 | 3.2 |
| (British India) | (151) | |
| France | 183 | —* |
| Britain | 240 | ( − 33) |
| (England and Wales) | (310) | |

*Sources*: R.M. Stern, 'A century of food exports', *Kyklos*, **13** (1960), pp. 44–64; *UK Statistical Abstract of Foreign Countries; Official Abstract of British India*; M.C. Urquhart and K.A.H. Buckley, *Historical Statistics of Canada* Toronto: Macmillan (1965).

* French grain exports were relatively small from 1854 to 1857, but increased greatly in 1858.

high and so were earnings. Hence workers in manufacturing industry had also to be paid similarly high wages. It was therefore worth developing more complex and expensive machinery to save labour in the United States than in Britain, as a group of Englishmen discovered when they came to see the Industrial Exhibition in New York in 1853. They arrived to find the exhibition was not ready and so instead they visited a number of American firms. Two of them, George Wallis, headmaster of the School of Art at Birmingham and Joseph Whitworth, one of the most prominent British engineers, wrote reports concerned with the manufactures and machinery they saw. Shortly afterwards, Whitworth testified to a parliamentary select committee on small arms that the American methods used to make small arms were worth further investigation. In 1854 a committee was sent to the United States to survey American methods, and to place orders for £10 000 worth of machinery. It is doubtful though that American superiority in labour-saving machinery extended much beyond light mass-production engineering; Whitworth's desire to boost his own achievement in machine tools, according to Musson, has led to an overestimate of American technology. Machine tools, which saved labour, originated earlier and in the first half of the century spread more extensively in Britain than the United States.

By the middle of the nineteenth century coal was, like land, a crucial natural factor of production. Some argued the British owed her prosperity entirely to her abundant coal resources which gave her cheap motive power for railways and steamships. Among them the Victorian economist, Jevons thought that the source of Britain's comparative advantage was her coal.[14] Because coal was a non-renewable resource, in contrast to climate, he thought that Britain's iron trade was suicidal from a national point of view. In 1865 the iron industry took between one-third and one-quarter of the whole national yield of coal, and at such a rate of consumption he forecasted Britain's stock of coal would soon be run down and her comparative advantage eliminated. The consequences of such a state of affairs he illustrated by an example of three economies, two with similar opportunity-costs. Then gains from trade could only be achieved by trading with the third country. The total trade, and therefore gains, would be shared between the two similar states in proportion to their absolute productivities.

This analogy, Jevons claimed, was appropriate to the international economy of the 1860s, which was in effect divided into five groups. First there was Great Britain with an advantage in coal-intensive products such as iron and steel. Secondly, there was continental Europe with an advantage in artistic and luxurious products, and lacking in coal. The third group was the tropical East, and other regions, supplying food and raw materials based on climate. Fourth, the Australia, Africa, and North American colonies group had plenty of raw materials, but no coal. Finally, there was the United States which had everything including coal, and as immigration boosted her population, she would soon become an impossibly powerful competitor to Britain in world trade.

Certainly the central importance of coal largely explains the pattern of French trade and technology. French engine drivers were given a bonus according to their fuel saving, while British and German engine drivers were merely required to arrive on time.[15] French ironmasters used less fuel per ton of pig iron smelted than British ironmasters throughout the second half of the nineteenth century. France's most important trading partners were Britain, the United States and Belgium. In trade with the US, France like Britain took advantage of the abundant land in America, but because of the paucity of her coal deposits, her imports from Belgium and Britain were coal-intensive products. Over 60 per cent of British exports to France in 1854 consisted of raw materials or intermediate goods, including coal, wool, iron, copper, semi-finished textiles, particularly woollen products; while over half of French exports to Britain took the form of finished manufactured goods and processed foodstuffs, such as silk, leather and cotton manufactures, wine, spirits, refined sugar and flour.[16] British industry sent machinery and intermediate goods to French industry which returned finished manufactured goods to British consumers. The French, having a comparative disadvantage in coal-intensive products, had a comparative advantage in skill-intensive processes (despite no higher literacy rates) which tended to involve finishing rather than basic manufacture.

## Trade and income gaps between countries

Because of the export possibilities for the wheat-growing areas of the United States, the price of wheat in terms of textiles was higher than it otherwise would have been, and therefore so also was the value of the wheat-growing land. Conversely, the availability of wheat imports to the United Kingdom reduced the market price of British wheat in terms of textiles, and thereby reduced the rent relative to wages that the British landlords could obtain, as they recognised in their opposition to the repeal of the Corn Laws in 1846. International trade then should tend to eliminate the differences in relative domestic factor prices that give rise to trade.[17] In fact similar logical difficulties occur with the factor price equalisation theorem as with predicting the pattern of trade from factor abundance and factor intensity. In the simple case of two countries and two goods, equalisation may not take place because each country stops producing the good in which it has a comparative coast disadvantage, importing it entirely; Britain might have given up all wheat production before rents had been driven down to American levels. Factor intensity reversals allow the possibility that even without complete specialisation, factor price equalisation may not occur. Transport costs and tariffs both prevent the emergence of a single price for internationally-traded commodities, and so also prevent the emergence of a single price for the factors used to produce these goods.

The technological changes giving rise to transport cost reductions mainly affected intra-European trade rather than longer distance routes. Hence regions within Europe were opened up to the international market in these years, and if the factor price theorem is true for this period there should have been a greater tendency to equalise wages within Europe, rather than between Europe and the rest of the world. However, even within countries the size of factor price differentials remained substantial. In England during the 1850s the money wages paid to farm labourers on Salisbury Plain, Wiltshire were half those paid in south Lancashire. Fitters' rates in central London were double rates in parts of Cornwall.[18] The differential was as great as the overall improvement between 1850 and 1914, and almost certainly exceeded the difference between the average British and American wage. Differences in male wage rates were not offset by compensating differentials in either the cost of living or family earnings. Apart from rents, there was a high degree of homogeneity in prices in the economy. Differences in male earnings were rarely compensated by earnings of wives and children and often reinforced. The demand for labour worked to supplement the advantages of already prosperous areas Hunt believes; capital was not drawn to low wage areas. Despite a high mobility of labour the reduction of differentials before 1914 was very slow; considerable mobility was needed merely to prevent a widening of differentials.

Similarly in the United States of 1860, personal money income per head was 65 per cent of the national average in the South Atlantic region, but 143 per cent of the average in New England.[19] By 1880 the differential had widened to 45 and 141 per cent, and the Pacific had become the richest region at 204 per cent of the average income. The extent to which regional prices offset or reinforced these money income variations is less certain. New England prices exceeded the national average probably by 7 per cent in 1851 and remained above it throughout the period.[20] Coelho and Shepherd's price index for the South Atlantic region is higher than that for New England despite the theoretical presumption that it would be lower. However the data on which the index is based may well be unrepresentative of the region as a whole. In any event there was no narrowing of price differentials between 1850 and 1880, and real income differentials therefore persisted.

This is a surprising conclusion in some respects in view of the results for India, which show a reduction in the inter-regional coefficient of variation of cotton prices from 0.441 in 1862/3 to 0.167 in 1874/5 as railways spread.[21] Grain, having a lower value in relation to bulk, only later showed a reduction in price variation. A study of the rye and wheat regional markets in Russia attributed 83 per cent of the decline in the inter-regional price differential directly to the railway-induced fall in transport costs.[22] In the light of this evidence, the persistence of wage and price differentials within countries must be explained partly by the importance in consumption

**Table 2.4** *European real incomes per head and their growth rates, 1850–70*

| | Real income per head in 1960 US dollar prices, (three-year annual averages) 1850 | Average annual growth rate 1850–60 | 1860–70 |
|---|---|---|---|
| Britain | 458 | 1.97 | 1.18 |
| Netherlands | 427 | 0.57 | 1.13 |
| Belgium | 411 | 1.75 | 1.53 |
| Switzerland | 391 | 2.04 | 1.34 |
| Norway | 350 | 1.36 | 0.49 |
| France | 333 | 0.92 | 1.80 |
| Spain | 313 | 1.00 | − 0.50 |
| Germany | 308 | 1.39 | 1.85 |
| Austria–Hungary | 283 | 0.18 | 0.57 |
| Italy | 277 | 0.83 | 0.36 |
| Portugal | 260 | 0.56 | − 0.18 |
| Denmark | 256 | 1.38 | 1.45 |
| Finland | 227 | 0.60 | 2.60 |
| Greece | 215 | 0.67 | 0.83 |
| Sweden | 211 | 0.64 | 0.89 |
| Romania | 190 | 0.51 | 0.49 |
| Russia | 175 | 0.17 | 3.36 |

*Source*: P. Bairoch, 'Europe's gross national product, 1800–1975', *Journal of European Economic History*, **5** (1976), pp. 273–340.

of goods that were not much traded between regions, and partly by a growth process that is not captured by the HO theorem on which factor price equalisation is based.

Under some circumstances a tendency towards factors price equalisation would be accompanied by the narrowing of gaps in real income per head between countries. But because economies have different resources per head of population, the equalisation of the prices of these resources and of labour through trade could widen the gap, even though all trading economies are made better off.[23] During the 1850s income gaps tended to widen. Britain, with the highest income, had the second highest growth rate, while Russia, with the lowest income, had the lowest growth rate (see Table 2.4). The next decade showed more signs of convergence. Russia now had the highest growth rate, and France and Germany also both achieved growth rates greater than those of the small open economies which took the top four places in the income per head league. That these countries, Britain, Belgium, Switzerland and Netherlands, were clustered together may itself be taken as evidence of the effects of trade, for being small and close to each other, regional differences within them may have been less persistent and the cost of trading between them was relatively low.

Divergent European income growths during the 1850s may be due to the elapse of time necessary for the railway network to spread and to generate trade and the consequent structural change, rather than to relative factor price changes and the pattern of resource endowments. Also other forces, institutions and political developments in particular, were working to influence national standards of living as well. The poor performance of the Spanish economy owed much to chronic banditry and endemic civil war which culminated in the fully-fledged revolution of 1868, in turn followed by nearly a decade of anarchy and civil war. Austria–Hungary also remained backward. Only in 1850 was the customs frontier between Austria and Hungary abolished, and the new tariff of 1852 was noteworthy merely because it replaced outright prohibitions on the importing of many articles with high duties. The unsuccessful wars with Piedmont and France in 1859 and with Prussia in 1866 similarly did not encourage economic development. On the other hand, from 1853 Austrian trade with the Zollverein was encouraged by large tariff reductions. Italy was not politically unified until 1861 and the relatively small size (and unprofitability) of her railway system indicated poor prospects for economic growth.

## Factor mobility

An alternative means of equalising factor prices in international trade is the mobility of factors of production. Capital was mobile between European nations despite many wars; the bankers Barings saw no objection to raising a loan for the Russian government in London during the Crimean War.[24]

The opportunities for the profitable mobility of free labour arose mainly from rural–urban migration, and between countries, from the old countries to the new. The movement of indentured labour from India and China to plantations was an exception to the rural–urban pattern. The time and costs spent on long-distance travelling were reduced by the steamship even when steam was uneconomical for long-distance freight. The simple Hecksher–Ohlin theory predicts that such migration would normally reduce the volume of trade, but the reverse was true because the natural resources of the United States, Australia and New Zealand were complementary to the mobile factors; without factor mobility there would have been less international trade because the natural resources on which it was based would not have been utilised.

The first major influx of immigrants to the United States was in the decade after 1844 when 2.87 million Europeans joined a population of only 19.5 million. Brinley Thomas offers some support for the natural resource hypothesis by pointing to a structural change in the American economy just after the Civil War, with the effect of changing the direction of the lag between immigration and American economic activity.[25] Before the war, immigration preceded railway building and followed coal output. After the war both immigration and coal output lagged behind railway building. The implication is that before the 1870s, when the exploitation of natural resources made transport developments of prime importance, the rate of American expansion was conditioned by new labour which built the railways. The second influx of migrants, from 1863 until 1873, also preceded fixed capital investment. Subsequently, railway building ceased to be the dominant force that it had been and changes in migration, for example the third expansion of 1878–88 were now induced by changes in the general level of investment.

The complementarity of natural resources and equipment also suggests why factor prices were not equalised by migration between Europe and the United States. Paul David has maintained that nineteenth-century mechanical technology happened to involve a greater input of 'land' per unit of output when operations were mechanised to save labour.[26] The woodworking machinery which was popular in America and neglected in Britain was not only labour saving but also wasteful of wood.[27] American cotton spinning machinery was not only more capital intensive than English equipment but also required a greater input of longer staple cotton (a more costly grade of raw material) per pound of yarn.[28] The efficient use of mechanical reapers required a level, stone-free farm terrain, arranged in large and regularly shaped enclosures, a specific natural resource input that in the mid-nineteenth century was obtained much more cheaply (relative to the price of grain) in the United States than in the British Isles.[29] Hence in America the capital formation encouraged by the greater possibilities of jointly substituting natural resources and capital for labour may have been responsible for driving up the relative price of labour on the demand side of the market.

New economies smaller than the United States were more dependent on international factor mobility. The movement of British factors of production to Australia, particularly to supplement local Australian savings, dominated economic development more than in any other growing new country.[30] During the 1860s overseas borrowing from Britain amounted to approximately half of total investment. British funds dominated financing of pastoral assets and were a major part of the finance required for communications development. This transfer, the selling of the greater part of exports to Britain, and the purchase of most commodity imports in Britain, all suggest a dependent relationship usually assumed to be exploitative. In fact Australian living standards appear to have been considerably above those of Britain (£46 GNP per head in 1861 at constant 1911 prices) and the rate of growth in Australia was higher than in Britain (1.4 per cent per annum in GDP per head between 1861–77). The flows of British capital and labour increased GDP at 4.9 per cent per annum by much more than labour productivity from 1861 to 1877. Population grew at 3.5 per cent per annum considerably above all other countries in the western world, and a substantial portion of the increase came from immigration. Between 1861 and 1890 about two-fifths of the addition to population was due to migration, almost all from Great Britain and Ireland. Australian colonial governments took a leading part in encouraging migration by directly offering help with cheap passages and land grants, (about 40 per cent of total immigration was assisted). To describe the Australian economy as subordinated to the British economy therefore seems inappropriate in view of the higher Australian income per head and growth rate, and bearing in mind the Australian government's policies that encouraged relations with Britain.

The effects of factor migration differed as between labour, with which the factor income moved, and capital, where it did not. In the case of labour migration the total effect is the sum of the factor supply increase in the regions of recent settlement and the corresponding reduction in Europe. The abundant natural resources of Australia and the United States meant that the productivity of labour was higher there than in Europe and therefore total world output increased. To a lesser extent this was true of foreign investment which provided a stream of profits for the home country.

Of the two main capital-exporting countries, the British tended to invest in the land-abundant regions, thereby reducing the costs of her food and raw material imports, and France tended to invest in Europe. By 1851 Frenchmen had lent about 2 billion francs to foreign governments and $\frac{1}{2}$ billion francs had been directed to private projects.[31] Spanish industry was almost wholly in the hands of the French. What marked a change after 1851 was the much increased proportion, almost one-half of new foreign investment, that went into enterprise. Railways alone, on the Iberian and Italian peninsulas, in Central Europe and in Russia, accounted for one-third of this investment. Banking, mining and metallurgy were also key sectors. Perhaps the most powerful institution for French foreign investment was the Credit Mobilier of the Pereire brothers.[32] This was a form of industrial bank intended to assemble resources by the sale of shares and obligations to small investors. At the height of its power it handled about 30 per cent of the new security business arising in Paris. It controlled a huge system of state-built Austrian railways and purchased another from the Russian government. Credit Mobilier set up subsidiaries in Spain and Holland with mines, gasworks, shipping companies and railways which they financed on their own responsibility.

British capital like French went mainly to foreign governments (often for expenditures of no benefit to the people, a matter discussed more fully in Chapter 5), secondly to railways, and then to public utilities. By the time Disraeli bought the Suez Canal shares without the consent of Parliament in 1875, Jenks estimated British earnings on foreign investment amounted to at least £50 million per annum and capital exports ran to £30 million more than this figure. The following year the position was reversed, and Britain collected the income from her foreign property for home consumption.

Direct investment in industry, rather than lending to governments, tended to follow the trading connections which first provided the information about investment opportunites. The Welshman, John Hughes, founded his New Russian Company in 1871 to take up a concession of coal- and ore-bearing lands in the Donetz basin, after originally becoming interested through supplying iron for the construction of a Russian battleship. A settlement he founded was named Yuzovka after him, although later the name was changed to Stalino and then to Donetsk.[33]

Where the regions of recent settlement were concerned, it seems likely that the complementarity of the factor flows from the Old World with the abundant natural resources resulted in persistently higher wages than in Europe, instead of factor price equalisation. In other areas, such as Russia, the informational difficulties and institutional restriction (Russian serfdom was only abolished in 1861 and the *mir*, village collective, was almost as restrictive) were probably too great to permit the equilibrating tendencies of the international market to operate.

## Income and welfare

The presumption that increased economic activity, such as that brought about by the extension of the international market, raises living standards requires that any associated changes in economic structure do not generate offsetting adverse effects. If they do then possibly relative incomes per head are poor guides to relative average levels of welfare. One of the most important structural changes associated with rising money incomes was urbanisation; Britain with the highest European income per head at the mid-century was also the most heavily urbanised. The greater part of the French population in contrast continued to live in the country. Thereby the French saved on investment costs of urbanisation, such as sanitation, which may have given an upward bias to British income, when counted as final goods.[34] Urbanisation also replaced unmeasured home production with measured output of market-produced goods, with the consequence that another upward bias may have been given to trends in measured British income. Even more fundamental is the possibility that the French land tenure system restrained population growth, while the British pattern of urbanisation and industrialisation encouraged an explosion of population.

These objections to income per head measures are of much wider significance than the comparison of Britain with France. Though Britain apparently had the highest standard of living in Europe as measured by money income, the life expectation of the British male was by no means the highest, despite the likelihood that this would have been regarded as one of the most important elements of living standards. French life expectations were lower than British as the income rankings predict, but the Scandinavians were well above, contrary to the income rankings.[35] In 1840 the Norwegian male at birth could expect to live 43, the English male, 40.2 and the French male, 38.9 years. Four decades later, the relative expectations, at 48.5, 42.4 and 41.1 years, had not altered.

Another source of bias arises from the use of exchange rates to compare one country's income per head with another.[36] The exchange rate is determined by the goods and services that are traded internationally but these usually amount to only a small proportion of the consumption of the average person. The prices of these non-traded goods can vary greatly from country to country precisely because they are not traded internationally. The poorer the country, the lower the wages which usually comprise most of the cost of these non-traded goods, and hence the lower are their prices relative to richer countries. Thus there will be a systematic tendency to understate the real income, the goods and services that can be bought with the available money income, of poor countries relative to rich. Countries with larger non-traded sectors will have a more biased income measure. If the traded sector is increasing, because for example productivity tends to increase faster in traded goods, there will be a tendency to overstate the growth of real income using exchange rate conversion factors. On the other hand if the size of the non-traded sector, housing, government administration, domestic service for example, is expanding in a poor country, the tendency for convergence of factor rewards is understated.

In a comparison of long-term growth rates of real per capita income between India and the United States, Heston and Summers investigate the order of magnitude of this bias.[37] Between 1870 and 1970 they calculate real income per head increased in India by 75 per cent and in the United States by 470 per cent, implying a relative decline in Indian income to 31 per cent of its 1870 standing in relation to the US. On the basis of exchange rate conversions, Indian income was 9.1 per cent of that of the United States in 1870. Using the prices of the two countries to calculate the relative purchasing power of the two currencies, Indian real income per head was perhaps one-quarter of US income in 1870. By 1970 instead of the 2.1 per cent of US income indicated by exchange rate conversions, the purchasing power method yielded 6.9 per cent. Exchange rate conversions of national income per head, as this example shows, must therefore be accepted only with reservations.

## Economic growth and international economic relations

The comparative advantage theory of trade suggests that income will be increased by opening an economy to trade but this does not constitute economic growth in the sense of a sustained rise in income per head. Roughly speaking theories of growth may be classified into those which are demand-led and those in which growth is generated from the supply side. An eighteenth-century idea of trade was that it increased the capacity and the income of the economy by providing 'a vent for surplus'.[38] This doctrine closely resembles the later export-led growth theory in which foreign demand encourages investment in export industries, which in turn raises income and stimulates further investment and increased income.[39]

Supply side growth theories usually emphasise the efficiency of the price system in balancing supply and demand. This balancing prevents the emergence of unemployed or underutilised resources on any substantial scale unless certain institutions prevent price adjustment. On this assumption an increase in the demand for exports would tend to divert investment and employment away from those industries mainly supplying the home market, so that there would be no increase in growth. Increased investment can temporarily increase growth rates but can only take place at the expense of a reduction in consumption, in current living standards. The only way in a closed economy that growth in income per head can occur is through increased technical progress. The introduction of foreign trade raises the growth rate of the economy temporarily as the gains from trade raise income and savings, and the savings are ploughed back into industry as investment. Diminishing returns to the increased investment set in and the growth rate falls back to that determined by technical progress.

Trade can permanently increase the growth rate when there is a natural input, such as ores, semi-processed metals or agricultural products, for which it is difficult to substitute other factors.[40] In this instance the long-term growth rate of the isolated country is set by the slowest growing natural input. The growth rate can be raised if opening the economy to trade increases the growth of available supplies of this input. This may be considered to be 'import constrained growth'. France's economic growth may have been raised by the opportunity to increase the supply of coal and British economic growth certainly owed something to imports of raw cotton. Indian economic growth may have been enhanced by the importing of railway equipment and Australian growth may have been constrained by imports of British capital goods.

If trade was important to growth we would expect to observe, as in fact we do for all countries growing economically 1850–73, a rise in the ratio of trade to national income. Export-led growth shifts resources into the export sector and in import-constrained growth the removal of supply constraints increases imports, which must be paid for by more exports or capital exports. But the same observation is equally consistent with increased trade in a static comparative advantage model, where growth is independent of trade in the long term. However when 'temporary' increases in growth may last half a century as seems possible in neo-classical supply side models,[41] the distinction between these static and temporary increases, and the permanent increases in growth rates, may not matter much in historical interpretation.

In the course of economic growth, comparative advantages will tend to change as different productivity increases occur between industries and the factors of production are accumulated at different rates. It is even possible that a country need not benefit from growth through the accumulation of its relatively abundant factor, for example labour in a densely-populated poor country ('immiserising growth'). The country will increasingly specialise in the production and export of goods which use a large proportion of the abundant factor, and increase imports of other goods. The price of exports relative to imports (the terms of trade) will fall and this loss of income may exceed the gain from the increased supply of the factor.

Bairoch invokes an immiserising growth model when he argues that the countries of continental Europe did not benefit from free trade in these years but were made worse off.[42] Railways can be regarded as effectively increasing the supply of land which was already abundant and forcing down food prices relative to manufactures. Agricultural productivity fell because the industrial sector could not absorb the labour force that was being made redundant by increased imports of cereals, and the labour remained on the farms. National income fell because agriculture was a large proportion of total output. The removal of protection from industry exacerbated the inability to absorb the surplus labour from agriculture.

The changing pattern of comparative advantage in economic growth is also associated with the changing relative importance of different economic groups and this importance is usually reflected in policy. By the mid-century only 20 per cent of British national income was earned from agriculture and 34 per cent from manufacturing, mining and building. Hence it is hardly surprising that a policy of protecting agriculture had recently been abandoned.

## Commercial policy

Although the twenty-five years after 1850 can reasonably be called the era of free trade, it is a matter of debate as to whether commercial policy was guided primarily, or even substantially, by a desire to reap the maximum gains from trade. From the government's point of view, the use of tariffs as a source of revenue often vied with their potential use as instruments of foreign policy. In some cases the government merely responded to pressure groups who stood to gain, or thought they did, from the imposition of a particular tax on imports. Those groups that stood to gain were producers expecting to sell at higher prices behind the tariff barrier. The losers had to pay the higher prices and included the ultimate consumers and the buyers of intermediate goods and raw materials. In addition mercantile interests suffered from the reduction in the carrying trade. The positive theory of tariff-making asserts essentially that where the numbers of producers expecting to gain are small, they will find it in their interests to co-operate in influencing the government to raise the relevant tariff.[43] Where the costs of the tariff are spread over a large number of losers, no individual will find it worth while to resist a change which has such a small effect on him.

Britain was the first country to adopt free trade and adhered to it most firmly, yet here the reductions were probably undertaken primarily because of budgetary policy rather than because of an ideological commitment to free trade or political lobbying, and arguably the impact of the reductions on the British economy were not ideal even though they were beneficial. Holding the composition of British imports constant, the reduction of tariff rates from 1841 to 1881 was 21 per cent.[44] The absence of major wars and the associated accumulation of debt, together with the Victorian views about the proper role of the state, combined to reduce the government's share of the growing national income. This reduced the share of national income that had to be financed by the tariff revenue, and anyway since the ratio of imports to income was rising, a given rate of tariff generated an increasing ratio of revenue to national income.

Although comparative advantage theory shows that free trade is better than no trade, free trade is not necessarily better than reduced trade. For a country large enough to affect world prices there is an optimum tariff which gives more benefit to the country which imposes it by reducing the price at which foreigners can sell than is cost by the fall in imports consumed by the domestic country. McCloskey argues that the 5.8 per cent average tariff rate in the Britain, on any plausible assumptions, was lower than ideal.[45] He dismisses the likelihood of retaliation against an optimum tariff as no defence, on the grounds that other European countries raised their tariffs anyway during the 1880s. This argument however neglects the 'most favoured nation' (MFN) clause in the treaties negotiated to reduce tariffs after 1860. This clause prevented discrimination in trade policy, because the reduction of duties to one country meant that they were automatically reduced to all other countries receiving MFN treatment from the country reducing them. Consequently the indirect consequences of a MFN treaty for trade expansion often exceeded the direct effects. Had Britain not reduced her average tariff to 5.8 per cent, other national tariffs would not have fallen by so much.

A benefit of the policy actually pursued, the move to virtually free trade, was cheaper food for the British consumer, and it was this that prevented the imposition of tariffs until after the first world war. Foreigners benefitted rather more than British consumers from the opening of the British market. The increased demand tended to raise world prices of cereals and of most transportable foodstuffs more to British levels than to reduce British prices down to former levels abroad.[46] In terms of national security, Britain's increased economic strength outweighed her increased dependence on the rest of the world which was, in any case, being forced on her by population growth. Jenks contests this view, asserting that

Britain's increased dependence upon food imports in exchange for manufactures left her vulnerable in the event of emergency such as harvest failure.[47] Without imports, harvest failures at home would have had much worse consequences.

Other states were less willing than Britain to move to free trade. Almost everywhere indirect taxes, such as excise and import duties, were the main sources of revenue and, while income from these sources expanded with prosperity, so also did state expenditure. The British example of using an income tax to supply the revenue requirements was not politically expedient.

The French liberalisation of trade policy was important for continental Europe, but the motives differed from the earlier British move.[48] Ideas played some part, and Michel Chevalier was an influential intellectual advocate of economic liberalism. The reduction in duties on coal, iron and steel in 1852 as the railway boom began showed an awareness of the national economic benefits of certain tariff cuts. Most significant in overcoming the weight of vested interests in protection was Napoleon III's foreign policy. The Emperor had the sole power to make treaties, including those dealing with trade. The British disapproved of his desire to rid Italy of Austrian rule by force. The Anglo–French commercial treaty of 1860 for reciprocal freer trade was designed to mollify British objections to the resulting war. Thereafter France, the Zollverein, Italy and Britain negotiated a whole series of reciprocal trade treaties with 'most favoured nation' clauses.

In Germany freer trade was one of the few liberal principles on which the eastern Prussian landed aristocrats producing agricultural products for export in these decades, could agree with the liberal western and urban classes who had contested their political predominance in 1848. Changes were made to reduce the Zollverein tariff after 1850 and continued until 1879. The objectives of Prussian foreign policy coincided with *Junker* interests. The main concern was the establishment of a unified Germany with Austria–Hungary excluded.[49] A trade treaty with France served to isolate Austria. Considerable financial concessions were made in order to achieve unification; Hanover, for instance, was bribed to enter the Zollverein customs union by being offered more revenue from the customs than she would get on the basis of population, the usual method of allocating receipts. In addition to the policy objective of unification the importance of the British market for German food grains meant that some attention had to be paid to sensibilities of the British government about the taxation of British exports to Germany. The British managed to foil proposals for a higher external tariff on textiles by referring to the benefits conferred on Germany by the repeal of the Corn Laws. The greatest obstacles for Prussian commercial policy were the protectionist south German states, who frustrated Prussian attempts to reduce the common external tariff. In fact the Zollverein was twice on the verge of collapse and it was only after the customs union had been formally (though not actually) dissolved as a consequence of the Austro–Prussian War of 1866 that Prussia was able to secure the founding of a new Zollverein with much needed reforms, including those affecting the powers of veto.

In contrast to the American tariff regime, the Zollverein drew most of its revenue (more than two-thirds in 1871) from the taxation of popular foods, drinks and tobacco, perhaps reflecting the differing degrees of political emancipation. Almost one-third of the receipts were derived from coffee alone. The protection of domestic industry was less important, though textile revenue was 10 per cent of the 1871 total, suggesting that tariff protection did not play a major part in the rapid industrial development of Germany during these years.

The independent states outside Europe were less affected by free trade doctrines, but in the United States the tendency towards lower tariffs in the late 1840s culminated in 1857, while southern cotton and tobacco interests were still politically strong, in the lowest tariff since 1816. The geographical position of the United States gave little incentive for the government to pay attention to foreigners in setting tariffs. Thus the forces at work on American tariff-making were perhaps to a greater extent than in other countries those of interest groups, though revenue needs were sometimes the justification. The financial crisis of 1857 and associated downturn in economic activity caused a falling-off in the revenue from the duties.[50] The reaction was embodied in the 1861 Morrell Tariff Act nominally intended to restore the rates of the 1846 Act, but the substitution of specific for *ad valorem* duties allowed rather higher rates. The Civil War produced an enormous requirement for government revenue; duties were increased every session until 1865, a huge debt was accumulated, and an inconvertible paper currency introduced.

Even after the war almost any increase of duties demanded by domestic producers was readily granted. A case in point was the wool producers who, in 1864, were protected by a 40 per cent *ad valorem* tariff which had allowed them to expand output greatly. With the end of the war and the re-emergence of the southern cotton economy, wool growers and manufacturers attempted to get more help from the government. A convention of wool growers and manufacturers was therefore held in Syracuse, New York in December 1865. The manufacturers agreed to allow wool producers to raise the duty on the raw material to any height they wished, expecting to be compensated in return. This was granted in 1867 when they were awarded 35 per cent *ad valorem* protection. The temporarily higher profits and increased sales allowed by this legislation did not serve the manufacturers' interests for very long because new entrants were attracted by the profits. The increased competition soon eliminated the excessive returns, and the industry found a new equilibrium in which it used more of the nation's resources than it would have done without protection.

Similar forces were at work to protect the iron and steel industry. By 1877 the duty on steel rails was effectively 100 per cent; as a result the price in the Great Britain was $36 a ton in 1880 and the American price was almost double at $67. The consumers who paid the higher prices of protected goods only gathered enough collective political impetus to object during years of agricultural depression. By 1872 all internal taxes raised during the Civil War had been abolished, yet there had been no corresponding reduction of the wartime tariffs. In that year agrarian unrest against the high price of manufactures, combined with the government budget surplus consequent upon the great volume of taxed imports, justified a tariff reduction of 10 per cent across the board. After 1873 imports declined and so did customs revenue. The reaction was to repeal the 1872 Act after only three years to restore the lost revenue.

Unlike the United States many countries outside Europe were unable to pursue an independent tariff policy in these years. Both China and Japan had signed treaties placing a low upper limit on their tariff rates. In the British empire, an Act of 1846 had given colonies freedom to pursue their own tariff policies. Canada raised duties on manufactures to around 20 per cent in 1859 and reduced duties on sugar, tea and coffee, despite the protests of Sheffield manufacturers, in order to raise money for the new railway system. The Australian colonies reacted to their freedom differently; New South Wales opted for free trade and Victoria for protection. South African colonists introduced a protective tariff in 1866/7. India was not given the same freedom in these years, not being a colony in 1846. This caused such indignation amongst nationalist Indian historians that the formation of policy has received much more intensive study than the effects.

Indian commercial policy was dictated by a combination of revenue requirements and the political pressures on the British government to maintain India as a market for British cotton textiles and prevent the emergence of Indian export competition. When the British government took control from the East India Company in 1858 the import duties consisted of $3\frac{1}{2}$ per cent *ad valorem* on cotton twist and yarns, and 5 per cent on other articles of British produce and manufacture, including cotton piece goods.[51] The duties were double on foreign articles. The heavy financial pressure after the Mutiny led to the abolition of all differential tariffs the following year. Beer, wine, spirits and tobacco were taxed at rates higher than the 10 per cent uniform rate established in 1860. Throughout the 1860s there was a general tendency to reduce tariffs, with cotton manufactures taking priority. This was made possible, as in the British case, by a rising revenue from trade. In 1856/7, customs revenue was £1.19 million of a total revenue of £31.92 million. By 1870/1 customs revenue was providing £2.61 million out of a total government revenue of £49.38 million. To prevent Indian mills competing in the finer cotton goods, a 5 per cent duty on long staple cotton imports was imposed in 1875. This was not deemed sufficient however, and Lord Salisbury, the Secretary of State for India, insisted on the repeal of the 5 per cent import duties on cotton manufactures. The Indian Viceroy, Lord Northbrook, resigned in protest, and subsequent financial difficulties prevented compliance for some years. In 1879 the duties were eventually repealed but the electoral advantage that the British government might have hoped to gain in Lancashire was not adequate, for they lost the General Election of 1880.

The consequences of the loss of tariff autonomy for Indian economic development are usually overstated. In other countries protective duties often merely allowed higher profits and prices, less effort, and the diversion of more resources than ideal to the protected industries. If there were economies of scale in cotton textile manufacture such that the larger output induced by tariff protection reduced unit costs and prices, then some benefit may have been forgone. Similarly the existence of cost reductions from 'learning by doing' could result in a net gain from the tariff protection that the Indian industry was denied. The evidence for the pre-Civil War American cotton textile industry suggests however that there were only small benefits at stake, and in any case there were alternative ways of ensuring the ideal amount of 'learning'.[52] Despite minimal tariff protection, a large modern Indian cotton textile industry did emerge.

Other dynamic arguments for net benefits from a high level protection can be found, though their relevance to the Indian case is doubtful. In a growing economy free trade is not the optimal policy for a large country because the growth of exports will cause an excessive deterioration in the terms of trade.[53] There is an optimum tariff which offsets this deterioration.

More important, perhaps, were the revenue limitations placed on the Indian government which remained limited to taxes, such as those on land, which did not increase their yield, unlike the import taxes, when the need for public expenditure also increased. Even this position loses some credibility if the charges of Government extravagence in the organisation of the construction of the Indian railway system, can be sustained.

## Summary and conclusion

The rapid expansion of international trade and economic development from 1850 to 1875 owed much to the application of steam technology to land and sea transport. Those countries whose incomes were growing experienced an increase in the 'openness' of their economies – in the ratio of trade to national income – largely because of transport cost and tariff reductions. These reductions expanded the demand for exports and for imports more than proportionately to the growth of income, which was itself enhanced by the increased productivity allowed by the extension of international specialisation. The pattern of this specialisation was largely determined by national endowments of factors of production especially climatic factors, arable or pastoral land, coal or labour rather than by the gradual diffusion of technical knowledge. A tendency towards the equalisation of national incomes per head as a result of trade and factor mobility was observed in the small open economies of Europe, Britain, Holland, Belgium and Switzerland, during the 1860s joined by France and Germany. In other European countries there were political and institutional barriers to this process. The regions of recent settlement, the United States and Australia in particular, had massive endowments of natural resources which, being complementary to capital equipment, allowed the persistence of higher returns to labour than were achieved in the countries from which so much of the labour migrated. Within countries there were also similar effects which allowed the persistence of wide interregional income differences.

The justification for believing in welfare gains from trade is the notion that being able to buy more of what one wants is an improvement in welfare. The structural changes associated with this process, especially urbanisation, meant that some things had to be bought which previously were either free or were unncessary. Hence it would be rash to assume without detailed consideration that higher incomes always permitted higher standards of living. However the higher incomes are evaluated, the increased international economic relations allowed Europe to support a larger population. The fundamental question, to which no answer has been attempted here, is whether that larger population would have been brought into existence anyway or whether it was, in some way, induced.

The process of economic expansion in these years resulted in a shift of resources and political power in response to the pressures of the international economy. The regulation of international trade was partly a response to the relocation of political power, or the changed objective of that power, partly to the needs for revenue to finance state activity, and partly to political beliefs. The general view of the consequences of economic liberalisation is that it was a great benefit to the European economies, though more recently it has been maintained that the gains to Britain were small and, for Europe, negative. The United States participated for only a few years in this movement, but foreign trade was sufficiently unimportant in national income for the gains or losses from protection in America to have been similarly small.

## Notes

1. R.W. Fogel, 'Notes on the social saving controversy', *Journal of Economic History*, **39** (1979), pp. 1–54. P.K. O'Brien, *The New Economic History of Railways*, London: Croom Helm (1977).
2. G.R. Hawke, *Railways and Economic Growth in England and Wales 1860–1870*, London: Oxford University Press (1970). T.R. Gourvish, *Railways and the British Economy 1830–1914*, London: Macmillan (1980).
3. W.J. Macpherson, 'Economic development in India under the British Crown 1858–1947', in A.J. Youngson (ed.), *Economic Development in the Long Run*, London: Allen & Unwin (1972), pp. 143–5.
4. C.K. Harley, 'The shift from sailing ships to steamships, 1850–90', in D.N. McCloskey (ed.), *Essays on a Mature Economy: Britain after 1840*, London: Methuen (1971).
5. D.C. North, 'Ocean freight rates and economic development 1750–1913' *Journal of Economic History*, **17** (1958), pp
6. P. Bairoch, 'Geographical structure and trade balance of European foreign trade, 1800–1970', *Journal of European Economic History*, **3** (1974), and 'Europe's gross national product, 1800–1975', *Journal of European Economic History*, **5** (1976), pp. 273–340.
7. D. Ricardo, *On the Principles of Political Economy and Taxation*, (1817), ch. 7.

8. D.A. Farnie, *The English Cotton Industry and the World Market 1815–1896*, London: Oxford University Press (1979), ch. 2.

9. D.S. Landes, *The Unbound Prometheus*, Cambridge University Press (1969), chs 3 and 4.

10. L.H. Jenks, *The Migration of British Capital to 1875*, London: Nelson (1971) (1st edn 1927), pp. 164–7.

11. E. Hecksher, 'The effects of foreign trade on the distribution of income', in H. Ellis and L. Metzler (eds), *Readings in the Theory* of International Trade, London: Allen & Unwin (1949). B. Ohlin, *Inter-regional and International Trade*, Cambridge, Mass: Harvard University Press (1933).

12. A.K. Dixit and V. Norman, *Theory of International Trade*, Cambridge: Cambridge University Press (1980), p. 8.

13. H.J. Habbakuk, *American and British Technology in the Nineteenth Century*, Cambridge: Cambridge University Press (1962). P. Temin, 'Labour scarcity and the problem of American industrial efficiency in the 1850s', *Journal of Economic History*, **26** (1966), pp. 361–79. R.W. Fogel, 'The specification problem in economic history', *Journal of Economic History*, **27** (1969), pp. 283–308. P. Temin, 'Labour scarcity in America', *Journal of Interdisciplinary History*, **1** (1971), pp. 251–61. P.A. David, *Technical Choice. Innovation and Economic Growth*, Cambridge: Cambridge University Press (1975), ch. 1. A.E. Musson, 'The engineering industry', in R.A. Church (ed.), *The Dynamics of Victorian Business*, London: Allen & Unwin (1980).

14. W.S. Jevons, *The Coal Question* (1906), pp. 369, 415.

15. A. Milward and S.B. Saul, *The Economic Development of Continental Europe 1780–1870*, London: Allen & Unwin (1973) p. 173.

16. P. O'Brien and C. Keyder, *Economic Growth in Britain and France 1780–1914*, London: Allen & Unwin (1978), p. 142.

17. P.A. Samuelson, 'International factor price equalisation once again', *Economic Journal*, **59** (1949), pp. 181–97.

18. E.H. Hunt, *Regional Wage Variations in Britain 1850–1914*, London: Oxford University Press (1973).

19. R.A. Easterlin, 'Regional income trends, 1840–1950', in S.E. Hanis (ed.), *American Economic History*, New York: McGraw Hill (1961).

20. P.R. Coelho and J.F. Shepherd, 'Differences in regional prices: the United States, 1851–1880', *Journal of Economic History*, **34** (1974), pp. 551–91.

21. M.B. McAlpin, 'Railroad prices and peasant rationality: India 1860–1900', *Journal of Economic History*, **34** (1974), pp. 662–84.

22. J. Metzer, 'Railroad development and market integration: the case of tsarist Russia', *Journal of Economic History*, **34** (1974), pp. 529–50.

23. A numerical example may clarify the point. Consider two economies, one labour-abundant, with 100 units of labour and 50 units of land, and the other land-abundant, with 30 units of labour and 40 units of land. Suppose that before trade the rent in the labour-abundant economy is 2

units of produce and the wage payment is 1, and that the opposite is true of the land-abundant economy. Then their incomes per unit of the labour force are respectively $(100 \times 1 + 50 \times 2)/100 = 2$ and $(30 \times 2 - 40 \times 1)/30 = 3\frac{1}{3}$. When factor prices are equalised by trade at $1\frac{1}{2}$ both for the wage rate and for the rent, the income gaps per unit of the labour force narrow to $2\frac{1}{4}$ and $3\frac{1}{2}$ units of produce respectively for the two economies. But when factor prices are equalised between the countries at a wage rate of $1\frac{1}{4}$ and a rent of $1\frac{3}{4}$ the gap is widened. The labour-abundant country benefits less from trade because wages have risen less than rents. Its income per labour unit is $2\frac{1}{8}$ compared with $3\frac{58}{100}$ in the land-abundant country.

24. Jenks, op.cit., p. 285.
25. B. Thomas, *Migration and Economic Growth: A Study of Great Britain and the Atlantic Economy*, 2nd edn, Cambridge: Cambridge University Press, (1973), pp. 92–4.
26. David, op.cit., pp. 87–91.
27. E. Ames and N. Rosenberg, 'The Enfield arsenal in theory and history', *Economic Journal*, **78** (1968), pp. 827–42.
28. L.G. Sandberg, 'American rings and English mules', *Quarterly Journal of Economics*, **83** (1969), pp. 25–43.
29. David, op.cit., ch. 5.
30. N.G. Butlin, *Investment in Australian Economic Development 1861–1900*, Cambridge: Cambridge University Press (1964), ch. 1.
31. R. Cameron, *France and the Economic Development of Europe 1800–1914*, Princeton, NJ: Princeton University Press (1961), p. 85.
32. Jenks, op.cit., pp. 242–5.
33. A. Milward and S.B. Saul, *The Development of the Economies of Continental Europe 1850–1914*, London: Allen & Unwin (1978) p. 407.
34. O'Brien and Keyder, op.cit., p. 188. Because public health expenditures in Britain were minimal at the mid-century, income then was biased downwards in relation to welfare, compared with French income.
35. M. Hart and H. Hertz, 'Expectation of life as an index of social progress', *American Sociological Review* (1944), quoted in Milward and Saul, op.cit. p. 135. H.J. Habbakuk and M.M. Postan (eds), *Cambridge Economic History of Europe*, vol 6, part. 1, pp. 72–88.
36. I. Kravis, *et al.*, 'Real GDP per capita for more than one hundred countries', *Economic Journal*, **88** (June 1978), pp. 215–42.
37. A. Heston and R. Summers, 'Comparative Indian economic growth: 1870 to 1970', *American Economic Review: Papers and Proceedings*, **70** (1980), pp. 96–101.
38. H. Myint, 'Adam Smith's theory of international trade in the perspective of economic development', *Economica*, **44** (1977), pp. 231–48.
39. W. Beckerman and Associates, *The British Economy in 1975*, Cambridge: Cambridge University Press (1965).
    R. Batchelor *et al.*, *Industrialization and the Basis for Trade*, Cambridge: Cambridge University Press (1980), ch. 7.

40. J. Black, 'Trade and the natural growth rate'. *Oxford Economic Papers*, **22** (1970), pp. 13–23.

41. K. Sato, 'On the adjustment time in neo-classical growth models', *Reviews of Economic Studies*, **33** (1966), pp. 263–8, suggests that 90 per cent adjustment in between 25 and 37.5 years is a plausible result from such models.

42. P. Bairoch, 'Free trade and European development in the nineteenth century', *European Economic Review*, **3** (1972), pp. 211–46.

43. J.J. Pincus, *Pressure Groups and Politics in Antebellum Tariffs*, New York: Columbia University Press (1977), ch. 5.

44. D.N. McCloskey, 'Magnanimous Albion: free trade and British national income, 1841–81', *Explorations in Economic History*, **17** (1980), pp. 303–20.

45. McCloskey's optimum tariff formula is:

$$t = \frac{1/e + 1/d}{1 - 1/d}$$

where $e$ and $d$ are respectively the (absolute values of the) elasticities of the foreign supply of British importables and of foreign demand for British exportables. An export elasticity formula is derived in M.E. Kreinen, *International Economics: a Policy Approach*, 2nd edn, New York: Harcourt Brace (1975), Appendix III. As the foreign demand for British exportables becomes more elastic, there is less opportunity for Britain to shift the terms of trade in her favour with a tariff: the optimum tariff rate falls. So if the foreign demand elasticity for exportables ($d$) rises from $(-)2$ to $(-)3$, the optimum tariff rate falls from

$$\frac{1/e + 1/2}{1 - 1/2} = (2/e) + 1, \quad \text{to} \quad \frac{1/e + 1/3}{1 - 1/3} = (3/2e) + \tfrac{1}{2},$$

or, if $e = 1$, say from 300 to 200 per cent. Similarly as the elasticity of foreign supply of British importables ($e$) rises from say 1 to 2 with $d = 3$, the optimum tariff falls from 200 to 125 per cent $= (3/2 \times 2) + 1/2$. These numbers are all high, well above the actual 5.8 per cent tariff rate for 1880, and McCloskey's conclusion is apparently supported. The problem is, however, whether the assumed elasticity values are plausible. If Britain in the nineteenth century were a small country, then it would face a perfectly elastic foreign demand for its exports and foreign supply of imports. With $e = d = \infty$, optimum $t = 0$; less than the actual rate for 1880. Using an export elasticity formula, McCloskey calculates $d = 17$. If the actual rate in 1880 was identical with the optimum rate, the value of $e$ can be inferred.

$$t = 0.058 = \frac{1/e + 1/17}{1 - 1/17}$$
$$1/e = (1 - 1/17) \times 0.058 - 1/17 = -0.0042$$

Therefore $e = -238$: colossal and absurd foreign economies of scale. If optimal $t$ were the 1841 actual of 0.34, the implied $e$ value is:

$$0.34 = \frac{1/e + 1/17}{1 - 1/17}$$
$$1/e = (1 - 1/17) \times 0.34 - 1/17 = 0.261$$

Hence $e = 3.8$, a rather more plausible number. Thus, although we are not able to assert the 1841 tariff rate *was* optimal, the above experiments show the robustness of the conclusion that the 1880 tariff rate was sub-optimal, in the *absence of matching behaviour by other countries*; McCloskey's conclusion is not sensitive to plausible changes in the parameters of the problem.

46. A. Imlah, *Economic Elements in the Pax Britannica*, New York: Russell & Russell (1969), ch. 6.
47. Jenks, op. cit., pp. 158–63.
48. C.P. Kindleberger, 'The rise of free trade in western Europe, 1820–1825', *Journal of Economic History*, **33** (1975), 38–41.
49. W.O. Henderson, *The Zollverein*, Cambridge: Cambridge University Press (1939), ch. 6.
50. F.W. Taussig, *The Tariff History of the United States*, New York and London: Putnam (1931), 8th edn.
51. R.C. Dutt, *India in the Victorian Age*, (first published 1904), 2nd edn, New York: B. Franklin (1970), chs. 10, 12, Book II.
52. David, op. cit., ch. 2.
53. M.A.M. Smith, 'Capital accumulation in the open two sector model', *Economic Journal*, **87** (1977), pp. 273–82.

# 3 The International Monetary System, 1850–1875

An expanding international division of labour was only possible because of the corresponding development of the international monetary system. Specialisation required exchanges between exporters and importers, often separated by great distances, so that goods spent a considerable time in transit and the contracting parties could have little direct knowledge of each other. As well as acceptable media of exchange, trust and finance were therefore essential to foreign trade. The international monetary system in the third quarter of the nineteenth century evolved to provide these needs. In many respects the international monetary system was merely the domestic monetary system writ large, and accordingly, though providing similar advantages, suffered from similar problems. Periodic financial crises convulsed the international economy; bankruptcies and defaults caused workers to be laid off, unemployment rose, and national incomes fell. One of the tasks of this chapter is to examine the extent to which crises were domestically, rather than internationally, generated, and whether they were exacerbated or alleviated by monetary institutions or policy. But first we describe the organisation of monetary relations and the way they worked.

## Merchant bankers and bills of exchange

Among the international monetary institutions of the mid-nineteenth century, their legendary private wealth made the Rothschild family the most glamorous. The Rothschilds were reputedly the best-informed men in Europe, using their knowledge to increase the mobility of European capital and to become even richer. The family fortunes can be traced to Meyer Amschel Rothschild, a dealer in coins, medals and antiques in the *Judengasse* of Frankfurt. Meyer died in 1812 leaving a vast fortune to five able sons. The eldest remained to manage the ancestral house in Frankfurt, while the others went separately to establish banks in Vienna, Paris, London and Naples. Because they lacked a house in Berlin, the Rothschilds adopted Bleichroder as their Berlin agent, thus contributing to the financial strength of Gerson Bleichroder which permitted him to become Bismarck's banker.[1]

Almost as powerful as the Rothschilds was the House of Baring. Baring also orginated in Germany; the House had been founded by an emigrant from Bremen to Exeter in 1717.[2] Baring however concentrated to a much greater extent on extra-European trans-actions. The bulk of their business in the 1850s arose from trade between the United States and Britain. They bought and sold merchandise and securities on commission as well as for themselves, they operated their own ships, kept the accounts of selected depositors, and acted as financial agents for business houses and governments all over the world, especially in Latin America and the British empire. But the mainstay of Baring was the 'acceptance' business, and here they had developed a system for assigning credit ratings to potential customers.

The acceptance business was the arrangement of short-term finance by granting 'acceptance credit'. Under these credits, bills of exchange were drawn out and accepted by Baring or another acceptance house, for a commission. The bill of exchange can be seen as a promise to pay a certain sum of money on a particular date – most usually in three months' time. A supplier would issue a bill for the value of goods he was shipping, and for which he expected to be paid at some definite future date; the supplier agreed to 'draw a bill' on the buyer, who acknowledged responsibility for eventual payment by writing on the bill his 'acceptance'. This 'acceptance' by a financial institution signified that the buyer was a good risk for a lender, because the acceptance house was liable in the event of default.

Just as the working of the banking system depended upon public confidence in the safety of their money, so did the bill of exchange system. Reputation and the availability of information as to the risk of lending were essential. Norwegian and Swedish bills during the 1860s were not regarded as first-class risks because the exports of these countries were almost entirely timber or shipping freight services, supplied by small firms without international reputations. In contrast the trade of the East Indies and China consisted of items of great value, and consequently was managed by large, wealthy houses, with established reputations, whose bills were first-class risks.

After acceptance the bill was sold to a financier; a lender would then 'discount' the bill (buy it for less than the sum payable in the future) and the supplier would thereby borrow. The difference between the purchase price of the bill and the value of the promise to pay was the interest charged on the loan. When the goods were sold, the supplier was able to pay the debt and withdraw the bill. The bill could change ownership (be rediscounted) during its currency should the original lender suddenly need cash. Bills of exchange therefore were a valuable means of facilitating both national and international trade at a time when transport was slow and communication difficult.

The London financial institutions accepted bills even for trade that did not touch British shores. In 1858 it was said that 'a man in Boston cannot buy a cargo of tea in Canton without getting a credit from Messrs. Mathieson or Messrs. Baring.'[3] This type of bill finance by London maintained its importance for trade between ports of small volume in the third quarter of the nineteenth century, but once the volume of trade increased and, along with it, information and confidence, the intermediation of London in trade not otherwise connected with Britain was no longer necessary. By the 1860s, the New York–Bremen trade was no longer mediated by London, but the Bombay–Bremen trade, being small, continued to use London bills.[4]

Not all types of bills had a good reputation. The finance bill issued, not to provide finance for a particular transaction but generally for working capital, on occasion was discounted without adequate attention to the collateral. Consequently, the over-issue of such bills, particularly international accomodation bills, was blamed for the financial panic of 1857.[5] The distinction between types of bill was however often misleading. Foreign bills were sometimes used to provide short-term capital, and inland bills were often drawn to finance foreign trade. The difference between types of bill was a legal one, not necessarily indicating the type of transaction financed. When the mail from Australia and New Zealand arrived only every few weeks, the failure of a London merchant to receive in one mail the payment for his goods would sometimes lead him to get new credit on bill finance until the next mail.[6]

As might be expected from this example, improved communications reduced the need for bills by cutting down the time spent by goods in transit. But the telegraph also allowed the money markets to finance the inventories previously held by great merchants by introducing greater certainty into international transactions.[7] The first direct communication between London and Paris by electric telegraph was in November 1852, through the lines of the Submarine Telegraph Co. and the European and American Telegraph Co.[8] Land communication by telegraph continued to be adversely affected by wet weather in the early 1850s, because of inadequate insulation of the cables. The first Atlantic cable of 1858 stopped working very quickly also because of an insulation fault. Not until 1866 did the Great Eastern manage to lay a cable that permitted permanent transatlantic communication. Fourteen years later there were nine cables across the Atlantic.

On 23 June 1870, the British Indian Telegraph Company's direct cable from Bombay to England was completed.[9] Soon afterwards the Great Northern Telegraph Company of Denmark extended the trans-Siberian line, which had been finished in the late 1860s, from Vladivostock to Shanghai and Yokohama. There the system linked up with the cables of the Eastern Extension Company which connected India with China, Singapore and Australia. The Indian exporter could now sell his cotton by contract even before it was shipped, and therefore had no need of bill finance.

## Exchange rates

Bills of exchange worked as a form of international money by acting as a medium of exchange between countries. The value of one currency in terms of another, the market exchange rate, was determined primarily by the buyers and sellers of these bills on the foreign exchange. Here debts and claims that originated from exporting or importing or from other international transactions, such as investment or foreign travel, were traded. If England were heavily in debt to France, but did not have claims on France falling due to an equivalent value, those few English merchants who had credits in their Paris accounts could obtain rather more for their credits than when debts and credits were more equally balanced; there was a tendency for the franc to rise against sterling.

A nation with a precious metal monetary standard undertook, at least nominally, to buy or sell gold or silver (or in the case of a bimetallic standard, both) at a fixed and predetermined rate against the national currency. Furthermore the precious metal was allowed to circulate freely within the national economy exchangeable against the domestic note issue. For every pair of nations that undertook this commitment against the same precious metal there was a 'mint par' exchange rate determined by the metal content of the two coinages. The franc–sterling mint par, for instance, was determined as follows:[10]

(a) The Bank of England coined 480 oz Troy of gold 11/12th fine into 1869 sovereigns.

(b) The Bank of France coined 1000 g of gold 9/10th fine into 155 Napoleons of 20 francs each.

(c) 1 oz Troy = 31.1035 g.

(d) The gold equivalent of the franc and pound was therefore such that $£1 = \dfrac{480 \times 11 \times 31.1035 \times 3100}{1869 \times 12 \times 900} = 25.2215$ francs

It was unlikely that the mint par exchange rate would usually correspond exactly with the market exchange rate. But if the divergence became anything more than slight then there were opportunities for profit from 'arbitrage' in precious metals, from buying bullion in one country and selling it in another. If the sterling rate against the franc fell below 25.10 francs, for example, gold would flow out of England in considerable quantities because a given quantity of gold had become more valuable in francs than it was in sterling at the prevailing rate of exchange. The 'specie points' were the exchange rates on either side of the mint par at which the import or export of bullion (or specie) became profitable. Because of different assaying and melting charges, the specie points depended on the form of the metal, as well as on the transport and insurance costs, as shown in Table 3.1.

Although the United States was also effectively on a gold standard in the 1850s, the great distance between America and Europe meant

**Table 3.1** *Specie points for sterling–franc exchange rate*

| | | | |
|---|---|---|---|
| above 25.35 f | Bank bullion sent from France to England | below 25.20 f | Refinable bullion sent to France |
| above 25.32 f | Shipments of market bullion from France | $25.17\frac{1}{2} - 25.15$ f | Market bullion leaves England |
| 25.20–25.30 f | Gold bullion from California or Australia bought by the Bank of England at 77/92 d per standard ounce | $25.12\frac{1}{2} - 25.10$ f | Bank of England reserves drawn down |
| | | $25.07\frac{1}{2} - 25.05$ f | Considerable withdrawals of reserves |

*Source*: E. Seyd 'On international coinage and the variation of the foreign exchanges during recent years', *Journal of the Statistical Society,* **33** (1870), pp. 42–73.

that most bullion arbitrage took place between European countries because between the time of shipment and arrival of bullion across the Atlantic the conditions that had made the operation profitable could well have changed. Changes in national holdings of American railway bonds were a common way of settling the foreign exchange balance, and later the securities of various governments were widely used in arbitrage operations.[11]

In the absence of exchange risk, bond arbitrage, like specie arbitrage, increasingly harmonised European interest rates as telegraph and railway networks spread. In 1869 discount rates in London were only about $\frac{1}{2}$ per cent higher than in Paris, Frankfurt, Hamburg and Brussels. At Berlin and Amsterdam, rates were between $\frac{1}{4}$ and $\frac{1}{2}$ per cent higher than in London. Neither Austria–Hungary nor Russia had currencies linked to precious metals and so interest rates there diverged from the rest of Europe because of risks of changes in exchange rates. Discount rates in Vienna were nearly $1\frac{1}{2}$ per cent higher than in London, and the St Petersburg rate was more than double the London rate. The money markets in Turin and Madrid were too small to exert much influence an European conditions.[12]

What was true of gold and bonds was also true to a lesser extent of goods. The international movement of goods ensured that usually there were no great divergences in the (wholesale) price levels of countries that maintained precious metal standards, and therefore that also maintained fixed exchange rates with each other

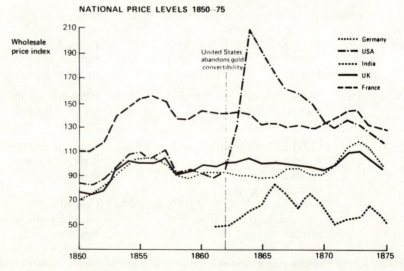

**Figure 3.1**　National price levels, 1850–75

(Figure 3.1). If prices are not equalised when exchange rates are taken into consideration, then there are profit opportunities to be had from importing or exporting as long as transport, tariff and information costs can be covered. Taking advantage of these opportunities tends to reduce price discrepancies, so that what can be bought with a sum in one currency is equivalent to what can be bought when that sum is converted at the prevailing exchange rate into another currency. This is the purchasing power parity theory.

## The new gold

Opportunities for the profitable international movement of precious metals, goods and bonds were expanded by the discoveries in California and Australia that massively increased the annual quantity of gold supplied to world markets. As Table 3.2 shows, the annual average supply from 1851 to 1855 was more than ten times that of 1801 to 1810, and over the half-century before 1849 supplies averaged only one-seventh of those available in the 1850s, barely sufficient to compensate for wear and tear of the coinage. At the time many had argued that prices in gold standard countries would rise greatly, from the simple notion that prices are merely a quantity of money against which goods are exchanged.[13] The contemporary economists Tooke and Newmarch however believed that the new gold stimulated economic activity (already encouraged by transport and communication improvements and the freeing of trade), so that output, rather than prices, rose.[14] The real danger, Newmarch thought, was that new gold supplies would fall. The evidence of the 1870s, Newmarch believed, confirmed his view: wholesale prices in London in the period 1831/45 to 1870/7 had risen only by 10 per cent which, considering the wars of the 1860s and 1870s (the American Civil War, the Franco–Prussian War, the Russo–Turkish War) and their disruption of production, was remarkably little. Newmarch's hypothesis that the increased spending permitted by the new gold primarily increased output rather than prices is a logical possibility, although it is one that modern monetarists would not maintain for such a long period.

Schumpeter plumped for a third causal pattern, suggesting that the period 1850 to 1870 was one of investment in the new opportunities in coal, iron, railways, steamships, textiles and clothing, leading to a rapid growth of production, which in turn caused a rise in prices.[15] Money, in Schumpeter's account, was passive. Output growth was independent of monetary expansion, although it may have encouraged the development of bank credit.

**Table 3.2**   *The relative value of production and market price of gold and silver, 1801–80*

| Period | Value of production (annual average) Silver (£m) | Gold (£m) | Proportion of silver to gold production | Average price of bar silver (d per oz) | Ratio of market value |
|--------|------|------|------|------|------|
| 1801–10 | 8.002 | 2.480 | 3.226:1 | 60 7/16 | 15.61:1 |
| 1851–55 | 8.019 | 27.815 | .228:1 | 61 3/16 | 15.41:1 |
| 1856–60 | 8.235 | 28.145 | .292:1 | 61 5/8 | 15.30:1 |
| 1861–65 | 9.965 | 25.816 | .386:1 | 61 1/4 | 15.40:1 |
| 1866–70 | 11.984 | 27.207 | .440:1 | 60 5/8 | 15.55:1 |
| 1871–75 | 17.232 | 24.260 | .710:1 | 59 1/16 | 15.97:1 |
| 1876–80 | 19.103 | 24.052 | .794:1 | 52 16/15 | 17.81:1 |

*Source: Final Report Royal Commission on Gold and Silver (1886), p. 6.*

**Table 3.3**   *The growth of money, national income and prices in Britain, 1846–80 (compound annual growth rates, per cent)*

|  | Gold and silver coin in Britain | Total money stock | GNP at factor cost, constant 1900 prices | Implicit price deflator |
|---|---|---|---|---|
| 1846/50–1856/60 | 5.2 | 4.7 | 2.3 | 0.49 |
| 1856/60–1866/70 | 3.1 | 3.9 | 2.5 | 0.82 |
| 1866/70–1877/80 | 2.8 | 2.8 | 2.0 | − 0.42 |

*Source*: M. Collins, 'The English Banking Sector and Monetary Growth 1844–80', University of Leeds, School of Economic Studies, discussion paper no. 102.

Consistent with this latter view, the period of the fastest growth in the British money stock, from the late 1840s to the late 1850s, did not correspond with the fastest growth of British GNP at current or constant prices, or in the price index, which was in the decade from the late 1850s (Table 3.3). It may therefore have been purely fortuitous that the period of rapid output growth (1846–73) in the premier gold standard nation coincided with the rapid growth of gold supplies.

The banking innovations and extensions probably took place in response to the rise in economic activity as Schumpeter proposed, because the share of bank and credit money in the money stocks of the United States, Britain and France increased from 37 per cent in 1848 to 59 per cent in 1872, when the total money stock grew faster than in any other period of the nineteenth century.[16] The decline in British monetary growth in the 1870s was primarily because of a fall in bank deposit growth rather than because of a fall in the growth of the coin circulation.[17] Similarly an estimate for the whole world shows bank deposits and capital growing at 5.6 per cent per annum in 1840 to 1870, but at only 3.5 per cent per annum from 1870 to 1890.[18] Had the new gold been the main cause of monetary growth bank deposits would not have increased their share of the money stock. If the new gold did not cause the monetary growth it is unlikely that it boosted total spending and output substantially. Hence the decline in monetary growth in the 1870s stemmed from a retardation of world economic growth not vice versa.

## The international transmission of price increases

Why then did prices rise so little in response to the new gold, if Tooke and Newmarch were mistaken? As long as a large part of the growing world economy was linked together by fixed exchange rates, prices of internationally-traded goods in one country could not rise because of the new gold faster than those of that country's partners on metallic standards. Therefore price increases depended mainly on the growth of the fixed rate world output and money stock, rather than on the output and money of any one country.

The initial impact of the new gold was to raise the prices of all domestic commodities in the mining economies of California and Australia as resources switched from agricultural to mining production. Australia quickly became a net importer of food instead of, as formerly, a net exporter. (Just as South Africa did with the gold discoveries later in the century.) Australia exported gold to Britain (with whom Australia effectively shared a common currency) in exchange for manufactures, as Chapter 1 showed, and to other countries in exchange for agricultural produce. Because the new discoveries made gold cheaper by about a half in terms of commodities, Australian prices, being gold prices of commodities, rose. Foreign goods therefore sold more easily in Australia than elsewhere, and their prices were accordingly bid up in gold terms. But many of these prices indirectly constituted a cost of gold mining, for miners had to buy the goods with their earnings. The costs of gold mining therefore rose, stimulating a diversion of resources back to agriculture. By 1870 gold production in Victoria had fallen to half the level of 1856, and exports other than gold had almost doubled, but at a now higher level of prices in Australia and in the rest of the world.[19]

The new gold had a lesser impact on prices than might have been expected also because of the bimetallism of France and until 1853, of the United States. It caused considerable difficulties for the monetary systems of the two countries. In the United States the divergence between the legal and market ratios of silver to gold had become sufficiently great for 'bimetallist arbitrage' to be profitable by 1849. The divergence between the ratios continued to widen until by 1853 the market ratio was 15.4 to 1 and the legal ratio 16:1.[20] Bimetallist arbitrage worked as follows: 1600 ounces of silver could be taken to the bullion market and exchanged for 100 ounces of gold with 60 ( = 1600 − 1540) ounces of silver left over. The payment of debts in gold rather than silver, as bimetallist legislation allowed, was profitable as the above examples shows, and this tended to increase the speed at which gold drove out silver. Equally profitable was the sale of silver for gold, and the sale of the newly acquired gold to the Mint. Congress reduced the mint ratio to less than 15:1 in 1853 to stop these arbitrage operations. Had the Mint been willing to take an unlimited amount of silver for coinage at this rate, silver would have tended to replace gold at the Mint, because the market gold–silver ratio was still above 15 : 1. However, the law provided that the Mint need only take the quantity of silver necessary for making small change. Since it no longer paid to melt down these devalued coins, a supply of them quickly came into use, but gold remained the main coin currency. In the ten years after the Gold Rush of 1849, $400 million of gold coins were struck. Legislation in 1873 dropped the silver dollar from the coinage list, but these pieces had disappeared from circulation many years before. The real abandonment of the bimetallic standard took place in 1853 not 1873, as was to be widely alleged subsequently by those who favoured monetary expansion (see Chapter 6). At the end of 1861 the link to gold and silver was in any case abandoned (except on the west coast) and not resumed until 1879.

As in the United States during the early 1850s gold was driving silver from the French currency circulation, and the silver was being shipped to the East. By the 1860s France was virtually on a *de facto* gold standard.[21] It was against this background that Chevalier's 'Parachute' thesis was formulated. The 'Parachute' limited the rise in the relative price of silver to the increase sufficient to displace silver by gold in the countries whose currencies were fixed in terms of both precious metals. When the displacement was complete, Chevalier predicted gold prices would fall substantially and silver prices rise.[22] In the meantime, however, prices and exchange rates of the major European gold, bimetallist and silver standard countries were all tightly linked, and the gold price of silver only declined a little (see Table 3.4).[23]

The German price level moved in parallel with those of France and Britain (Figure 3.1) even though Germany held to a silver standard until 1871, France remained with bimetallism until 1874

**Table 3.4**  *Average annual exchange rates against sterling, 1845–59*

| Year | Paris (franc = £1) | Hamburg (mark = £1) | Amsterdam (guilders = £1) | Calcutta (rupee) | London silver prices |
|------|------|------|------|------|------|
| 1845 | 25.92 | 13.135 | 12.725 | $22\frac{1}{4}$d | $59\frac{1}{2}$d per oz |
| 1850 | 25.40 | 13.11 | 12.15 | $24\frac{3}{4}$d | 60d per oz |
| 1855 | 25.50 | 13.8 | 11.19 | $25\frac{1}{2}$d | $61\frac{1}{2}$d per oz |
| 1859 | 25.35 | 13.55 | 11.16 | $24\frac{3}{4}$d | $61\frac{1}{2}$d per oz |

*Source*: W. Newmarch, 'Reports of the character and results of the trade of the United Kingdom during the year 1859', *Journal of the Statistical Society* (1860), p. 109.

and Britain maintained a gold standard. The silver that France lost
from circulation mainly went to India, a silver standard economy.
Because India did not produce silver itself in any great quantities,
perhaps 30 million rupees in silver were needed each year merely
to provide for wear, losses and population growth, if prices were
to be maintained at the same level.[24] The large imports of silver
from 1855 to 1866 were mainly due to borrowing to meet expenditure incurred because of the Mutiny, to the foreign investment in
building the railway system, and to the increased value of cotton
exports as a result of the blockade of the southern cotton ports
during the American Civil War. Unlike Germany, however, as far
as can be judged, the parallelism of Indian prices with European
prices was much weaker; between 1864 and 1869 the two sets of
prices diverged probably because of the effects of foreign investment, famines and the foreign demand for cotton in India, as well
as the greater distances involved in trade. The rupee showed a rise
against sterling in the period 1845 to 1855 proportionately greater
than the rise in the gold prices of silver. So also did the silver
standard Dutch currency. As long as exchange rates moved, then
price levels had some freedom to diverge.

## Floating exchange rate regimes

The exchange rate of a country with an inconvertible currency gave
the greatest freedom to national price movements. An inconvertible
currency could not be changed into a precious metal at a legal rate.
The value was determined solely by the goods and services that
could be bought with it, both in the present and in the future. The
external value of the currency, the exchange rate, was similarly
determined by the relative strengths of foreign demand for the
currency and by domestic demand for foreign currency. A government therefore had the power to alter the domestic and external
value of inconvertible money by changing the quantity in circulation,
a power which to European liberalism was an 'intolerable evil',
because of the disturbance to contracts and expectations caused by
the consequent changes in the price level.[25] This doctrine had been
'tolerable effectually drummed into the public mind' of industrialising countries, but even there, the exigencies of war finance could
necessitate the abandonment of the precious metal standard.

In Latin America and in Central and Eastern Europe the liberal
strictures against currencies and exchange rates influenced by the
governments' financial needs seemed to have been borne out. The
failure to reform the money market was an important factor in the

long-term retardation of Brazil.[26] The Bank of Brazil received extraordinary privileges which allowed it to supply one-third of the banking services in Brazil as well as being responsible for financing the government's budget deficit and the resulting inflation. The growth in the national money stock was absorbed by rising prices, rather than by increases in productivity. Even after reforming her currency in 1843, Russia continued to increase her issue of paper roubles unbacked by gold, and the foreign exchange value of the rouble declined on trend against the metal-backed currencies. The rouble exchanged for 35d British in 1844 but for only 24d in 1880. Austria–Hungary was in a similar but less extreme position. During the 1870s, with an uncovered paper currency issue of over 600 million florins, the exchange rate of the florin fluctuated around 20d, only five-sixths of the value of the gold florin. Both Austria–Hungary and Russia suffered from erratic development during these years.[27]

The experience of the United States with floating exchange rates, on the other hand, suggests that the liberal argument may have confused cause with effect. Convertibility of the currency into precious metals was not a means of disciplining governments so much as a manifestation of a governmental desire to conform to the liberal ideas of good behaviour. The costs of financing the Civil War meant that from 1862 to 1879 there was no official link between the US dollar and gold, and therefore no fixed parity between the US currency and the pound sterling. The average monthly dollar ('greenback') price of gold, and hence of sterling, varied widely, reaching a peak in 1864 corresponding to a price of more than $12 per pound, or $2\frac{1}{2}$ times the previous and subsequent fixed exchange rate.[28] Prices in the United States had to fall if the exchange rate was eventually to return to the previous parity, and the massive expansion of national output, especially agricultural production, combined with monetary restraint, achieved this goal. The decline in prices hurt farmers already loaded with debt, and fuelled the Greenback Party, which agitated for a plentiful supply of money to raise prices. This unsuccessful movement was surprisingly the only major political reaction under the floating exchange rate regime; by comparison with the twentieth century the pressures for government spending in excess of tax receipts, which would have been possible, were small.

A second criticism of floating exchange rate regimes is the charge that they are prone to destabilizing speculation. The forces which determined the actual exchange rates of the gold and silver standard countries within the specie points, could not be counted on to stabilize the exchange rate in the absence of these points. The

American crisis of 1869 has been instanced as a classic example of the instability of floating exchange rates and the detrimental consequences for trade.[29] During August and September 1869, Jay Gould led a determined attempt to increase the greenback price of gold in the New York gold market. This was equivalent to attempting a depreciation of the exchange. The gold dollar had been $1.31 in greenbacks. By 23 September the price had reached $1.41. The following day the greenback price fell from $1.62 to $1.34 in half an hour when the President authorised the sale of Treasury gold dollars. Gould claimed he was trying to ease the massive US harvest exports by forcing down the exchange rate. Gold inflows into New York in September were a major impediment to Gould's speculation. The success that he achieved was due to the market's belief that the govenment supported his activities. Had the government stated their neutrality, the movement would have been broken earlier. Under a fixed exchange rate regime the government would have been forced to act earlier by the gold outflow which would have threatened the convertibility of the currency. To this extent the 'discipline' argument of European liberalism is supported.

Much of the public distrust of floating exchange rates was based not on the objections already discussed, but on a mistaken theory of value. A study of the Austro–Hungarian floating exchange rate shows that the contemporary debate on restoring the gold standard centred on a belief that it was precious metals that conferred value rather than the goods and services that could be brought with the currency.[30] In turn this might be accounted for by the comparatively late development and use of general price indices which measured the value of money.[31]

## Monetary unions

The use of the same precious metal as the basis for national currencies made the creation of unions of states sharing the same currency system a relatively simple matter. The problems of the changing relative prices of gold and silver were instrumental in the formation of the largest monetary union of bimetallist states. Better communications and increasing trade were also major forces behind the establishment of monetary unions. Perhaps the single most important cause though was the shared political values of the ruling groups in Europe, a belief in the benefits of trade and industry, and in progress. Mill for example asserted 'political improvement' would eventually lead to one world currency as nationalistic irrationalities disappeared.[32] In these circumstances the general economic policies that different nations wished to pursue could be very similar, so that a monetary union might involve little effective loss of sovereignty. Even so the desire to link political objectives with the formation of economic institutions was paramount in two of the three unions of the period and greatly reduced their effectiveness. The benefits of a monetary union were similar to those arising from trade in general: the integration of national monetary units was merely one facet of the integration of national economies by factor mobility, trade and the establishment of common institutions so that resources were put to their best possible use.

In 1857 Austria and the Zollverein founded the Austro–German Union with a common unit of account, the silver mark. Three distinct units with a fixed rate of exchange provided the medium of exchange.[33] No real integration of money and banking systems took place, however, and the Union was dissolved in 1866 with the outbreak of the Austro–Prussian War. The Union was primarily a means of achieving political domination over the German states, and when Prussia clearly won this fight, Austria had no place in the Union.

The Latin Monetary Union proved more durable. The falling price of gold relative to silver during the 1850s produced difficulties for the French bimetallic monetary system. In response to the export of silver, the French adjusted the silver content of their coinage thereby creating problems for economic relations with Belgium, Switzerland and Italy.[34] In 1860 87 per cent of the circulation of subsidiary coin in Belgium was French, the Swiss had adopted the French standard of 1850, and the Italians had done the same in 1862. The Monetary Convention of November 1865 met to resolve these difficulties. France wanted to maintain the *status quo* according to Willis because the Bank of France and French financial leaders found bimetallist arbitrage profitable. The other countries wanted to standardise on gold, as did a good part of the French delegation. The political domination of the French ensured that the Latin Monetary Union of 23 December 1865 codified the *status quo*, although it also militated against the success of the Union, because it inhibited voluntary coordination within the Union. The last important state to join the Union was Austria in 1867, and the terms of the treaty specified gold as the medium of exchange. The falling value of silver led to the Treaty of 1874 restricting silver coinage, and in 1878 silver coinage was suspended by the Union.

The ultimate cause of the collapse of bimetallism on which the Latin Monetary Union was based was the strong mercantile preference for gold, arising from the increase in large-scale commerce which favoured the metal with the greatest value for the smallest bulk.[35] Germany moved from silver to gold between 1871 and 1873 and sold substantial quantities of silver. India could not absorb it all because of a growing indebtedness to Britain, and because the introduction of a note issue in 1862 and improved transport reduced the need for silver for transactions. The value of silver relative to gold began to fall but not, judging by the timing, as a response to German silver sales, or to the demonetisation of silver by the Latin Union in 1878.

Italy continued to be unwilling to subordinate national policies to those of France or to wider international concerns throughout the Union period. From 1860 to 1865 Italian government spending, including expenditure on railways and the 'pacification policy' in the newly-conquered south, was twice that of tax revenues.[36] In 1866 the Italian government had declared its currency inconvertible. Italy did not acquiesce in the 1874 decision to move to a *de facto* gold standard, and at the 1878 conference announced its intention to continue coining silver. The Union managed to place a restriction on the amount coined and extracted a pledge that this would be the last silver issue.

The Scandinavian Monetary Union formed towards the end of the third quarter of the nineteenth century, proved to be the most successful of the three Unions, lasting until the disruptions caused by the first world war.[37] The success was due to the essentially similar character of the economies of Norway, Sweden and Denmark, based upon agriculture, extractive industries, forestry, fishing and trade. The gains from specialisation did not as a result require very great reallocation of resources. Germany's move to gold and the French adherence to bimetallism discouraged the Scandinavians from joining the Latin Monetary Union. Instead, the Scandinavian Monetary Union between Sweden and Denmark was created in 1873, and was joined by Norway in 1875. Identical style gold coins circulated freely within the Union, but by 1885 gold was essentially a reserve currency, with more than half of Sweden's money stock being uncovered notes. A rudimentary clearing scheme for notes established by the central banks further helped monetary integration.

## International fluctuations in economic activity

So far, this chapter has been principally concerned with the structure of the international monetary system and its normal working. We now consider the pathology of monetary relations. Ultimately the ills of the system can be traced to the structure of bank and trade credit built on the cash base – precious metal coinage for those countries on metallic standards. Monetary policy was directed to ensuring this structure did not become too large or too small for the needs of the economy, but the main focus was on the bullion reserves of the central bank, for those countries that had such banks. When reserves began to the depleted either because of foreign demands (an 'external drain') or domestic demands (an 'internal drain') this was a signal for a rise in the price (discount rate) at which the central bank would lend funds to selected borrowers caught short of liquidity. A higher cost of credit reduced the demand for funds and reduced the credit pyramid relative to the cash base. Thereby the central bank ensured convertibility of claims into precious metal, while at the same time preventing widespread bankruptcy and loss of confidence in the monetary system, by acting as a lender of the last resort. Lacking a central bank in these years, the United States was a source of instability for the international monetary system and was dependent on Europe for funds during crises.[38] The Banks of England and France were the chief regulators of the system, although in 1870 France ceased temporarily to maintain convertibility of her currency and so lost influence.

Under fixed exchange rates, crises were transmitted from one economy to another more strongly than under floating rates. A crisis and depression in one country lowered the demand for imports and attracted bullion and foreign assets. Fewer imports allowed more room for expansion for domestic production and employment. The balance of trade surplus tended to lower interest rates and expand the money supply with similar effects. By contrast under floating rates, a crisis and depression caused a rise in that country's exchange rate, when import demand fell relative to foreign demand for exports, and the domestic currency therefore became scarcer in term of foreign currency in the exchange markets. This higher exchange rate reduced the marketability of exports and prevented monetary expansion; both forces tended to ensure the depression continued.

The United States in 1857 offers an example of the first case, and in 1873 of the second. From the viewpoint of the rest of the world, the United States with a floating exchange rate in 1873 was less harmful than with a fixed rate in 1857, for in 1857 she could export her unemployment to the rest of the world by reducing her imports, whereas in 1873 until 1879 she could not. The greenback appreciated a small amount between 1873 and 1876, and in the following year appreciated almost 7 per cent more. The forces that caused appreciation under a paper standard would have been channelled into stimulating the domestic economy or arresting the fall of prices under gold standard conditions. In 1877 there were signs of an upturn in railway investment, building, manufacturing and mining. This indicates that under a gold standard deflation might well have ended by 1877 instead of 1879, as it actually did.

The classification of exchange rate regimes assumes implicitly the absence of a central bank policy, which is appropriate for the United States but not for Western Europe. Though central banks could prevent widespread financial collapses, so long as they maintained precious metal standards with small reserves, they could not prevent the international transmission of crises. In many instances the crises occurred simultaneously from similar causes in different countries and it is therefore difficult to distinguish the extent to which a depression originated at home or abroad. However the political crisis of 1861 in the United States supplies a clear-cut instance of unemployment being forced upon Britain from abroad, and the 1866 collapse in Britain had a similar impact on Australia. Probably the German crisis of 1873, a direct consequence of the receipt of French reparations, was responsible for the rise in British unemployment then. The French remained largely immune because they had not then resumed convertibility.

The important role of British finance in world trade and the consequent impact of British interest rates on the rest of the world has sometimes led to the inference that the rest of the world had to suffer unemployment forced on it by Britain. Such an interpretation mistakenly assumes British interest rates were uniquely controlled by British conditions and policy. The majority of the crises that required adjustment of national economies originated outside Britain in these years, that of 1866 being the exception.

## The 1857 crisis

The state of the national harvest was an important determinant of national fluctuations in this period, and sometimes good harvests coincided in the major exporting countries. In 1857 there were good harvests. The re-establishment of normal commercial relations between Russia and Western Europe after the Crimean War and the construction of new railways in the fertile Hungarian plain further increased the amount of grain on the world market.[39] The price of wheat fell and the whole US market was affected. The failure of the Ohio Life Insurance and Trust Company in August 1857 was the signal for a general panic. The fall of agricultural prices left farmers unable to service their debts and institutions that had lent them the money as a result were endangered. Panic withdrawals of bank deposits in the United States required the supply of cash from abroad, primarily from Britain. Sterling fell against the dollar and gold was exported to the United States. To protect its reserves, so that Britain could remain on the gold standard the Bank of England raised bank rate (the rate at which it was prepared to act as lender of the last resort) to 10 per cent by November 1857. The banking panic spread to British and Irish depositors who demanded their money back; from the Bank's view there was now an 'internal drain' on their reserves as well as an 'external drain'.[40] In Britain two Scottish banks, one Liverpool and two leading London bill brokers failed between 12 October and 11 November 1857. These and other firm failures, with the increase in bank rate, had very serious results on the commerce of Hamburg in Germany; 150 firms with total liabilities of £15 million failed. The 1857 crisis then clearly originated in the United States and the wheat-exporting economies, but was exacerbated by a contraction of demand associated with bank failures, other bankruptcies, and a failure to renew bill finance. Under the bill system, a trader was liable to postpone purchases that would commit him to finding cash in three months' time, if there was a risk of other traders being insolvent, because his ability to meet his commitments depended on the bills he held for the sale of his goods being met on maturity. During the 1857 crises there was a general reluctance to buy goods by bill acceptance, orders for manufacturers therefore fell, unemployment rose, and consumers' incomes fell. High discount rates had the same effect of reducing traders demands, and lowering consumers income.

## The crises of the 1860s

Lincoln's election as President of the United States in November 1860 precipitated the secession of the slave-owning southern states. New York had financed the greater part of southern exports. The approach of secession by removing this finance caused a banking crisis in the South, and the North began to absorb gold. This reversal of the United States from being a gold exporter to a gold importer disrupted the European monetary system at a time when the Bank of France was in any case short of gold.[41] The Bank of England took over 50 million francs of silver from the Bank of France in exchange for gold. The US gold demand only ended when the greenback issue in summer of 1861 got underway. A high bank rate

and other interest rates in England had been deflationary; unemployment rose in 1861 and 1862.

Recovery began in 1863. Continental Europe suffered a set back
in 1864 (bank rate reached 9 per cent in November) but British
activity continued to expand. The 10 per cent bank rate following
the failure of Overend and Gurney in 1866 remained in force for
three months and gold did not flow in even though the Bank of
France discount rate was $3\frac{1}{2}$–4 per cent.

The failure was regarded so seriously that the British Foreign
Secretary unprecedentedly sent circular telegrams to the embassies
stating that the national finances were in no danger.[42] Many other
firms, mainly those associated with railway contracting (including
Peto's) went bankrupt at the same time. The subsequent recession
was however mild, and the United States also experienced only a
mild decline in economic activity from April 1865 to December 1867.
Railway construction continued to increase. The other major
economy with a floating exchange rate, Austria–Hungary, also
experienced expansion in 1866–7 with the recovery from the Austro–
Prussian War.[43] France and Germany experienced a recession in
1867 as might be expected with their fixed exchange rates. The
Austro–Prussian War of 1866 finally ended the career of the Pereire
brothers. Credit Mobilier held large quantities of Austrian securities
which depreciated with the Austrian defeat. In 1866 the bank lost
8 million francs and French financial confidence was shaken.[44]

The more distant countries linked to the British economy by fixed
rates, in particular India and Australia, suffered a similar recession
with a lag, though there were also important endogenous influences
arising from the reduced profitability of raw cotton. The blockade
of the South during the American Civil War had caused a land
boom on the other side of the world, in Bombay, as Indian cotton
exports expanded to replace those lost to Lancashire. With the
ending of the war, the boom collapsed, taking with it a large number
of banks that had been engaged in speculation.

In Australia the shock was amplified further by the failure of the
London bank through which the Queensland government had been
raising capital to build railways.[45] When news of the crisis reached
Queensland in July 1866 there was immediate panic because it was
thought the government would no longer have funds to spend on
railway construction, unemployment would rise and social disorder
would quickly follow. Money was nevertheless raised without
adopting the inconvertible paper currency which would allow the
offsetting monetary policy, and exchange depreciation, that local
politicians wanted.

*The crisis of 1873*

The next slump was precipitated on 9 May 1873 by the inflation of German credit from the payment of the French indemnity of 5 billion francs.[46] Vienna also was quickly involved. The British bank rate reached $7\frac{1}{2}$ per cent in June (in 1873 it changed twenty-four times – a record) and gold imports occurred. On 19 September the American crisis broke. By 1878 there were said to be 1.2 million unemployed able-bodied men roaming the US.[47] One-fifth of the railways were foreclosed or under proceedings.

Because of the inconvertible US currency the reaction on Great Britain was less severe than in 1857, but there was still a panic and bank rate reached 9 per cent November 1873 to staunch the outflow of gold. In Paris and Brussels the discount rate reached 7 per cent. In the most important South American economy, Brazil, the banks almost ceased lending. In Buenos Aires the private banks actually did so, and property values fell between 30 and 40 per cent.[48]

As with the 1857 depression but to a greater extent, transport improvements caused marked and unexpected price declines. The Suez Canal had been opened in 1869 and the railway system of the world had been rapidly extended. In Austria the system had increased from 2200 miles in 1865 to 6000 in 1873, almost all the Russian system had been built after 1868, and the railway system of the United States had doubled in the seven years before 1873. Bad harvests in Britain in 1873 and 1876, together with cattle disease, forced food prices up there and reduced the demand for manufactures. The depression in Britain was however less deep than in many countries, at least until 1879. Despite the decline in export demand (of more than 50 per cent to the US 1872–6) the British economy experienced no increase in pauperism or decline in state revenues as had occurred in 1857 and 1866.

The depression was felt much more severely in raw material producing than in manufacturing countries, because the transport improvements immediately affected the earnings of the first group more. These transport improvements often depended on foreign investment. The collapse of foreign investment was occasioned by the falling agricultural prices and became the proximate cause of the collapse, in Australia and in the United States as well as in South America and in Russia. In Britain the crisis was largely endogenous from the realisation of the unsound nature of so many of the foreign loans recently advanced; the foreign loans to Turkey, for instance, had been used to pay interest on previous loans until Turkey defaulted in 1875. Spain also went bankrupt.

The depression that began in 1873 was the second severest in the history of the international economy both in its depth and duration, being exceeded only by that beginning in 1929.[49] The earliest investigators into these cycles thought they were caused by fluctuations in the supply of money or credit. Rostow and Lewis believe that these influences were not fundamental.[50] The great financial crises generally òccurred after the downturn in economic activity and resulted from changes in expectations generated by the downturn, they assert. The ensuing panic accelerated the decline but did not initiate it. Changes in the determinants and directions of investment, especially in transport improvements, with the consequences for relative prices and economic activity already described, were fundamental. Even so exchange rate regimes and monetary policy (or its absence) influenced the severity and transmission of these fluctuations.

### Summary and conclusion

The international monetary system throughout the third quarter of the nineteenth century depended to a considerable extent on the money and credit of the world's largest trader, Britain. Even trade which did not touch British shores was often financed by British institutions. The acceptability of British money and finance owed much to its apparently unbreakable link with gold for a number of reasons: a belief that gold itself conferred value on money, not social acceptability; the guarantee that the British government could not reduce the value of the money by increasing the stock, as long as the commitment to gold was maintained; and a strong mercantile preference for gold over other precious metals because the higher value in relation to weight made gold more suitable as an ultimate means of payment for the increasing value of international trade.

The system of commercial banking and bills of exchange, helped by the international spread of the electric telegraph, in fact ensured that very little gold was needed for international exchange. As long as confidence in the financial institutions was maintained, the pyramid of credit built upon the gold base served as a means of exchange. The gold discoveries of the late 1840s were less responsible for the monetary growth of the period than was the development of the commercial banking. There was only a gentle rise in prices from this monetary growth because of the relatively rapid accompanying expansion of international and domestic trade. The greater availability of gold provided the opportunity for the major industrial powers to move to gold standards whether *de jure* or *de facto*. This increased demand for monetary gold provided another reason why prices in the industrial world rose very little. France and the United States, whose currencies were linked to both gold and silver, found that the price of gold fell in response to the increased gold supplies sufficiently to drive silver coins out of circulation. But bimetallism seems to have prevented a great rise in the price of silver relative to gold and therefore limited the appreciations of the silver standard exchange rates, such as those of India and Germany.

The tendency of trade to unify international markets was helped by the formation of monetary unions in Europe, in turn a manifestation of the prevailing liberal internationalist beliefs, and in the case of the Austro–German and Latin Unions an attempt to enhance one nation's international influence. The Scandinavian Monetary Union was the most successful because political considerations were not paramount and there was genuine integration of financial institutions between the countries.

Monetary unions were made easier because adherence to a common metallic standard already provided a fixed exchange rate between the different currencies within the limits set by the specie points. Although monetary unions and fixed exchange rate regimes created a stability of international relative prices that facilitated trade, they also potentially allowed the international transmission of recessions and booms from which an economy could in principle be insulated under a floating exchange rate regime. Fluctuations in international economic activity seemed to have been caused by discontinuities in the profitability of investment, largely in transport facilities, in agricultural and raw material producing areas. When the investments began to come to fruition the prices of agricultural products tended to fall, creating difficulties for financial institutions which had lent to primary producers and which now found their assets illiquid or reduced in value; hence the financial crises, especially those of 1857 and 1873.

It is doubtful that the exchange rate regime made a great difference to the transmission of these crises, because international capital movements and domestic monetary policies were so important. The depression in the United States after 1873 was probably exacerbated by the floating exchange rate and the contractionary monetary policy designed to allow to return to the pre-Civil War fixed exchange rate. Economic recovery tended to raise the exchange rate at the expense of expanding domestic capacity utilisation. However, in this instance the forces making for depression originated in the United States to a much greater extent than they were transmitted from abroad. Britain suffered relatively little initially, despite maintaining a fixed exchange rate with countries such as Germany which were hard hit, because she had, by the 1870s, a relatively small commitment to primary production. What probably was of more importance than the exchange rate regime was the willingness of the Bank of England to act as lender of last resort and to control domestic monetary conditions. This facility provided some contribution to preventing marked contractions of the money stock by controlling and reducing internal and external 'cash drains' when residents or foreigners panicked and demanded gold rather than bank deposits or bills.

The severity and duration of the depression of 1873 began the undermining of the liberal consensus amongst industrialising nations about the benefits of international trade and investment. A belief that the international market would not raise or preserve living standards adequately became more widespread. Instead, governments or other corporate forms of organisation such as trade unions and cartels were increasingly expected to take remedial or positive action in the face of market forces. Even in Britain the verities of free trade seemed less than permanent. Giffen remarked on the 'continual references to the increase in manufactures abroad', and it was true that by the 1870s Britain no longer occupied the same dominant position in the international economy that she had in the 1850s. In the new era that was beginning the industrial capacities of the leading nations were more equal, trade was less free and the international economy was increasingly used to achieve objectives of foreign policy.

## Notes

1. E. Corti, *The Reign of The House of Rothschild*, London: Gollancz (1928). F. Stern, *Gold and Iron*, New York: Alfred Knopf (1977).
2. R. Hidy, *The House of Baring in American Trade and Finance*, New York: Russell & Russell (1970) (first published 1949).
3. *UK Select Committee on the Operation of the Bank Act of 1844* (1858), Minutes AA 1699–1792, quoted in W.T.C. King, *History of the London Discount Market*, London: F. Cass (1972).
4. Rt Hon. Viscount Goschen, *The Theory of Foreign Exchanges*, London: Wilson 3rd edn (1866) is a useful contemporary account.
5. J.H. Clapham, *An Economic History of Modern Britain: Free Trade and Steel*, Cambridge: Cambridge University Press (1952), pp. 370–1.
6. S. Nishimura, *The Decline of Inland Bills of Exchange in the London Money Market 1855–1913*, Cambridge: Cambridge University Press (1971).
7. W. Newmarch, 'On the progress of the foreign trade of the United Kingdom since 1856...', *The Journal of the (Royal) Statistical Society*, **41** (1878), pp. 187–282.

8. J. Kieve, *The Electric Telegraph: A Social and Economic History*, Newton Abbot: David & Charles (1973), pp. 106–15.
9. C. MacKenzie, *Realms of Silver*, London: Routledge & Kegan Paul (1954), p. 40.
10. G. Clare, *A Money-Market Primer and Key to the Exchanges*, London: Effingham Wilson (1891), p. 74.
11. ibid.
12. *The Economist: Commercial and Financial History for 1869.*
13. For example, W.S. Jevons, 'A serious fall in the value of gold ascertained', in *Investigations in Currency and Finance*, London: Macmillan (1909).
14. T. Tooke and W. Newmarch, *A History of Prices* (1857).
15. J. Schumpeter, *Business Cycles*, New York and London: McGraw-Hill (1939). W.W. Rostow, *The British Economy of the Nineteenth Century* London: Oxford University Press (1948), adopts a similar line of argument. The Cambridge quantity theory of money assumes the demand for money equals the supply of money ($M$). Demand is determined by the product of the price level ($P$) and level of income ($Y$) and $K$ the fraction of money income averagely held as money balances. The fraction varies with the rate of interest and the state of monetary institutions among other things. Using lower case letters to indicate proportionate rates of growth of the upper case letter variables, the Cambridge relation can be written $M = K \cdot P \cdot Y$

    or $m = k + p + y$

    The second equation can represent the first hypothesis of the text as $m \rightarrow p$, the second (Newmarch) hypothesis as $m \rightarrow y$, and the third (Schumpeter) hypothesis as $y \rightarrow p$ and perhaps $m$, where '$\rightarrow$' indicates causal direction.
16. R. Triffin, *Our International Monetary System*, New York: Random House (1968), Table 1.2.
17. M. Collins, 'The English banking sector and monetary growth 1844–80', University of Leeds, School of Economic Studies, discussion paper 102.
18. M.G. Mulhall, *Dictionary of Statistics*, London: Routledge (1892).
19. M. Bordo, 'John E. Cairnes on the effects of the Australian gold discoveries 1851–73: an early application of the methodology of positive economics', *History of Political Economy*, 7 (1975), pp. 337–59.
20. J.L. Laughlin, *The History of Bimetallism in the United States*, New York: D. Appleton (1897), pp. 75–82.
21. H. Parker Willis, *A History of the Latin Monetary Union: A Study in International Monetary Action*, New York: Greenwood Press (1968) p. 9.
22. R.S. Sayers, 'The question of the standard in the eighteen fifties', *Economic History* 2 (1933), pp. 575–601. Sayers shows that Chevalier was wrong. When displacement was complete, prices may not fall much because of the size of the new gold area relative to increments in the gold stock.

23. This was the view of the *UK Royal Commission on the Precious Metals* (1886), Final Report, part 1, p. 64.
24. D. Barbour, *The Theory of Bimetallism*, London: Cassell (1886), ch. 2.
25. J.S. Mill, *Principles of Political Economy* (ed. W.J. Ashley) London: Longmans Green (1929), ch. 13, esp. pp. 544–6.
26. C.M. Pelaez, 'A comparison of long-term monetary behaviour and institutions in Brazil, Europe and the United States', *Journal of European Economic History*, 5 (1976), pp. 439–50.
27. Mulhall, op. cit.
28. M. Friedman and A. Schwartz, *A Monetary History of the United States 1867–1960*, Princeton: Princeton University Press (1963), p. 85.
29. L.T. Wimmer, 'The gold crises of 1869: stabilising or destablishing speculation under floating exchange rates?', *Explorations in Economic History*, 12 (1975), pp. 105–22.
30. L.B. Yeager, 'Fluctuating exchange rates in the nineteenth century: the experiences of Austria and Russia', in R.A. Mundell and A. Swoboda, *Monetary Problems of the International Economy*, Chicago: University of Chicago Press (1969).
31. I. Fisher, *The Making of Index Numbers*, Boston: Houghton Mifflin (1922), Appendix 4. Fisher states that Jevons' work of 1863 entitles him to be called 'the father of index numbers'.
32. Mill, op. cit.
33. R.J. Bartel, 'International monetary unions: the 19th century experience', *Journal of European Economic History*, 3 (1974), pp. 689–704.
34. Willis, op. cit., ch. 4.
35. Laughlin, op. cit., pp. 167–9.
36. Willis, op. cit., ch. 7.
37. Bartel, loc. cit.
38. Latham has suggested another major source of business fluctuation, namely the failure or success of the Asian rice harvests. The high prices of rice when the harvest failed increased the income available to the rice farmers and merchants who typically demanded British manufactures and semi-manufactures. An increase in the demand for exports tended to send the whole British economy into a boom. The view would have more credibility for the third quarter of the nineteenth century if Asia, and particularly India, was more important in British, European or American trade, but as the figures given in previous chapters have indicated, the poor countries probably accounted for too small a proportion of world trade to be a major cause of fluctuations. A.J. Latham, *The International Economy and the Undeveloped World 1865–1914*. London: Croom Helm (1978), ch. 5.
39. W.O. Henderson, *The Zollverein*, Cambridge: Cambridge University Press (1939). J.R.T. Hughes 'The commercial crisis of 1857', *Oxford Economic Papers*, 8 (1956), pp. 194–222.
40. R.G. Hawtrey, *A Century of Bank Rate*, London: Longmans Green (1938), pp. 25–7.

41. ibid., pp. 78–81.
42. L.H. Jenks, *The Migration of British Capital to 1875*, London: Nelson (1971), p. 261.
43. W.L. Thorp, *Business Annals*, NBER (1926), p. 77.
44. Corti, op. cit., p. 406.
45. L.S. Pressnell, 'The sterling system and financial crises before 1914', in C.P. Kindleberger and J.P. Laffargue, *Financial Crises: Theory, History and Policy*, Cambridge: Cambridge University Press (1982).
46. Hawtrey, op. cit., pp. 92–3.
47. Newmarch, op. cit.
48. R. Giffen, 'The liquidations of 1873–76', and 'Why the depression of trade is so much greater in raw material producing countries', in *Essays in Finance*, London: Bell (1880).
49. For the United States, a rapid expansion of output occurring despite the marked decline in prices made the depression probably less severe than that of the 1890s.
50. W.W. Rostow, *The World Economy: Theory, History, Prospects*, London: Macmillan (1978), ch. 22. W.A. Lewis, *Growth and Fluctuations 1870–1914*, London: Allen and Unwin (1978).

# 4 International Trade and European Domination 1875–1914

European political and economic power reached its zenith in the last quarter of the nineteenth century and the years before the first world war. Those Europeans who had settled in temperate zone lands outside Europe, where necessary displacing the indigenous population with superior military organisation and technology maintained a high living standard often by participation in international trade. Europeans also assumed political control over most tropical regions with which they traded, without settling there.

Within Europe the changing economic and political balance created potentially explosive tensions. The rise of Germany to challenge Britain's former economic supremacy and to displace France from the political leadership of continental Europe was the most fundamental change of the period. The United States' massive economic strength had much less international impact because of its direction westwards across the prairies and mountains of North America. Europe's now delicate balance of power between France, Germany, Britain, Austria–Hungary and Russia, as it turned out, preserved the world from major wars for forty years, but contemporaries had no belief in the inevitability of peace. Some feared a German annexation of Holland, others a Russian invasion of India, and most widespread was anxiety about a general European war over the decaying Turkish empire.

As chimerical as the late nineteenth-century Pax Britannica, was the belief that this was the time when capitalism functioned best. For the sixteen wealthiest economies that accounted for one-sixth of the world's population, growth in real output per head averaged only 1.5 per cent per annum between 1870 and 1913, a performance that was dwarfed by that after the second world war; in the twenty years after 1950[1] the growth of output per head averaged 3.8 per cent per annum. Similarly, the rate of growth of world trade averaged 3.3 per cent per annum compared with 8 per cent between 1953 and 1973.[2] What was striking about the late Victorian epoch was that economic growth, at a rate unprecedented for most countries, had spread so widely through the international economy. The following sections discuss some of the international causes and consequences of this growth. First, the changes in manufactures' trade are analysed; second, temperate zone primary product trade is considered; and third, tropical primary exports. Then movements in the terms of trade between primary and secondary goods are described and explained. Colonisation, the political consequence of much tropical trade in these years, forms the next topic, and finally the political responses in the industrial countries to the declining prices after 1873, in the form of tariff policy and cartelisation, are described.

## The changing pattern of comparative advantage in manufactures

The mid-century pattern of comparative advantage in manufactures, described in Chapter 2, shifted as Germany, the United States and other countries industrialised. Nowhere was this more apparent than in iron and steel. By 1913, German iron and steel exports exceeded British, with American exports not far behind, and Britain had become a major importer of steel. Had Britain dominated the world iron and steel market in 1913 as she did before 1870, she would have supplied the exports actually provided by Germany and America. In so doing the relative output levels of Britain and Germany would have been reversed, with British production half as large again as that of the German iron and steel industry.[3]

The combination of changing technologies with international differences in endowments of natural resources and of specialised human capital made changes such as this inevitable. German iron and steel producers had been handicapped by shortages of indigenous ores until 1879 when the Gilchrist–Thomas process was patented.[4] This process permitted the use of phosphoric ores with which Germany was richly endowed. A scientific chemical education was cheaply available in many German universities, whereas in Britain and France it was expensive, difficult to find, and almost non-existent within the universities. Very quickly the German chemical firms established a monopoly of knowledge which was maintained by the availability of appropriate education. The German chemical industry was quite different from those of France and Britain, being based much more heavily on applications of organic chemistry, a branch of the industry insignificant elsewhere except in Switzerland. In addition, the much more rapid accumulation of capital in Germany and the United States than in Britain was bound to affect international competitiveness. Nevertheless, the extent of these changes was sufficient to disturb some contemporaries, and subsequent analysts concluded that there was some failure of British industry. Allen estimated the British iron and steel industry was about 15 per cent less efficient than the German and American industries in 1901–4 in addition to the burden of now higher raw material prices.[5]

The growing competition from Germany in Britain prompted the publication in 1896 of E.E. Williams' *Made in Germany*. The attention drawn to the German 'commercial invasion' encouraged a xenophobic scare out of all proportion to the size of the challenge. Five years later, W.T. Stead's *The Americanisation of the World* similarly painted a picture of Britian's commercial decline amidst a flood of American imports.

The change in relative coal prices from the period of Britain's industrial supremacy shows one basis for a shift in comparative advantage. By 1900 the price advantage that British coal possessed in the 1860s had disappeared. Pennsylvanian coal was cheaper, and German coal was no more expensive (see Table 4.1). The advantages that British industry had gained from cheaper power and heat than elsewhere in the world had disappeared. Britian's production possibilities resembled more those of her European partners, diminishing the scope for trade of the mid-century's pattern.

As Levine has pointed out, the high concentration of British exports on coal and cotton textiles did not provide much opportunity for productivity increases based upon the available science and technology.[6] By contrast, in Germany exports of chemicals and machinery were proportionately much more important, and textiles and coal less so. Hence, Levine argues, the increasingly poor British economic growth which reached its nadir in the decade after 1900. Such an analysis tends to distract from the structural change that was taking place, and from the causes of the pattern of international specialisation. As Table 4.2 demonstrates, British exports did show some of the changes that are more usually attributed to the German economy. Chemicals quadrupled their export share over the twenty-year period, and machinery exports also increased at a rate faster than total exports. When ships are included in the iron

**Table 4.1**   *The pit price of coal in various locations, 1861–1901*

|  | c. 1861 | 1901 (average) |
|---|---|---|
| France | 6–14s | 12s 7$\frac{1}{2}$d |
| Germany | 7–10s | 9s 4$\frac{1}{4}$d |
| England | 6–10s | 9s 4$\frac{1}{4}$d |
| Pennsylvania | na | 8s 4$\frac{3}{4}$d |
| Pennsylvania (anthracite) | 8–9s | 2–4s |

*Source*: W. Jevons, *The Coal Question* (1906 edn), p. 343.

and steel manufactures category for 1900 there is a slight increase in the share of that class. Textiles, on the other hand, especially cotton, showed a marked decline in export value share, though not in total value. Thus, although British exports were still less diversified than German in 1900, they were reducing the difference. In 1900 78 per cent of British merchandise exports were manufactures, whereas the proportion for Germany had risen from only 26.4 per cent in 1880 to 39.2 per cent in 1900.

**Table 4.2**   *The changing composition of British exports, 1880–1900*

| | | 1880 (%) | 1900 (%) |
|---|---|---|---|
| Primary products {coal | | 3.7 | 13.3 |
| | cotton & wollen textiles | 43.1 | 32.1 |
| inc. { wollen mfrs | | 7.7⎫ | 8.2 |
| wool yarns | | 1.5⎭ | |
| cotton mfrs | | 28.5⎫ | 23.9 |
| cotton yarn | | 5.3⎭ | |
| Manufactured goods | iron, steel & mfrs | 12.7 | 10.8 |
| | machinery | 4.1 | 6.7 |
| | linen manufactures | 2.6 | 2.1 |
| | chemicals | 1.1 | 4.5 |
| | ships | — | 2.9 |
| | wearing apparel | 1.4 | 2.7 |
| | Total export value | £ 223 million | £ 291.2 million |

*Source*: *Statistical Abstract for the United Kingdom.*

Germany to a much greater extent remained an agricultural country, with 35 per cent of the employed population, over 10 million people, officially still working in agriculture in 1913. There was virtually no reduction in the area of arable land because of protective tariffs, in marked contrast to Britain, although there was a decline in the land area devoted to agricultural use. Food exports declined in absolute value as well as in market share because of the rising population and capital accumulation on a relatively fixed agricultural area (see Table 4.3). Sugar exports are an exception to this rule because of the payment of an export subsidy.

The low costs of water transport meant that Ruhr coal could often be sold more cheaply in Western Europe than in Berlin and north-eastern Germany.[7] Consequently, these latter regions imported British coal.

Within the total of German manufactured goods exports, cotton textiles greatly increased their share, and the proportion of wollen textiles declined. But cotton and wollen textiles together slightly raised their percentage between 1880 and 1900. Machinery, iron and steel manufactures, dyestuffs and books all increased dramatically. In machinery both Germany and Britain exported their own specialities to each other and the trade was almost balanced.[8] The steel industries of the two countries also developed complementarily with each country exporting semi-manufactures to the other.

Britain's declining international competitiveness in manufactures and the consequent decline in exports was probably not itself the cause of Britain's slow growth, even though the same slow productivity growth may have been responsible for both phenomena.[9] Because Britain was a much more open economy than France, Germany or the United States, the foreign trade sector may still have exercised an exogenous influence over Britain's poor performance, but the transmission is likely to have been through the monetary influences discussed in Chapter 6.

In the United States changing specialisation resulted primarily in increased inter-regional, rather than international trade. Though the USA was a great world exporter of wheat and meat, as well as of the older staples, cotton and tobacco, the greater part of the farm output of the newly settled mid-west and western states was sold in the north-east of the country. Hence her participation in international trade was proportionately lower. The rapid growth and sheer size of the economy (a population of 76 million by 1900) nevertheless meant that the overall impact of the United States on the international economy was immense. The American tendency to engage in import substitution, increasingly to produce

**Table 4.3**   *The changing composition of German exports, 1880–1900*

| | | 1880 (%) | 1900 (%) |
|---|---|---|---|
| Primary products | grain & flour | 6.4 | 2.9 |
| | sugar | 3.6 | 4.7 |
| | coal | 1.5 | 4.7 |
| | animals | 3.6 | 0.04 |
| Manufactured goods | cotton & woollen textiles | 10.5 | 11.0 |
| | inc. { wool mfrs | 5.6 | 3.8 |
| | cotton mfrs | 1.8 | 5.2 |
| | yarn | 3.1 | 1.9 |
| | silk manufactures | 6.7* | 3.0 |
| | iron, steel & mfrs | 3.1 | 8.2 |
| | machinery | 1.4 | 4.7 |
| | wearing apparel | — | 2.8 |
| | books, etc. | — | 3.2 |
| | dyes | — | 1.7 |
| | *Total export value* | 3046 million marks | 4611 million marks |

*Source: UK Statistical Abstract for Foreign Countries*
* Silk manufacture exports in 1880 were triple those of 1879.

domestically-manufactured goods formerly imported, slowed the growth of world trade. The proportion of manufactures and semi-manufactures in US exports rose throughout the years 1880–1914 as the American economy experienced a process of industrialisation, capital accumulation and population growth similar to the German pattern. Industrialisation and population growth in the United States altered the relative factor endowments so that her comparative advantage was ceasing to be based on abundant natural resources. The natural resource content of US exports, both renewable and non-renewable, declined markedly. Imports of resource products, mainly industrial raw materials such as wool, silk, rubber, hides and skins, increased by more than the decline in imports of crude foodstuffs.[10] Variations in the price of resource products relative to the general price levels of exports and imports were not important in explaining this tendency. Around the time of first world war these trends resulted in the United States becoming a net importer of natural resources as far as direct requirements were concerned.

The transformation of comparative advantages in manufactures in the last part of the period under consideration can be further analysed using the work of Maizels.[11] Maizels divides the changes in the exports of manufactures, measured at constant prices into three parts:

(a) *The market growth factor*: the growth consequent upon the change in the size of the world market for manufactured goods as a whole (this measures how exports from each country would have moved if the area and commodity pattern of trade, and the share of individual markets had remained unchanged), assuming equal commodity supply elasticities.

(b) *The diversification factor*: the change in exports due to changes in the area and commodity pattern of trade. (This measures how exports would have moved if the world total, and each country's share of each market, had remained unchanged).

(c) *The competitiveness factor*: the change in exports resulting from the change in the share of each exporting country in imports of each commodity group into each market. (This measures how exports would have moved if the world total and the area and commodity pattern of trade had remained unchanged.)

One of the more surprising results in Table 4.4 is the small decline in the United States' 'revealed comparative advantage' in

**Table 4.4** Changes in the volume of export of manufactures attributable to changes in the world market, in the pattern of trade and in market shares, 1899–1913 ($ billion constant 1913 prices)

| | Britain | France | Germany | Other W. Europe | Canada | US | India | Japan | Total |
|---|---|---|---|---|---|---|---|---|---|
| 1899 exports | 1.33 | 0.50 | 0.78 | 0.46 | 0.02 | 0.42 | 0.11 | 0.06 | 3.68 |
| Change due to (a) market growth | +1.02 | +0.39 | +0.60 | +0.35 | +0.01 | +0.32 | +0.08 | +0.04 | +2.82 |
| (b) diversification | −0.02 | −0.07 | +0.02 | −0.05 | — | +0.17 | −0.03 | −0.01 | — |
| (c) competitiveness | −0.36 | −0.03 | +0.33 | +0.07 | −0.01 | −0.07 | −0.01 | +0.06 | — |
| Total | +0.63 | +0.29 | +0.95 | +0.37 | +0.02 | +0.43 | +0.04 | +0.09 | 2.82 |
| 1913 Exports | 1.96 | 0.79 | 1.73 | 0.83 | 0.04 | 0.85 | 0.15 | 0.15 | 6.50 |

*Source:* A Maizels, *Industrial Growth and World Trade* (1963), ch. 8.

manufactures, the competitiveness factor.[12] US exports expanded much more proportionately and absolutely than those of other economies because of the change in the type of manufactured goods exported into the fast growing categories and into the more rapidly growing markets. The growth of the adjacent Canadian market provided a strong reason for diversification. Japan increased her comparative advantage as measured by market share proportionately by the greatest amount because she was industrialising most rapidly. Germany gained the most trade from an improved competitive position. Britain lost almost exactly the amount Germany gained because of a deteriorating comparative advantage in manufactures.

The 'normal' pattern of development however implies that an increasing proportion of resources is allocated to services in the economy because of their high income elasticities of demand and, therefore, Britain's comparative advantage might change in that direction. Where such services as insurance and banking are concerned this may well have happened, but other (personal) services such as those provided by government are not tradeable and so could not affect comparative advantage. French national income per head was close to Britain's and, therefore, France might reasonably be expected to experience a similar shift in comparative advantage away from manufactures, but the French decline in competitiveness was smaller even than that of the United States. Thus the 'normal' process of development of the economy is less satisfactory as an explanation for Britain's declining manufactures trade than is low productivity growth in manufacturing shifting her comparative advantage towards natural resources, in particular coal.

## The temperate zone primary product exporters

Low and falling long distance freight rates, analogously to the decline in short distance rates in the third quarter of the century, were major contributory factors to an aspect of the late nineteenth-century international economy that was unique in historical experience; the availability of vast amounts of temperate zone agricultural land that could be brought into use to supply food to the world. These freight rate reductions in particular benefitted the long-distance wheat trade. The British wheat price fell and the Chicago wheat price rose, the gap between them becoming almost negligible by 1880.[13] The refrigerator ships of the 1880s allowed Australia and Latin America to supply Europe with meat products. Despite the raising of the general level of tariffs these changes presented the temperate zones possessing abundant land with an opportunity for expansion. The low density indigenous population could be relatively easily displaced by the threat or use of superior western military technology and organisation. By the 1890s in the mid-western states:

Across the plains where once there roamed
The Indian and the scout,
The Swede with alcoholic breath
Set [s] rows of cabbages out.[14]

The displacement did not invariably proceed smoothly though; Custer's cavalry was wiped out by the Sioux Indians at Little Big Horn in 1876.

The temperate regions of recent European settlement, Argentina, Australia, New Zealand, Canada, South Africa and the west and mid-western United States all shared the common characteristics of receiving labour and capital from the industrialising or developed world and exporting, in return, a variety of primary products that allowed the migrants to maintain high standards of living. By 1895 a contemporary estimate placed the Argentine income per head on the same level as those of Germany, Holland and Belgium and higher than those of Austria, Spain or Italy. At £24, however, the Argentine figure was below those of Canada (£36), the United States (£44) and Australia (£51).[15]

Despite their different living standards the Argentine and Australian economies showed similar export development. Both exported large quantities of wool at the beginning of the last quarter of the nineteenth century when land was by far the most abundant factor of production.[16] Australia had the largest national flock of sheep in the world until drought halved the sheep population, which did not reach its 1892 peak again until 1931. Then, with the development of infrastructure, grain exports became the dynamic sector at the expense of pastoral farming. At the same time, chilled and frozen beef exports grew rapidly in both countries. The differences in living standards between the two economies persisted in part because, unlike Argentina, Australia had a valuable mining sector. Gold mining began to revive again in 1886, first in Queensland, then in Kimberly in Western Australia and finally in Kalgoorlie. Broken Hill proved a valuable source of silver in 1887–8. These discoveries were so fortunate at a time when Australia was facing a severe balance of payments crisis that their exploitation may have been induced by the contemporary underemployment of labour and capital.

Much more dependent on non-renewable resource exports was

the similar South Africa. Small in population (about $\frac{1}{2}$ million whites and $1\frac{1}{2}$ million blacks) but large in area, 475 000 square miles in 1890, this vast agricultural and pastoral area imported nearly all its own food; wheat from Europe, tinned and frozen meat from Australia and preserved fruit.[17] The paradox is a measure of the magnitude of the demands made upon here resources by the diamond industry in the early 1870s and by the gold industry in the late 1880s. The chief consuming areas were connected with the ports of Cape Colony and not with South Africa's producing areas; Johannesburg was economically nearer to Australia by railway and steam ship than she was to many parts of the Transvaal. The influx of foreign capital and labour to exploit South Africa's natural resources caused greater political disturbance than in any other area of recent European settlement as Boer farmers resisted giving up political power to the immigrant English-speaking miners. The Boers defeated the British at Majuba Hill in 1881 and inflicted many reverses on them during the Boer Wars of 1899–1902.

Just as Australia had provided the food for the South African miners in the 1890s, so New Zealand had entered into foreign trade by supplying the Australian gold fields in the 1850s with grain and potatoes. In the next decade New Zealand exported gold from her own fields and then followed the pattern described for Argentina and Australia, with exports of wool, wheat and refrigerated foods.[18]

The pull of the colossal United States' economy delayed Canadian economic development relative to other regions of recent European settlement. During the last three decades of the nineteenth century Canada lost population to the United States as emigration exceeded immigration (see Figure 5.2). But the closing of the American frontier gave Canada her economic opportunity, and in the first decade of the twentieth century the remarkable Canadian wheat export boom pulled over 700 00 immigrants (net of emigration) mainly into the Canadian prairie provinces.

With the exception of the west and mid-west regions of the United States, the temperate zone exporters clearly depended for their high living standards on their relations with the international economy. The nature of this dependence is less clear. Nurkse, among others, asserted that international trade was the engine of growth of these recently settled areas (including the United States).[19] Rising populations, incomes and industrial growth in the countries of the 'industrial core', Nurkse believed, caused an expanding demand for primary products. This demand raised the returns to labour and capital in the 'countries of the periphery' and thereby stimulated international factor flows to satisfy this demand with the abundant land. The influx of labour and capital boosted economic growth, even in America after the Civil War, according to Nurkse.

For the smaller economies Nurkse's views are almost certainly correct. In New Zealand life at a European standard of living would have been impossible without international trade. For South Africa growth was clearly based on exports of gold and diamonds from the 1880s. 48 per cent of the variation in the growth of Argentine national income in the period 1906 to 1940 could be explained by variations in export growth.[20] The Canadian experience is more difficult to interpret despite the wheat export boom. Chambers and Gordon estimated that the spectacular expansion of Canadian agriculture between 1900 and 1910 contributed only 5.2 to 8.4 per cent of the increase in per capita income.[21] The income per head of Canada would have been between 1.2 to 1.94 per cent lower at the end of the decade without the agricultural expansion, even though agriculture was more important to Canada than to other high income economies. On the other hand the marked rise between 1890 and 1900 and 1910 and 1920 in international commodity flows as a percentage of commodity output suggest that export-led growth had a role in Canadian development, although not in the decade chosen by Chambers and Gordon.[22]

The larger temperate zone economies were much less dependent on the international economy. Australia was unusual among primary product exporters in the very high proportion of the population urbanised: two-thirds of the population were town-dwellers in 1890, whereas this proportion was not attained by the United States until 1920. Hence, it is difficult to see exports of rural products providing the dynamic element to an economy so highly urbanised. As indicated in the previous section, the much larger American economy grew mainly on the basis of inter-regional, rather than international trade. The European economies tended to grow more slowly than the temperate 'peripheral' economies, and because therefore European imports similarly grew more slowly than the national products of the peripheral countries, the European 'core' is unlikely to have been the engine of growth.[23] A purely demand-oriented expansion would have allowed the traditional suppliers of primary produce to benefit proportionately to new producers and maintain their market shares. Yet, in the case of wheat especially, the share of Britain's imports supplied by the new producers increased considerably. The extensively farmed prairies produced wheat at much lower prices than the British farmer. Between 1873 and 1894 British wheat production fell by 60 per cent, the United States accounting for 80 per cent of the increase in exports. The traditional suppliers, such as Russia, lost much of their market share. Supply side changes in the regions of recent European settlement were therefore providing much of the impetus of international growth.

Although Britain was the world's largest wheat importer – by 1914 importing 80 per cent of her wheat supplies – it was not British conditions that were the most important determinants of world wheat demand. British wheat consumption was only about 10 per cent of total consumption in 1896. The British increase in wheat imports only amounted to 6.7 per cent of the total increase in world production and demand in the period 1885–9 to 1909–14 because Britain's GNP and population were not rising as fast as those of most other comparable nations.[24] In the same period, Germany increased her demand for wheat sixfold, meeting it, unlike Britain, mainly from expanding home production. The exporting countries raised their own wheat consumption greatly during these years: the US by 167.7 million bushels and Russia by 359 million bushels. The four decades before 1914 were therefore not as favourable to economies that sought to grow on the basis of wheat exports as Nurkse's views imply.

## Tropical trade and the less developed countries (LDCs)

Both the temperate zone primary product exporters and the manufacturing economies maintained high living standards and positive rates of economic growth. Despite the growth of the international trade of the tropical countries at the same rate as industrial production expanded in the main industrialising countries and Britain from the 1880s to 1914, the tropical countries failed to match the income levels of the western world.[25] For many subsequent observers this failure has demonstrated that the effects of trade on less developed countries differ from the effects on higher income economies, and theorising has been directed to explaining why that should be. Enterprises producing for export constitute enclaves of modernity throwing 'backwash effects' on the rest of the economy, it is asserted, bringing about an over-rapid depletion of non-renewable resources, encouraging foreign consumption patterns which increase the demand for imports, and tending to lower the propensity to save, thereby reducing capital accumulation and growth. Indigenous industries are allegedly destroyed by competition from imports, and the resources they formerly used remain unemployed. Because the market forces these countries to specialise in primary products which have low price and income elasticities, the prices of their exports have a chronic tendency to decline relative to import prices. These primary products are also often subject to uncontrollable fluctuations in supply conditions, because of drought or disease, and the associated variability of export earnings further constrains economic development by limiting the ability to import capital goods.

The foregoing analysis, as will be shown, is considerably more pessimistic about trade than warranted by historical experience. Trade almost certainly had a beneficial impact on tropical countries, although it had costs as well. But except for small economies specialising in products that were not closely competitive with the exports of other low income countries, the impact was small.

The late nineteenth-century Jamaican economy suffered costs of international trade different from those listed above: the cost of obsolete specialisation. The protection of Western European beet sugar production meant that Jamaica could no longer profitably provide sugar from its plantations, and the economy became depressed. Only with the economy's switch to banana production was there any recovery.[26]

The benefits of trade (compared to no trade) are analogous to an increase in productivity of an economy. Exports are the inputs into the 'trade process' and imports are the outputs. For tropical countries, as for others, trade is worth while if the resources used to provide the exports are less valuable than the imports obtained in exchange. The more productive the economy, the fewer are the resources needed to supply a given quantity of exports. The problem of the late nineteenth-century tropical economies, according to Lewis, was ultimately low productivity in their agricultural sectors which engaged the great bulk of their labour forces, and that the price at which the products of tropical agriculture could be sold on the international markets was held down by perfectly elastic world supplies of Indian and Chinese willing to travel anywhere to work on plantations for a shilling a day, and by the abundance of tropical land.[27] Because the factors were in elastic supply, so were the products. As demand grew, tea production spread from China to new plantations in India and Ceylon. Burma, Thailand and Indo-China multiplied their exports by four or five times, as they sent rice to feed the plantation workers of Ceylon, Java and Malaya. The rubber plantations of Malaya expanded from 5000 acres in 1900 to $1\frac{1}{4}$ million acres by 1913. The Gold Coast (Ghana), which had supplied virtually no cocoa in 1883, had become the world's largest producer by 1913, as northerners migrated to the wetter south.

Increased productivity, as against increased output, in tropical agriculture would have allowed some of the agricultural labour force to move into manufacturing industry, but this did not happen to any significant extent. Instead, the opening of new tropical areas to international trade by falling freight rates increased the supply of tropical produce and lowered prices relative to temperate zone agricultural goods, whose suppliers had alternative employment opportunities in manufacturing and service sectors.

The export growth of tropical countries was low, or the share of foreign trade in their national product was small (or both) and foreign trade therefore could not be expected greatly to effect the tropical economies.[28] But this small importance of foreign trade was usually because of the fundamental low productivity problem of tropical agriculture. As with the larger temperate zone economies, supply was more important for development than demand.

Even so demand from industrial countries made a difference to the growth of tropical trade. The export growth and diversification of less developed countries was most pronounced in the second and third quarters of the nineteenth century when high income countries were pursuing liberal trade policies, and the most open high income country, Britain, was growing fastest.

Hanson maintains that demand around the mid-century was strongest because of changes in British supply conditions as well as in British demand.[29] The switch to land-economising methods of cultivation in Britain helped create a strong demand for Peruvian guano (see Chapter 1) while the gradual exhaustion of indigenous deposits of copper ore simultaneously with rising demand for copper in the railway and shipbuilding industries fostered the expansion of Chilean copper exports. However, developments in the last quarter of the nineteenth century brought increasing competition for tropical exports, actual or potential. Sugar prices were forced down by the expansion of subsidised beet sugar exports from continental Europe from the 1870s; new copper deposits were discovered and exploited in the US and other countries, and the invention and commercialisation of synthetic dyes greatly reduced exports of Indian indigo. The US became the world's leading producer of cotton and tobacco, Japan became an important exporter of silk and tea, and the United States, continental Europe and Japan all developed advanced textile industries.

In the later decades of the century the rate of growth of British consumption of many LDC products fell because of the retardation of British growth of income and of population. Maizels' analysis of Indian exports of manufactures in Table 4.4 supports the position that the declining growth rate of the open British economy was harmful for the exports of less developed countries. India showed the greatest proportionate decline in exports due to the country of destination and product composition, of all the manufactured goods exporters considered, and Britain was India's most important market, once the opium trade with China declined, as it did in these years.

With the retardation of the growth of tropical trade, diversification of exports of less developed countries almost ceased in the last quarter of the century. Diversification will usually take place when the relative factor endowments of an economy are changing, as will occur with economic growth. The typical LDC, as judged by the mean, earned 58 per cent of its export proceeds from one product in 1860, and 52 per cent in 1900. Yates showed that in 1913 twenty-two LDCs in his study depended on one product for more than 50 per cent of export proceeds; in 1900 this was true for 20 out of 49 LDCs.[30] The deconcentration of developed country exports was faster than for LDCs, but several important LDCs such as British India, China and the Dutch East Indies underwent substantial declines in export concentration while others, such as Brazil and Egypt, experienced increasing concentration.

One of the beneficial effects of export diversification is usually a greater stability of export earnings, because uncontrollable supply or demand side influences are less likely to affect all export products at the same time. The slower diversification rate and lower level of diversification of less developed countries meant that the group of non-European countries which in the twentieth century can be classified as developed (NEDCs) (Argentina, Australia, Canada, Cape of Good Hope, Japan, New Zealand, US and Uruguay) experienced less export instability than the LDC group.[31] On the other hand, the NEDCs experienced more instability than the industrial countries of Western Europe in every decade from 1850 to 1906. Nevertheless, the NEDCs generally maintained higher growth rates than industrial countries. Hence, the instability of export earnings is unlikely to have been an insurmountable obstacle to the economic growth of the less developed countries.

Was there something about the nature of the export enterprises in tropical countries that prevented economic development? The production function of the primary commodity or commodities a region first exports, it has been argued, governs the region's prospects for future development.[32] Labour-intensive, plantation commodities, such as cane sugar, restrict economic development, while non-plantation crops, such as wheat, which provide the right technological and institutional factors, encourage development. In many, if not all, primary products there was a choice of production technique. Tea was not a plantation crop in China but became one in the nineteenth century for India and Ceylon. In Brazil, rubber was not a plantation crop but was introduced into Malaya as one. Cotton was grown on plantations only in the United States. Thus it is not so much the product that is fundamental, but the forces that make for the choice of plantation production. In any event, several products representing a large share of LDC foreign exchange earnings in the nineteenth century had good production functions as judged by this criterion, and yet countries expanding these products did not obviously experience higher rates of economic development than others.

The tropical countries as a whole in 1913 were participating more fully in the international economy than ever before, and their economies almost certainly showed higher living standards (although redistributed among different groups) and improved infrastructure as a result. As for the larger high income countries, trade was not a major stimulus to tropical economic growth (nor was it generally harmful).

## The commodity terms of trade

Writing at the end of the period under consideration, J.M. Keynes speculated that the operation of Malthusian pressures would turn the terms of trade permanently against the manufacturing countries and in favour of the primary producers.[33] The limited availability of land and minerals restricted the scope for increasing the supply of products based mainly on natural resources, whereas technical progress could expand manufactured goods supply without bounds. Admittedly, this did not seem to have happened in the preceding forty years, but eventually the fundamental economic truths would assert themselves, bringing the possibility that economic growth in Britain and industrial Europe would be choked off.

Since then the most popular predictions about movements in the terms of trade have been exactly the opposite of Keynes' view, and based largely upon the experience of the years 1875–1914. The Singer–Prebisch thesis emphasised the demand side of the relationship between primary and manufactured goods, rather than the supply side, drawing attention to the low income elasticities of demand for food and raw materials.[34] As productivity increases raise real incomes, the demand for manufactured goods will expand considerably faster than the demand for primary products, tending to push up the relative price of manufactures. In addition, the greater monopolisation of the secondary sector, both in the goods and the labour markets, will allow that sector to capture most of the gains from technical progress.

The data originally used to support the Singer–Prebisch thesis were based on the import prices of Britain from 1876 to 1914. Because these were prices of primary products and these prices fell relative to British exports of manufactures, it was inferred that primary exporters must have experienced an adverse movement in their terms of trade, corresponding to the favourable movement of the British terms of trade. Since exports are valued exclusive of transport costs but import values include them, a reduction in transport charges could improve the terms of trade for one country without causing a deterioration for its trading partners. It has been argued that the whole of the apparent deterioration of the terms of trade of primary producers in the period 1871 to 1905 could be accounted for by this valuation bias.[35] But thereafter the valuation bias was in fact reversed by rising transport charges, until by 1946 there had been a complete offset.[36] Furthermore, if the unit cost saving from progress in transport technology was equal to the relative fall in price of primary products including transport costs, the importers of the primary goods appropriated the entire gain. That is largely to be expected because importers have price inelastic demands for primary products. Whether or not it is just, bearing in mind the manufacturing countries were the ones devoting resources to transport improvements, is open to debate.

The concern with these particular terms of trade arose originally from the belief that they were representative of industrial countries and less developed countries as a whole. Critics of the Singer–Prebisch thesis point out that primary products imported by industrialised countries included commodities predominantly produced in developed countries and that British data were not necessarily representative of all industrial countries. What evidence there is shows that *these* objections do not invalidate the thesis. The unit value index for industrial Europe's combined exports and imports of primary products fell by 22 per cent between 1872 and 1938.[37] Over the same period the unit value index for industrial Europe's imports of primary products from poor countries fell by 38 per cent. Poor countries therefore experienced a greater fall in their export prices of primary products than those of industrialised or high income countries, as Lewis's argument reviewed in the preceding section implied, although the difference may not be significant in view of the sensitivity of the calculation to the choice of initial and terminal years. As to the second objection, Spraos reduced the dependence of the terms of trade index on British data after 1900 and showed that this reduced but did not eliminate the significant trend in the data.[38].

Yet another attempt to invalidate the Singer–Prebisch thesis has drawn attention to the entry of new manufactures into international trade with the passage of time, while the quality of existing products improves. However, the bias introduced into the terms of trade index on this account cannot be ascertained *a priori* because the quality of primary products also is improved, for instance through processing, and that of manufactures may even decline if durability is reduced, for example.

Lewis thought that what movements there were in the commodity terms of trade of tropical primary producers were relatively unimportant compared with the factoral terms of trade (the value of a factor's export production in terms of imports), and in any case the available evidence suggests that it was only in the twentieth century, and then mainly in the interwar years, that there was a deterioration for primary producers as a whole.[39] The policy implication drawn from the Singer–Prebisch thesis was that specialisation in the production and export of primary products was not beneficial, or at least not optimal. Instead, more resources should have been devoted to the development of domestic manufacturing industry and reducing dependence on international trade. Until the interwar years, such a policy would not have been justified by the decline of primary product prices, and only then because of the collapse of international trade in general, in part a consequence of the pursuit of autarkic policies as were implied by the Singer–Prebisch view.

## Trade and colonisation

A relationship between trade and colonisation was by no means novel at the beginning of the fourth quarter of the nineteenth century, as Chapter 1 has shown, but the speed of the 'scramble for Africa' and other colonial acquisition in the last two decades of the century was sufficiently remarkable to initiate a spate of theorising about the economic causes of this new colonisation, beginning with Hobson, Luxemburg and Lenin.[40] Map 4.1 shows the pattern of African colonisation. Colonies had become, according to Hobson, necessary as a source of demand because the unequal distribution of income in industrial countries gave too little spending power to those who needed to spend. Colonial markets then were allegedly a new way of maintaining demand. According to Lenin, the con-

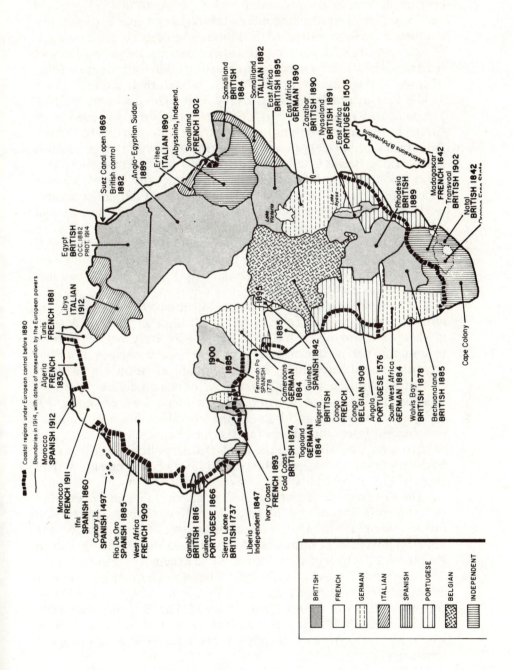

Coastal regions under European control before 1880

Boundaries in 1914, with dates of annexation by the European powers

Suez Canal open 1869
British control 1882

Anglo-Egyptian Sudan

Eritrea ITALIAN 1890
Abyssinia, Independ.
Somaliland FRENCH 1802

Somaliland BRITISH 1884

Somaliland ITALIAN 1882

East Africa GERMAN 1890
Zanzibar BRITISH 1890
Nyasaland BRITISH 1891
East Africa PORTUGESE 1505

East Africa BRITISH 1895

Melanesians & Polynesians

Madagascar FRENCH 1642
Transvaal BRITISH 1902

Rhodesia BRITISH 1889

Natal BRITISH 1842
Orange Free State

Egypt BRITISH OCC.1882 PROT. 1914

Lake Victoria

Lake Nyasa

Cape Colony

Libya ITALIAN 1912

Tunis FRENCH 1881

Algeria FRENCH 1830

Morocco SPANISH 1912

1900

1885

Fernando Po. SPANISH 1778

1895

1885

1885

Guinea SPANISH 1842

Cameroons GERMAN 1884

Nigeria BRITISH

Congo FRENCH

Congo BELGIAN 1908

South West Africa GERMAN 1884

Angola PORTUGESE 1576

Walvis Bay BRITISH 1878

Bechuanaland BRITISH 1885

Morocco FRENCH 1911

Ifni SPANISH 1860

Canary Is. SPANISH 1497

Rio De Oro SPANISH 1885

West Africa FRENCH 1909

Gambia BRITISH 1816

Guinea PORTUGESE 1866

Sierra Leone BRITISH 1737

Liberia Independent 1847

Ivory Coast FRENCH 1893

Gold Coast BRITISH 1874

Togoland GERMAN 1884

BRITISH
FRENCH
GERMAN
ITALIAN
SPANISH
PORTUGESE
BELGIAN
INDEPENDENT

centration of industry allowed the monopolists to divide the world between them, first into commercial empires and then into political empires, in order to safeguard their monopoly of markets and sources of raw materials. A first step towards assessing these doctrines of the necessary connection between trade and colonisation is an outline of some of the main events of the process and their timing.

The year after Stanley's discovery of the Congo basin in 1877, Leopold II of Belgium set up a Studies Committee for the Upper Congo to further his designs for a free trade colony in central Africa. An international treaty guaranteeing free trade and navigation was signed at the Berlin Congo Conference of 1885.[41] At the same time Bismarck created a German empire five times the size of the new Reich over infertile lands where there were few German economic interests. 1884 had been an election year for Bismarck and foreign adventures were therefore useful to him, especially as the French desire to find new access to the Chinese market had embroiled them in Indo-China at the time, and the British were preoccupied in Egypt (see Chapter 5) for strategic reasons.[42] By 1886 Bismarck had lost interest in his colonial empire.

The larger French colonial empire of nearly 1.2 million square miles at the end of the century was, with the exception of Algeria in the 1830s, mainly conquered since 1880. Italy belatedly tried to emulate her northern neighbours, despite a parlous financial condition, until defeated by the Abyssinians at Adowa in 1896.

British colonial activity seems to have followed a different pattern, most probably because British economic interests were already well established overseas, and because the liberal tradition of minimal government intervention was more firmly established. When other countries were colonising in the 1880s British policy was still to hold back on grounds of expense. Just as in 1859 when the most powerful chief in Fiji offered sovereignty over the islands to Great Britain, and the British government declined, so also in 1883 the Queensland government's annexation of south-east New Guinea (to prevent further German and Dutch acquisitions) was not ratified by the imperial government until Queensland agreed the following year to guarantee a portion of the administrative expenses.[43] Similarly, the British procrastinated in early 1883 when the German government indicated they would be glad to see British protection extended to German settlers in South-West Africa.[44] The British policy only changed in the 1890s when British trading interests were apparently in danger of losing out through other countries' annexation of territories.

All these colonial acquisitions, and most of those of Russia in

**Table 4.5**  *Total trade compared with colonial trade (annual average), for selected countries, 1892–6*

| Imperial power | Imports (%) | Exports (%) | Colonial area (000 sq. miles) | Colonial population (m) |
|---|---|---|---|---|
| Britain | 22.5 | 33.2 | 11 090 | 325.1 |
| France | 9.5 | 9.5 | 1 195 | 36.15 |
| Holland | 14.5 | 5.0 | 785 | 34.5 |
| Portugal | 15.8 | 9.2 | 834 | 7.9 |
| Spain | 9.7 | 24.0 | 323 | 8.5 |
| Denmark | 1.1 | 1.6 | 41 | 0.127 |
| Germany | 0.05 | 0.09 | 1 026 | 9.8 |

*Source*: A.W. Flux, 'The flag and trade' *Journal of the Royal Statistical Society* (1899).

Asia, differed from most of the temperate zone settlements in having substantial indigenous populations and climates uncongenial to Europeans. As a result, the motives for colonisation and the pattern of economic development imposed on them also necessarily differed. Trade with the new colonies was relatively unimportant for the European powers as Table 4.5 shows for the 1890s.

Britain was most reliant upon colonial trade, which accounted for one-third of her exports and over one-fifth of her imports. The only other power as closely dependent upon the trade was Spain, with almost one-quarter of her exports going to her colonies. Germany, the most vigorous industrial state, was distinguished by the tiny percentage of her trade with her colonies. The new colonial empires were in fact even less important to the imperial powers than Table 4.5 suggests because colonial trade was concentrated usually on one or two possessions. Nearly two-thirds of French trade with French possessions were with Algeria and Tunisia, India dominated British colonial trade, East India the Dutch, Angola was much the most important for the Portuguese colonial trade, and Cuba for the Spanish.[45] All of these colonies (except Tunisia) had been held long before the wave of colonisation of the last two decades of the century. Theories that link this colonisation with the economic necessities of the capitalism of the time are on thin ground because the trade involved was so small.

If imports from the colonies provided raw materials for the industrial powers and exports to them provided markets, then market factors dominated British and Spanish relations with their colonies, and raw materials dominated Dutch and Portuguese relations. The relative unimportance of French colonial trade in total French trade, at less than 10 per cent, is at first sight surprising in view of France being an imperial power second in importance only to Britain. This can however be explained by the different ways in which the two countries came to acquire colonies in the 1880s and 1890s, as well as by earlier mercantile history.

Cain and Hopkins link the search for new markets with imperialism as joint consequences of Britain's failure to maintain her position in the markets of her major rivals, but over a much longer period than the 1880s and 1890s.[46] They emphasise that Britain's leadership in exports by 1913 had come to rest upon her ability to sell to the large group of semi-industrialised countries, most of which were either formally controlled or under the direct economic influence of Britain. In this category they include the Dominions and Latin America which pursued independent tariff policies, as the next section shows, yet the implication of their argument is that had there been no formal or informal British empire, British exports would have been much lower, because presumably of the pursuit of different commercial policies in the export markets. In fact, Britain's ceasing to be a technological leader in this period inevitably meant a loss of markets in advanced countries, but that does not imply an independent British drive to colonise in these years; rather, as suggested above, British colonisation, unlike French or German, was defensive rather than offensive.

Even granted this motivation, the effects of the new colonialism do not suggest that it was justified by trade increases. Table 4.4 shows that the pattern of products and of markets was not responsible for any increased sales of manufactured goods by the main colonial powers, Britain and France, during the period 1899–1913. As well as the small importance of the colonial trade, there is little evidence of the exclusion of one European country's traders from another's colonies. Germany increased her exports to other West African colonies from 1889 to 1911 by more proportionately than she did to German West Africa in the same period (535 and 310 per cent, respectively). British exports to German South-West Africa increased by proportionately more than German exports from 1900 to 1911 (530 as against 454 per cent, admittedly starting from a low base). French exports to British possessions in Africa rose by 60 per cent from 1889 to 1911, while French exports in total rose by almost the same proportion, by 64 per cent.[47] Hence, it is more appropriate to see the trading patterns of colonial areas as the cause, rather than the consequence of, colonisation. The imperial powers staked their territorial claims where their nationals already had trading interests, however small these were.

This is borne out by the dependence of colonies on trade with the imperial power. 55 per cent of British colonial imports came from Britain in the period 1892–6, and 49 per cent of exports went to Britain. These percentages were a slight decline from those of twenty-five years earlier. An even larger percentage of the external trade of British colonies, 65 per cent, was conducted within the British empire. The dependence of the French colonies on trade with France at 61 per cent for 1896 was of a similar order of magnitude.

Although colonisation did not in fact enhance the trade of the imperial powers, the administration of the colonies became for most of them a considerable financial drain. The excess of colonial expenditure over colonial receipts in 1898 cost France more than 108 million francs.[48] Between 1894 and 1913 German expenditure on colonies, excluding defence, amounted to 1002 million marks compared with total colonial trade of 972 million marks.[49] The latest addition to the imperial powers, Italy, spent 6586 million lire on the direct cost of colonial government compared with a value of colonial trade of 5561 million lire between 1893 and 1932. The Dutch had obtained a financial surplus from the Netherlands East Indies until 1874, but thereafter it was eliminated because of the rebellion in Northern Sumatra.[50] The other Dutch colonies of Surinam and Curacao demanded subsidies. Great Britain, in contrast to most other powers, required its dependencies to be self-supporting. Loans were expected to be repaid eventually. The British West Indies were an exception in the 1890s because the economy was so depressed that the British Colonial Secretary could not envisage the colony becoming self-supporting for many years. A military contribution to Britain was paid by the colony where its own interests were concerned, but wherever ports were fortified with reference to the interests of the empire as a whole, Britain bore the expense.[51]

The impact of colonialism on the colonised territory has almost invariably since 1945 been represented as harmful. Colonialism has come to mean exploitation by a foreign society and its agents who occupy the dependency to serve their own interests, not that of the subject people. That was not how it was seen at the time. The eminent Victorian economist, A. Marshall, thought the colonies received very good value in the services of the British administration whose salaries they paid:[52]

we export to India a great number of prime young men. If their value was capitalised as it would be if they were slaves, it would be several thousand pounds a piece. We bring them back afterwards, if they come back at all, more or less shrivelled and worn out. Those are a vast unreckoned export.

The colonial impact, considered in more detail in Chapter 7, is usually denounced on three dubious assumptions: first, that some better alternative was available; second, that the undesirable features of colonialism were deliberately intended; and third, that the effects were universally deplorable.[53] Fieldhouse concludes that the alternative to formal imperial rule was widespread anarchy, because the economic dynamism of Europe and North America was so strong and the capacity of most other societies to resist or make constructive use of that force was so limited. Colonialism was not a system of international servitude but a solution on both sides of the relationship to acute problems of international relations. It was not, for example, a one-sided response by the industrial powers to the slump of the 1870s.

## The response to depression

The depression of 1873 and after, described in Chapter 3 nevertheless did provoke a political reaction, but in the form of higher tariffs. Industrial interests reacted to lower prices by demanding tariff protection and by forming cartels to restrict output in order to maintain prices. Higher tariffs provoked retaliation and the ensuing tariff wars reduced trade.

Under pressure from industrialists and the agrarian interests, Bismarck introduced a new German tariff in 1879 which imposed relatively low duties on a wide range of imported manufactures and heavier duties on agricultural produce. No major charge occurred in the 1880s, but in 1890 higher rates were imposed on many articles. In 1893 a tariff war with Russia began, culminating in Russian breadstuffs paying 115 per cent higher taxes in Germany than did American, and with German imports to Russia paying 50 per cent more than those from elsewhere. Both sides eventually concluded that the resulting paralysis of trade was dangerous to the peace of Europe, and reached agreement.[54]

The movement to protection in France began at the same time as in Germany, when the flood of US wheat increased agricultural agitation for a tariff in 1878, and the 'American peril' became a matter of popular debate. The 1881 tariff raised rates on manufactures by an average of 24 per cent, but only as a basis for negotiations with other countries. At the same time the French introduced state subsidies for shipbuilders and for owners of ships engaged on long voyages. The agricultural interests were disappointed in the tariff of 1881 and managed to raise rates on various agricultural products during the 1880s. The French duty on cattle imports annoyed the Italians, who in any case in their search for revenue proposed to revise upwards their tariffs to an average level of 60 per cent *ad valorem* in 1886. Negotiations between France and Italy over the new tariffs broke down in 1888, and each country successively increased duties on each other's products until 1892. French exports to Italy approximately halved although they were recouped in other markets. Italy suffered much more, her exports to France falling by more than half and the decline was not compensated by increased sales elsewhere. The 1892 French tariff raised duties further – on agricultural produce to an average level of 25 per cent, and on textile manufactures. A $2\frac{1}{2}$ year tariff war with Switzerland followed this increase.

Russia and the United States had always been protectionist but increased the height of their tariffs. Russia did so in 1881/2 and 1890/1, and the United States behaved similarly with the McKinley Tariff of 1890 and the Dingley Tariff in 1897. The average US tariff level rose from 47 per cent in 1869 to 49.5 per cent in 1890 and 57 per cent in 1897. The new justification for the American tariff, replacing infant industry arguments, was the need to protect the highly paid US workmen against the products of the poorly paid Europeans.

Britain continued to keep to free trade despite the founding of the Fair Trade League in 1881. The Conservative Party lost the election of 1906 fought on a platform of protectionism. The prospect of higher food prices for the greater part of the electorate employed outside agriculture was sufficient to sway their vote. Those parts of the empire without tariff autonomy therefore had to follow suit. Although India was allowed a 5 per cent import duty in 1893 for revenue purposes, Lancashire cotton manufactures were able to secure a 5 per cent excise duty on cotton goods made in India to eliminate any protective effect on Indian textiles.[55] The Dominions, on the other hand, were able and anxious to promote manufacturing industry by tariff protection. Canada unilaterally granted a tariff preference to British goods in 1897.[56] Unlike Canada, Australia and South Africa were relatively late even in securing free trade between their component states. In Australia this was not achieved until 1900 and in South Africa in 1903.[57] Taking the total tariff revenue in relation to the total value of imports as a measure of the height of a national tariff, Australia, Canada, the United States and Argentina in 1913 all had tariffs of about the same level — 16.5 to 17.7 per cent.[58]

Argentina has often been classified as part of Britain's informal empire, and described as a country whose policy was distorted in the interests of the agricultural landowners and British exporters of industrial goods. It is true that British exports were disproportionately represented on the free import list, yet the two items which dominated duty free imports, railway equipment and coal, were intermediate goods in which Britain had a strong comparative advantage. These goods would have been prohibitively expensive to supply domestically, and would have raised the costs of many other Argentinian products.[59] As it was, from the 1880s, the tariff had been sufficient to create viable factories, such as those making galvanished iron. If the Argentinian tariff had been within the British sphere of influence a lower level or a wider duty free list would have been observed on many other items, especially on textiles.

Increasing protectionism must have reduced world trade, though it is less clear that economic welfare consequently declined. Protection in Germany reduced the relative decline of the agricultural sector and therefore cut the migration from the country to the towns. This migration was not necessarily beneficial if it was taking place at a rate faster than could be accommodated by the expansion of social overhead capital – schools, roads, sewers. In the British case, there is not only the optimum tariff argument of Chapter 2 to suggest the economy might have benefitted from protection, but also the existence of economies of scale in some of the new industries in which Britain was weak. Had tariff protection been given to the young motor industry early in the twentieth century it may well have been able to reduce costs as a result of the increased home market sales to an extent which would have offset the higher prices that consumers would have had to pay for the imports they would otherwise have bought.[60]

Among businesses there was a parallel movement to restrict the play of market forces. The Nobel Dynamite Trust Company, one of the first of the international cartels to regulate prices and output, was formed in 1886.[61] Alfred Nobel, a Swede brought up in Russia, prone to relieve his feelings by writing in English, and who eventually gave his fortune to establish the Nobel Prizes, had set up a number of companies in different countries in partnership with natives, largely to avoid tariff barriers. In a later period the Trust would have developed as a multinational company.

One of the problems the Trust was supposed to solve was the elimination of competition between companies which he had founded and on whose boards he still sat. The General Pooling

Agreement of 1889 between the Trust and the German powder companies was to obtain a wider market sharing agreement. The American market proved more difficult to control and was the subject of long negotiations between the European companies and the American firm Du Pont, from 1897 until 1914. The agreements were that Europe was to be reserved for the European firms, North America for the Americans and the British empire, including Great Britain, for the British. Rights elsewhere, as for instance in South America, were negotiable. The basis of these agreements was a shared belief that the market for explosives could not be increased by any action which the companies themselves could take. This belief was almost certainly correct. Because explosives were an intermediate good for other industries, and because the costs were a very small part of mining costs, reductions in price would not induce the mining companies to use more than they otherwise would.

The average annual rate of return for the Nobel–Dynamite Trust over the whole of its life from 1887 to 1914 at a little over 8 per cent hardly suggests that the market regulation was used to make monopoly profits. The only question then is whether the market sharing agreements reduced the stimulus to innovate and increase efficiency. A detailed study of the United Alkali Company's choice of technique for producing soda showed that they did indeed forgo profits by failing to replace Leblanc process plant with Solvay process plant early enough, and that the likely reason is that they operated a market sharing arrangement with continental producers which reduced the incentive.[62] Perhaps in the absence of the Trust, Nobel would have been forced to try to diversify and would have developed the chemistry of dyestuffs which German companies were using in the 1870s. On the other hand, improvements in operating efficiency were steadily bringing down the costs of production, and possibly this was the best that could be done.

Anyway the international economy was little affected by any stultification of innovations by cartels because few had successfully divided up the international market entirely among their members; the zinc and lead syndicates, the European plate-glass agreement, and the international pipes and rails cartels were the most important successful examples.[63] In 1883 the British Railmakers' Association was formed and soon after combined with German and Belgian manufacturers into the International Rail Syndicate. The stability of published steel prices in the following two years does suggest they were set by a committee rather than the market. This syndicate collapsed in 1886. Ten years later the British Railmakers' Association was officially revived and in 1904 joined again in an International Railmakers' Association.[64]

More usual were cartel agreements concluded between firms in different countries. According to one estimate there were at least one hundred agreements in which Germany was concerned, most of these applying to the chemical industry.[65] Writers on cartels were inclined to include companies owning plants in different countries in the same category on the grounds that they were aiming to produce the same effect. Thus Coats, the British multinational thread manufacturer, controlled spinning mills and thread factories in many countries and was a cartel in intention. The American cigarette trust almost entirely controlled the English cigarette industry and had also established itself firmly in Germany. The substitutability between mergers and cartels as alternative means of securing market power explains the strength of the American merger boom of 1899–1900 in comparison to the British. In the United States the anti-trust legislation of 1890 made cartel agreements more difficult and therefore encouraged mergers.[66] The division of international markets by large firms and the tariff wars of governments brought to the fore the element of conflict in international economic relations, that had been largely absent in the twenty-five years or so before 1875. The mid-century vision of the free-trade liberals was receding.

## Summary and conclusion

The economic development of the industrialising countries shifted the pattern of comparative advantage as well as the political balance of power. Britain's unique mid-century position in manufactured goods based upon cheap coal was eroded and her share of foreign markets began to decline in the face of German and American competition. However, it was lower long distance freight rates rather than increased demand by manufactures exporters that encouraged the extension of arable farming for export by European migrants in the American mid-west, in Canada, Australia, Argentina and New Zealand. These temperate zone countries were able to provide high standards of living for their agrarian population working for the world market but the tropical countries were not able to emulate this performance despite a substantial growth of exports. Ultimately, this failure was because of the low productivity of tropical agriculture which precluded any substantial development of a modern manufacturing sector, but the lower rate of expansion of the British economy reduced in the last quarter of the nineteenth century the growth rate of tropical exports, further limiting the possibilities for development of the tropical economies. Virtually all the tropical countries had either a low growth of exports or a low ratio of export value per head of the population. The commodity terms of trade of the tropical economies may have deteriorated slightly during these years, but in that case the fall was mainly after 1900.

European trade with many tropical areas led to a variety of problems, which often from the viewpoint of the European powers could best or most simply be dealt with by the extension of formal political control. The expense of doing so usually meant that the industrial powers preferred 'spheres of influence' to protectorates, and protectorates were preferred to formal colonisation. Nevertheless, by the turn of the century, except where there were what Europeans could recognize as responsible governments, for example in Siam and China, most areas of the tropics had been converted into formal colonies. The effects of colonisation was not, however, significantly to increase the trade of the imperial power.

Lower freight rates increased the effective supply of agricultural land and brought down agricultural prices. This provoked a demand for protection against food imports in continental Europe, where sufficient numbers were still employed in agriculture to be an important political force. With the slowing down of world trade growth the benefits forgone by industrial protection seemed to diminish. The raising of tariffs and the associated tariff wars further reduced the volume of trade relative to what it would have been. The protected nations grew faster, by and large, than when they had been committed to free trade, although the association would not seem to be causal. Businesses also tried to ameliorate the impact of competition by agreeing the division of international markets, but with a few notable exceptions they were not particularly successful.

## Notes

1. A. Maddison, 'Phases of capitalist development', *Banca Nazionale del Lavoro Quarterly Review*, **30** (1977) pp. 103–38.
2. W.A. Lewis, 'The rate of growth of world trade 1830–1973', in S. Grassman and E. Lundberg (eds), *The World Economic Order, Past and Prospects*, New York: St Martins Press (1981).
3. R.C. Allen, 'International competition in iron and steel, 1850–1913', *Journal of Economic History*, **39** (1979), pp. 911–37.
4. A. Milward and S.B. Saul, *The Development of the Economies of Continental Europe*, London: Allen & Unwin (1977), p. 27.
5. Allen, loc. cit.

6. A.L. Levine, *Industrial Retardation in Britain 1880–1914*, New York: Basic Books (1967), pp. 133–5.
7. Milward and Saul, op. cit., p. 30.
8. S.B. Saul, *Studies in British Overseas Trade 1870–1914*, Liverpool: Liverpool University Press (1960), p. 32.
9. Or so McCloskey argues on the basis of the size of the British foreign trade sector and likely movements in the British terms of trade, in R. Floud and D.N. McCloskey (eds), *The Economic History of Britain, Since 1700*, Cambridge: Cambridge University Press (1981), vol. 2.
10. J. Vanek, *The Natural Resource Content of United States Foreign Trade 1870–1955*, Cambridge, Mass: MIT Press (1963).
11. A. Maizels, *Industrial Growth and World Trade*, Cambridge: Cambridge University Press (1963), ch. 8.
12. The term 'revealed comparative advantage' for trade shares was coined by B. Balassa, 'Trade liberalisation and 'revealed' comparative advantage', *The Manchester School*, 33 (1965), pp. 99–123.
13. C.K. Harley, 'Transportation, the world wheat trade and the Kuznets Cycle 1850–1913', *Explorations in Economic History*, 17 (1980), pp. 218–50.
14. Quoted in M. Cunliffe, *The Age of Expansion 1848–1917*, Springfield, Mass.: Merriam (1974), p. 152.
15. M.G. Mulhall, *Industries and the Wealth of Nations*, London: Longmans (1896).
16. C.F. Diaz Alejandro, *Essays on the Economic History of the Argentine Republic*, New Haven: Yale University Press (1970), ch. 1.
17. D.M. Goodfellow, *A Modern Economic History of South Africa*, London: Routledge (1931), pp. 7, 96–7.
18. J. Gould, *Economic Growth in History*, London: Methuen (1972).
19. R. Nurkse, *Equilibrium and Growth in the World Economy*, G. Haberler and R.M. Stern (eds), Cambridge, Mass.: Harvard University Press (1961).
20. Diaz Alejandro, op. cit., ch. 2.
21. E.J. Chambers and D. Gordon, 'Primary products and economic growth', *Journal of Political Economy*, 74 (1966), pp. 315–32.
22. A. Green and M. Urquhart, 'Factor and commodity flows in the international economy of 1870–1914: a multi-country view', *Journal of Economic History*, 36 (1976), pp. 217–52.
23. I. Kravis, 'Trade as a handmaiden of growth', *Economic Journal*, 80 (1970), pp. 850–72.
24. M. Olsen, 'The UK and the world market for wheat and other primary products 1885–1914', *Explorations in Economic History*, 11 (1974), pp. 352–6.
25. W.A. Lewis, *Growth and Fluctuations 1870–1913*, London: Allen & Unwin, (1978a).
26. G. Eisner, *Jamaica 1830–1930: A Study in Economic Growth*, Manchester: Manchester University Press (1961). D. Hall, *Ideas and Illustrations in Economic History*, New York: Holt Rinehart (1964).

27. Lewis (1978a), op. cit., and W.A. Lewis, *The Evolution of the Internatinal Economic Order*, Princeton, NJ: Princeton University Press (1978), ch. 3.
28. J.R. Hanson II, 'The Leff conjecture: some contrary evidence', *Journal of Political Economy*, **84** (1976), pp. 401–5.
29. J.R. Hanson II, 'Diversification and concentration of LDC exports: Victorian trends', *Explorations in Economic History*, **14** (1977), pp. 44–68.
30. P.L. Yates, *Forty Years of Foreign Trade*, London: Allen & Unwin (1959).
31. J.R. Hanson II, 'Export instability in historical perspective', *Explorations in Economic History*, **14** (1977), pp. 293–310, Table 1.
32. R.E. Baldwin, 'Patterns of development in newly settled regions', *Manchester School*, **24** (1956), pp. 161–79.
33. J.M. Keynes, *An Essay on Indian Monetary Reform*, London: Macmillan (1913).
34. H.W. Singer, 'The distribution of the gains between investing and borrowing countries', *American Economic Review, Papers and Proceedings*, **40** (1950), pp. 473–85. R. Prebisch, 'The economic development of Latin America and its principal problems', *Economic Bulletin for Latin America*, **7** (1962), pp. 1–22.
35. P.T. Ellsworth, 'The terms of trade between primary producing and industrial countries', *Inter American Economic Affairs*, **10** (1956), pp. 47–65.
36. J. Spraos, 'The statistical debate on the net barter terms of trade between primary commodities and manufactures', *Economic Journal*, **90** (1980), pp. 107–28.
37. C.P. Kindleberger, *The Terms of Trade: A European Case Study*, London: Chapman and Hall (1956).
38. Spraos, loc. cit.
39. Lewis (1978a), op. cit.
40. J.A. Hobson, *Imperialism: A study* (first published 1902), London: Constable Revised ed. (1905). R, Luxemburg, *The Accumulation of Capital* (first published 1913), London: Allen Lane (1972). V.I. Lenin, *Imperialism, the Highest Stage of Capitalism* (first published 1916), London: Lawrence & Wishart (1934).
41. D.K. Fieldhouse, *Economics and Empire 1830–1914*, London: Weidenfeld & Nicolson (1973).
42. F. Stern, *Gold and Iron*, New York: Alfred Knopf (1977), p. 409.
43. *Essays in Colonial Finance*, Members of the American Economic Association, New York: Macmillan (1900), pp. 283, 287.
44. Stern, op. cit.
45. P.J. Cain and A.G. Hopkins, 'The political economy of British expansion overseas, 1750–1914', *Economic History Review*, **33** (1980), pp. 463–90.
46. A.W. Flux, 'The flag and trade', *Journal of the Royal Statistical Society*, **62** (1899), pp. 489–522.

47. Calculated from *Statistical Abstract for the United Kingdom* and *UK Statistical Abstract for Foreign Countries*.
48. American Economic Association, op. cit., p. 27.
49. C. Grover Clark, *The Balance Sheet of Imperialism*, New York (1936).
50. American Economic Association, op. cit., pp. 73–104.
51. ibid., pp. 302, 168–9.
52. A. Marshall, *Official Papers*, London: Macmillan (1926), pp. 312–13, 290–1.
53. D.K. Fieldhouse, *Colonialism 1870–1945: An Introduction*, London: Weidenfeld & Nicolson (1981), pp. 8, 48. This work contains a valuable bibliography and a chronology of colonialism.
54. P. Ashley, *Modern Tariff History: German, the United States, France*, London: John Murray (1904).
55. R. Dutte, *India in the Victorian Age*, New York: B. Franklin (1970).
56. O.J. McDiarmid, *Commercial Policy in the Canadian Economy*, Cambridge, Mass.: Harvard University Press (1948).
57. C.F. Bastable, *The Commerce of Nations*, London: Methuen, 9th edn, (1922), pp. 118–19.
58. A Leage of Nations study, quoted in C. Diaz Alejandro 'The Argentine tariff, 1906–1940', *Oxford Economic Papers*, **19** (1967), pp. 75–98.
59. Diaz Alejandro (1967), op. cit.
60. J. Foreman-Peck, 'Tariff protection and economies of scale: the British motor industry before 1939', *Oxford Economic Papers*, **31** (1979), pp. 237–57.
61. W.J. Reader, *Imperial Chemical Industries: A History*, vol. 1, London: Oxford University Press (1970).
62. P. Lindert and K. Trace, 'Yardsticks for Victorian entrepreneurs', in D.N. McCloskey (ed.), *Essays on a Mature Economy: Britain after 1840*, London: Methuen (1971).
63 League of Nations, *Cartels and Combines* (by K. Wiedenfeld), Geneva (1927).
64. H. Macrosty, *The Trust Movement in British Industry*, London (1907).
65. League of Nations, op. cit.
66. L. Hannah, 'Mergers in British manufacturing industry 1880–1918', *Oxford Economic Papers*, **26** (1974), pp. 1–20.

# 5 International Factor Mobility, 1875–1914

The great nineteenth-century migrations were unique in international economic relations both in the numbers involved and in the fundamental reasons for the movements. Accompanying the people were enormous quantities of capital, equally motivated by the search for gain, but directed by different groups. The previous chapter has discussed one of the elements that underlay these movements, the opening up of new lands by new transport technology and the consequent change in the pattern of international specialisation. In this chapter a more detailed explanation is offered of the great migrations of labour and capital, together with an account of their consequences and an assessment of their desirability. The first section discusses the forces underlying national supplies of, and demands for, capital, and the differences and similarities among receiving and sending countries. The focus shifts in the next section to the capital exporters, Britain and France, and to what determined the size and distribution of their foreign investment. The political impact of foreign investment on receiving countries which did not wholly share western institutions and attitudes forms the subject of the third section. The distribution of the gains from foreign investment between the borrowers and the lenders is considered next, and to conclude the discussion of capital movements there is an analysis of the distinctive nature and problems of foreign direct investment, as distinguished from portfolio investment. Moving on to the international mobility of labour, the pattern and measurement problems are described. Next is discussed the causes that were powerful enough to make so many people permanently uproot themselves and travel often thousands of miles to the New World. Finally an evaluation of the gains and losses of international labour migration is attempted.

## International capital mobility

If ever a world capital market existed then it was in this period. Though domestic and foreign assets did not become perfect substitutes, they became sufficiently close to permit the assumption for long-term flows that international capital moved because of imbalances between domestic savings and domestic investment at the internationally-determined, risk-adjusted, interest rate. Countries with a strong demand for capital relative to their savings tended to receive capital from abroad. Urbanisation made the greatest demands upon capital and therefore those countries which had the largest movements of population from the country to the town, or from abroad into the towns, usually received some foreign investment.[1]

The demand for real capital then can be divided into two components: the first associated with the growth or redistribution (urbanisation) of the labour force, and the second associated with technical progress.[2] Higher proportions of population increase were absorbed into urban areas in Britain, France, Spain and Germany than in most receiving countries. In these four international suppliers of capital urban growth typically accounted for not more than two-thirds of total population growth. But each sending country had substantially lower rates of growth of population than had the United States and Australia. Until 1900 Canada's population growth was only slightly above those of the sending countries, but it rose dramatically after the turn of the century. Several of the supplying countries in various decades had rates of productivity growth greater or equal to the rates of receiving countries. As for total growth rates, those of the United States were generally greater than those of the sending countries.

The proportion of investment (gross domestic capital formation) to GNP tended to be higher the greater was the growth rate of national income, for the various countries and time periods. For this reason, the proportion was generally higher for the faster growing receiving, than for the sending, countries. The proportion of this investment that was devoted to construction of various sorts, varied with the differing national population growths.

The supply of capital can be divided into that portion originating from domestic savings and that arising from international capital flows. The more industrially advanced countries, Britain, the United States and France, had relatively high and steady savings ratios. The savings ratios of the industrialising countries, Italy, Sweden, Canada and Australia, by contrast rose, and to a lesser extent this was also true of Germany. These observations are consistent with Rostow's views on economic growth, but unfortunately Rostow does not explain why savings rates should have risen.[3] One possible explanation can be given in terms of the life-cycle savings hypothesis,

INTERNATIONAL CAPITAL FLOWS AS A PERCENTAGE
OF GROSS NATIONAL PRODUCT, SELECTED COUNTRIES
BY DECADE 1870–1910

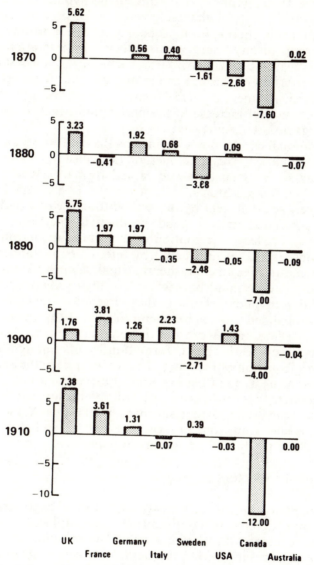

**Figure 5.1**     International capital flows as a percentage of gross national
product, selected countries, 1870–1910

which asserts that households save or dissave in order to eliminate discrepancies between their consumption plans and their expected income over their lifetimes.[4] According to this hypothesis the savings rates will be highest for the age group 25–45, because this is the maximum earning period for most people. The proportion of people in this group in any country was affected by migration and by natural increase. Receiving countries such as the United States had a high proportion of this age group in the labour force because of immigration, and therefore had a high savings ratio until 1900, when the rate of natural increase in the population began to slow, and the savings ratio fell somewhat.

International capital flows, defined as the net foreign balance on current account (the 'residual' method described in Chapter 1), are the difference between domestic capital formation and domestic savings. The United States, Italy (from the 1890s) and Germany were largely self-sufficient by this period, because of a high rate of growth combined with a good productivity performance. (see Figure 5.1). The large and continuous export of capital from Britain was a consequence of unusually (by international standards) low rate of domestic investment rather than high savings. Countries with the largest international borrowing had high growth rates and a high immigrant inflow relative to the indigenous population. In this group are included Canada between 1900 and 1914, Australia in the 1870s and 1880s and Argentina throughout the period. Here the demands on domestic capital formation by the immigrants could not be met from domestic savings. France was one of the anomolous countries, being a major net exporter of capital, but not of people. The French savings rate was unexpectedly high, more than offsetting the higher than expected domestic investment ratios. At the opposite end of the spectrum from France were Sweden and Russia which imported capital, but sent migrants overseas.

### The capital exporters

The foreign investments of the two major capital exporters, Britain and France, differed markedly in their geographical distribution, and this, together with their relatively slow growth rates, has been the basis of accusations that the capital markets of these countries were biased, directing too many resources overseas, and not necessarily to the most profitable projects. Whereas in the third quarter of the nineteenth century French economic activity abroad had been located mainly in Central and Western Europe, from the early 1880s the centre of gravity moved away, to Eastern Europe, Latin America,

Asia and the colonies.[5] More than 90 per cent of French foreign investment was in Europe (including the Turkish empire and Egypt) in 1881, but thereafter almost half the new investment went to other continents. Russia, the Balkans and Scandinavia were important areas. In part this was merely the shifting locus of opportunities as old areas became self-sufficient in technical knowledge and capital. There was also an important political factor deriving from the French government's search for security against what they perceived as the German threat.

From 1887, any new issues on the French stock exchange had to be acceptable to the Russian Foreign Ministry as well as to the French, because Russia had become allied to France.[6] So, for example, in 1901 Japan was unable to raise a loan in Paris because Russia feared Japanese expansion in China. The other side of the coin was the welcome given to French investment in Russia, the largest European borrower, where France accounted for by far the greatest proportion of foreign investment. Although Britain was a much larger foreign investor in total, her investments in Russia remained small until after the signing of a treaty in 1906. The greater government involvement with the French capital market also enhanced the opportunities for pressure groups with access to the government to influence the market. Organised employer groups sold their consent to foreign loans for promises that foreign borrowers would give French lenders special consideration in their expenditure, or for tariff concessions. Loans to directly competing industries were sometimes kept off the French market, as in the refusal in 1909 to grant official listing to the common stock of the US Steel Corporation.

The policy of securing orders in return for loans was most consistently and effectively applied in loans to the Balkan states and Turkey. Often in these negotiations a representative of Creusot, France's greatest manufacturer of steel and war materials, or some bank on whose board Creusot was well represented, took a direct part. Such tying was frequently justified by reference to German demands. The Germans similarly justified their own restrictions. Because of the 1870 Franco–Prussian War, Germany was forbidden territory for French investment despite its proximity. Similarly, as Austria–Hungary allied herself more closely with Germany, she ceased to be a favourite field for French investment as a result of government restrictions.

These were some of the biases imparted by politics to the French capital market. Instances can be found of political interference in the British capital market. The withdrawal of British government support for the trunk railway line across the Turkish empire from Constantinople to the Persian Gulf in 1903 led to the withdrawal of the British banks that had arranged to participate in the finance and operation of the line. The signing of the Anglo–Japanese Treaty in 1902 was immediately followed by the granting of loan arrangements to the Japanese on the London market. It may be that the close social connections of the major figures in the London capital market with leading statesmen of the day meant that overt political control was unnecessary in achieving what the government saw as the national objectives by means of international finance. But the British capital market was generally subject to far less overt political control, for whatever reason, and channelled investment very differently from the French. Between 1882 and 1914 38 per cent of new foreign investment went to Eastern Europe from France, and half went to Europe as a whole. In contrast British foreign investment went mainly to the regions of recent European settlement, mainly inhabited by people with British traditions, though Argentina was an important exception.

Approximately 10 per cent of Britain's national income in 1913 came from foreign investment. It has been argued that this investment would have been more productive and perhaps earned higher returns at home, had it not been for the peculiar nature of the London capital market.[7] This market, the largest in the world, sold primarily safe, well-known securities, many of which happened to be foreign; in order of increasing expected risk these were colonial government securities, foreign government securities, colonial rails, US rails, foreign rails and finally, foreign company issues. Domestic British firms did not in fact raise money on this market. Edelstein maintains that this was not a consequence of the rigidity of London's capital market facilities, or of the unwillingness of domestic industrial borrowers to offer debt instruments of the type desired by the new 'trustee' investor, or of a British preference for overseas assets, however.[8] Rather, provincial capital markets and wealth were quite adequate to satisfy cheaply and flexibly the usually small-scale needs of domestic industry, without recourse to London. As the scale of domestic industry and commerce rose, the London market eventually became involved in long-term funding of industry. American securities on the London market in particular filled a gap in the security market for high returns and medium risk. If there was a failure, Edelstein believes it to be in excessive risk aversion among investors which may have deterred them from lending to domestic manufacturing industry.

The differences between Britain on the one hand, and the United

States and Germany on the other, was that the British capital market with its excellent facilities for trading first-class securities, allowed British lenders to indulge their risk aversion. In the United States and Germany banks played a much more important role in allocating funds, and directed them towards the newer, advanced technology industries which were also riskier, argues Kennedy.[9] The published data on firms in Britain before 1914 were so bad that shareholders depended almost entirely on their personal knowledge of the men who ran the business. Such information was harder to come by than information about the reliability of first-class foreign securities. Hence, given that these securities were available, more resources were directed towards foreign investment than if the same information was provided about domestic firms. One caveat to this argument is the use of the London capital market by foreign lenders as well as British, which allowed American and German savers also to trade off risk against return. But to the extent that their banks provided them with a different range of assets, or supplied information, or intermediated between them and the firms, the German and American savers had less need to do so.

## The political impact of foreign investment

The difference between investment within a national economy and international investment arises from the different legal, institutional and social environment of the host country compared with the country of origin. It is these differences that created substantial problems in the forty years before the first world war. In countries with similar social frameworks to those of the Western European investors, such as the USA, Canada, Argentina and Australia, the problems were minimal. Countries less committed to economic advancement experienced more difficulties.

Within a national capitalist economy, an investor is prepared to lend for a project if he has reason to believe it will be sufficiently profitable to repay his capital as well as interest and profits on it. He will also usually be concerned to have a claim on some asset which will allow him to recover his money in the event of the failure of the project. If a firm defaults on its obligation to pay interest on loans, then it can be declared bankrupt, and a Receiver will be appointed to sell off the assets of the firm so as to earn as much as possible to repay the firm's creditors. Where a nation is concerned matters are rather different. A government may borrow money from foreign countries and then find itself unable to pay the interest or repay the capital, but a Receiver cannot be appointed. As long as the economy continues to work, revenue can be raised from taxation. The problem for the foreign creditor is how to get access to these tax receipts. The private citizen who goes bankrupt can be coerced by the state to conform to the bankruptcy laws, which in the nineteenth century often included going to a debtors' prison. The foreign creditor could only appeal to the borrowing country's government, or his own government, to have his interests considered.

In fact many defaulting countries in the nineteenth century did submit to treatment much like that of a firm. Foreign commissioners were appointed to administer certain tax receipts, such as the customs duties, and to appropriate some or all of the revenue for the repayment of interest and capital on the debt. Just as under the Bretton Woods system of the post-second world war period, these countries had to relinquish some sovereignty as a result of their economic mismanagement until the mistakes were rectified. What was more offensive to national feeling was that the commissioners were appointed by the few great powers as national representatives rather than as representatives of an international body in which the recipient country participated, at least nominally. Worst of all was the case where the previous government that incurred the debt was regarded as decadent and corrupt by a new government that had to bear the cost.

Other defaulting countries had no sanctions brought to bear upon them, other than the difficulty of raising fresh international loans as long as they remained in default. Since default was often caused by the vagaries of international economic fluctuations, payments were frequently resumed as soon as conditions allowed; a form of unilateral rescheduling of debt.

The use of military or naval superiority by the lending governments was usually eschewed, unless, as in the case of Egypt, important political objectives were also thought to be threatened. The apparent major exception to this rule in Britain's case would appear to have been governmental support of its investors in the Boer republics in South Africa, which eventually led to war. Here the pursuit of wealth in the diamond and gold fields brought British colonials and nationals into conflict with pioneer farmers of a different nationality, determined that their land should not be dominated by the new-comers. Even here the intervention can be interpreted politically as a defence of subjects oppressed in a foreign land, with the British government goaded by the threat of German intervention. France dispatched a naval division to Turkey in 1901 to seize the Customs at Mytilene to discourage default. And neither country was averse by the early twentieth century to sending a battleship to the

Caribbean to remind foreign governments of their international financial obligations. There was, however, some difference in attitude between the two major lending powers, Britain and France, in their approach to foreign investment.[10] The French capital market was more closely regulated to achieve government objectives, and because such foreign investment as was allowed served these ends it could usually count on official support where necessary. The competitive effort of Italy in Tunis to procure entry for Italian enterprise was among the influences which decided the French government to assume political control.

The contrast between the successful and unsuccessful use of foreign capital by countries outside the legal and institutional tradition of Western Europe is most clearly shown by China and Japan. Although by the outbreak of the first world war foreign investments in China were half as large again as those in Japan, with a population perhaps as much as seven times the size of Japan's, China's foreign investment per head was very much smaller.[11] China's inability to absorb foreign capital stemmed mainly from the attitude of the government and society. This is well illustrated by the fate of the first railway built in China (with foreign capital). Within a short time of opening a Chinese citizen was accidentally killed. In response to the public outcry, the Chinese government bought the line and pulled it up in 1877.[12] Compare this with the accidental death of the Trade Minister of Britain, Huskisson, in 1830 when opening the Liverpool–Manchester railway. This tragedy was not allowed to prevent the regular earning of 10 per cent dividend on capital in subsequent years. As a result of ruling Chinese attitudes, China was poorly served by transport facilities in 1914 and had little need of capital to build them in relation to the size of the country.

Chinese foreign trade remained small in relation to her population and with imports exceeding exports, at least where visible trade was concerned, there was nothing to service any foreign debt acquired. The continued depreciation of silver against gold also meant the Chinese exchange rate depreciated against the currencies of the western powers. Between the 1880s and the first decade of the twentieth century the rate of exchange of the Haikwan tael halved against sterling. Foreign debts denominated in gold standard currencies therefore became increasingly expensive to service.[13]

Before the 1894–5 war with Japan these problems did not matter because the Chinese government contracted almost no debt, spending as it did very little on administration, economic development or defence. When the indemnity had to be paid to Japan after the war, the Chinese government first sought to borrow from its own citizens.

But the wealthy Chinese merchants did not trust their government to repay them any advances they made, and only foreign lenders came forward. These lenders could bargain for security against their loan and the Chinese Maritime Customs proceeds were pledged. Set up under the control of a foreign inspectorate in accordance with the Treaty of Tientsin in 1860, the Chinese Customs had become an efficient internationally manned body, generating a revenue higher than was previously available to the Chinese government, that increased with the passage of time.[14]

Because of the Boxer Uprising, and the subsequent occupation of Peking by the western powers, China had to pay another indemnity for the death and destruction of European citizens and property. Once again the Chinese government had to borrow foreign capital. The revolution of 1911 which overthrew the Manchu dynasty, required the republican government to sign yet another loan contract in 1913 primarily to finance the costs of the revolution and for troop disbandment. Thus, to a large extent, China was forced to borrow abroad because of circumstances rather than because of predetermined policy. Nevertheless, direct foreign investment in businesses greatly exceeded government foreign borrowings as Table 5.1 shows. This investment probably financed most of the balance of trade deficit also shown in the table, the remainder being due to the remittances of Chinese living abroad.

The Japanese attitude to foreign investment was to use it to achieve

**Table 5.1**   *Foreign investment in China and Chinese trade*

| Year | Foreign investment in China (£m) | | Total |
|------|------------|-----------------------------------|-------|
|      | *Business* | *Chinese government obligations* | *Total* |
| 1902 | 116 | 66 | 181 |
| 1914 | 250 | 121 | 371 |

| *Chinese trade (£m annual average)* | | |
|------|------------|-----------|
| *Years* | *Net imports* | *Exports* |
| 1882–86 | 21 | 19 |
| 1902–06 | 54 | 32 |
| 1912–16 | 76 | 60 |

*Source*: Allen and Donnithorne, op. cit., Appendices and B.

economic development without losing control over national resources. Direct investment was an extremely small proportion of
the total. Railways were nationalised and foreign rights of ownership
in land and mining properties was forbidden by law, although long
leases could be bought. The government subsidised iron and
steelworks, shipping companies, banks and telephone companies in
order to accelerate the diffusion of western technology.[15] To the
same end they employed foreign technicians whose salaries in the
1880s amounted to about 20 per cent of government expenditure.
This positive approach to development required finance, and in 1867
the Japanese government floated their first loan, on the London
market, for the construction of the Tokyo–Yokohama railway. In
1872 they returned to launch a pension loan to commute feudal
obligations, but thereafter the onset of the depression, and the default
of Turkey and Egypt with their associated loss of sovereignty, for
Egypt culminating in occupation by a foreign power, made the
Japanese less willing to borrow. As with China, the depreciation of
the silver standard yen was also unhelpful to foreign borrowing.
Domestic inflation, a large budget deficit and national debt during
the late 1870s made Japan a poor risk for lending countries.[16] After
the deflation and financial reforms of Count Matsukata (who had
been impressed by the ideas of the French Finance Minister, Say)
it was possible to raise another foreign loan for building the
Nakasendo Railway in 1885.

The successful war with China brought Japan into direct rivalry
with Russia in northern Asia and led her to undertake a heavy
armaments programme. The annexation of Formosa also committed
Japan to paying substantial annual development subsidies. Another
loan was therefore raised abroad in 1897 and again in 1902. The
cost of the 1905–6, Russian war amounting to about 1500 million
yen, was also financed by foreign borrowing.[17] Table 5.2 shows
Japanese foreign debt held abroad, after a decline from a peak in
the mid-1870s. It grew very much faster than Japanese trade from
the 1890s, which in turn showed a phenomenal growth. Nevertheless,
the excess of exports over imports in the years when Japan was not
involved in major hostilities demonstrates that this debt was being
serviced other than by the increasing foreign investment. By 1913
more than half of the government debt of Japan was held by
foreigners. The ratio of Japanese foreign debt to exports can be seen
from Table 5.2 to suggest that the interest payments were considerably safer than the Chinese (Table 5.1).

The defaults on payments on foreign borrowings by Egypt and
Greece show the slow emergence of international financial bodies

**Table 5.2** *Foreign investment in Japan and Japanese foreign trade (m. gold yen)*

| | Govt loans issued abroad | Total portfolio investment | Direct and short-term (liquid) investments 1904 |
|---|---|---|---|
| 1894 | 2 | 2 | 40? |
| 1913 | 1525 | 1970 | 70? |

*Japanese trade (m. yen, annual averages)*

| | | |
|---|---|---|
| 1883–87 | 33 | 42 |
| 1904–08 | 442 | 377 |
| 1914–20 | 1 300 | 1 434 |

*Source*: Allen and Donnithorne op. cit.; G.C. Allen, *Short Economic History of Japan*.

in the last quarter of the nineteenth century, each one set up to deal with a particular problem. In this respect they differed from the institutions established in the interwar period and as part of the Bretton Woods system. They also differed in that they were not truly international, being managed only or mainly by representatives of the lending powers or powers who had substantial political status. The comparison of the experience of the two countries with foreign investment illustrates the process by which a country could lose its sovereignty. In the case of Egypt, default was associated with massacres of Europeans and a perceived military threat linked with a loss of access by Britain to the Suez Canal, deemed crucial to communications with the Indian empire. In the case of Greece, bankruptcy led only to the imposition of international control over certain tax administrations and the obligation to control the money supply and the government's budget until the creditors were satisfied. There was no breakdown of law and order and no important perceived political threats that warranted intervention by the western powers.

The depression of 1873 and after ushered in the defaults on their foreign obligations of a considerable number of states. Italy restricted payment, and Greece had to be persuaded to resume payment on her long outstanding debts. Only with these two countries did the British government take part in negotiations on behalf of bond-holders. With the other major European powers, the British government signed a declaration at the Congress of Berlin in which Turkey acquiesced by creating an international debt administration to manage the tax receipts assigned to the foreign debt. Egypt proved more of a problem.

Under the Khedive, Ismail Pasha, from 1863 the national debt had more than quadrupled. The money had been used to rebuild Cairo in imitation of Paris, to extend Ismail's properties until they included 20 per cent of Egypt's arable land, to build a road system, and to operate factories. Loans had been raised to pay interests on earlier loans and the tax system had become a system of arbitrary tribute and confiscation.[18] Ismail appointed a receivership in 1876 which put under control of the representatives of creditors the taxes, such as Customs duties and the salt and tobacco taxes, which had been assigned as securities for loans. The receivership was composed of four representatives appointed by the Khedive on the separate recommendation of the French, British, Austrian and Italian governments. They were to have the status of Egyptian officials who could not be recalled by their governments without the consent of the Khedive. Debts were unified at a lower interest rate. Another Khedival decree named two European controllers, one French and one English, to watch over the state finances. Interestingly, in the light of later developments, the British government refused to make its nominations, but did not object to them.[19]

In view of the parlous state of the nation's finances – the debt charges were over £8 million, while total government revenue was only about £9 million –it is not surprising that the system did not work. A Commission of Inquiry in 1878 recommended as a solution the dismissal of army officers, the taxation of the upper classes and further restrictions on the powers of the Khedive, thereby securing an alliance of all three parties against the European creditors. Although Ismail was deposed in 1879, the foreign controllers became locked in dispute over financial matters with the Egyptian Assembly and the strength of nationalist sentiment had by 1881 virtually made ruler an Egyptian of peasant origin, Colonel Ahmed Arabi. Throughout the country there was a breakdown of order. The murder of Europeans in Alexandria, together with the fortification of the town, precipitated occupation by the British who feared their access to the Suez Canal would be stopped.

Under the Constitution of 1883, the British Consul General was the real governing power. The Egyptian representative bodies could advise and criticise, but not directly oppose. Their consent was necessary to new taxes but not to the spending of the revenue from existing taxes. Between 1882 and 1913 the British administration reduced taxes per head but almost doubled net revenue. This was done by regularising tax collection, revising the system of public accounts and enforcing Treasury control of expenditure. Out of the limited budget surplus, roads, railways, irrigation and drainage canals were built and the external debt slightly reduced. Until 1914 the improvements in financial administration were matched by a rising standard of living amongst the peasantry.[20] In 1923 Egypt regained her formal political independence.

Greece had unilaterally reduced interest payments on her external debt in 1893, by which time the national debt was absorbing one-third of the revenue, without causing any international reaction. But in 1898 her defeat by Turkey necessitated more foreign financial aid and the creditor powers therefore established an International Financial Commission to control the revenues pledged to the defaulted loans.[21] The six members of the Commission were appointed directly by their governments. Political considerations accounted for the representation given to the Russian, Austrian and Italian governments, in addition to the English, German and French representatives, because their citizens held very small amounts of the Greek debt. The pledged revenues were similar to the Egyptian, and these revenues was directly administered by an organisation with a Greek staff and a director elected by the bondholders subject to the Commission's veto.

The debt settlement also included provisions calculated to improve the nation's finances. Restrictions were placed upon government borrowing and the money supply was to be controlled. These measures raised the foreign exchange value of the drachma. The yield of the taxes did not rise, except for the Piraeus Customs revenue, in contrast to the Egyptian case, either because the administration was less chaotic and thus had less scope for improvement, or because no direct foreign control was placed over the tax systems. In any event, the very existence of the Commission enhanced the foreign borrowing power of the Greek government. Whether this was desirable is a moot point for it meant the government's capacity to renew the war with Turkey was increased. Between 1905 and 1911 Greece spent 193.7 million drachmas, and the cost of the Balkan wars was about 411 million (25 drachmas = £1 in 1913).

If it is possible to leave aside nationalist sentiment and instead use the welfare of the people as an evaluative criterion, then the loss of sovereignty by Egypt as a consequence of foreign lending was, until the first world war, desirable. For Greece, which maintained control over most of its policy, foreign investment increased the ability to pursue policies which could well not have been desirable for the great majority of Greeks. When foreign investment is put to productive uses it almost certainly increases world output. What makes the rate of return on investment higher in the host country than in the country of the donor is the greater contribution of the marginal unit of capital to real output. Thus the increase in output in the recipient country brought about by foreign investment must be greater than the reduction in output in the investing country. This conclusion does not hold when the foreign investment is directed to unproductive purposes, such as war for Greece, or extravagant building programmes in Egypt.

## The gains from foreign investment

One of the central controversies about the effects of foreign investment when it is devoted to productive purposes is the distribution of the increased output that results between the lending and the borrowing country. Foreign-owned enterprises have often been accused of exploiting labour in the host country or taking away natural resources at less than market value. Such exploitation can occur only when there is monopoly power such as conferred by the exclusive rights of the British chartered trading companies, the British South Africa Company and the Royal Niger Company (these powers were conferred to compensate the companies for bearing administrative costs normally borne by governments). Most foreign investment during these years was the result of competitive bidding for contracts, examples of which are given below, and hence exploitation was unlikely to occur. The Balkans, discussed above, were an exception. On theoretical grounds there are reasons to think that the distribution of the benefits depended upon the type of investment. Investments complementary to the labour and capital employed in the donor country, such as those calculated to increase the availability of raw materials, or reduce the price of food, especially by improving foreign transport facilities, must offer gains to the investing country, as well as to the private investor who receives a higher return on his capital than if it was confined to the domestic economy. Because so much of British and French investment was of this nature during these years, especially for the provision of foreign railways, these economies must have gained. On the other hand, when foreign investment reduces labour costs, the savings occur in the employment of factors that are competitive with domestic resources. Such foreign investment enhances the productivity of domestic capital, but lowers the productivity of domestic labour relative to what it would have been if similar investment had been undertaken in the domestic economy.[22] American investment abroad tended to be in manufacturing industry and thus, in contrast to British and French investment, is less likely to have benefitted the American investing economy.

A widely-alleged gain from foreign investment to the donor country, and source of exploitation to the host country, is increased demand for national exports as a result of preferential treatment. In fact it will be argued that the relationship between trade and foreign direct investment is exactly the other way round. In the years before the first world war, the allegation of preferential treatment was most frequently heard about investments in China and Latin America. An investigation of railway contracts in these countries showed that competitive bids were normal both for the loans and the construction.[23] The lender's nationality was uniformly denied a preference over better offers from other sources in seventeen important Chinese government railway loan contracts with Americans and Europeans between 1898 and 1914. And these were the majority in which the informal tying of investment with trade by the great industrial powers could occur, amounting to about 2800 miles out of a total of 6000 miles of railway. Of the remainder, 1000 miles were built with Chinese capital, 1900 miles by the Russians and the Japanese, and 600 miles were built by French and German companies, their purchases being closed to international competition by the terms of their charter. Table 5.3 shows that the smallest investor in Chinese railway loans, the United States, obtained the second largest exports of rails and rolling stock to China, and the largest investor, Great Britain, obtained the second smallest value of export orders.

**Table 5.3**   *Railway loans and exports to China, 1898–1912*

| *From* | *(1)* *Railway loans to Chinese govt* *($m)* | *(2)* *Exports of rails and rolling stock to China (value $m)* | *(3)* *(2) as % of capital loaned for rail* |
|---|---|---|---|
| US | 3.0 | 11.48 | 382.8 |
| Germany | 29.76 | 9.47 | 31.8 |
| Britain | 52.39 | 6.90 | 13.2 |
| France | 27.1 | 0.65 | 2.4 |
| Belgium | 11.6 | 12.85 | 110.8 |
| Total | 123.85 | 41.35 | |

*Source*: A.P. Winston, 'Does trade follow the dollar?' *American Economic Review*, (1927).

In Latin America the experience was similar. Three-quarters of Argentine railways were owned by the British, yet British companies secured less than half the imports of railway equipment. The French owned almost half of the Brazilian railway system, yet their share of railway imports into Brazil remained smaller than into Argentina except where rails were concerned, with just over one-quarter of Brazilian imports. The United States, with only a small investment stake in Brazil, secured more than half the imports of railway engines.

Rather than the relatively small trade of France and the United States with Argentina being a consequence of their small investment stake, their investments were a consequence of their lack of interest in trade with that country. Argentina was a temperate zone region of recent European settlement and therefore was a potential supplier of beef and wheat. Britain was far more dependent on basic foodstuff imports than France and the United States, and therefore was the major trading partner of the Argentine. As nations of coffee-drinkers the French and Americans were much more interested in the Brazilian trade which the tea-drinking British neglected. The citizens of each country stood to gain from lower import prices from these countries, and investments in improvements in, or construction of railways, ports and public utilities in Brazil and Argentina were the means of doing this. Trade provided the information about investment opportunities.

## Direct and portfolio investment

Just as investment was encouraged in the country of origin of imports so it was in the country of destination of exports, though here the Americans led. Partly this was because the United States was the country in which the large-scale, multi-unit industrial firm first emerged. By the 1880s, the telegraph, cable, railways and steamships were sufficiently widely diffused to allow the control of these enterprises. Foreign direct investment was one manifestation of the enhanced technology of communication and control. The large firm often moved overseas by first setting up branch offices and warehouses abroad. Then with the expansion of demand and the appearance of local tariffs, the enterprise built plants abroad which it soon began to supply from nearby sources.[24] By 1914 at least forty-one American companies, concentrated in machinery and food industries, had built two or more operating facilities abroad. The largest number of these were in Canada, but by 1914 twenty-three had factories in Britain, and twenty-one in Germany, with a small number scattered in other countries. Transport costs and problems of the scheduling of shipping could be as important as tariffs in the foreign investment decision as shown by the importance of Britain, still a free-trade country.

The large-scale firm in Britain flourished in the consumer sectors of chemicals and food, and in the processing and distribution of perishable goods – meat, dairy products and beer. Not surprisingly then, when these firms first moved branches overseas, it was to areas with similar tastes and income where competition was less – Australia, Canada, New Zealand and South Africa. In the twentieth century more ventured into the United States and continental Europe. Occasionally before the first world war, overseas sales grew to a size that warranted building factories abroad, usually prompted by tariffs rather than by transport costs.

The Japanese reliance on portfolio investment to the virtual exclusion of direct investment might seem to warrant claims that nineteenth-century foreign investment was preferable to twentieth-century, largely direct investment, on the grounds that national control of resources is maintained by portfolio investment and nineteenth-century investment was largely indirect. As the cases of Greece and Egypt show it was just as easy to lose control of the economy with portfolio investment if the borrowing country defaulted. But, more importantly, recent research suggests that there has been little if any increase in the proportion of direct investment since 1914. Svedberg found that the share of direct investment in all private investment in the Third World was between 44 and 60 per cent in 1914.[25] The share had previously been underestimated first, because two criteria had been used to separate the two types of investment, namely the *medium* through which shares were distributed and *control* by the investor in the undertaking in which the capital was embodied. The present-day definition uses only the second criterion. Thus investments floated on stock exchanges and controlled by foreign investors have been counted as portfolio under the earlier definition. Secondly, coverage of government and municipal bonds was easy to achieve and therefore to compute, but this was not true of direct investment. Finally, the methods of valuation of private investment have changed. The earlier method used only the nominal value of new issues, while the later method used the book value of total assets, which tends to be much greater.

## The international mobility of labour

The task of identifying and measuring the permanent movement of people from one country to another in the four decades before the first world war is one that is extremely difficult to perform with any degree of accuracy. Nevertheless, whatever the inadequacies of the available statistics, these years saw an unprecedented volume of long-distance migration from Europe to the New World, and from Asia to countries around the Pacific that would allow immigration. Within Europe the flows of people across land borders, seasonal and permanent, were even more difficult to measure than migrations across oceans, but clearly the movements were also substantial.

The main source of data on international migration for this period is the compilation by Ferenczi and Wilcox.[26] An indication of the magnitude of error in these volumes is that the gross outflow overseas for all countries is recorded as 46 million, while total immigration is apparently $51\frac{1}{2}$ million. Because the definition of an immigrant varied between countries many of those who left their native country returned and so the gross outflows are in any case an overestimate of permanent emigration. In fact ocean transport had become sufficiently cheap by the end of the nineteenth century for many agricultural workers from Spain and Italy to go to Argentina every year, work on the wheat harvest there, and then return in time for the harvest in their native lands.[27]

Figure 5.2 gives Green and Urquhart's summary of best estimates for decadal emigration and immigration for selected countries. Unfortunately, only gross migration figures are available for Germany, Spain, Russia and Brazil. Total emigration from Europe grew in each decade until the outbreak of the war, although the outflow in the 1890s was little higher than in the previous decade. Britain ceased to be the largest sender after the 1880s, being overtaken by Italy and Spain in the 1890s, and also by Austria–Hungary in the first decade of the twentieth century. The United States was the largest recipient of migrants throughout the period, so much so that despite the almost trebling of Brazilian immigration with the coffee boom of the 1890s, total emigration fell because of the fall in US immigration. The effect of the US 'magnet' on Canada is shown by the slight decline in Canadian emigration in the 1890s, which normally went to the United States. Thereafter, the Canadian wheat boom got under way and Canadian immigration became strongly positive. South Africa also experienced a massive inflow of people as a result of the expansion of mining after the Boer War. The depression of the 1890s followed by drought kept Australian immigration at a low level for twenty years, apparently less than the level experienced by New Zealand (although the New Zealand data are suspect because virtually all arrivals were included in the immigrant category).

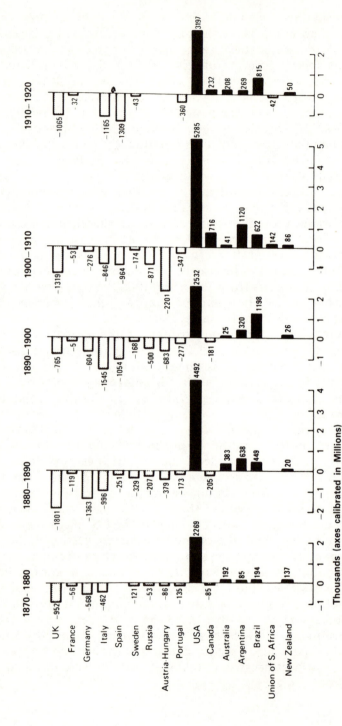

**Figure 5.2** International migration, selected countries, 1870–1920 (in thousands)

Rates of population growth were considerably lower in sending than in receiving countries. Partly this was because of the higher rates of natural increase in receiving than in sending countries, a part which diminished in importance over time as rates of natural increase converged. Britain had a higher population growth than most other sending countries, despite substantial migration, and despite population decline in Ireland. Russia had one of the lowest proportion of migrants in the population despite the highest rate of population increase of all sending countries, a result which can be attributed to the system of collective responsibility for the village land established after the emancipation of the serfs in 1861 and to ignorance of opportunities abroad amongst Russian peasants. The similarly low proportion of migrants from France can also be explained by the land tenure system, but here the family farm arrangement probably constrained fertility to give France the lowest population growth rate in nineteenth-century continental Europe.

France, in fact, was an important host country for European migrants. In 1881 there were a million foreigners living in France, and in the first decade of the twentieth century 330 000 immigrants came into France (although this was less than emigration), more than half of them from Belgium and Italy.[28] Similarly, the summer census of 1907 showed 1.3 million of the German residents were born abroad. Some were alien seasonal migrant agricultural labourers. In 1910 639 000 of these entered Germany and received identification cards. They came mainly from the East, from Russia and Poland.[29] Seasonal agricultural labourers, perhaps 30 000 a year, at the end of the century, also emigrated from Ireland to Great Britain at harvest time.[30]

Lewis probably overstates his case when he asserts that the number of Chinese and Indians moving into the tropical countries (gross migration) exceeded the numbers of Europeans migrating to temperate zone countries after 1870. The evidence for this view is that between 1871 and 1915 15.8 million people left India, 11.7 million returned, leaving 4.1 million as net migrants.[31] The much greater proportion returning is to be explained by the indenture system which bound a migrant to work for a plantation employer for usually five years in return for the cost of his passage. By the end of the century 30-day verbal contracts for work in Ceylon and Malaya were increasingly common.[32] Figures for the gross migration of Chinese are not available, but the number of Chinese living abroad increased by perhaps 5 million between 1880 and 1922. As with Indian migration contract labour was important and therefore the gross flow may be expected to have been some multiple of this approximate net flow. Even so, as a proportion of the total Indian and Chinese populations, migration was very small compared with the European experiences because the populations were so large; probably over 400 million for China and over 250 million for India. The benefits to the economies were also accordingly proportionately small.

The countries of destination of Asian migrants, like those of European emigration, had lower population densities than the donor country. Ceylon therefore escaped the famine and disease that regularly checked the nineteenth-century Indian population, and the new tea plantation, among other activities, attracted a net immigration of 1.275 million between 1871 and 1911. Burma increased her population by more than half over the same period, compared to a 20 per cent increase for all British India, suggesting a similar flow of immigrants. Indians also went in considerable numbers to East and South Africa, to Mauritius, Fiji and the Caribbean. Chinese net migration was concentrated on southern Asia, especially the Dutch East Indies and, to a lesser extent, Malaya.

Although industrialisation was beginning in Japan, as in Europe, it came too late to prevent an outflow of people, given late nineteenth-century transport technology. Beginning in the mid-1880s, emigration reached about 1 million in total by 1913, mostly going to temperate zone countries, to Hawaii and to Brazil.

## The causes of international migration

Why did all these people move so far away from the places where they were born? A conceptual apparatus similar to that used in the analysis of capital moved can be deployed to answer this question. Immigration can be represented as the consequence of a stronger national demand for labour than supply, given the prevailing wage rates, conditions of work and leisure, availability of information, the prevailing transport costs and legislations. Conversely, emigration stems from a stronger national supply of labour than demand, given these conditions. The relative strengths of national supplies of, and demands for, labour determined the late nineteenth- and early twentieth-century patterns of migration. People moved to 'equalise the net advantages' of the jobs and life-styles, given various conditions. Changes in these conditions, or those determining national labour supplies and demands, 'pushed' or 'pulled', increased (or decreased) numbers of migrants between countries.

The general pattern of migration, from higher to lower population density economies, was because of the high productivity of labour in the areas of recent settlement. This high productivity was based on new technology which lowered transport costs and which could make good use of relatively abundant land. High productivity meant high earnings, but migrants tended to drive down these earnings to the point where the present value of the differential in earnings between the receiving and sending economies was sufficient to compensate for the relative advantage in the sending and receiving countries. Other things being equal, the differential had to cover the costs of transport and the earnings forgone while travelling. Again, if Europeans had regarded the United States in the nineteenth century as a land of religious and political freedom compared with Europe – and they highly valued those freedoms – then a lower American wage than the European earnings would have been established by immigration, other things being equal.

The costs of passenger transport across the Atlantic at least did not show a pronounced increase or decrease in these years, varying between £3.10s and £5 steerage class from Liverpool to the United States. What did change was speed of passage and the conditions. In 1867 the average crossing-time by sail was forty-four days and by steam about fourteen days. By 1875 the White Star Line had reduced this to 9 days $16\frac{1}{2}$ hours and to 7 days $15\frac{1}{2}$ hours by 1890. These changes reduced the time when the migrant would not be earning and so reduced the costs to him of moving.[33]

One of the biggest alterations during the period was in the information available to potential migrants. The profitability of steamship lines and of railway companies came to depend upon a continuous flow of migrants and so they pursued a positive advertising policy to ensure the numbers were maintained. Probably more important though was the knowledge of conditions provided by friends and relatives who had already migrated or who had returned from the prospective host country. As this stock built up overseas the information about opportunities for improvement became more widely spread across Europe and this, more than anything else according to Gould, explains the pattern of inter-continental migration.[34]

The highest emigration as a proportion of the population was typically found in the mountainous areas and smaller islands of Europe where the pressure of population upon resources was greatest. Information about conditions abroad was sent back to these areas from where it slowly diffused outwards to other areas where the need to migrate was less compelling. The migration rates of these areas began to rise as those that with full information would migrate, did so. By 1914 Ireland, Sweden, Switzerland

and West Germany had virtually exhausted their stock of potential emigrants. This diffusion theory has the advantage of explaining the boom in migration from Southern and Eastern Europe in the years immediately before the first world war. Restrictions on movement, such as were imposed by serfdom, had been removed some years before the boom, and income differentials were little if at all wider in the boom years than before. Hence, the notion that the boom was stimulated by the accumulation of knowledge from previous migrants seems a satisfactory explanation for the change in the origin of migrants. It also has considerable value in explaining the destination of migrant groups. Even in the 1890s Wisconsin and Iowa accounted for 52 per cent of Norwegian-born American residents, because of the pull of kinsfolk, soil and climate, together with the availability of free land on the frontier in the 1850s. The United States remained the main destination for migrants from Norway, Sweden and the Balkans. For British migrants, the attraction of empire countries, which often subsidised fares, reduced the proportion going to the United States as the period wore on, while the opposite was true of the Italians. The Italians, formerly migrating to Latin America, increasingly went to the United States. Citizens of Spain and Portugal consistently avoided the United States and went to Latin America.

The diffusion model does not necessarily explain changes in the total volume of migration, which can still be understood in terms of the 'push' and 'pull' doctrine; that is the strength of changes in the excess demand for labour in the receiving country and changes in the excess supply of labour in sending countries.[35] When it is available the most obvious indicator of 'push' and 'pull' is unemployment, and unemployment in the receiving country has proved a consistently good predictor, in a statistical sense, of immigration.[36] Unemployment in the sending country is a less satisfactory variable because while high unemployment may increase the desire to migrate, it will also reduce the ability to move of those with the greatest need. Changes in the population structure might also be expected to 'push' people out of sending countries; a large number of people coming up to, or arriving at, working age might not be potentially absorbable into domestic employment without a radical realignment of wages. This shift in labour supply in the sending country would increase that in the receiving country as migration occurred, tending to reduce wages relative to what they would otherwise have been, and in the sending country wages would also be reduced, but by less than if there had been no migration.

Both Williamson and Gould conclude that immigration into the

US in the last quarter of the nineteenth century was reduced because the North–West European 'push' declined by more than the increase in American 'pull'.[37] Industrialisation in North and West Europe had raised relative wage incomes and increased jobs well before the first world war. Switzerland had become an area of net immigration from 1888, the western industrialised German states from the 1890s and the Po valley in Italy also before 1914 were receiving migrants from outside the region. If Sweden had industrialised twenty years earlier there would have been no emigration from that country. The retardation of the British economy, by contrast, explains the rise in migration from the Britain in the decade before the war.

Williamson reached his conclusion by econometrically estimating US migration equations for Sweden, Denmark, Britain and Germany, assuming the outputs of the sending and the receiving countries determined the respective demands for labour to produce that output. Migration was determined by the national demands for labour relative to national supplies. Emigration from the four countries to destinations other than the United States, and immigration to the United States from countries other than the four, were treated as being determined outside the model. Although one-third of the increase in the American labour force between 1870 and 1910 came from immigration, since none of the four countries alone supplied the major proportion of this increase, it was possible to neglect the causal influence in the opposite direction to that specified in Williamson's equations, that of immigration on US output. Similarly, the relatively small proportion of sending country output accounted for by emigration (calculations for Germany in the 1880s are presented below) implies that the estimated coefficient on the sending country output in the migration equation was unlikely to be subject to significant simultaneous equation bias.[38]

Rapid industrialisation in North-Western Europe, apart from Britain, required the new immigration to the United States in the first decade of the twentieth century increasingly to come from new sources. The diffusion of information in Southern and Eastern Europe about employment prospects abroad provided these sources. Piore's alternative explanation for the new immigration emphasises instead changes in demand in the receiving country.[39] Just before the Civil War the extension of the division of labour began to reduce skill requirements as production expanded in the American shoe and textile industries. This expansion created a demand for unskilled and more or less transient immigrants. Towards the end of the nineteenth century the consolidation of American industry by trusts segmented the labour market into a stable section and an unstable part where the immigrant jobs were to be found. The new immigration consisted of unskilled and often illiterate workers, mainly from Southern and Eastern Europe, who were deliberately recruited on a temporary basis to fill these jobs at the bottom of the labour market. Of the $1\frac{1}{2}$ million employed by United States railways in 1910, immigrants amounted to only one-fourteenth of the ticket and station agents, and one-tenth of the engineers, but one-quarter of the track foremen and one-half of the labourers.[40] One-quarter of the total United States labour force consisted of immigrants.

Piore assumes implicitly that these unskilled and unstable jobs were essential to the economy. Though it is true that industrialisation and higher incomes in one country of emigration would have meant that other sources of migrant supply would have been found to fill these jobs, it is not necessarily true that the US economy would have collapsed if the restrictions on immigration in 1921 had been passed earlier. There would have been other adjustments as Piore recognises in his analysis of black migration from the southern states. He sees this black migration as the most likely alternative response in the nineteenth century as it turned out to be in the twentieth century. But what if, as Lewis argues, racial discrimination had prevented migration to the North? Then the development of labour displacing technology by industry, for which the United States had been noted in the middle of the nineteenth century, would have proceeded faster. And the prices of services which were difficult to mechanise would have been higher.

More fundamentally, this demand side explanation founders when it is recognised that there were other countries to which migrants went apart from the United States, with different levels of industrial and agricultural development. In terms of illiteracy, on Piore's account there is reason to expect that Spaniards would be attracted to the United States as were Italians, but this did not occur. The increasing transitory component of migration can equally well be explained by the reduction in transport time and costs as by changing industrial structure, especially when the seasonal agricultural migrants to Argentina, and the Asian plantation workers are recalled. Thus it is plausible to regard the unskilled jobs in American industry as more of a response to the elastic supply of migrants than as a cause of migration.

## The gains and losses from migration

International migration redistributed the European population so that they could take advantage of the land which had been very sparsely occupied by nomads and hunters. The Asiatic population was not redistributed to anything like the same extent in proportionate terms. Lewis believes that Asian migrants were excluded from the empty lands because of the recognition by the white workers that their living standards would otherwise be forced down to Asiatic levels.[41] Chinese miners had been excluded from the gold fields of Victoria, Australia, by a heavy poll tax in 1857, but a much stronger effort to exclude the Chinese from all of Australia began in 1878 when the Australasia Steam Navigation Company tried to employ coolies. The unions with their headquarters in Sydney began a bitter thirteen-week strike in protest. Eventually, in 1901, the White Australia Policy was officially implemented, based on a language test for prospective immigrants. The proportion of Australians of Asian birth declined from 1.25 to 0.82 per cent ten years later.[42]

California had the largest concentration of Chinese immigrants in a temperate zone region of recent European settlement at the beginning of the last quarter of the nineteenth century; perhaps 148 000 in 1876. Accordingly, legal exclusion occurred earliest, in the form of the Chinese Exclusion Act of 1882. In Canada, as earlier in the United States, many Chinese first came to build railways; the Canadian Pacific Railway in 1883 brought in 5–6000 coolies as construction labour. As California had, British Columbia showed strong anti-Chinese sentiments. In an Act of 1883 imposing an annual tax on Chinese immigrants, the legislature described these immigrants as

not disposed to be governed by our laws, ... dissimilar in habit and occupation from our people, evade [rs] [of] the payment of taxes justly due to the Government, ... governed by pestilential habits.

Although Chinese immigrants were not totally excluded by law from Canada, in 1903 a poll tax of $500 was levied on each immigrant.

Why was what was true of Asian migration not also true of European migration? In some instances there was similar pressure. The Member of Parliament for Stepney, East London, a destination for Russian Jewish immigrants, conducted extensive investigations in 1903 in an attempt to exclude these people, arguing that their migration was more economic than political ('From an English point of view everyone in Russia is more or less persecuted').[43] Opposition to Jewish, Chinese and East European migrants could draw upon racial prejudices supported by the scientific endeavours of 'craniologists' who believed they had closely associated racial skull types with brain sizes and intelligence.[44] Restriction of immigration to a *limited* (and familiar) group (West Europeans) could enhance land values. The landowners who stood to gain had political influence which they used to get tax-financed subsidies for this group of immigrants at various times in Brazil, Australia and New Zealand. In addition *some* immigration was beneficial for many economies because facilities such as ports, railway systems and other types of infrastucture could supply services for a larger population at a lower unit cost per head, at least until a certain level was reached.

A short-run benefit to the receiving countries and corresponding loss to the sending countries arose from the concentration of migrants in the young adult age groups. The sending countries bore the costs of supporting and training from infancy, but reaped little benefit when they reached working age, except through payments sent back to relatives (which however could be very large). An estimate of the cost to Germany of emigration took into account the above costs, and the effects of the age structure of migrants. The study assumed that each worker generated a surplus of production over consumption that would have repaid the present value of early education and maintenance costs by the age of 60 to 65. Emigration then cost Germany over 4 billion marks in the 1880s, nearly 1.7 billion marks in the 1890s and over 1 billion in the following decade. In addition, the money that immigrants took with them was thought would probably have raised the loss to the German economy by another 10 per cent. In 1880 and 1913 German net social product has been calculated at about 17 and 52 billion marks, respectively. As a proportion of social product over the decade of the 1880s, the costs of emigration from Germany was a little over 2 per cent.[45]

Conversely, the receiving countries obtained the benefits of this injection of human capital without bearing the costs. Population pressure was temporarily relieved in the sending countries and wages and the productivity of labour were at least temporarily raised. Whether there was any permanent effect depends upon whether birth rates rose to compensate for the emigration, on Malthusian lines. The evidence of falling birth rates in the last quarter of the nineteenth century suggests there probably was a lasting impression on European populations.

Even if these various effects could be accurately measured, an estimation of the gains and losses from the great migrations depends upon what standpoint is adopted; that of a person in a sending country, in a receiving country, or of the international economy as a whole.

## Summary and conclusion

The forty years before 1914 probably saw the greatest migration of people and capital that the world has ever experienced. Many millions crossed the Atlantic to settle temporarily or permanently in North and South America. Substantial numbers temporarily left China and India to work on plantations around the world. Smaller numbers of Europeans also went to Australasia and South Africa. Malthusian pressure was thereby relieved in Europe, but not in Asia. Much of the pattern of the origin and destination of migrant nationalities is to be explained by the information flows sent back by nationals already abroad. The timing of migration depended upon economic conditions in the sending and the receiving countries, but the decline in migration to the United States towards the end of the nineteenth century is attributable mainly to the reduced pressure to emigrate with the industrialisation of Western Europe. The increase in the first decade of the twentieth century was mainly from Eastern and Southern Europe. It has been suggested that Australia would have had a higher income per head if it had received fewer immigrants.[46] The natural resources would have been shared among smaller numbers. There are, however, certain minimum size populations necessary to make some services viable, and it is a question of whether the gains from increasing these types of services offset the losses from sharing the natural resources with more people.

The demand for internationally mobile capital was due largely to the high rates of population growth and urbanisation in land-abundant countries. The supply came mainly from Britain and France. Britain had an unusually low demand for investment in the home economy, rather than a high savings ratio. By contrast, France did have a high savings ratio and a relatively strong demand for domestic investment. French investment seems to have been more subject to political influences than British. Russia became the major destination for French capital exports because of the alliance of the two countries against Germany. The London capital market dealt in foreign investment to the exclusion of all but the largest domestic manufacturing concerns, probably less because of a structural bias than because for most of the period domestic capital requirements were adequately supplied through the provincial stock exhanges.

In the receiving countries, major problems occurred among those states that did not share western attitudes and institutions. Here the borrowing abroad of money for unproductive purposes could easily result in the loss of national control of taxes, the financial adminstration or, in extreme cases, of sovereignty. The gains from such foreign investment to the borrower in such instances were negligible, except in so far as the consequent foreign administration increased governmental efficiency once and for all. Whether the foreign investment was direct or portfolio made no difference to the chances of these problems occurring, but the proportion of investment that was direct was much closer to that of the post-1945 period than has previously been thought. The means of dealing with national default on foreign financial obligations also bore a close similarity to post-1945 methods, although the groups of national representatives that took steps to rationalise defaulters' financial policies were constituted for the occasion rather than originating from permanent institutions, such as the IMF and the World Bank,

## Notes

1. W.A. Lewis, *Growth and Fluctuations 1870–1914*, London: Allen & Unwin (1978), pp. 148–50.
2. A. Green and M. Urquhart, 'Factor and commodity flows in the international economy', *Journal of Economic History*, **36** (1976), pp. 217–52.
3. W.W. Rostow, *The Stages of Economic Growth*, Cambridge: Cambridge University Press (1972).
4. A. Ando and F. Modigliani, 'The "life cyle" hypothesis of saving', *American Economic Review*, **53** (1963), pp. 55–84.
5. R. Cameron, *France and the Economic Development of Europe*, Princeton NJ: Princeton University Press (1961), p. 485.
6. H. Feis, *Europe, the World's Banker 1870–1914*, New Haven: Yale University Press (1930), p. 134.
7. For example, *Britain's Industrial Future*, London (1928) (the report of the Liberal Industrial Inquiry).
8. M. Edelstein, 'Rigidity and bias in the British capital market 1870–1913', in D.N. McCloskey (ed.), *Essays on a Mature Economy*, London: Methuen (1972); and 'The determinants of UK investment abroad', *Journal of Economic History*, **34** (1974), pp. 980–1007.
9. W. Kennedy, 'Institutional response to economic growth: capital markets in Britain to 1914' in L. Hannah (ed.), *Management Strategy and Business Development* (1976), London: Macmillan, pp. 151–83.
10. Feis, op. cit. chs 4 and 5.
11. G.C. Allen and A. Donnithorne, *Western Enterprise in Far Eastern*

*Economic Development*, London: Allen & Unwin (1954), Appendices B and C.

12. A.J.H. Latham, *The International Economy and the Undeveloped World*, London: Croom Helm (1978), p. 20, and generally this section; A. Feuerwerker, 'Economic trends in the late Chi'ing empire 1870–1911', in *The Cambridge History of China*, Cambridge: Cambridge University Press (1980).

13. C.F. Remer, 'International trade Between gold and silver countries: China 1885–1913' *Quarterly Journal of Economics*, **40** (1926) pp. 597–643.

14. Allen and Donnithorne, op. cit. p. 21.

15. ibid. ch. 11.

16. H. Rosovsky, 'Japan's transition to modern economic growth', in H. Rosovsky (ed.), *Industrialisation in Two Systems*, New York: Wiley (1968).

17. Feis, op. cit., ch. 18.

18. ibid. ch. 15.

19. ibid.

20. Despite asserting that Egypt's lack of political autonomy constrained her economic development, C. Issawi concedes that living standards did rise, as did population until 1914. 'Egypt since 1800: A Study in Lopsided Development', *Journal of Economic History*, **21** (1961), pp. 1–26.

21. D. Dakin, *The Unification of Greece 1770–1923*, New York: St Martins (1971), pp. 146–8, 154–5, 201; Cameron, op. cit., pp. 497–8; Feis, op. cit., pp. 284–92.

22. M. Kreinen, *International Economics*, 2nd ed., New York: Harcourt Brace (1975), pp. 394–400.

23. A.P. Winston, 'Does trade follow the dollar?' *American Economic Review*, (1927), pp. 458–77.

24. A.D. Chandler, *The Visible Hand: The Managerial Revolution in American Business*, Cambridge, Mass: Harvard University Press, (1977); and 'The growth of the transnational firm in the United States and the United Kingdom', *Economic History Review*, **33** (1980), pp. 396–410.

25. P. Svedberg, 'The portfolio-direct composition of private foreign investment in 1914 revisited', *Economic Journal*, **88** (1978), pp. 763–77.

26. I. Ferenczi and W. Wilcox, *International Migration*, vols I and II, NBER (1929) and (1931).

27. C. Diaz Alejandro, *Essays on the Economic History of the Argentine Republic*, New Haven: Yale University Press (1970), p. 22.

28. H. Bunde, 'Migratory movements between France and foreign lands', in W.F. Wilcox (ed.), *International Migrations: Interpretations*, New York: NBER (1931).

29. F. Burgdorfer, 'Mirgration across the frontiers of Germany', in Wilcox, op. cit.

30. D.A.E. Harkness, 'Irish emigration', in Wilcox, op. cit.
31. Lewis, op. cit., pp. 185–7.
32. Latham, op. cit., ch. 4.
33. J.D. Gould 'European intercontinental emigration', *Journal of European Economic History*, **8** (1979), pp. 593–679.
34. ibid.
35. H. Jerome, *Migration and Business Cycles*, New York: NBER (1926).
36. A.C. Kelley, 'International migration and economic growth: Australia 1865–1935', *Journal of Economic History*, **25** (1965), pp. 333–54. L.E. Gallaway and R.K. Vedder, 'Emigration from the UK to the USA 1860–1913', *Journal of Economic History*, **31** (1971), pp. 885–97. M. Wilkinson, 'European migration to the United States', *Review of Economics and Statistics*, **52** (1971), pp. 272–9. M.J.A. Tomaske, 'The determinants of inter-country differences in European migration 1881–1900', *Journal of Economic History*, **31** (1971), pp. 840–53. H.W. Richardson, 'British emigration and overseas investment 1870–1914', *Economic History Review*, **25** (1972), pp. 99–113. M.M. Quigley, 'A model of Swedish emigration', *Quarterly Journal of Economics*, **86** (1972) pp. 111–26.
37. J.G. Williamson, *Late Nineteenth Century American Development*, Cambridge: Cambridge University Press (1974), ch. 11.
38. The estimation technique involves finding the parameters of the migration equation which minimises the variation in migration that is not associated with, or explained by, the variables (such as outputs) in the receiving and sending countries. An assumption underlying the method is that the explanatory, or independent, variables (output, etc.) can be thought of as fixed and determining the dependent variable (migration) with a random error. If the dependent variable also influences the independent variable with a random error in another relationship (immigration increases national ouput), then the techique will produce biased estimates of the parameters in the migration equation. Hence inferences drawn about the strengths of 'push' and 'pull' forces on the basis of these parameter estimates may be incorrect.
39. M.J. Piore, *Birds of Passage: Migrant Labour and Industrial Societies*, Cambridge: Cambridge University Press (1979), ch. 6.
40. P. Taylor, *The Distant Magnet: European Migration to the United States*, London: Eyre & Spottiswoode (1971), pp. 197–8.
41. Lewis, op. cit., p. 192.
42. P.C. Campbell *Chinese Coolie Emigration to Countries Within the British Empire*, London: P.S. King (1923), pp. 33, 39–40 fn 2, 56, 63, 76.
43. C. Erickson, *Emigration from Europe 1815–1914: Selected Documents*, London: a. & C. Black (1976), Document 13. For a fictional but realistic description of the persecution of the Jews in Russia before 1914, see B. Malamud, *The Fixer*, London: Penguin (1967).
44. S.J. Gould, *The Mismeasure of Man*, New York and London: Nelson (1981), p. 115.

45. Burgdorfer, loc. cit. and calculated from B.R. Mitchell *Abstract of European Historical Statistics*, Cambridge: Cambridge University Press (1975).
46. For example, J.D. Gould, *Economic Growth in History*, London: Methuen (1972), p. 188.

# 6 The Heyday of the International Gold Standard 1875–1914

By adopting or returning to the gold standard in the four decades before the first world war, the majority of the world economies established fixed, or 'par', exchange rates with each other. This replacement of the changing exchange rates associated with the bimetallist, silver and paper standards of the third quarter of the nineteenth century helped international investment and trade by increasing the predictability of the returns and costs of transactions between countries. The voluntary move to an impersonal international monetary system convinced many among later generations that this was a golden age in more ways than one. But the gold standard was not adopted in a pure form. Only Britain, the Netherlands and the United States (New York) had free markets in gold.[1] Many governments, including those of Japan, Austria–Hungary, the Netherlands, Scandinavia, Canada, South Africa, Australia and New Zealand, operated a gold exchange standard, keeping mainly foreign currencies that were linked to gold as foreign exchange reserves, rather than gold, to maintain their fixed exchange rates. Despite this economy, the spread of the gold standard and the reduced expansion of gold supply until the 1890s encouraged many to attribute the simultaneous downward drift of world prices to monetary causes. An assessment of the relationships between money and prices in these years, of central importance in today's economic controversies, forms the subject matter of the first section of this chapter. A discussion of the consequences for the low income countries of the changing relative scarcities of gold and silver follows.

The fixed exchange rate regime of the gold standard was in some respects similar to the shorter-lived Bretton Woods system after the second world war (see Chapters 9 and 11). The third section compares and contrasts the different aspects of the two systems: parity changes, liquidity and reserve currencies. The fourth section examines whether the impossibility of changing the exchange rate because of the link with gold was made easier by contemporary attitudes towards public finance, or constrained government expenditures. Another difference between the gold standard era and the years after 1945 lay in the greater instability of banking and financial institutions in the earlier period. Most of the downturns in the international economy in these years began with banking collapses. These and other determinants of international business cycles are discussed in the fifth section. Finally, the role and methods of monetary policy in coping with these disturbances are analysed, and an example of the benefits of a policy of going onto the gold standard is described.

## Money and the international price level

The price trends of the gold standard era offer valuable evidence for testing competing theories of economic behaviour. Broadly speaking those modern economists who adopt a Keynesian position maintain that prices, output and employment vary because of 'real' changes in the economy and that monetary influences are of secondary importance. These conclusions follow from the assumed inability of prices and wages to clear markets. As their name implies, modern monetarists assert the primacy of monetary forces in influencing monetary variables, such as prices and interest rates, and of supply side forces, including institutions, in determining output and employment over long periods.

Figure 6.1 shows for the gold standard countries declining prices until 1896 and then rising prices. Silver standard India exhibited the reverse pattern until the closing of the Mints in 1893, with the price level rising as silver fell in value relative to gold, although the trend is somewhat obscured by famines pushing up the price level: food prices soared in 1878, 1897 and 1899. The gold standard economies show fairly close synchronisation of price movements – France and Germany being particularly highly correlated and, to a lesser extent, Britain and the United States. This synchronisation was noted also in the third quarter of the century (Chapter 3). The rise of the American price level in the early 1880s, not matched by a British increase, may be explained by the excessive price fall in the years immediately before the return to gold, and a subsequent reaction.

The controversial question is whether these price trends originated in monetary or in 'real' changes. A second question is what the consequences of the price movements were, for some argued the results were dire.

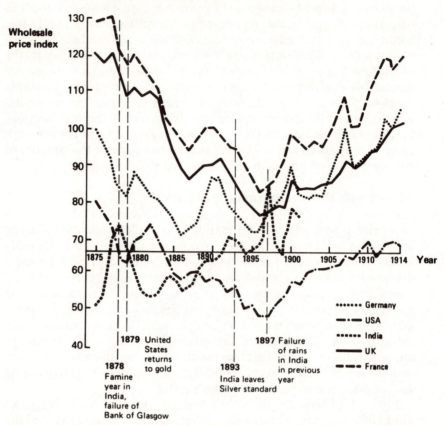

**NATIONAL PRICE LEVELS 1875–1914**

**Figure 6.1**　National price levels, 1875–1914

The growth rate of the world money supply, as measured by Triffin's calculations for Britain, France and the United States, fell from 4 per cent per annum between 1848 and 1872 to an average of 3.2 per cent per annum between 1872 and 1892.[2] The figures for uncovered credit money (that portion of credit money, bank deposits and notes in excess of total gold and silver reserves) showed a similar fall in growth rate from 6.5 to 4.0 per cent per annum over the same period. The slowing of monetary growth has been widely attributed to the decline of gold production and to the demonetisation of silver. The simultaneous depression of prices in the last quarter of the nineteenth century invited an explanation in terms of the quantity of money.[3] Gold discoveries, especially those in Transvaal in 1886, were interpreted as easing the monetary restraint from the mid 1890s. Between 1893 and 1913 Triffin's measure of the world monetary gold stock growth averaged 3.6 per cent per annum, more than double the rate of the preceding twenty years and, from 1896, prices began to rise again. The growth rates of the total money supply and of uncovered credit money also rose to 4.3 and 5.4 per cent per annum respectively.

The growth of the money supply could differ from the growth of the monetary gold stock because of changes in all or any of the three proximate determinants of the money supply; the relationship between high-powered money (currency and bank reserves) and the money supply, the deposit–reserve ratio determined by the banking system, and the deposit–currency ratio, which depended upon the preferences of the public. Bordo's recent recalculation of the British money supply shows the value of gold coins in circulation actually fell in the two decades after 1872, and the total British money supply only increased because of a greater willingness of the public to hold bank deposits relative to cash, and a willingness of the banks to supply this demand.[4] The proximate cause of the more rapid growth of the British money supply after 1896 was the expansion of high-powered money because of the state of the balance of payments and Bank of England policy. The findings for both phases are consistent with a monetary interpretation of price movements; in the first phase the effects of gold on the money supply were only partly offset by changes in the banking system and in the second phase the link between gold expansion and monetary expansion was precise and central. Similarly, Friedman and Schwartz attributed virtually all of monetary expansion in the United States between 1879 and 1914 to the increased output of gold.[5]

## Keynesian-style theories of price changes

Keynesian-style explanations for the depression of prices after 1873 and the turnaround after 1896 have followed a number of routes. Laughlin pointed out, on the basis of US Mint estimates, that in the period of rising prices from the turn of the century until the first world war, the percentage of new gold in relation to the existing stock was not much greater than for the last quarter of the nineteenth century when prices were falling.[6] He believed it was the total gold stock as well as additions to it, that influenced aggregate demand (or total spending), and therefore the changes in the price level could not be attributed to the new gold, nor were other components of the money stock of causal significance. Banks made increased loans, not because gold reserves were more readily available, but because of greater secure trading opportunities that warranted bank advances. Real factors changed prices in these years. Prices in the US in 1896 were exceptionally low because of the industrial depression there. The subsequent rise in American prices, according to Laughlin, was explicable by high tariffs, agricultural readjustment, higher wages and the increasing expenditure of the rich.

Monetary causes cannot explain the movement of prices according to Phelps-Brown and Ogza, because of the parallel movement in interest rates; Gibson's paradox.[7] When monetary expansion drives prices *up* by increasing expenditure on goods, it should also increase the supply of loanable funds and thereby drive interest rates *down*. But falling prices in the last quarter of the century were associated with falling interest rates. Lenders are interested in what their money will buy when it is returned and, in choosing the interest rate at which they are willing to lend, they therefore make a judgement about future price levels. If they expect prices to fall in the future, they will accept a lower nominal than real interest rate. Similar considerations apply on the demand side of the market. Only if the slower monetary expansion than output from 1873 to 1896 was not anticipated to lower prices (regardless of whether or not it did) would it have raised interest rates.

Like Phelps-Brown and Ogza, both Lewis and Rostow attempt to explain the price trends of the period in terms of output movements.[8] The turnaround of prices in the 1890s can be explained, argued Lewis, by a decline in the rate of growth of supplies of wheat, wool and cotton. Prices fell too much in the 1870s, rose too slowly in the first half of the 1900s, and rose too much thereafter. This, Lewis believes, is attributable to the slowness of reaction at turning-points in the relative supplies of agricultural and manufacturing products, followed by over-reactions. Changes in the gold stock cannot explain these price movements because the relationship between gold and the total money supply was unstable; other factors caused the relationship to vary, Lewis asserts. Both in Britain and the United States the velocity of circulation contributed more than the stock of money to explaining the turnaround in prices; the ratio of money incomes to money accounted for more of the change than did the variation in money stock. Changes in the demand for, and supply of, money were induced by the more fundamental changes in agricultural supplies.

Both Lewis and Rostow have been criticised for using a short-run theory to explain long-term phenomena. Supply side shocks, with which they are concerned, cause a once-and-for-all change in the price level, rather than trends lasting two decades.[9] An opposing view is that, given the lesser price flexibility of manufactured than agricultural goods, it is quite possible that one or more supply side shocks could generate such a price rise or fall. A model of this nature has recently been used to provide a non-monetary explanation of British inflation during the Napoleonic wars.[10] Even so, either the money supply must be passive or the velocity of circulation must be variable.[11] Whatever the cause of price changes, since prices are denominated in money terms exactly the money necessary to buy the goods at those prices must be available, either by the existing money stock being used more or less intensively, or by the money supply contracting and expanding as required, for example, through the operation of the banking system, as Laughlin believed. Bordo and Schwartz deny that either of these conditions was fulfilled, and assert that the monetary explanation continues to hold the field.

## Price changes and policy

A belief in the relationship between the gold base and prices was sufficiently strong and widespread in the United States to encourage continual agitation by small farmers, silver miners and great landowners during the period of falling prices for the remonetisation of silver to reverse the trend. The United States in 1878 therefore passed the Bland Act requiring the coining of not less than 2 million dollars in silver every month at a ratio with gold of 1: 16.[12] The Act was a response to the 'Crime of '73' by which America had altered her nominally bimetallic currency to a nominal gold standard, although her currency was not then fully convertible. At the same time as the Bland Bill became law, the United States vainly tried to bring the Latin Union back to its former bimetallism at the International Monetary Conference in Paris, also to prevent the decline of prices. Despite the disruption of Franco–Italian relations over Tunisia, the Union presented a united front against silver at the 1881 International Monetary Conference.

Another American Silver Purchase Bill was passed in 1880, and the gold price of silver began to rise, helped by the formation of a silver cartel. The cartel could not, however, hold the market because European governments took the opportunity to rid themselves of their demonetised silver stocks. There were wide oscillations in the price of silver which convinced Hungarian farmers of the need for the stability of the gold standard even if it did mean lower prices and, in 1892, Austria–Hungary adopted the gold standard. Japan went on to gold in 1886. In 1893 the US Silver Purchase Act was repealed. India closed her Mints to the free coinage of silver in the same year and in 1896 the United States survived the last serious attempt to return to silver in the presidential campaign of that year. Russia also went on to the gold standard in 1895–7. Thus, the main trading nations of the world by the end of the century had turned to gold, increasing the demand for it even faster than the growth in world trade, tending to depress prices of gold standard countries further and to raise prices in the remaining silver countries. Between 1896 and 1915 world monetary gold demand rose probably by more than $4 billion, whereas silver demand fell by about $1.8 billion.[13]

## The silver standard economies

The impact on the silver standard countries of the fall in the gold price of silver was dramatic.[14] Most of the less developed economies were linked to silver and they found their exchange rates continuously depreciating between 1873 and 1894 against gold standard countries, in total by about half. If resources were unemployed or underemployed in these countries, depreciation will have raised national incomes by increasing the demand for exports, and for import substitution. In turn higher incomes might have induced more invesment, making exports more competitive and further raising incomes. Without this induced investment, higher exports paid for in silver must have inflated the money supplies of silver standard countries and raised their prices, thereby eliminating the competitive advantage of the initial depreciation. Silver countries with obligations denominated in gold to other countries were less fortunate. In India a major government concern was the payment of the 'home charges', the interest on debt, civil servants' pensions, and so on, which were denominated in gold, so here the burden increased as silver depreciated. In general, importers, who had to pay higher prices, objected to the depreciations, and exporters, whose products became more competitive, did not.

Nugent has compared the export performance of silver and gold standard countries in these years as a measure of the effects of the depreciation.[15] The 'average' gold country in Nugent's data set achieved a growth in the gold value of its exports of barely 1 per cent per annum, although as world prices were falling steadily at about 2 per cent per annum over the period, in real terms the increase in exports was higher. Exports from the silver countries present a very different picture. Even when Korea and Bolivia (the two fastest growing countries) are excluded, the average silver country's exports grew at more than 4 per cent per annum in gold values, and there is no evidence that any silver country experienced a decline in the gold value of its exports. Depreciation, therefore, seemed to favour silver standard countries where their trade was concerned. The impact on foreign investment could well have been harmful though.

These results may, of course, have been purely fortuitous. In any case, in examining particular economies it is necessary to bear in mind that other major and relevant changes were possibly occurring at the same time. For instance, regardless of the depreciation of silver exchange rates, productivity and population growth in the gold standard countries from which India imported exceeded those in India. Hence, the otherwise unexpected observation that the price of Indian imports fell by more than silver fell in relation to gold, or by the rupee–sterling exchange rate, so they became cheaper despite depreciation. Some Indian export prices rose, but in general they did so by less than the fall in the exchange. Therefore, the competitive advantage conferred by depreciation was maintained.

The general Indian price level was a little higher in the mid-1890s than in the beginning of the 1870s. Net imports of silver were especially heavy in the quinquennium ending 1893/4 and probably pushed the general price level upwards.[16] If the rupee had not depreciated, the growth of exports from India between 1873 and 1895 would have been even further below the growth of imports than it actually was, (respectively 89 and 108 per cent). This would have tended to lower prices as silver flowed out of the country. At least prices would have been lowered as long as the outflow did not push down further the silver price in terms of gold, as gold standard exporters exchanged silver for gold and further depreciated the rupee exchange rate. As expected from an export stimulus with sticky prices, there was some evidence of rising real incomes. In the interior of India the money wages of skilled labour tended to rise without a corresponding increase in food grain prices, although unskilled rates showed little improvement. The rapid growth of Indian state revenues since the fall of silver indicated general prosperity, as did the increased imports of luxury items such as clocks and watches, corals and glass.[17] Numbers of spindles in cotton mills increased from 1.23 million in 1876/7 to 2.05 million in 1884/5. But it would be rash to attribute this prosperity solely to the depreciation of the exchange rate.

In China the inflow of silver following the depreciation of the exchange rate similarly does not seem to have raised prices in the country as a whole to offset the depreciation. So China also must have maintained an export advantage.[18]

## The working of the gold standard

The unthinkability of changing the exchange rate once it had been linked to a precious metal meant that different rates of growth of productivity between countries had to be met by price or output changes, not by exchange rate changes as were allowed under the later Bretton Woods system. If prices and wages were sticky downwards in the slower growing economy as Keynesians expect, the gold outflow consequent upon the balance of trade deficit, by reducing the money supply, would raise unemployment which in turn might discourage investment and growth. Such an observation has led Lewis to propose that devaluation would have been a solution to slow economic growth in Britain from the mid-1880s.[19]

An alternative solution might have been to increase international liquidity. More liquidity may have delayed the raising of interest rates and the reduction of business activity so early on in the expansionary phase of the business cycle as to prevent the loss of international reserves. Concern was often voiced about the inadequacy of the Bank of England's gold reserves, the frequent rises in bank rate, the contrasts with the stable, cheap money regime in France, and the constraining effect on economic development.[20] Anxiety continued to be expressed into the twentieth century after gold production had accelerated. Between January 1904 and December 1914 the Bank of France changed its interest rate eight times, the Bank of England forty-nine times and the Reichbank thirty-seven times. In 1907 the raising of the bank rate to 7 per cent worried the Bank sufficiently to institute an inquiry about the effects outside the London money markets.[21] The conclusions were generally that only an increase above 5 per cent had prejudicial effects on business activity, but even then the banks tempered the wind, charging less than the bank rate. In some country areas in the North, notably Yorkshire, the traditionally fixed 5 per cent still reigned. The Bank's actions might have impinged on internal business activity also through the cash reserve of the domestic banks. But the Bank only tried to influence these reserves to affect the market rate of discount, not the level of bank lending.

*Reserve currencies*

For most countries the problems for international liquidity that the move to gold generated were partly met by the use of the key or reserve currencies; these currencies were 'as good as gold'. Countries needed reserves or liquidity to be able to finance unforseen fluctuations in their balance of payments under fixed exchange rates, without resort to deflationary measures. Most private international settlements were conducted in sterling, French francs or German marks, and these key currencies composed a share of the world's official reserves as well – about 20 per cent by 1913.[22] Their use economised on the gold that was becoming scarcer in relation to economic activity. Slightly over half of the known official foreign balances were held in Russia, India and Japan, with some countries, most notably Britian and the United States, holding no official exchange assets at all.

A consequence of the key currency system was that Britain's liquid liabilities to foreigners were several times greater than the Bank of England's gold stock (for which the liabilities could in principle be exchanged), even when the sterling balances of the colonies were excluded. This position was closely analogous to that of the United States in the late 1960s. Germany to a lesser extent, though not perhaps France, similarly had an excess of liquid foreign liabilities over the gold stock. Although there was an association between the capital exports and the payments deficits for Britain, France and Germany as a group, and only these lending countries registered payment deficits over the first fourteen years of the century, the transactions themselves ultimately failed to worsen the balance of payments of Britain or France sufficiently to explain the overall imbalance, because of the profits and dividends yielded by the investment. Before 1914 the international economy was willing to accumulate the reserve currencies, and the central banks of these countries, especially the Bank of England, saw little wrong as long as their own gold reserves were not declining relative to their own liabilities. Under these conditions the declining competitive position of certain British export industries and the rapid rise of imports were not countered so vigorously by deflationary measures as they would have been if the Bank had adopted the payments equilibrium goal of the post-1945 period.

The international use of sterling raised British and world incomes by foreigners effectively giving Britain interest-free loans by holding sterling, and by sterling's enhancement of world liquidity. Against this must be set any repercussions on British industry from the frequent rises and falls in bank rate, already discussed, which were consequences of the size of the Bank's own gold reserves and the key (or reserve) currency role of sterling.

By analogy with the role of the US dollar after 1945, the key currency system contained the seeds of its own destruction. The dominant role of sterling in the international economy had evolved from Britain's unchallenged superiority in international trade from the mid-nineteenth century. As confidence in the international role of sterling grew so did foreign holdings of sterling. British industry had to export less in order to buy a given quantity of imports than if sterling had not been a reserve currency. The adjustments of prices in the British economy and of the industrial structure, necessary to maintain a balance of payments equilibrium, were reduced. If Britain had been forced to adjust faster the structure of her industry, not only would the eventual adjustment have been less wrenching, but the rate of industrial growth in the late nineteenth century may have been higher as the demand expanded for the products of the new industries, which had much greater scope for productivity increases than the old staples located in Britain.[23]

Instead, British trade competitiveness declined, as described in Chapter 4, and the currencies of other countries came into increasing use as reserves. Eventually confidence was lost in sterling convertibility and the British economy had to adjust radically in the interwar years. Undoubtedly, the financial and political consequences of the first world war and the rapid economic development of the United States were responsible for the timing and much of the magnitude of the changes. But the reserve currency role of the US dollar in the 1960s and 1970s, which was substantially reduced without the interruption of a world war, seems a compelling analogy; eventually, even without the war, sterling's international role would have been questioned.

A difference between the fixed rate regime of Bretton Woods and of the gold standard, which may explain the greater longevity of the gold standard system, and so argue against the 'internal contradictions' interpretation of the reserve currencies, is the different scope for speculation. Since exchange rate changes were not allowed under the gold standard, speculators' beliefs in the viability of the system encouraged short-term capital flows that allowed the maintenance of the chosen rate. By contrast, since rate changes were permitted under Bretton Woods, speculative capital flows tended to precipitate them.[24]

## The gold standard and public finance

Perhaps the less all-embracing role of government in the heyday of the gold standard made unchangeable exchange rates more feasible than under the Bretton Woods system. Exchange rate changes may have been less necessary because of the absence of differential rates of inflation resulting from the financing of some government expenditure by monetary expansion. But it is by no means certain for there were strong pressures to increase government spending in the late nineteenth century. Budget deficits were financed by debt accumulation, which may have crowded out private investment and certainly increased the tax liability of future generations with possible inflationary consequences. The causality may have worked in the opposite direction; the need to maintain currency convertibility into gold at a fixed price may have restrained the growth of government expenditure. The continuing deficits of the Austrian Treasury and the privileged position of the government in the money markets that allowed the payment of up to 8 per cent on long-term issues, almost centainly excluded private investment unable to pay these rates.[25] Austria–Hungary did not go on to gold, abandoning its floating exchange rate, until 1892. Even so, the money supply had increased only slowly in the previous decade.[26] Neither was the gold standard necessary to impose financial probity on the Russian government in this period, despite an inconvertible paper currency until 1895–7. During the Russo–Turkish war of 1877–8 there were large increases in the paper money circulation, but then, from 1880 to 1885, the money supply was contracted. The money supply similarly grew rapidly in 1905 to 1906 during the war with Japan, despite the existence of nominal gold convertibility (severely limited in these years).[27]

According to Ford, there is little question of the gold standard constraining government budgetary policy in Argentina either.[28] Rather it was a tool to serve the dominant political groups. Once inflationary finance had caused the collapse of the standard, a depreciating exchange rate moved the distribution of income in favour of exporting and landed interests and the representatives of these interests saw no reason to return to the standard. Stabilisation in 1900 was engineered by these groups largely to stop the unfavourable redistribution of income they were experiencing from the appreciating exchange rate, once the foreign investment began to lead to higher exports, and primary product prices rose.

Both in the weight of taxation and in the propensity to abandon convertibility Argentina resembled Italy, which according to Mulhall's data in Table 6.1 paid the greatest amount of taxation in proportion to earnings. High taxation was necessary because budget deficits had quadrupled the Italian national debt in the first twenty years after unification. Similarly Spain and Serbia had penchants for unproductive government expenditures that slowed their economic development and kept them off the gold standard.

Even in sounder economies there were powerful forces operating to push up public expenditure. Germany introduced old age pensions and unemployment insurance in 1888, and Britain did the same two decades later. Armaments became increasingly important in the German budget as the German navy was expanded to become

**Table 6.1** *Taxation and national debt, 1888–90*

| Country | Taxation (national and local) (shillings per inhabitant) | Taxation as a percentage of earnings | National debt per head (£) | Debt Service per head (£) | Approximate income per head (£) | Approximate $1960 per head (£)[b] |
|---|---|---|---|---|---|---|
| Britain | 63 | 9.3 | 18.3 | 0.73 | 33.7 | (785) |
| France | 74 | 13.6 | 32.7 | 1.36 | 27.8 | (575) |
| Germany | 45 | 10.4 | 8.9 | 0.34 | 22.2 | (537) |
| Russia | 16 | 7.4 | 8.2 | 0.30 | 11.5 | (182) |
| Austria–Hungary | 28 | 9.5 | 14.5 | 0.40 | 15.5 | (361) |
| Italy | 54 | 22.0 | 15.2 | 0.68 | 12.2 | (311) |
| Spain | 41 | 12.3 | 14.7 | 0.62 | 16.5 | (321) |
| Portugal | 33 | 14.0 | 24.0 | 0.76 | 12.1 | (270) |
| Sweden | 28 | 6.7} | | | 22.0 | (356) |
| Norway | 24 | 6.0} | 2.1 | 0.07 | 20.5 | (523) |
| Denmark | 35 | 5.5 | 5.2 | 0.23 | 32.5 | (502) |
| Holland | 64 | 15.1 | 19.3 | 0.67 | 22.6 | (536) |
| Belgium | 36 | 6.0 | 12.6 | 0.63 | 28.0 | (630) |
| Greece | 24 | na | 10.4 | 0.68 | na | (290) |
| United States | 40 | 5.4 | 3.6 | 0.16 | 39.0 | |
| Australia | 60 | 7.2 | 53.5 | n.a. | 40.2 | |
| Canada | 24 | 4.6 | 9.8 | n.a. | 26.0 | |
| Argentina | 54 | 11.2 | 42.7 | n.a. | 24.0 | |
| India | 5 | n.a. | 0.8 | n.a. | n.a. | |

*Source*: M.G. Mulhall, *Dictionary of Statistics*, London: Routledge (1892).

[a] Population of British India excluding native states.

[b] P. Bairoch, 'Europe's gross national product, 1800–1975', *Journal of European Economic History* (1975).

capable of challenging the British. German expenditure on the army and navy in 1909 was half as high again as it had been in 1905, and the national debt increased by the same proportion.[29] In the sixteen years after 1893 the German national debt increased at an annual average rate of 6.4 per cent, considerably faster than national income. Between 1904 and 1913, the budget was in surplus for only three years.

Not all gold standard countries financed their increased expenditure by increasing their debt. Italy raised her military expenditures by more than a third between 1905 and 1909, but slightly reduced her outstanding debt, as did France, whose military expenditure rose 14 per cent between 1905 and 1909. Russia reduced her military expenditure by 20 per cent between 1905 and 1909 after defeat in the war with Japan, but debt nevertheless rose 15 per cent.

Those countries which did raise the ratio of debt to national income faced the prospect either of reducing expenditure on other items to pay for the debt charges, finding other sources of taxation, raising existing tax rates, or abandoning the convertibility of currency into gold and printing money. Germany, because of its federal structure, faced particular difficulties in getting more revenue from taxation, but this does not seem to have constrained debt expansion.[30] The experience of hyperinflation after the first world war suggests the gold standard would have been abandoned first, and that for Germany at least the gold standard did not inhibit government expenditure, though it did restrain the expansion of the domestic money supply.

As will be shown in the next section there were considerable benefits from foreign investment for some countries from being on the gold standard. Among the benefits were easing the financing of budget deficits within limits. The scope for taking up this option by productive public sector investment clearly differed between countries, as did the willingness to use state finance. With their abundant natural resources the regions of recent European settlement had greater opportunities for profitable investment in infrastructure than the older European countries. The remarkable contrast between the debt per head in Australia and Argentina on the one hand, and the United States and Canada on the other, indicates the varied possibilities of the extent of state involvement in economic development (Table 6.1). There were limits to which the state could depend on foreign investors underwriting development though. It was the size of national debt held by foreigners, and the problem of earning the foreign exchange to service the debt, that forced Argentina off the gold standard from 1885 to 1900. By the late 1880s Argentina therefore had to pay twice the interest rate on government borrowing as did Britain.

Table 6.1 shows that gold standard countries adopted a wide variety of financial strategies; taxation, debt and debt service differed greatly between them. Different pressures of aggregate demand and therefore pressures on the balance of payments must therefore have resulted. This explains the varying extents to which countries maintained a pure gold standard. The Italian exchange rate fluctuated widely because the National Bank only paid out gold in small quantities and refused to sell large quantities for export. Little restraining influence on public finance seems to have flowed from the gold standard, nor were the underlying pressures to raise state spending particularly weak. By comparison with the years after 1945, the doctrine of the balanced budget except in wartime undoubtedly made unchanging exchange rates more viable. But even in the most prosperous industrial countries, the disintegration of the nineteenth-century liberal consensus on government expenditure was making the maintenance of the gold standard more difficult by 1914.

## Fluctuations in economic activity

Though the persistence of the fixed or 'par value' exchange rate regime of the gold standard with small international reserves has been described as the product of unusually favourable historical circumstances, the international economy experienced sizeable fluctuations in economic activity and severe financial crises to which gold standard countries had to adjust. The absence of an American central bank to act as lender of last resort, and to provide seasonal elasticity to American money and credit, exacerbated world economic disturbances. Some have seen the business cycles in these years as different for each country.[31] But the pervasiveness of relatively fixed exchange rates implies that, wherever the cycles originated, they would be transmitted, perhaps with diminished intensity and some delay, to other economies. During the 1870s the attempts of Germany, the United States and France to accumulate gold caused a slump in Britain in 1878. British interest rates were raised to protect the gold reserve and then the City of Glasgow Bank failed.[32] Until then British industries mainly dependent on trade with the empire were largely insulated from depressed conditions elsewhere.

Another slump began in 1882. In France the ravaging of the vineyards by disease was at its peak, the Freycinet plan to spend massive sums of public money on transport improvements was cut, and the Union Générale failed. Gold flowed from London to Paris to assuage the panic demands for cash and the Bank of England's discount rate reached 6.6 per cent. Germany, Britain and the US moved into recession and in the Spring of 1884 the American banking system experienced problems arising from railway finance, although on a smaller scale than in 1873. The recession soon spread to Canada and to South America but empire demand remained buoyant. A redirection of British foreign investment stimulated activity in India and Australia. After 1886 the United States economy recovered, gold was discovered in the Transvaal, and Indian demand stagnated.

The collapse of an attempt to rig the copper market and the bankruptcy of the Suez Canal enterprise in 1889 in France was a prelude to the Baring crisis in London the following year. The French crises also provided a blueprint solution when the Bank of France collaborated with leading finance houses to support the Comptoir d' Escompte.[33] Massive British investment in Argentina initially generated rising incomes and imports there, only later supplying the exports from the pampas.[34] Much borrowing was at fixed interest, denominated in gold or sterling and payable or guaranteed by public authorities. Domestic inflation was stimulated by irresponsible banking and weak corrupt financial administration. In 1889 a bad harvest signalled problems in paying for the overseas debt and the following year there was a *coup* and a temporary default. The Argentinian default found Baring in a position of having lent for long periods and borrowed for short periods. To save such a prestigious firm from bankruptcy, the Bank of England did what it had not been prepared to do for the 'Norwich upstarts' Overend and Gurney in 1866, organise a consortium of financiers to set up a rescue operation. This consortium, however, excluded a more powerful and more recent group of upstarts, the joint stock banks, whose exclusion from the financial management system was to have awkward consequences in 1914.

The problems of the 'external drain' of gold prompted by the panic could not however be dealt with by the consortium. The Bank of France disliked the disruption to the loan operations in Paris that high interest rates would cause and was easily persuaded to allow Rothschilds to ship £3 million in gold across the Channel.[35] The Bank of England itself purchased some £$1\frac{1}{2}$ million in German gold coins from Russia, which offered more. This the Bank declined, but Russia supported the reserve position by agreeing not to withdraw substantial deposits from Baring as had been their intention. The Governor of the Bank of England assured the Russian ambassador of the safety of these deposits.

The Bank of England and international co-operation prevented the Baring crisis from becoming a national and international monetary crisis. Prosperity therefore continued until two years later. The American depression began in 1893 when the Australian land boom also collapsed. For the first time since 1853 annual gold output exceeded £30 million in 1892, continuing to rise rapidly. Low discount rates in London from 1893 to 1896 were made possible by the new gold easing the Bank of England's reserve position and the British slump was therefore not severe.

By now multilateral trade had become important: no longer was Britain at the centre of the majority of international transactions. Hence empire countries could expect to share more in the booms and slumps of the United States.[36] Intra-European trade was more important than European trade with the United States so that if conditions were right elsewhere, an American recession, such as that of 1903/4, could pass unnoticed in Europe. In 1907 conditions were not right. Financial panics occurred in Egypt in April, in Japan in May and in Germany in October. The Knickerbocker Trust failed in New York and in October and November the US banking system suspended general cash payments. This was the climax of an increasing demand for gold imports which the Bank of England met by raising the Bank Rate through 1906 and 1907.[37] The drain of gold was met by temporarily reshuffling the destinations of newly-mined gold to such an extent that Britain remained a net importer. Temporary accommodation came from Europe, in particular from the Bank of France and the Reichsbank, not merely because of a change in short-term interest rate differentials, or because of the German financial collapse, but because of central bank co-operation. The Bank of France placed resources at the disposal of the Bank of England for fear that if England had to resort to further rises in the discount rate, France too would have to increase her rates exorbitantly and injure her own trade and industry. Short-term interest rates dropped in 1908 and British exports recovered in 1909.

In 1914, fear of war caused heavy sales of internationally traded securities in the European stock exchange which in turn caused a partial breakdown of long-term capital markets.[38] Short-term international credit also collapsed. The London bill market and the London stock exchange no longer provided the London clearing banks with liquid assets. The Bank of England could not supply enough cash to the bill market to prevent new business there drying up on Thursday, 30 July. On Friday morning the Stock Exchange did not open and gold moved from London to Paris. Imports from

New York would take some days to arrive. Despite their substantial gold reserves, the clearing banks refused to pay out sovereigns, passing the burden on to the Bank of England. The Bank Holiday of Monday, 3 August was extended for three more days, by which time war had been declared.

Although de Cecco sees the financial crises of 1914, as breaking the gold standard before war was declared, and marking the end of the system because of its internal contradictions, this would seem to misunderstand the fundamentally political cause of the crisis.[39] The crisis was caused by the war scare, and if war had not broken out it would have been remedied by the arrival of gold from New York. In any event, British gold convertibility was not abandoned in 1914, and the joint stock banks' refusal to pay out gold sovereigns was the consequence of their battle for power over monetary policy with the Bank of England, not an intrinsic inability of the gold standard institution to cope with the crisis.

The central role of confidence in shoring up the pyramid of credit inevitably rendered international monetary relations vulnerable to war scares. And not only to war scares but also to the prospective illiquidity of financial institutions. The contrast between the Baring crisis and the rescue operation of the Comptoir d'Escompte on the one hand, and the failure of the Knickerbocker Trust on the other, implies that proper monetary management and regulation could alleviate downturns in the business cycle that originated domestically. The cycle may have had an underlying structure of long swings in investment, perhaps induced by some sort of multiplier–accelerator interaction, but the instability of financial institutions almost certainly increased the severity and duration of slumps. The British slumps of the late 1870s, the early 1880s and 1907 owed much to the transmission of foreign disturbances through the gold outflows and high interest rates. But low Bank of England reserves left little discretion to British monetary policy to offset these shocks.

## Monetary policy under the gold standard

National monetary policy under the international gold standard was primarily concerned to maintain the convertibility of national currencies into gold in the face of international or domestic disturbances. The 'rules of the game' to achieve this end were that a drain on gold reserves was to be countered by an increased discount rate and that a rise in the reserves was met by a reduced rate.[40] The bank of England however followed rather than led the market down in the latter case. These interest rate changes were to attract or repel short-term assets that would restore equilibrium in the balance of payments and eliminate the accommodating gold flows. Actual practice differed somewhat from the 'rules' because central banks had other objectives as well as maintaining the reserves. They were, for example, concerned to insulate the domestic economy from foreign disturbances as far as possible.

The Bank of France regarded its gold reserves more as a national war treasure, and therefore it tended to prevent an outflow by paying a premium on gold. Large withdrawals for export required special permission. The French did not like to raise the discount rate to protect gold reserves because of the impact on domestic industry. From 1885 to 1888 the Bank of France did not alter the rate from 3 per cent. After 1900 at least, when gold did flow out of the country, reserves were so high that a higher discount rate was unnecessary. The premium policy to prevent a gold outflow was of doubtful effectiveness because by contrast with Britain, in France the cheque system was almost unknown and trade was conducted with gold or notes. Gold could therefore be withdrawn from circulation and exported, if exchange rate depreciation made it profitable, without having to go to the central bank. When the Bank of France did choose to raise the discount rate it could count on attracting gold from Belgium and Switzerland.

Berlin in the late 1880s operated a discount policy similar to the British. Gold could be drawn into Germany from Denmark and Scandinavia, but the Reichsbank was loathe to let gold leave the country. Although it had never refused gold (and had no power to do so) there was a general impression that when the Reichsbank agreed to gold exports, it generally took action to indicate disapproval when inconvenienced by requests for gold. In the struggle to accumulate gold in the 1880s the Reichsbank was more ingenious than the Bank of England, allowing importers of gold free finance. Thereby Germany's gold reserves rose by one half between 1884 and 1890. Nevertheless during the 1907 crisis, when there was almost a flight from money in Germany, none of the Reichsbank's devices, including a higher discount rate than in London, prevented a massive outflow of gold.

The United States handicapped itself and created problems for the rest of the world by not having a central bank. Lacking a 'lender of last resort' domestic banking crises were more intense, depressions were therefore deeper, and American seasonal and panic demands for gold had to be met by other countries. But interest rates in the United States did follow the rules of the game, rising rapidly when the reserves of the principal banks, especially in New York, fell to the legal one quarter of deposits. Government policy exacerbated the difficulties of monetary control through the national budget. Whereas in Europe tax revenues were paid into the central banks and recirculated, in the United States the receipts were drained from the economy into the Treasury vaults. The unwillingness of the Republicans to reduce the Customs revenue and objections to increased government expenditure combined to produce budget surpluses of over $100 million in the late 1880s. This surplus was eventually used to retire the national debt, but as the debt diminished the policy became increasingly difficult to pursue.

Bloomfield's wider study of central bank policy showed an ambivalence towards the 'rules'.[41] For only six out of the eleven central banks studied was there a close inverse correlation of discount rates and reserve ratios (on the basis of annual average monthly statistics) between 1880 and 1914. For five of these six banks, reserve ratios tended to move inversely with domestic business cycle fluctuations. Discount rates therefore moved positively with the cycle, consistent with a policy of domestic stabilisation.

## Bank of England policy

The Bank of England's behaviour confirms this latter pattern.[42] During an upswing in income the banking system accommodated the increased demand for money. Consequently there was an 'internal' drain on the Bank's reserves. A larger trade deficit also accompanied the rise in economic activity, but did not cause an 'external' drain of gold. Instead the increases in interest rates largely brought about by the Bank of England to protect its reserves, led to such inflows of short-term capital that gold actually flowed into the Bank from abroad during periods of increased domestic activity and thus partly, but not entirely, offset the internal drain of reserves from the Bank.

To make the Bank of England's discount rate effective, the Bank had to ensure sufficient monetary scarcity that the bill market would be forced to borrow from it. It had to engage in open market operations. The Bank did not sell bills to make bank rate effective because it carried no suitable portfolio.[43] The supply of Treasury bills was insignificant. Instead it sold securities, thereby affecting the bill market indirectly through the stock exchange. Another method of making bank rate effective was by the direct control of funds, that would have been otherwise directly lent to the bill market, such as those of the Council of India. In the 1890s, the Bank of

Japan's funds also became subject to Bank of England's direct borrowing. The ability of the Bank of England to control the British and the international monetary system by 1914 had been reduced by the rise of ten large British joint stock banks. The Bank's power to build up its own gold stock had come to depend to some extent on their goodwill. To make the bank rate effective, the Bank tended to borrow from the clearing banks from 1905. Larger gold reserves, which everybody agreed were necessary, required that the clearing banks place bigger reserves with the Bank of England, but the Bank was unwilling to concede any power over the gold reserves that the banks wanted in exchange for the deposits.

Sometimes the Bank experimented with methods more direct than discount rate policy to influence international gold flows. The Bank was left a free hand in fixing its buying and selling prices for foreign gold coin – the most readily available gold – subject always to the limits implicit in the possibility of melting these coins into bars. To check an export of gold to the USA the Bank would raise the selling price of American gold coins or refuse to sell them at all, forcing a diversion of demand to bar gold. Interest-free advances on gold shipments were another option, as was paying over the odds for bar gold, especially at the weekly South African gold sales from 1903.

The Reichsbank also borrowed in the market to make its discount rate effective, by selling Treasury bills in 1901, 1903, 1905 and 1906. Like the Bank of England, it did not engage in open market operations to ease the money market.[44]

A recent interpretation has cast doubt on whether central bank policy could influence events at all. McCloskey and Zecher maintain that Britain was too small to influence the world money supply significantly, yet that it would have to do so if it wished to influence British monetary variables; they show on the basis of the strong association of price changes for various commodities between countries that there was an international market for goods no more imperfect than national markets in the period 1880–1913.[45] Thus, contrary to the view of Keynes and many others, London's influence on credit conditions throughout the world in the second half of the nineteenth century was not paramount; the Bank of England could not influence rates of interest or prices.[46] The Bank could only contract the money supply growth into line with the values of these variables for the rest of the world.

All this follows from the implication of the simple monetary theory that the balance of payments is merely the difference between the national demand for money and the national supply of money. The level of national income influences the demand for money but is not itself influenced by the balance of payments adjustment process. During an upswing the tendency for excessive credit expansion was checked by a gold outflow as national monetary growth exceeded the world average. The contraction of the monetary base tended to cause financial stringency putting up interest rates, unless rationing of now scarcer loans was preferred, and the rise in bank rate merely reflected and signalled this stringency.

The great limitation of this model is the assumption that there is effectively only one type of asset apart from money. However, as Edelstein has shown (see Chapter 5) British domestic investment was not a perfect substitute for British foreign investment, and this imperfect substitutability was also true of short- and long-term assets and of the assets of different countries. Hence, it was possible for the different market interest rates on different types of assets to prevail and for the Bank of England to influence rates on one of the types of asset.[47] It is certainly true that interest rates in different financial centres did diverge during crises, an event that could not occur if McCloskey and Zecher's model was completely correct.[48]

## The benefits of the gold standard

One of the choices of monetary policy that countries had to make was whether to go onto – and stay on – the gold standard. The benefits to be had from submitting to gold convertibility are shown by the Russian experience. The main costs of Russian convertibility was the two-thirds of official borrowing abroad between 1885 and 1897 which was used to acquire gold reserves, rather than being diverted to productive investment. The benefit was the increased attraction of foreign capital by the reduction in exchange risk.[49] The influx of foreign capital into Russia after convertibility increased over the earlier period by at least half. If this is attributed to the introduction of the gold standard, then the consequent Russian net national product (NNP) growth can be found using a Harrod–Domar type calculation. Foreign investment as a proportion of NNP rose from 0.5 to 1.5 per cent between the two periods. The marginal Russian capital–output ratio was about 2.5:1. Hence the percentage increase in national income from the rise in foreign investment, being the product of the increased investment share of income and the marginal product of capital (1 per cent × 1/2.5), was about $\frac{1}{2}$ per cent per annum. If Russia had not gone onto the gold standard the growth rate of the economy would have been 3.5 per cent per annum instead of 4 per cent per annum, and by 1913 national income would have been approximately 7 per cent lower. Using the same method to assess the maximum costs in terms of growth of the official borrowings from 1885 to 1897, growth would appear to have been 0.2 per cent per annum higher if the gold reserves had been devoted to productive investment. Since 0.2 per cent is less than 0.5 per cent, there was a net benefit to the economy from the gold standard.

## Summary and conclusion

The thirty years before the first world war saw the establishment and working of an international fixed exchange rate regime, unprecedented in history. The linking of national currencies to gold made the international price level vulnerable to changes in world gold supplies. An explanation in these terms has been offered for the depression of prices between 1873 and 1896 and the subsequent rise to 1914. On the other hand, in the most advanced economies the greater part of the money supply consisted of bank deposits, the supply of which, some have maintained, responded passively to changes in world output. Changes in relative supplies of agricultural and manufacturing products, according to this school of thought, were the main influence on world prices.

The demonetisation of silver caused a decline in the demand for silver and hence a fall in its price in the last quarter of the century. The demand for gold was correspondingly increased so that countries remaining on a silver standard experienced a depreciation of their exchange rates with gold standard countries. On average the growth of exports from silver standard countries exceeded those from gold standard countries. For which reason there probably were some beneficial consequences from the depreciation for the silver economies.

The gold standard offered no remedy for an overvalued exchange rate other than price or wage deflation, or persistent unemployment. In this respect the standard differed from the international monetary regime established after 1945. The same feature may account for its relative longevity by encouraging stabilising speculative capital flows in contrast to the Bretton Woods system. Like that system the gold standard saw the emergence of reserve or key currencies that economised on the use of gold, and reduced the problem of international liquidity.

Just as after 1945, during the late nineteenth century there were strong pressures to increase government expenditures, which threatened the viability of the fixed, exchange rates for some countries. There is little evidence that the link to gold constrained public finances.

The working of the gold standard was not dependent on a tranquil international economy. World trade and finance were convulsed by periodic crises, exacerbated by inadequate financial institutions, especially in the United States. Harvests, capital movements and income effects all played a part in synchronising fluctuations in national economies.

Central banks pursued monetary policies calculated both to maintain currency convertibility into gold and to avoid as far as possible adverse repercussions of international fluctuations on their domestic economies. The use of high discount rates to attract gold from abroad when reserves fell was the main instrument of policy. Open market operations to 'make the rate effective', gold devices and direct borrowing from the market were subsidiary instruments. During crises there was a certain amount of central bank co-operation, stemming from a recognition of the interdependence of the national economies.

# Notes

1. C. Rosenraad, 'The international money market – discussion', *Journal of the Royal Statistical Society*, **63** (1900), p. 33.
2. R. Triffin, *Our International Monetary System*, New York: Random House (1968), p. 28.
3. For example, A. Marshall, 'Remedies for fluctuations of general prices', in A.C. Pigou (ed.), *Memorials of Alfred Marshall*, London: Macmillan (1925).
4. M.D. Bordo, 'The UK money supply 1870–1914', *Research in Economic History*, **6** (1981), pp. 107–25.
5. M. Friedman and A. Schwartz, *A Monetary History of the United States*, Princeton, NJ: Princeton University Press (1963). For a somewhat different interpretation, see B.B. Aghlevi, 'The balance of payments and the money supply under the gold standard regime: The United States 1879–1914', *American Economic Review*, **65** (1975), pp. 40–58.
6. J.L. Laughlin, *Money and Prices*, London: P.S. King (1919).
7. E.H. Phelps-Brown and S.A. Ogza, 'Economic growth and the price level', *Economic Journal*, **65** (1955), pp. 1–18.
8. W.A. Lewis *Growth and Fluctuations 1870–1913*, London: Allen & Unwin (1978), ch. 3. W.W. Rostow, *The World Economy: History and Prospects*, London: Macmillan (1978).
9. M. Bordo and A. Schwartz, 'Money and prices in the nineteenth century', *Journal of Economic History*, **40** (1980), pp. 61–7.
10. J. Mokyr and R.E. Savin, 'Stagflation in historical perspective: the Napoleonic wars revisited', *Research in Economic History*, **1** (1976) pp. 198–259.
11. Bordo and Schwartz, loc. cit.

12. D. Barbour, *The Theory of Bimetallism*, London: Cassell (1886), p. 67.
13. Laughlin, op. cit.
14. A.G. Latham, *The International Economy and the Undeveloped World 1865–1914*, London: Croom Helm (1978). Chapter 2 provides a useful summary of the experience of LDC silver standard economies.
15. J.B. Nugent, 'Exchange rate movements and economic development in the late nineteenth century', *Journal of Political Economy*, **81** (1973) pp. 1110–35.
16. B. Narain, 'Exchange and prices in India 1873–1924', *Weltwirtschaftliches Archiv*, **23** (1926), pp. 246–92. Barbour, loc. cit. ch. 21.
17. ibid., p. 149.
18. C.F. Remer, 'International trade between gold and silver countries: China 1885–1913', *Quarterly Journal of Economics* (1926), pp. 597–643.
19. Lewis, loc. cit.
20. A.I. Bloomfield, *Monetary Policy under the International Gold Stock 1880–1914*, New York: Federal Reserve Bank (1959).
21. R.S. Sayers, *The Bank of England 1891–1944*, Cambridge: Cambridge University Press (1976), vol. 1, pp. 43–5.
22. P.H. Lindert, *Key Currencies and Gold 1900–1913*, Princeton: Princeton University Press (1969). See also J.M. Keynes, *Indian Currency and Finance* London: Macmillan (1913) on the emergence of the key currency system.
23. See M.C. Kirby, *The Decline of British Economic Power Since 1870*, London: Allen & Unwin (1981), pp. 14–16 maintains the deformation of industrial structure was because of overseas investment.
24. J. Williamson, *The Failure of World Monetary Reform*, Sunbury-on-Thames, Middlesex: Nelson (1977) believes this to have been the main reason for the failure of the Bretton Woods 'adjustable peg'.
25. R. Cameron (ed.), *Banking and Economic Development: Some Lessons of History*, Oxford: Oxford University Press (1972).
26. L.B. Yeager, 'Fluctuating exchange rates in the nineteenth century: the experiences of Austria and Russia', in R.A. Mundell and A. Swoboda (eds), *Monetary Problems of the International Economy*, Chicago: Chicago University Press (1969).
27. ibid., and I. Drummond, 'The Russian gold standard 1897–1914', *Journal of Economic History*, **36** (1976), pp. 663–88.
28. A.G. Ford, 'Flexible exchange rates and Argentina 1885–1900', *Oxford Economic Papers*, **10** (1958), pp. 316–38.
29. *UK Statistical Abstract of Foreign Countries*.
30. T. Balderston, 'Inflation in Britain and Germany 1908–23: a comparative study', University of Manchester, History Department, mimeo.
31. Lewis, op. cit.,
32. R. Hawtrey, *A Century of Bank Rate*, London: Longmans Green (1938).
33. L. Pressnell, 'Gold reserves, banking reserves and the Baring crisis of

1890', in C.R. Whittesley and J.S.G. Wilson (eds), *Essays in Money and Banking*, Oxford (1968), p. 205.
34. A.G. Ford, 'Argentina and the Baring Crisis of 1890', *Oxford Economic Papers*, **8** (1956), p. 133.
35. Pressnell, loc. cit., p. 199.
36. S.B. Saul, *Studies in British Overseas Trade 1870–1914*, Liverpool:Liverpool University Press (1960) ch. 5.
37. A.G. Ford, 'Bank rate, the British balance of payments, and the burden of adjustment 1870–1914', *Oxford Economic Papers*, **16** (1964), pp. 24–39.
38. Sayers, op. cit., pp. 43–5.
39. M. de Cecco, *Gold and Empire*, Oxford: Blackwell (1974).
40. G. Clare, *A Money Market Primer*, London: Effingham Wilson (1891); and H.M. Neuberger and H.H. Stokes, 'The relationship between interest rates and gold flows under the gold standard, *Economica*, **46** (1979), pp. 261–79.
41. Bloomfield, op. cit.
42. C.A.E. Goodhart, *The Business of Banking 1891–1914*, London: Weidenfeld & Nicolson (1972), chs 14 and 15. See also W.E. Beach, *British International Gold Movements and Banking Policies 1881–1913*, Cambridge, Mass.: Harvard University Press (1935).
43. Sayers, op. cit.
44. Bloomfield, op. cit.
45. D.N. McCloskey and J.R. Zecher, 'How the gold standard worked, 1880–1913', in J. Frenkel and H.G. Johnson (eds), *The Monetary Theory of the Balance of Payments*, London: Allen Unwin (1975).
46. J.M. Keynes, *Treatise on Money*, London: Macmillan (1930), vol. II, pp. 306–7.
47. R. Dornbusch, *Open Economy Macroeconomics*, New York: Basic Books (1980) ch. 10.
48. For example in 1907. Ford (1964), loc. cit, p. 34.
49. P.R. Gregory, 'The Russian balance of payments, the gold standard and monetary policy: a historical example of foreign capital movements', *Journal of Economic History*, **39** (1979), pp. 379–99.

# 7 International Trade in the Twilight of Liberal Capitalism

Named after the two most destructive wars the world has so far seen, and dominated by the greatest economic depression, the period 1919 to 1939 has a poor reputation for achievements in the fields of economics and politics. What were later regarded as the mistakes then made greatly influenced policy-makers at the end of the second world war and subsequently. These were years of great change in institutions and in beliefs. The old international liberal economic order seemed to many to be unable to cope with the disruptions of the 'war to end all wars' and then with the Great Depression. Rival doctrines of Fascism and Communism both offered remedies which emphasised greater state control of economies. And all economies moved to some extent in that direction during these years both in national and international relations.

This chapter analyses the period by outlining the disruptions caused by the first world war and then by examining the subsequent tendency for international trade to decline. Whether this decline mattered much for well-being is considered in the third section on overall economic performance. Contemporaries felt that among the failures of the market economies the persistence of agricultural trade depression was prominent. The chapter therefore goes on to assess the relative importance of deficient demand from industrial countries, technical progress and the expansion of colonial supply as explanations for the agricultural distress. In the same section on primary products we discuss the impact of the oil trade on the coal exporters and some of the political elements of the young oil trade which were to continue into its middle age. Like the primary product sector manufactures also experienced substantial technical progress, and the differing extents to which countries took advantage through trade of the developments is described next. The 1930s saw international trade fall to one-third of its 1929 gold value as the Depression ushered in a host of controls and alliances intended to raise domestic prosperity regardless of the rest of the world. These policies and their impact are the central concern of the final section.

## The first world war and European economic relations

The tremendous death and destruction caused by the first world war marked such a break in the pattern of life that many people of the 1920s and later were encouraged to see the years before 1914 almost as a golden age which the war had destroyed. The war and its aftermath caused a structural maladjustment of the international economy, it was widely thought, and hence economic policy among the victorious powers was largely an attempt to return to pre-war conditions.[1] Others have seen the old order (variously defined) as on the verge of disintegration or radical change quite independently of the war and the associated political changes. Thus de Cecco argued the gold standard was no longer viable by 1914. Dangerfield asserted that the liberal consensus in England had disappeared, leaving the country on the verge of civil war over Ireland, while the rapid industrialisation of the United States was eliminating British and French trade supremacy and potentially causing balance of payments problems.[2] German industrialisation and trade expansion was another possibly destabilising influence on international economic relations before 1914.

Largely on the basis of German experience, Lenin formulated his hypothesis that the war was a part of the economic and political change of the years before 1914, and not an exogenous event.[3] Lenin represented war and territorial acquisition as the result of the influence of monopoly finance and the struggle of capitalists to avert the tendency for the rate of profit to fall. The state, according to Lenin, was necessarily the instrument of the predominant type of economic organisation. In their attempts to secure raw material supplies such as oil and iron ore, the monopolists enlisted the state to acquire territory by force. The German invasion of Belgium in 1914 was a manifestation of this tendency, as were most of the international conflicts in the previous four decades. In fact the part played by finance in the international disputes leading up to the war, and in the outbreak of war itself, was almost the reverse of that proposed by Lenin.[4] Between strong states there was hardly any evidence of finance causing friction or war. Rather finance was continually used as a pawn, as suggested in Chapter 5, and the employment by governments of commercial policy to enhance national security helped to create a climate in which war could break out.[5]

International economic relations were thoroughly disrupted by the war because of the central importance of Europe in trade before 1914. First the currencies of the European belligerents ceased to be reliable international media of exchange as panic seized traders and bankers. Then trade became further disturbed by the naval blockades and the sinking of merchants ships by submarines. International migration and investment slowed to a trickle as the former lending nations, Britain and France, became net debtors to pay for the war. Resources were reallocated to provide war materials and expand the armed services, to the benefit of heavy industry – steel, coal, shipbuilding and heavy engineering – while domestic agriculture in industrial Europe was encouraged to replace imported foods.[6]

The destruction of life probably had a greater economic impact than the destruction of capital; perhaps $8\frac{1}{2}$ million European military and 5 million civilian dead. Nevertheless, nature exceeded man's brutality with the influenza pandemic of 1918, estimated throughout the world to have killed as many as 20 million.[7]

The shock of the level of mortality was reinforced by far-reaching political changes. In 1917 the Russian empire finally collapsed with the strains of three years of total war, and, on the promise of 'Bread and Peace', Lenin and the Bolsheviks came to power. The existence of a major communist state directly or indirectly influenced economic policy in the non-communist world for the rest of the century. Fear of further communist revolutions encouraged expansionary monetary and fiscal policies in Britain after the war. Boom conditions were maintained during demobilisation to minimise the chances of insurrection. A corporatist political response to what was perceived as the communist threat, was the rise of Fascism in Europe, emphasising isolation from international trade and a much greater role for the state in economic life. The peripheral states of the Russian empire – Poland, Lithuania, Latvia, Estonia and Finland – all managed to gain independence with the breakdown of central Russian authority. (Poland was also helped by the dismemberment of Austria–Hungary and the German empire.)

The Turkish empire, known for much of the nineteenth century as 'the sick man of Europe' and requiring support against Russian expansion, lasted one year longer than the Russian. Under the peace settlement the former Turkish empire in the Middle East was divided between Britain and France as League of Nation mandate territories.[8] The search for oil in these territories became yet another source of international friction.

Neither the dismemberment of the Russian nor the Turkish empires were of great importance to international economic relations, but the treatment of the German and Austrian empires at the Versailles peace settlement certainly were. The treaty-makers of the victorious powers were determined not to repeat what they saw as the mistake of the Treaty of Vienna in 1815 at the end of the previous European war – the neglect of the aspiration for independence of national groups.[9] In avoiding this mistake and dividing Europe into a large number of small nation states they made a different error; they neglected the economic unity of European regions which they disrupted by creating the new states, hedged with barriers to trade and investment (see Map 7.1). Out of the Austro–Hungarian empire were created the states of Austria, Hungary and Czechoslovakia. Austria was in particular difficulties, her economy and railway network having developed as the centre of a great empire. Of her textile industry, the yarn spinning and finishing mills remained, but the weaving mills were in Czechoslovakia which protected her own infant spinning industry.[10] Though Austria's major coal deposits were given to Poland and Czechoslovakia, the Alpine ironworks that used the coal were still in Austria. Similarly Hungary's great flour mills lost their sources of supply and the market for their products.

The treatment of Germany was determined primarily by a desire for retribution. Alsace–Lorraine was returned to France, thereby increasing French exports of iron ore and increasing German imports, purely because of a definitional change. Under the terms of the Peace Treaty Germany ceded 13 per cent of her territory, and with it 10 per cent of her population. She lost three-quarters of her potential output of iron ore, one-third of her potential output of coal, and 15 per cent of the area under cultivation. In terms of income per head, the loss of the poor agricultural territories in the east may have made her richer.[11] Part of East Germany was given to the new Polish state. Poland was given access to the Baltic at Danzig by a corridor which separated East Prussia from the rest of Germany. This was to provide a proximate cause of the next world war.

Had the opportunity been taken to create a sounder world economic order at the same time, the multiplication of national boundaries might not have had adverse repercussions. But the universal insistence on unfettered national economic sovereignty, Arndt argues, together with a strong belief in the recuperative power of private enterprise and automatic economic forces, continued to choke international economic recovery in the interwar years.[12] Assertions such as Arndt's, with their policy implications of state central planning and import controls, give the debate on economic

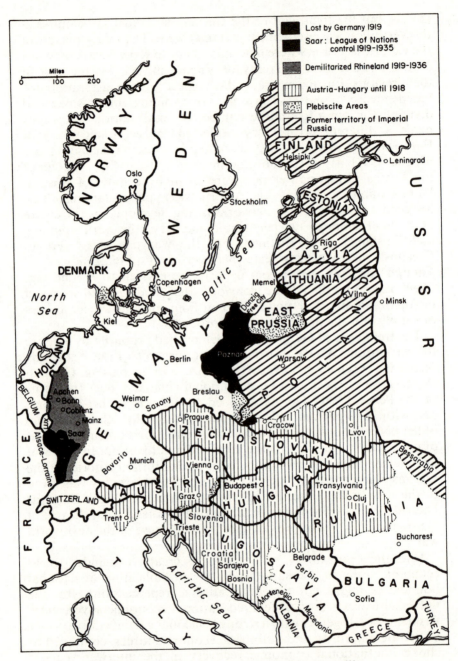

**Map 7.1**   European frontiers after Versailles

problems between the wars a much wider relevance. The apparently powerful growth of the centrally-planned Russian economy, largely independent of economic relations with the market economies throughout the 1920s and the Depression of the 1930s, added more grist to the anti-capitalist mill. After 1945 the prestige so acquired for central planning and control of international trade was a major stimulus to the import-substituting industrialisation policies of the less developed countries (see Chapter 10). The Royal Institute of International Affairs recognised the political importance of Arndt's interpretation and added an appendix to his book maintaining that it was the strangling of market forces by the post-war boundaries settlement, as described above, and war debts and reparations (see Chapter 8) that were the root cause of interwar economic difficulties.

## The decline of international trade

Purely because of the great increase in national boundaries in Europe, the volume of international trade and investment, at least relative to domestic economic activity, should have increased. In fact the pursuit of nationalist commercial policies reduced the volume both absolutely and relative to national income. The mean trade–income ratio for Great Britain, Italy, Sweden, Norway and Denmark fell from 43.7 per cent between 1905 and 1914, to 35.7 per cent between 1925 and 1934, and to 26.7 per cent between 1935 and 1944.[13] The American decline in the trade–income ratio began from a lower level and the rapid phase occurred earlier. From 12.4 per cent between 1915 and 1924, the mean American trade–income ratio reached 7.7 per cent between 1925 and 1934 and 6.8 per cent between 1935 and 1944.

Not all of this decline by any means was caused by commercial policies. The rest of the world was becoming more independent of Europe as a source of supply of manufactures and especially of some traditional types of export product such as cotton textiles.[14] The war had meant that overseas markets, cut off by submarine warfare and military demands on shipping space, were stimulated to start industries of their own. Partly under this influence the industrial development of overseas competition, especially in the United States and Japan, was given a boost. Even so, from the 1870s until the end of the 1920s, industrialisation had increased such countries' ability to export and to buy increased imports of manufactures.[15] The United States by now was anyway largely economically independent of the rest of the world, except in certain tropical products. Consequently the stagnation of the open

European economies while the United States grew in the 1920s inevitably lowered the world trade–income ratio.

The small increase in agricultural raw material trade was to a considerable extent because these materials competed against each other and because of the accidents of the locations of sources of supply and demand in relation to national borders. Rubber displaced leather in some uses, and wood pulp in the form of rayon competed against and partially displaced cotton. There was also the beginning of competition from minerals, with light metals replacing wood in many constructional jobs, petroleum-based compounds being made into nylon or synthetic rubber, and dyes and drugs being made from synthesised chemicals, rather than from the juices of plants.[16] Whether these technological changes expanded or contracted the demand for imports depended upon whether they brought into use materials plentifully available within the frontiers of the major manufacturing countries. The United States lacked natural rubber, but had the raw materials for synthetic rubber and wood. Britain depended almost entirely on imports of pulp and pulp wood as well as rubber. Hence Britain's propensity to import these items exceeded that of the United States in the interwar years (as Hanson argued also for the period 1880–1914). Similarly the growth of the Indian cotton textile industry did not cause a parallel increase in world raw cotton trade because raw cotton supplies were available in the country. The Japanese cotton industry though had similar consequences for international trade as had the rise of the European cotton industry.

Nevertheless it was on commercial policies that most contemporaries concentrated in their diagnosis of the decline of trade, the problems of the interwar years and the causes of the 1929 Depression.[17] Both Arndt and Lewis suggest however that tariffs and the decline of trade were an inevitable concommitant of industrialisation and that they need not have greatly harmed international economic relations under 'normal' conditions.[18] The paralysing restrictions of the interwar years were a consequence of instability and unemployment which had their root cause in domestic economic management. Indeed restrictive trade policies which were associated with attempts to restore domestic employment, such as Schacht's 'New Plan' in Germany of 1934, were amply justified in the absence of international reflation. The central problem of the international trade of Western Europe was that trade in manufactures was low because the industrial countries were buying too little from the primary producers and paying too low a price, Lewis maintains. Expansionary fiscal and monetary policies in industrial Europe, by implication, would have boosted demand and prices even with an unchanged level of protection.

Although the United States tariff policy has often been blamed for exacerbating interwar trade policies, the Fordney–McCumber duties of 1922 which raised tariff levels steeply did so on products which would not have been imported in large quantities anyway. For instance on sewing-machines a tariff of 15–30 per cent was imposed, yet under free trade the previous year exports totalled $7.3 million and imports, a mere $0.4 million. The development of the vast resources of the United States meant that the economy had little need to import manufactures from Europe, or primary commodities from the temperate zone exporters. Falkus suggests the US price elasticity of demand for imports and the price elasticity of demand for United States exports were sufficiently low for a reduction in tariff protection or a revaluation not to have had much of a beneficial effect on the American trade balance with Europe, and the associated accumulation of US short-term claims on Europe.[19] The relationship between the relevant elasticities which must be fulfilled if a revaluation of the currency is to diminish the current account surplus, is the Marshall–Lerner condition. If export and import supply are perfectly elastic then the condition is that the sum of the absolute value of the price elasticities of demand for imports and for exports should exceed one, a condition satisfied by the US and UK elasticities Falkus reports. They imply that a 10 per cent US revaluation would have reduced the current account surplus by 2.5 per cent. Because it operated only to increase American imports, not to contract American exports, a 10 per cent reduction in the United States tariff would have had a lesser effect.

Falkus believes the solution was for the European deficit nations to cut their imports from the United states by strict quantitative controls, further reducing international trade. Had they done this in the early and mid-1920s there might have been less economic dislocation in Europe at the end of the decade as a result of the withdrawal of American funds. An alternative policy similar to Lewis's recommendation, and consistent with Falkus's diagnosis, would have been the pursuit of a more expansionary US domestic economic policy. This would have drawn in imports, especially luxuries, probably more than proportionately to the growth of income, and eased the chronic imbalance in the international accounts with Europe.

As with the Fordney–McCumber duties so also the British deviation from free trade with the 1921 Safeguarding of Industry Act, and the continuation of the McKenna duties cannot be regarded as a major influence on the contraction of trade. These duties covered only a small number of commodities and the tariff rates were not prohibitively high. Dyestuffs imports were prohibited for ten years except under licence because of their relationship with explosive technology, the dominance of Germany, and the weakness of British industry in the field. Duties imposed on German imports in part-payment of war reparations averaged 26 per cent, yet by 1930 only 17 per cent of imports by value were dutiable. Protective tariffs, in contrast to low duties designed merely to earn revenue, did not affect more than 2 to 3 per cent of imports.[20] With low price elasticities for British trade, these tariffs would have had little effect.[21]

Contrary to the predictions of the simple factor price equalisation theorem, but consistent with the analysis of earlier chapters, declining trade was matched by diminished factor movements between the world wars.[22] The great intercontinental migrations before 1914 did not diminish the need for trade, so also the contraction of trade in the 1930s did not increase the need for factor mobility. Intercontinental migration declined to around 6.7 million in the 1920s little more than half the outflow of 1901–1910 (11.6 million), and to 1.9 million in the 1930s.[23] The United States recorded the greatest drop in immigration numbers in the 1920s at least partly because of the quota restrictions imposed in 1921 and 1924. During the 1930s migrant numbers did not reach the quota limits, because of very high American unemployment; there was actually net emigration from the United States between 1930 and 1934. Southern and Eastern Europe, as before 1914, continued to provide more than half the immigrants, though Britain remained the largest single source. Within Europe about 7 million people were transferred or fled as consequences of wars, persecutions and boundary changes. In many instances it became difficult to distinguish flights of refugees from normal migration.

In Chapter 5 we discussed Gould's hypothesis that potential migrant numbers in most countries were falling as a result of the relatively full diffusion of information about opportunities in traditional areas of emigration, and because of industrialisation in these places. This offers an alternative to the quota limitation view, which can then more fundamentally be interpreted as the political *response* to the ending of opportunities for extensive expansion in the United States, or to the instability of employment. Only if the quota limitation was an important *cause* of the reduction in migration could trade be expected to increase according to the factor price equalisation theorem.

## Economic performance in the interwar years

Despite the decline in international trade and factor mobility, the unemployment and the instability of the period, real incomes in most countries rose quite considerably so that those in employment (and sometimes the unemployed) had a higher living standard in 1938 than in 1913.

Higher living standards were based upon a variety of technical developments which were so important as to be comparable to the techniques of the first industrial revolution. The most fundamental developments were in new applications of electricity and the combustion engine which transformed mechanical motive power sources for transport, agriculture and industry. The basic innovations had been achieved several decades before the war. But continued progress after the war had, for example, halved the coal required to generate a given output of electricity in a decade and greatly widened the radius around primary energy sources within which electricity could be cheaply supplied, by the development of high voltage transmission.[24] More flexible transport of goods and people was made possible by the motor vehicle in the form of the lorry, the bus or the private car. Between 1919 and 1928 the number of motor vehicles, excluding lorries, registered in the United States tripled to over 21 million and the number registered in the United Kingdom rose fourfold to 1 million. In the three years before 1929, African motor car registration almost doubled to about 350 000 vehicles.

The consumption of other goods rose with the higher incomes created by the new technologies during the late 1920s. In 1927 there were $2\frac{1}{2}$ million wireless sets in Great Britain, 2 million in Germany and over $\frac{1}{4}$ million each in Japan and Australia. The diet of the West became lighter and more varied, with more fruit and dairy produce being consumed.[25] State education and insurance against unemployment, sickness and old age diverted a part of national income from investment to consumption. The changing age structure induced by falling population growth increased the proportion of the population that earned a living in the market, as did the greater female labour force participation. Hence family income and consumption rose by more than wages did.

The interwar growth experience varied greatly between nations. For the United States and the regions of recent European settlement the 1920s was a relatively prosperous time, and the 1930s a period of acute depression. Most of the former belligerent states of Europe took longer to recover from the war. Civil war with outside intervention continued in Russia until 1922, by which year Greece was again at war with Turkey. In Hungary and in Ireland also there was civil strife. France's rapid recovery from the war can be explained by an undervalued franc, an expansionary fiscal policy and the benefits of the Versailles Treaty. Table 7.1 shows the contrast in growth rate of France and the US between 1913 and 1925 on the one hand, and Germany, Hungary, the United Kingdom and the USSR on the other.

Taking the interwar years as a whole, Bairoch's national income figures for Europe imply that the poor reputation of the period is not justified by the growth performance compared with the pre-war decades.[26] In drawing conclusions from Table 7.1 it is important to be aware of the way in which the measurement of growth rates may be affected by the choice of initial or terminal years. If the terminal year for one country is a recession, whereas for the country with which it is being compared that terminal year is a boom, then,

**Table 7.1.** *Annual growth rates of real GNP per head, 1913–38 (percentages)*

|  | *1913–25* | *1925–38* | *1913–38* Bairoch's estimates | Maddison's estimates |
|---|---|---|---|---|
| France | 2.1 | 0.4 | 1.2 | 0.8 |
| Germany | − 0.5 | 3.6 | 1.6 | 1.1 |
| Hungary | − 0.1 | 3.8 | 1.8 | — |
| Italy | 0.7 | 1.1 | 0.9 | 1.0 |
| UK | − 0.2 | 1.5 | 0.7 | 0.7 |
| USSR | − 2.8 | 5.4 | 1.4 | 1.9 |
| Sweden | 0.8 | 2.8 | 1.9 | 1.3 |
| USA | 2.1 | 0.4 |  | 0.8 |
| Australia |  |  |  | − 0.1 |
| Canada |  |  |  | 0.0 |
| Japan |  |  |  | 2.6 |
| Argentina |  |  |  | 0.6[a] |
| India |  |  |  | 0.2[b] |
| Brazil |  |  |  | 2.0[c] |

*Source*: A. Maddison, *Economic Growth in Japan and the USSR* (1969); and P. Bairoch, 'Europe's gross national product 1800–1975', *Journal of European Economic History* (1976).

*Notes*: [a] C. Diaz Alejandro, *Essays in the Economic History of the Argentine Republic* (1970).

[b] A. Maddison, *Class Structure and Economic Growth*, Allen & Unwin (1971).

[c] A. Fishlow, 'Brazilian development in long term perspective', *American Economic Review* (1980).

even if the two economies had identical growth rates on trend, the second country would seem to have grown faster than the first. Similar considerations apply to the comparison of different periods for the same country.[27] Bearing in mind these caveats, France averaged a growth rate of 1.18 per cent per annum from 1900 to 1910 and a similar rate between 1913 and 1938. Germany improved on the 0.98 per cent per annum in that pre-war decade as did Britain (0.26 per cent per annum). However Maddison's earlier figures for European growth of real GNP per head are all lower than Bairoch's, except for the USSR and Italy, and more consistent with the traditional interpretation of the interwar years.[28] The United States showed the same growth rate as France between 1913 and 1938. The agricultural regions of recent European settlement did worse than Europe or the United States; in the case of Argentina only marginally so, but the Australian economy performed catastrophically, with 1938 income per head below the 1913 level.

Outside Europe and the European offshoots the growth experience was mixed. The Indian figure is extremely low but compared with the other mainly primary producers in Table 7.1, Australia and Canada, the performance is almost respectable.[29] Brazilian economic growth, according to Fishlow, almost rivalled Japan's at about 2 per cent per annum, despite the disastrous earnings of the major export crop, coffee (see below).[30] But the coffee sector accounted for little more than 10 per cent of national income, and the ratio of exports to GDP was only about 15 per cent. The growth in the Brazilian manufactures sector (and that of Indian manufactures) was based upon massive substitutions of domestic goods for imports.

Export performance (Table 7.2) varied between countries as much as income growth. Japan experienced the fastest increase in income of the economies listed and also the greatest expansion rate of exports. Japan and probably Malaya were exceptional in the interwar years in showing the characteristics of export-led growth; an increasingly open economy growing rapidly. Otherwise there seems to be an inverse association between growth and export orientation. Both Germany and Britain grew faster in the 1930s when world trade and their participation in it, was greatly reduced. The USSR is the most extreme example of this phenomenon. Most of Europe was less dependent on trade in 1938 than in 1913. Apart from Canada, the top six export growth economies had low incomes, and were all initially mainly exporters of primary products. The large economies of industrial Europe which exported manufactures, Britain, France and Germany, by contrast all had declines in their

**Table 7.2.** *Growth rates per annum in the dollar value of exports, 1913–37*

|  | Total | per head |  | Total | per head |
|---|---|---|---|---|---|
| Japan | 5.2 | 3.85 | USA | 1.4 | 0.25 |
| Malaya | 4.2 | n.a. | World | 1.4 |  |
| Canada | 3.7 | 2.2 | Belgium | 0.7 | 0.35 |
| Indonesia | 3.0 |  | Italy | 0.5 | − 0.15 |
| China (inc. | 2.4 |  | UK | 0.1 | − 0.3 |
| Manchuria) |  |  |  |  |  |
| Thailand | 2.4 |  | Germany | − 0.1 | − 0.6 |
| Australia | 2.2 | 0.7 | India (inc. | − 0.1 |  |
|  |  |  | Burma) |  |  |
| Netherlands | 1.8 | 0.4 | France | − 1.3 | − 1.3 |
| Argentina | 1.6 | − 0.7 | USR | − 12.4 | − 13.2 |

*Source*: Maddison (1969), op. cit., Table 10 and Appendix C1.

dollar values of exports per head. A cursory examination of the evidence then suggests the effects of trade in primary products in the interwar years was rather different from trade in manufactures. The experience contributed much to the later distrust of primary product trade as a means of economic development.

## Trade in primary products

The distrust was largely based upon misinterpretation. This section will show that though technical change did adversely affect some primary products, especially coal, the main problem was the low demand from the industrial countries because of their increasing agricultural protection and their high and persistent levels of unemployment. In the following section we demonstrate how the introduction of agricultural price support policies by the primary product exporters exacerbated their problems.

Within the category of primary products there were substantial differences in growth rates that reflected the buoyancies of the demands of the industrial economics. As Table 7.3 shows, the volume of total primary exports grew faster between 1913 and 1937 than did manufactures. Trade in cereals however actually declined while the value of trade in fuels doubled. The greater expansion of primary product export volume compared with manufactures export volume, with similar value increases, shows that the commodity terms of trade moved against primary products and in favour of manufactures between 1913 and 1937. The pattern

**Table 7.3** *The composition of world exports, 1913–37 (Index nos 1913 = 100)*

| Year | | All manufactures | All primary products | Cereals | All food | Agricultural raw materials | Fuel | All minerals |
|---|---|---|---|---|---|---|---|---|
| 1913 | | 100($6855m) | 100($12248m) | 100($1784m) | 100($5535m) | 100($4040m) | 100($919m) | 100($2673m) |
| 1929 | (a) | 129 | 138 | 107 | 136 | 128 | 173 | 155 |
| | (b) | 180 | 164 | 115 | 153 | 161 | 224 | 191 |
| 1937 | (a) | 107 | 129 | 98 | 133 | 111 | 171 | 151 |
| | (b) | 133 | 131 | 85 | 113 | 122 | 205 | 184 |

*Source*: P. Yates *Forty Years of Foreign Trade*, London: Allen & Unwin (1959).
Notes:
(*a*) = 1913 constant prices (*b*) = actual values, $m

of international specialisation was such that the open 'non-industrial' countries were dependent on the demand from industrial countries to which 85 per cent of their exports were sent in 1913, but the industrial countries depended on other industrial countries for two-thirds of their export demand.[31] A stagnation or decline in industrial countries therefore greatly hurt primary exporters. The industrial countries in the interwar years wanted to prevent a further decline in their agricultural sectors and introduced measures which reduced their primary imports. The move to agricultural protectionism was in part a response to the disruption of supplies caused by the war, which had shaken the assumptions on which the nineteenth-century pattern of food production was based. Britain started a state-aided sugar beet industry in 1925 and the same year Italy began her battle for self-sufficiency in wheat.

Technical progress in temperate zone agriculture further acted to worsen the terms of trade by increasing supply. The use of the tractor and the combine harvester expanded rapidly in late 1920s. In 1928 over 140 000 tractors were sold in the United States or exported.[32] Two-thirds of the 68 000 American combine harvesters in use in 1929 had been bought within a year. Argentinian annual purchases of these harvesters doubled to over 6000 between 1928 and 1929. Over 20 000 tractors were sold in Canada in 1928. Nevertheless, cereals exports were lower in 1937 than in 1913 and so a demand side explanation for the decline in the terms of trade is more plausible than a supply side explanation.

Colonial economic policy accentuated the increase in primary product export supply. The rapid expansion of cocoa, oil seeds and fats sales raised Africa's share of world exports. In the French African colonies the use of administrative measures to enforce the planting of coffee, cocoa and cotton was common, but not very successful.[33] Imperial tariff preference on exports to France offered another incentive to increase agricultural production for export as did the African peasants' need to earn the cash to pay taxes. French colonial public expenditure was also directed towards agricultural exports. By 1942 8455 million francs had been allocated by the central government for the development of the colonies (£ 113 million at the 1935 exchange rate) of which 1153 million francs represented unstarted projects.[34] Forty per cent went to French West Africa. Most projects were public works or agricultural processing, mainly peanut shelling.

Precisely what contribution the British African colonial governments made to export growth, other than through the maintenance of law and order, is still a matter of dispute, as is the desirability of that pattern of development.[35] The construction of a railway in Kano, Nigeria in 1911 allowed a groundnut boom which tripled the tonnage exported between 1916 and 1929. In 1920 the Empire Cotton Growing Corporation was established and cotton cultivation for export was encouraged in Uganda. In Kenya, Africans were denied access to land which would allow the profitable cultivation of coffee for export on the grounds that the fertility of the soil had to be protected to prevent the emergence of another US 'dustbowl'. This restriction also had the effect of keeping down the wages of labour employed by the white farmers. The Colonial Development Act of 1929, permitting the disbursement of up to £1 million a year, provided assistance mainly to small-scale transport and public health schemes, 60 per cent in the form of grants. A colonial policy which prevented colonial industrialisation by expecting colonies to maintain an 'open-door' tariff policy, despite Britain's abandonment of free trade, it has been argued, helped increase the supply of primary exports.

A decline in the commodity terms of trade because of increased supply in any case does not necessarily imply a loss from that increased supply, only a decrease in the share of the gains from trade. Objections to primary product exports, rehearsed in Chapter 4, are based upon other, usually erroneous, beliefs and often go hand-in-hand with a distrust of international economic relations altogether, linked to the fear of dependency. Birnberg and Resnick in this spirit formulated and estimated econometrically an ingenious model of colonial development based upon exports, to explain primary product exporters experience during the interwar years (and, in most cases, from the end of the nineteenth century).[36] The colonies for which they estimated their model were Ceylon, India, Nigeria, the Phillipines and Taiwan. They also included countries which were not formal colonies, Chile, Egypt, Thailand and Cuba because they believed that foreign influence, though exercised more subtly through international trade and finance, subjected these countries to the same internal and external forces which determined their pattern of development. The argument can of course be reversed; formal political control did not involve distortion of the colonial economies, as shown by the development of independent economies.

The structure of Birnberg and Resnick's model is given in Figure 7.1. The volume of colonial exports is determined by increases in accumulated real government expenditures oriented towards export growth, for example, the provision of transport facilities, irrigation, education and public health. Colonial export volumes depend also upon import prices, reflecting the costs of export

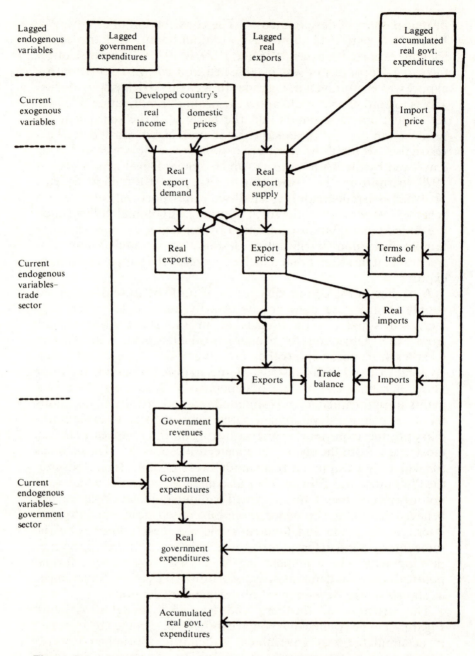

**Figure 7.1**  Arrow diagram of Birnberg and Resnick's model of colonial
development

*Source:* T.B. Birnberg and S.A. Resnick, *Colonial Development: An Econometric
Study*. New Haven and London: Yale University Press, (1975)

production (for example, capital goods, transport equipment, fertilisers). The demand for colonial real exports depends upon the real income, domestic prices and trade policies of the developed country to which the colony is tied. Export price is determined by the balancing of colonial export demand and supply. The colonies did not balance their commodity trade so colonial import demand is determined by exports, import prices and export prices. Nominal government revenues are generated from the direct and indirect taxation of real exports and nominal imports. Nominal government expenditures depend upon government current revenues and lagged expenditure.

Birnberg and Resnick obtained low supply and demand price elasticities for colonial export volumes. Thus changes in supply or demand conditions caused large changes in export prices. The average real income elasticity of demand for colonial exports was approximately equal to one in the long run implying, contrary to many assertions, that the growth prospects were reasonable. Birnberg and Resnick found a wide range of estimated coefficients of the response of exports to long-run accumulated government expenditure. They maintain that these values are as important for explaining the low export growth of India and Egypt as for the high export growth of Ceylon and Philippines. The response coefficients, they believe, take their particular values because of the uses to which government expenditure was put. Almost one half of the Indian budget was devoted to military expenditure and Egypt's government expenditures were largely allocated to paying interest on previous international loans. Hence the low productivity of these expenditures in total in boosting Indian and Egyptian exports. On the other hand a measure of the openness of the economy to trade, for example proxied by population size, is likely to alter this conclusion markedly. A very small proportion of Indian output was exported and so government expenditure mainly increased the ability to supply at home not abroad.

Two colonial characteristics, the developed country to which a colony was tied and the productivity of government expenditures directed towards development, are key explanations for the similarity and differences of the colonial development process, Birnberg and Resnick maintain. The economic losses from the first world war were greatest for the UK bloc. Their terms of trade deteriorated because of the post-war rise in import prices and the weakness of the British economy. Those linked to the United States and Ceylon suffered most from the Great Depression because of the decline in the demand for rubber. The inclusion of rubber-exporting Malaya in the sample would have shown, as Ceylon did show, that political links were not necessarily coterminous with economic links.

Probably the most adverse effects of primary product export oriented development in the interwar years were not experienced by any of Birnberg and Resnick's sample, but by Japan. The collapse of Japanese silk exports and the political repercussions in the 1930s eventually resounded around the world.[37] Raw silk was second only to rice in importance as an agricultural crop to Japan. Between 1914 and 1929 production had tripled to supply the American demand for silk stockings. With the collapse of the United States market, the export price of silk fell by 1932 to almost one quarter of the 1929 level. Farmers' cash incomes from this source were thereby greatly reduced just at the time the price of rice (the other peasent income earner) had fallen. The peasants attributed responsibility to the politicians and to the *zaibatsu* (the financial/industrial conglomerates of the modern sector). They communicated their discontent to the army (largely recruited from the agricultural sector), and thereby contributed to the overthrow of the liberal government and the transference of power to those who favoured military aggression. In 1931 Japan invaded Manchuria, and in 1937 the Sino–Japanese War broke out. Correctly understood, the Japanese experience occurred because of export concentration rather than the nature of the product itself. But like the late nineteenth century West Indian experience with sugar, Japanese specialisation served to underline the element of uncertainty and instability in international trade which the classical analysis of the gains from trade had neglected.

## The fuel trade

The secular impact of a weak demand for a primary product was felt strongly in the interwar years by one of the foremost industrial powers, Britain. In contrast to the pre-war increase of 4 per cent per annum, the demand for coal remained stable in the 1920s. Oil and hydroelectricity reduced the demand for coal and prevented rising industrial production boosting coal sales.[38] In 1913 the international trade in coal and coke had ranked third in importance to cotton and wheat. Even at the lower 1938 level, the coal trade was surpassed only by cotton. Britain, Germany and Belgium provided the import needs of the Netherlands, France, Italy, Austria, and others. The United States exported a little to Canada, and the European surplus, together with small amounts from Japan and Australia, supplied the needs of other continents.[39] These were however relatively small because coal was a motive force for industry, steamships and railways; the industrial countries therefore consumed 93 per cent of the world's coal output. Coal prices, especially British, rose relative to commodity prices after 1928, reinforcing the switch to oil for power and heat that was already occurring. This was one of the reasons for the concentration of long-term unemployment in the British coal industry.

Despite the decline in the coal trade, Table 7.3 shows a substantial increase in the fuel and mineral trade between 1913 and 1937 mainly because of oil. The politics of the oil trade in these years in some respects was a dummy-run for the era after the second world war, and in other respects laid the ground for the post-war trade. Though the trade in oil was small in 1919, it was regarded as a matter of extreme national importance because of the vital role oil had played in the war and because of the recognition by the British that the nineteenth-century technology which had made their indigenous deposits of coal so valuable was nearly obsolete.[40]

At the San Remo conference of April 1920 Britain and France divided the Arab territories of the Turkish empire between them as League of Nations mandates, a division which was to give them control over much of the Middle Eastern oil. Throughout 1919 British officials had been refusing to allow Standard of New York to resume its pre-war explorations in Palestine while Shell geologists were at work in Mesopotamia. The US State Department believed the British were planning to use their military presence in the Middle East to exclude US interests from promising oil areas. Between 1914 and 1920 US domestic demand had more than doubled and the tripling of crude oil prices since 1913 convinced many Americans their domestic fields would soon be exhausted. The Americans were therefore extremely concerned to find new sources of supply. Eventually an agreement was reached in 1922 which allowed the American firms to participate in the development of the Mesopotamian oil fields.

By then the oil crisis was almost over. In December 1922 a massive oil discovery was made in Venezuela near the shores of Lake Maracaibo which enabled Venezuela to replace Russia as the world's second largest producer in 1928. New reserves were discovered in the United States where, from 1922, more oil was produced than the refineries could handle.

## Commodity control schemes

The small number of companies engaged in the oil trade made the creation of a cartel or price agreements relatively easy. To end an international price war, in 1928 the companies signed the Achnacarry agreement. The weakening of primary product prices and the larger number of producers in other sectors increased the electoral advantage from governments' introducing price support or output control schemes during the 1920s. As a result, for much of the interwar years market prices were not necessarily market-clearing prices. Stocks were accumulating during the late 1920s and the impossbility of financing them any longer contributed to the onset and severity of the Depression after 1929. Stocks were only a problem for some commodities, however, such as sugar, wheat and coffee, for which there was a strong increase in supply relative to demand, because of technical progress or, in the case of coffee, because of a price support scheme.[41] The area planted with coffee in Columbia increased by one-third between 1926 and 1928 because of the Brazilian scheme.[42] The wheat fields of the United States and Canada especially were being mechanised, sugar costs in Cuba were reduced by the introduction of large-scale mills, and in Java by the use of improved varieties of sugar cane. For many products the evidence of imbalance pointed the other way – copper, tin, petrol, meat, dairy products and wool, for example.

One of the more successful attempts to raise primary products prices was the Stevenson rubber output restriction scheme of 1922. The success of the scheme in achieving its objective of increasing the dollar earnings of the British empire was a source of friction with the United States, whose motor industry was the major user and which had, by 1919, become extremely concerned about its supply of raw materials. During and immediately after the war the allied governments operated a number of control schemes for the benefit of consumers, which were the forerunners of post-war cartel agreements in copper, tin and rubber.[43] A rubber tree takes about seven years to reach a tappable size. Those trees planted in the boom of 1909–10 were coming into production in 1917, a time when the war was causing a shortage of shipping space. A voluntary scheme to restrict output to 75 per cent of plantation company capacity was introduced for twelve months. With the ending of the post-war boom of 1920 the price of rubber more than halved in four months, and voluntary restriction was again introduced. After a year the lack of support for the scheme's continuance led to a compulsory restriction scheme both for Malaya and Ceylon in 1922. By November 1925 the restriction scheme had raised the price of rubber to double the 1920 peak.

A Brazilian scheme in 1923 regulated the flow of coffee on to the market at a rate estimated to stabilise the price independently of good and bad crops. By 1925 the price had risen substantially, mainly because of market conditions rather than the valorisation scheme. Bumper crops occurred in 1927, 1928 and 1929, when finance for stockholding ceased to the available and prices collapsed. The Cuban government was encouraged to restrict sugar output in 1926 after a bumper harvest, and significantly influenced the price of sugar until 1929.

In contrast to rubber, coffee and sugar, governments played no part in the establishment of the international copper cartel in 1926. This was an attempt to gain monopoly profits for the American capital controlling about 75 per cent of world mine production and for the Union Minière du Haut-Katanga in the Belgian Congo, then supplying about 15 per cent of world exports. Within three years by rationing the European market and restricting output, the cartel doubled copper prices, until March 1929 when a buyers strike began. The cartel's price policy undoubtedly encouraged the development of the new copper fields in Northern Rhodesia. There had been a similar response to the British rubber control. Production in the Netherlands East Indies expanded to take advantage of the high prices, and the formation of a centralised buying pool by the large American consumers in 1926 forced down prices after that date, until the abandonment of the scheme in 1928.

Nevertheless control schemes continued to proliferate. The Canadian wheat pool in 1928, faced with a large crop, decided to hold back part of it to prevent prices falling unduly low, just as the Brazilians had done. These stocks were successfully financed but, though the 1929 crop was smaller, they were not reduced in August 1930. The collapse of wheat prices made further private finance impossible and the Canadian federal government took over the selling side of the pool's business. In the United States the fall in wheat prices in 1930 led to heavy government purchases, which kept Chicago prices above the world level, and eliminated exports. Direct acreage control was introduced by the Roosevelt administration in 1933 to keep prices up by restricting output. This was achieved so successfully that the drought in 1934 turned the USA into a net importer of wheat for the first time in its history.

Perhaps the most interesting commodity control scheme of the 1930s was for tin. Certainly it had more claimed for it than most such schemes. 'If such machinery had existed in 1929 there would have been no major slump, much higher living standards all round, and no Second World War.'[44] The machinery in question was the tin buffer stock of 1934, financed by the producer governments, to be released on to the market when demand was high and accumulated when it was low, holding the price in the market on its long-term trend or level. If this could have been successfully done the costs of buying would have been covered by the earnings from selling at an earlier or later period, assuming the correct price had been chosen as the long-term price, and buyers would have been better off because of the reduction in fluctuations. Unfortunately the size of the buffer stock was too small.[45] When prices rose in 1935 the stock was released and the scheme ended. In mid-1938, with falling prices, a stock was again accumulated and held until the war scramble for raw materials the following year when the sale of all the stock was quite insufficient to have any effect on prices.

The commodity control schemes of the 1920s generally suffered from an inability to control total output. They therefore tended to raise world output by temporarily raising particular commodity prices and to introduce more volatility into prices when the schemes collapsed. This often made the forming of informed expectations about future prices very difficult and exacerbated speculation, of which the most extreme example occurred outside the commodity markets on the Wall Street stock exchange in 1929.[46]

## Trade in manufactures

As did primary products, some sectors of manufactures trade showed a rapid growth, and others declined. Those countries with a comparative advantage in the dynamic sectors benefitted accordingly. The United States showed the greatest expansion in competitiveness between 1913 and 1929, in the growth sectors of machinery, transport equipment and chemicals.[47] (See Table 7.4.) In 1913 a far higher proportion of manufactured exports of the United States (over 40 per cent) and of Germany (about 35 per cent) than of other industrial countries consisted of the 'expanding' commodity groups. This reflected to a large extent the more dynamic character of the economies of these two countries and their higher technical level. At the other extreme, Japan had only 5 per cent of her manufactured exports in the 'expanding' groups in 1913.

Turning to the main markets for imported manufactures, in Canada the rise of the United States' market share was accounted for by America's predominant position as a supplier of the three growth sectors. The rise in Canada's share of the American import market was almost wholly in newsprint and non-ferrous metals. The fall in Britain's share of that market was mainly in textiles, but the fall in the German share was spread across all groups, reflecting US import substitution. In the British import market the rise of the

**Table 7.4** *Changes in volume of export of manufactures, 1913–37 ($ billion, constant prices)*

| | UK | France | Germany | Other Western Europe | Canada | US | India | Japan | Total |
|---|---|---|---|---|---|---|---|---|---|
| 1913 exports | 1.96 | 0.79 | 1.73 | 0.83 | 0.04 | 0.85 | 0.15 | 0.15 | 6.50 |
| Change to 1929 attributable to: | | | | | | | | | |
| market growth | + 0.74 | + 0.30 | + 0.65 | + 0.31 | + 0.02 | + 0.32 | 0.06 | + 0.06 | + 2.44 |
| diversification | − 0.01 | − 0.03 | − 0.09 | − 0.08 | + 0.02 | + 0.26 | − 0.04 | − 0.02 | — |
| competitiveness | − 0.86 | − 0.01 | − 0.43 | + 0.26 | + 0.24 | + 0.65 | + 0.03 | + 0.14 | — |
| Total | − 0.14 | + 0.25 | + 0.12 | + 0.49 | + 0.27 | + 1.22 | + 0.05 | + 0.18 | + 2.44 |
| 1929 exports (values at 1913 prices) | 1.82 | 1.04 | 1.85 | 1.32 | 0.31 | 2.07 | 0.20 | 0.33 | 8.94 |
| 1929 exports (values at 1955 prices) | 5.18 | 2.76 | 4.76 | 3.95 | 0.93 | 5.09 | 0.42 | 0.76 | 23.84 |
| market growth | − 0.86 | − 0.46 | − 0.79 | − 0.65 | − 0.15 | − 0.84 | − 0.01 | − 0.13 | − 3.94 |
| diversification | + 0.21 | − 0.08 | − 0.10 | − 0.05 | 0 | − 0.04 | + 0.02 | + 0.06 | — |
| competitiveness | − 0.50 | − 1.07 | − 0.63 | + 0.62 | + 0.38 | − 0.13 | + 0.10 | + 1.20 | — |
| Total | − 1.14 | − 1.61 | − 1.52 | − 0.08 | + 0.23 | − 1.02 | + 0.05 | + 1.13 | − 3.94 |
| 1937 exports | 4.03 | 1.15 | 3.24 | 3.87 | 1.16 | 4.08 | 0.48 | 1.89 | 19.9 |

*Source:* A. Maizels, *Industrial Growth and World Trade* (1963).

Canadian share was, as in the United States, due to the greater sales of resource-based manufactures, and the sharp fall in the French share was mainly in textiles, this last being associated with the devaluation of sterling in 1931 and the Import Duties Act of 1932. France's traditional exports of silk fabrics were facing a secular decline because of competition from the textiles, especially cotton and rayon (developed in the 1930s particularly by Germany, Italy and Japan to lessen dependence on imported raw cotton). A second reason for the French decline was the overvaluation of the france during the 1930s.

Before the first world war Britain had been the major supplier of manufactured goods to Japan. Many of the Japanese warships that destroyed the Russian fleet at Port Arthur in 1905 had been built on the Tyne, and over half of Japanese imports of manufactures in 1913 came from Britain. By 1929 this component had fallen to one-quarter, the decline taken up by American exports. A similar decline occurred in the British share of manufactures exported to the Southern Dominions, Australia, New Zealand and South Africa, from three-quarters in 1913 to three-fifths in 1929, though Imperial Preferences may have reduced this decline during the 1930s (see below). The British share in the Indian market for imported manufactures showed a similar pattern during the interwar period, offering evidence against the view that India was a captive market for British goods. Britain did not use her influence over the Indian Tariff Board which was implementing a policy of selective protection, without any preferences for British goods during the 1920s and granting very few during the 1930s.[48] Britain supplied 80 per cent of India's imports of manufactures in 1913, a similar proportion to that in the politically autonomous Southern Dominions. The composition of these exports was different however, the greater part supplied to India being textiles. The growth of factory production of cotton textiles in India in the interwar years reduced the level of imports, mainly to Britain's loss. By 1937 British textile exports to India were only one-seventh of their 1913 volume.

## Changes in competitiveness

The lower level of British exports in 1929 than in 1913 was almost entirely due to the loss of market share (Table 7.4) conventionally attributed mainly to the overvaluation of sterling. Canada and the smaller industrial countries of Western Europe made significant gains in the share of individual markets between 1913 and 1929, and this trend continued into the 1930s. By 1934 the yen had been devalued to 36 per cent of its 1929 gold parity compared with a devaluation to 60–62 per cent of parity for Britain and the US. Hence Japan achieved a major increase in her market share by 1937.[49] The main losers in 'competitiveness' were France, (the franc was overvalued), Britain and Germany, which suffered from Britain's tariff as well as from overvaluation during the 1930s.

Japanese international competitiveness in textiles was mitigated during the 1920s by the Japanese ability to finance raw material imports largely from the proceeds of growing sales of raw silk to the United States, and by drawing upon foreign currency holdings which had accumulated during the first world war. Late in the decade the price of raw silk collapsed in the US, and Japanese currency holdings were exhausted. Japan therefore became increasingly dependent upon the export of manufactured goods. The new competition was sharpened by the depreciation of the yen. The main adverse element in this competition was its erraticness which could not be offset by price adjustment in the short run. Even so there may have been beneficial secondary effects. Between 1929 and 1935, in the Central American republics of the Dominican Republic, Haiti and Honduras there was a change from the United States or Britain to Japan as the principal supplier of cotton piece goods, the Japanese share of imports in Haiti rising from 0.1 to 17.7 per cent.[50] Although trade in general was declining and the quantity of most manufactured goods imported into these countries declined also, the low Japanese prices stimulated a rise in cotton piece good imports. By raising the demand for raw cotton, the pressure on raw material prices was reduced, and the income of primary producers, and their demand for manufactured imports, was enhanced.

By and large, however, it was more difficult during the 1930s for older industrial countries to profit from their sales to primary producing regions from industrial expansion elsewhere, and previous gains were often wiped out. The United Kingdom was particularly dependent on selling manufactures to countries which depended on exporting primary products to all parts of the world. The collapse of international lending and multilateral trade greatly reduced this option.

## Multinational companies and trade in manufactures

Large companies which formerly exported to foreign markets were often encouraged to invest in them during the interwar years by tariff policies such as India's. One of the largest of these companies was Unilever, a manufacturer of detergents and edible oils. The deterrent to direct investment in most colonies was the limited size of the market, but in India the lack of local competition with imports deterred Unilever from the expense until the 1920s. Sales and profits slumped between 1921 and 1922 because of the post-war depression, but William Lever wrongly attributed his firm's misfortunes to Gandhi's call for a boycott of imports from Britain.[51] So in 1922 Lever acquired a controlling interest in two local companies. The boycott ceased and, because soap was not tariff protected, soap imports rose to an all-time peak in 1928. Production in Unilever's Calcutta factory remained small, limited to local not Unilever brands. The boycott revived during the slump, soap received a 25 per cent tariff in 1931, and sales of imported soap almost halved between 1929 and 1932. Early in 1933, these events persuaded Unilever to build a substantial factory in Bombay, alongside another factory making *ghee* substitute, which had been begun the year before on the same grounds – that the established market would otherwise be lost.

American exports in the dynamic sector of transport equipment were particularly prone to be replaced by multinational production abroad. The motor industry was the basis of two of the largest US multinationals, General Motors and Ford. In the first quarter of the twentieth century the US motor industry built up a massive technological lead over the European industries, at least as judged by output per man, despite the invention of the petrol-driven motor vehicle in Europe in the 1860s and 1870s. General Motors and Ford, therefore, had an established advantage over their European rivals when they began production overseas. As with Unilever's decision to produce in the Indian market, it was tariff barriers that were important in setting up production plants rather than exporting, although Ford produced in Britain before tariff protection.[52]

The bulkiness of motor vehicles had always justified assembly plants overseas when the market was large enough, because it was so much cheaper to ship the vehicles 'completely knocked down'. By the end of 1926 General Motors had invested $30 million in plant, equipment inventories and working capital (overseas sales were $100 million), and the following year increased this sum by the acquistion of Opel, which already had 40 per cent of the German market. General Motors were more sensitive to the trend of economic nationalism, attempting to acquire established national names as facades for their products. This they had already done in Britain with the purchase of Vauxhall and Bedford. In Australia they formed an alliance with the indigenous body-building firm, Holden. Even in India General Motors (and Ford) established subsidiaries to get round the tariff barrier and to receive advantages in Indian government orders, when to the chagrin of the British Board of Trade, Morris, the largest British motor manufacturer, declined to do so.[53]

Ford was a larger investor overseas than General Motors initially. By 1923 Ford's assets in foreign plants totalled almost $50 million, but these assests were almost entirely paid for from overseas profits. American multinational motor vehicle production abroad in 1928 at 309000 in total was greater than the output of any single national motor industry outside the United States.

Not all states that wanted to use their technology for import substitution were favourably inclined to the permanent presence of American firms. Ford's exports to the USSR were sufficient for the company to boast in 1927 that 85 per cent of the tracks and tractors in the country were Ford's.[54] In 1929 Ford contracted to supply the technology for a factory at Nizhni Novgorod (Gorki) to produce 100 000 units a years in return for a commitment by the Russian government to buy a total of 72 000 Ford units on a four-year schedule. What happened to this contract provides an insight into why multinationals have been unwilling to take out licensing agreements in the face of economic nationalism. Ford lost over $\frac{1}{2}$ million on the $18 million sales and Ford officers thought that the products were below standard. Sub-standard Ford products could have adversely affected sales elsewhere had the Soviet economy been less closed to international relations.

## Commercial policy and the Depression of 1929

Ultimately far more important than multinational production for the trade in manufactures were the 'beggar-my-neighbour' commercial policies of the 1930s that contracted income and employment. The decline in agricultural prices during the 1920s in the United States prompted Hoover, during his presidential campaign of 1928, to promise to raise tariffs to help farmers. Political lobbying extended the promised Smoot–Hawley Tariff Act of 1930 to non-agricultural products. Although some countries had already raised tariffs, the passage of the Act caused a wave of foreign protest, a boycott by Switzerland, and tariff reprisals. The timing of the Act was most unfortunate. In the middle of a world depression it exported unemployment, but the size of the effect, Kindleberger thought, was not great.[55] What mattered, he believed, was that the Act signalled the United States was not taking on the leadership of the world economy that her economic importance required.

Between 1929 and 1931 agricultural prices fell by about one half. Wheat export prices fell by more in the twelve months after December 1929.[56] With specific duties in force, that is duties fixed in money terms, the actual tariff percentage on agricultural products rose as a result of the price fall. Nominal tariff levels and trade restrictions increased markedly, raising trade barriers even higher. Just as the protectionist Meline Tariff of 1892 reversed the increase in agricultural imports of the 1870s and 1880s, so the French government again took drastic action in 1931 when the proportion of agricultural imports rose above 25–30 per cent of the total, threatening the agricultural interests. From 22.8 per cent in 1928–30 agricultural imports as a proportion of the total rose to 34.5 per cent in 1930–1 and, after the introduction of quotas, declined to 25.3 per cent in 1937.[57]

Quotas were preferred to tariffs because they gave better control of imports in the face of the massive price declines. Though they better protected internal economic activity, the main reason for the introduction of quotas (their secondary use as an instrument for bargaining with other states) was less satisfactory.[58] Whereas in a tariff war between two countries the welfare of the country initiating the war may be improved in the end, this does not happen in a quota war.[59] The successive retaliations to the other country's quota limitations leads asymptotically to the complete elimination of all trade between the two states. Italy was the first important country to use quotas as reprisals, on French exports of wines, liquors, perfumes and soaps.[60] The French retaliated in July 1932 with limitations on Italian exports of fruit and vegetables. The Italians replied with restrictions on their imports of French cars and clothing. In June 1933 the French reduced the Italian meat quotas. A week later French cotton, yarn, lace, tools, machinery and hides exports to Italy were further limited.

The vast amount of administration involved in the allocation of quotas at first required the delegation of powers to distribute import licences. In Greece the Chambers of Commerce distributed them, while in France 'Inter-Professional Committees' of traders and producers were consulted about the distribution. Some co-operation facilitated the formation of import monopolies, which in order to maximise profits could sometimes find it advantageous to import less than the full quota, limiting trade even further.[61] In Germany imports were restricted by tariff increases, quotas and exchange control, introduced originally to prevent to flight of capital. The amount of foreign exchange which importers could buy was reduced by an amount deemed to correspond to the decrease in foreign prices and domestic incomes since 1931. Regional Chambers of Commerce were consulted about currency quotas by the Ministry of Finance acting for the Reichsbank.

Europe had been divided into two main trading blocs; the industrial countries of Europe trading with each other, and industrial Europe trading with the agrarian 'border Europe'.[62] Britain's departure from the gold standard (while France, Switzerland, Netherlands, Italy and Belgium did not devalue) and Britain's new tariff barrier of 1931/2, reduced her usefulness as a market in the first bloc. The British emergency Tariff Act of 1931 allowed *ad valorem* duties of up to 100 per cent. The Import Duties Act of 1932 did not apply to empire goods at that time nor to important industrial raw materials or food. Otherwise a general 10 per cent tariff was imposed and an Import Duties Advisory Committee was appointed to suggest alterations.[63] The recommendations of the Committee, in contrast to US tariff-making bodies, do not seem to have been greatly influenced by the lobbying of interested industrial groups.[64] After alterations agreed to at the Empire Conference at Ottawa, about one-quarter of imports remained duty free (though many were restricted by other methods), one-half payed 10–20 per cent, 8 per cent payed over 20 per cent, and the remainder payed the old duties of the 1920s.

Similarly drastic Italian and Czech protection reduced the viability of these countries as markets in the first bloc. Among the remaining states industrial exports, which were still liable to moderate duties, kept up fairly well. Any substantial agricultural exports of these countries had already been largely eliminated by 1931. The connections between Central Europe (Germany, Austria and Czechoslovakia) and 'Border Europe' were threatened by the central agricultural protectionism and by the industrial protectionism of eastern and south-eastern Europe and Spain. The trade of northern and north-eastern countries and Holland with Germany and Britain, based mainly upon the exchange of timber and timber products, dairy produce and meat for industrial products, was well maintaned up to 1931, duties on these articles remaining moderate. Trade between the Mediterranean border states and industrial Europe (England, Germany and France) also remained relatively unaffected because the major export, fruit, was less badly hit by duties.

The worst happened between 1932 and 1935 when quota and tariff barriers escalated. By 1935 world trade had fallen to one-third of the 1929 level in gold dollars, and even measured in paper pounds trade had lost 45 per cent of the 1929 value.[65] The proposals for tariff reductions at the Economic Conference at Geneva in 1930 had failed because the bilateral negotiations violated the 'most favoured nation clause' which most nations had in their commercial treaties, (stating that any tariff reduction granted to one state should equally be granted to all others). The proposed Austro–German customs union failed because of French and Italian objections, based nominally on this clause but really motivated by political considerations (as was the proposal). As a result previous commercial treaties were renounced and exchange control and bilateral agreements replaced free market trade. The decline of international monetary relations meant that barter agreements became a major means of conducting trade; in December 1932, for example, Hungary agreed to exchange eggs and pigs for Czech coal.

The general increase of trade restrictions after 1929 could have been beneficial: by cutting imports they may have arrested the secondary decline in domestic income and employment and so prevented production falling in the same proportion as exports.[66] But a test of this hypothesis by modelling the interaction of foreign trade and national income among the European economies, refuted it.[67] The effects of lower levels of trade on income generally, swamped the tendency of national policies to stimulate domestic economic activity. This conclusion was strengthened when industrial and agricultural European economies were compared, and when the effects of alternative policy measures were considered.

*After the deluge*

Those European nations with empires, Britain, France and Holland, could respond to these policies of trade destruction by tightening their commercial links with their overseas territories, as they had already been doing. French exports to her empire had risen from 12.4 per cent of the total in 1913 to 15.2 per cent in 1928–30. The British political move towards closer economic ties with the empire can be dated to 1917 when the United Kingdom committed herself to encourage empire settlement and to introduce preferential tariffs. Significantly, the initiative for the policy came from the Prime Minister of New Zealand and subsequent moves towards closer union also originated from the Dominions. A Canadian lead of 1929 resulted in the Imperial Economic Conference the following year, which in turn led to the Ottawa Conference of 1932.[68] The conferees extended to each other reciprocal tariff preferences intended to increase trade between empire countries, and proclaimed that the consequent increase in empire purchasing power would also expand the trade of the rest of the world.

Throughout the interwar period the empire drew a decreasing proportion of its imports from Britain. However in 1932–5 the proportion was slightly higher than might be expected from the trend. If this was the result of Ottawa then the agreements raised British exports by 3.5 per cent in 1933 and by 5.4 per cent in 1937. With a multiplier of two, output and employment might have been $\frac{1}{2}$ and 1 per cent higher in the two years. British imports by a similar method were 7.2 and 10.3 per cent higher in 1933 and 1937 as a consequence.[69] Much of the trade diversion did not involve a loss of income or employment to foreign countries because when empire countries sold more primary products to Britain, they sold less in foreign markets, allowing room for import substitution to raise foreign income and employment. In any case empire imports of foreign goods rose by three-quarters in value terms in 1933–7, and British foreign imports increased by a half.

In view of the measures taken to reinforce empire economic ties in the face of increasing economic nationalism in the 1930s, it is not surprising to find the share of trade and investment of imperial countries in their colonies was higher than the share of the country in all LDC trade and investment by 1938. The foreign direct investment share was considerably higher than the trade ratios. In Madagascar, Indo-China and British Crown colonies, foreign investment in extractive industries was banned. The investor countries, Britain and France, also imposed restrictions on direct investment in non-associated countries. In British, American, Belgian and Dutch colonial territories, few outright limitations were levied upon investment from third countries in non-extractive sectors.[70] After decolonisation in 1967, compared with 1938, the British share in foreign direct investment in ex-dependencies actually increased, while in French former colonies, the French share fell slightly. Either in the British case there was no imperial distortion of investment during the 1930s, or influence was later retained through neo-colonialism, or inertia, or exchange controls precluded a search for new opportunities by the investors of the former imperial power, who instead ploughed back their retained profits.

For those countries, such as Argentina and Denmark, outside the British empire to whom Britain was an important market, trade agreements had to be reached as best they could.[71] Agricultural 'Border Europe' was drawn further into the German sphere of influence to form another quasi-imperial grouping. Under Schacht's 'New Plan' of 1934, twenty-five supervisory centres allocated foreign exchange for import transactions approved by the state. Bilateral clearing agreements were concluded especially with Central Europe and South America in which German purchases were credited against offset purchases by foreigners in German markets. By the Spring of 1938 more than half of Germany's foreign trade was carried on through these agreements.

If Germany used her market power to exploit agrarian Border Europe through these arrangements, her terms of trade should have risen; instead they fell. Neal argues this monopoly/monopsony framework is not appropriate in the conditions of widespread unemployment of Germany and south-eastern Europe.[72] The foreign goods Germany brough from Europe were 20–40 per cent above world market prices, and on average Germany paid more for the same commodity from a clearing agreement country. Neither did Germany secure higher prices for her exports; even when she reached full employment German purchasing agencies offset the effects of higher prices by offering Yugoslavia very generous deferred purchase terms with almost negligible down-payments. It is possible that future economic or political gains were being purchased at the expense of present gains, but then this investment was undertaken for at least five years and the monopoly position never exploited. Most probably it was Germany's desire to get foreign exchange by any means possible that was responsible for these generous arrangements. Effectively, a two-tier exchange rate was introduced, with German ASKI (Auslander-SonderKonten für Inlandszuklungen) marks received by an exporter to Germany being sold to an importer from Germany at a discount, so that although the overvalued gold mark was still used to make payment on foreign debt, the ASKI mark floated in these 'private organisation agreements'.

More important for the states of south-eastern Europe were the clearing agreements. Germans exported little but imported much so that Germany accumulated large debts in blocked marks in these countries, which exporters tried to sell in their own countries. If the central bank supported the exchange rate agreed upon in the bilateral agreement, they paid out domestic currency at that rate for claims on blocked marks. In one sense this was an extension of credit to Germany and raised the domestic price level or employment (the Hungarian, Greek and Bulgarian cases). Alternatively, the central bank could refuse to buy blocked marks from exporters until they received a request for the marks from domestic importers of German goods (as in Romania and Yugoslavia), effectively a devaluation of the mark or a revaluation of the domestic currency which had no expansionary effects.

The increasing politicisation of international trade associated with these bilateral agreements was matched by the first important collective use of trade sanctions as a political weapon during the 1930s. On 11 October 1935 fifty of the fifty-four League of Nations members agreed to apply sanctions against Italy for her invasion of Ethiopia.[73] The members stopped arms sales to Italy but not to Ethiopia, cut off credit to the Italian government and to Italian businesses, prohibited imports from Italy and placed an embargo on the export to Italy of strategic raw materials (including rubber, tin, aluminium and manganese) which were substantially controlled by the boycotting states. Within a few months the Italian gold reserves were dangerously low and the lire had to be devalued. Italian foreign trade was greatly reduced. The measures were insufficient to prevent the conquest of Ethiopia however and more effective sanctions such as embargoes on food, coal, steel and oil, and refusal of Italian access to the Suez Canal, were rejected. Two months after Mussolini's announcement of victory, sanctions were abandoned in July 1936 at the initiative of the British. The British wished to secure Italian support in resisting Germany in Europe, following Hitler's remilitarisation of the Rhineland in 1936.

The sanctions were not allowed to achieve the success of the commercially motivated trade quotas because political stability in Europe was judged to be of overriding importance. The history of Europe in the interwar period suggests that the commercial policies pursued were equally unconducive to political stability, encouraging the building of 'siege economies' which made easier restrictions on personal freedom and the waging of aggressive wars. In 1944 Hayek wrote that 'the experience of most continental countries has taught thoughtful people to regard foreign exchange control as the decisive advance on the path to totalitarianism and the suppression of individual liberty.'[74]

## Summary and conclusion

Whether or not the pre-1914 trading system would have been maintained if there had been no world war, it is fairly certain that the peace settlement exacerbated already existing problems of international economic relations by greatly extending the lengths of national boundaries in Europe. The increasing self-sufficiency of the United States in the products that Europe could supply was an independent problem which required an adjustment in European trading relations and those of the temperate zone primary commodity exporters outside Europe and the United States, which was not made. Had America pursued more expansionary monetary or fiscal policies, or revalued or reduced tariffs, the necessity for such adjustment would have been greatly reduced.

The poor economic reputation of the interwar years is due to the instability, the unemployment and the decline of trade. For many countries that reputation is not justified on the grounds of increased real incomes per head which compared favourably with the pre-war experience. This observation casts doubt upon the role of inter-national trade and factor flows in generating higher incomes. At the most it can only be said that incomes would have been higher if trade had been less restricted, and even the value of this proposition is called into question by the Depression after 1929 which, by suddenly cutting off foreign markets, caused great hardship and an increase in political extremism.

Japan suffered as much as most countries from the trade effects of the Depression yet Japanese exports grew faster than national income which in turn grew faster than those of other countries. During the 1930s this export growth was associated with a devaluation of the yen relative to other currencies and so the growth was to some extent at the expense of employment in other countries, a tendency reinforced by the virtual disappearance of multilateral trade.

The one area in which the by now massive US economy was not self-sufficient was in certain raw materials. About the time of the war the US ceased to be a net exporter of natural resources as judged by the resource content of its trade, and became a net importer. The rapid growth of the US motor industry was responsible for the oil crisis of the early 1920s and for providing the opportunity for the rubber output restriction scheme to push up rubber prices markedly. Other primary commodities, especially cereals were not so favoured and countries, such as Canada, to whom wheat exports were important, accordingly stagnated. A major reason for the poor performance of the international trade in food was the increase in agricultural protection by the industrial countries, unwilling to accept the structural readjustments required by an expanding international division of labour. This protection became very serious from 1930 and helped to increase to severity of the depression. The use of quotas, rather than tariffs, was especially destructive of trade once quotas became instruments of economic warfare and bargain-ing.

The weakness of some primary commodity prices encouraged the establishment of a number of schemes to raise prices. Though successful for a few years these schemes usually stimulated the expansion of supply elsewhere and the accumulation of stocks during the 1920s. Consequently, when the stocks could no longer be financed during the Depression, the fall in prices and incomes of the primary commodity exporters was the more acute. During the 1930s more control schemes were tried, usually with government support, but only the prices of tin, tea and rubber were decisively influenced.

The volume of trade in manufactured goods declined by more than the volume of primary products partly because the location of such production was more 'foot loose' in response to barriers to trade. Companies which formerly exported to a large market often preferred to manufacture there rather than be excluded by tariffs and exchange controls. Also the industrialisation of lower income countries such as India and Brazil led to import substitution, which was not offset in the 1930s by the increased imports generated by higher incomes. The biggest change in manufactures trade compared with the pre-war era was the removal of the German challenge to British supremacy. However by the end of the 1920s the United States was exporting more manufactures than Britain, largely by virtue of her comparative advantage in the rapidly growing sectors of chemicals, machinery and transport equipment, while the British industrial structure heavily weighted towards textiles, suffered from the import-substitution and international competition of the newly industrialising countries.

The rise in trade barriers during the Depression after 1929 prompted a tightening of economic ties within empires and of bilateral agreements between other countries. The effect of the 1932 Ottawa agreement was probably temporarily to halt the decline in Britain's share of the Dominion markets, and to raise Britain's imports from the empire possibly by as much as 10 per cent of total imports in 1937. Though creating difficulties with outsiders, especially the Americans, the net result of the agreement was probably expansionary for the world as a whole, because the higher British import of primary products meant the empire countries exported less than they would have otherwise done to foreign markets, thereby allowing room for import-substitution to raise foreign incomes and employment. Germany established bilateral trading agreements with Central Europe and South America which were very important to those economies. The effects of the agreements depended on the central bank policy of the dependent states; some countries, notably Hungary, Greece and Bulgaria, benefitted substantially from the boost to aggregate demand from their exports, while others, Romania and Yugoslavia, did not gain because their banks did not engage in monetary expansion.

Just as international economic policy was used to bolster the system of alliances in Europe before 1914 and thereby contributed to the increase in tensions that eventually resulted in war, so the abandonment of the market for government controlled international economic relations in the interwar years also became a source of friction and often in addition, a means of supressing individual freedom.

## Notes

1. The report of the British Cunliffe Committee of 1919 exemplifies this tendency, with its advocacy of a return to the pre-war gold standard at the earliest possible opportunity. The majority report of the Gold Delegation of the Financial Committee of the League of Nations in 1932 for example emphasised the changes in economic structure caused by the war. See also J.M. Keynes, *The Economic Consequences of the Peace*, New York (1920), p. 10, for nostalgia.
2. M. De Cecco, *Gold and Empire*, Oxford: Blackwell (1974).
3. V.I. Lenin, *Imperialism the Highest Stage of Capitalism*, (First published 1916) London: Lawrence & Wishart (1934).
4. L. Robbins, *The Economic Causes of War*, London: Jonathan Cape (1939). See also M. Staley, *War and the Private Investor*, Chicago: University of Chicago Press (1935).
5. It would be out of place to discuss in detail what were the proximate causes of the war, but Taylor believes the most responsible person was Schlieffen (already dead by 1914) who had prepared Germany's war contingency plans which made certain that once Germany began to mobilise, war was inevitable, and that any war in Europe would be a general war. A.J.P. Taylor, *Europe, Grandeur and Decline*, London: Harmondsworth (1977).
6. G. Hardach, *The First World War 1914–1918*, London: Allen Lane (1977), chs 2–6.
7. D.H. Aldcroft, *From Versailles to Wall Street 1919–1929*, London: Allen Lane (1977), pp. 13–23. H. Mendershausen, *The Economics of War*, New York: Prentice Hall (1941), p. 260, quotes a world total mortality from influenza of 15 million. Added to other civilian deaths he makes a civilian total of 28 million and a civilian and military total of 41 million.
8. Hardach, op. cit., p. 243. Aldcroft, op. cit., pp. 26–30.
9. E.H. Carr, *What is History?*, Cambridge University: Trevelyan Lectures (1961) Carr was present at the Versailles negotiations in a diplomatic capacity.
10. D. Mitrany, *The Effects of the War on South Eastern Europe*, New Haven: Yale University Press (1936), pp. 172–3. See also Aldcroft, op. cit., chs 2 and 3.
11. Hardach op. cit., p. 244. Aldcroft, op. cit., p. 23.
12. H.W. Arndt, *Economic Lessons of the Nineteen Thirties*, London: F. Cass (1972) (first published 1944), ch. 9. pp. 296–7.
13. S. Grassman, 'Long-term trends in openness of national economies',

*Oxford Economic Papers,* **32** (1980), pp. 123–33. Trade, in these ratios, is the sum of exports and imports.

14. I. Svennilson, *Growth and Stagnation in the European Economy,* Geneva: United Nations Economic Commission for Europe (1954), p. 22.
15. League of Nations (F. Hilgerdt), *Industrialization and Foreign Trade,* Geneva (1945). Subsequent, more detailed analysis by A. Maizels, *Industrial Growth and World Trade,* Cambridge: Cambridge University Press (1963), confirmed his analysis.
16. P.L. Yates, *Forty Years of Foreign Trade,* London: Allen & Unwin (1959).
17. The World Economic Conference of 1927 was unanimous in condemning tariffs.
18. W.A. Lewis, *Economic Survey 1919–1939,* London: Allen & Unwin (1949), p. 164. Arndt, op. cit., p. 271.
19. M.E. Falkus, 'United States economic policy and the "dollar gap" of the 1920s', *Economic History Review* **24** (1971), pp. 599–623; and 'Comment', S. Glynn and A. Lougheed, *Economic History Review,* **26** (1973), pp. 692–4. The rationale of the Marshall–Lerner condition can best be understood by an example. Suppose the price elasticity of demand for US exports was − 1, and the US price elasticity of demand for imports was zero. A 10 per cent revaluation of the dollar, by raising the foreign price of American goods by 10 per cent, therefore reduces their sales by 10 per cent, exactly offsetting the greater American foreign currency earnings from the higher foreign price. American foreign currency earnings from exports are therefore unchanged. So also are American foreign currency requirements to buy imports, because although each dollar will now buy more foreign goods, Americans choose to purchase the same quantity as before, spending fewer dollars, but the same amount of foreign currency. In this example, where the two elasticities sum to one, there is no change in the trade balance from a revaluation then. Suppose now the American price elasticity of demand for imports is − 0.25 instead of zero. Then a 10 per cent revaluation increases the imports demanded and the foreign currency required by 2.5 per cent. In this case the two elasticities sum to 1.25 and a 10 per cent revaluation reduces the current account surplus. Changing the assumption about the supply elasticities can increase or decrease the responsiveness of the trade balance to changes in the exchange rate with given demand elasticities, depending on the assumptions chosen. See P.H. Lindert and C.P. Kindleberger, *International Economics,* Homewood, Illinois: Irwin (1982) 7th edn. ch. 15.
20. **S. Pollard, *The Development of the British Economy 1914–1950,*** London: Edward Arnold (1962), p. 194.
21. Elasticity pessimism – a belief in the low responsiveness of international economic relations to relative price changes – was widespread between the world wars. See, for example, B.J. Eichengreen,

*Sterling and the Tariff*, Princeton, NJ: Princeton University Press (1981), p. 25. That such pessimism has not been confirmed in more recent years suggests the estimates of low price elasticities were due to faulty techniques.

22. Compare R.A. Mundell, 'International trade and factor mobility', in J.N. Bhagwati (ed.), *International Trade: Selected Readings*, Cambridge, Mass.: MIT Press (1981).
23. W.S. and E.S. Woytinsky, *World Population and Production: Trends and Outlook*, New York: Twentieth Century Fund (1953), pp. 75, 82, 95–7.
24. Svennilson, op. cit., pp. 20–21.
25. B. Ohlin, *The Course and Phases of the World Depression*, League of Nations (1931), p. 19.
26. P. Bairoch, 'Europe's gross national product, 1800–1975', *Journal of European Economic History*, **5** (1976), pp. 273–340.
27. So, for example, Maddison's use of the period 1913 to 1950 as one of his growth phases, including as it does two world wars, inevitably biases his conclusion towards finding the interwar growth experience to be worse than that of any other period since 1870. A. Maddison, 'Phases of capitalist development', *Banca Nazionale del Lavoro Quarterly Review*, **30** (1977), pp. 103–38.
28. A. Maddison, *Economic Growth in Japan and the USSR*, London: Allen & Unwin (1969).
29. The Indian growth rate figure is in any case controversial. Mukherjee shows a substantial rise in Indian income per head, but Maddison notes this is inconsistent with Blyn's finding of a fall in agricultural output per head. Heston and Summers also report virtually no growth in income per head between 1911 and 1946 in their study of Indian national income. A. Maddison, *Class Structure and Economic Growth: India and Pakistan since the Moghuls*, London: Allen & Unwin (1971). M. Mukherjee, *National Income of India: Trends and Structures*, Calcutta (1969). G. Blyn, *Agricultural Trends in India 1891–1947; Output. Availability and Productivity*, Philadelphia: University of Pennsylvania (1966). A. Heston and R. Summers, 'Comparative Indian economic growth 1870 to 1970', *American Economic Review, Papers and Proceedings*, **70** (1980), pp. 96–101.
30. A. Fishlow, 'Brazilian development in long-term perspective', *American Economic Review, Papers and Proceedings*, **70** (1980), pp. 102–8.
31. Yates, op. cit., pp. 56–7, 62. The industrial countries of 1913 were the US, the UK, Belgium, France, Germany, Austria, Hungary, Netherlands, Italy, Sweden, Switzerland and Japan, in this calculation.
32. Ohlin, op. cit., pp. 91–4.
33. J. Suret-Canale, *French Colonialism in Tropical Africa 1900–1945*, London: C. Hurst (1971).
34. C. Coquery-Vidrovitch, 'Industry and Empire', in P. Bairoch and M. Levy-Leboyer, *Disparities in Economic Development since the Industrial Revolution*, London: Macmillan (1981).

35. C. Ehrlich, 'Building and caretaking: economic policy in British Tropical Africa 1890–1960'. *Economic History Review*, **20** (1973), pp. 649–63. I. Drummond, *Imperial Economic Policy 1917–1939*, London: Allen & Unwin (1974), ch. 9. C.C. Abbot, 'A re-examination of the 1929 Colonial Development Act', *Economic History Review*, **24** (1973), pp. 68–81. D. Meredith, 'The British government and colonial economic policy 1919–39', *Economic History Review*, **28** (1975), pp. 484–99.
36. T.B. Birnberg and S.A. Resnick, *Colonial Development: An Econometric Study*, New Haven and London: Yale University Press (1975).
37. G.C. Allen, *A Short Economic History of Modern Japan*, London: Macmillan, 4th edn (1981), pp. 120–1.
38. Ohlin, op. cit., p. 60.
39. Yates, op. cit., p. 150.
40. C. Tugendhat and A. Hamilton, *Oil, the Biggest Business*, London: Eyre Methuen (1975). S.H. Longrigg. *Oil in the Middle East*, Oxford: Oxford University Press 2nd edn (1961). E.T. Penrose, *The Large International Firm in Developing Countries: the International Petroleum Industry*, London: Allen & Unwin (1968).
41. J.W.F. Rowe, *Primary Commodities in International Trade*, Cambridge: Cambridge University Press (1965), ch. 7.
42. Ohlin, op. cit., pp. 51–4.
43. Rowe, op. cit., ch. 10.
44. Lewis, op. cit., p. 174.
45. Rowe, op. cit., p. 143.
46. J.S. Davis, *The World Between the Wars 1919–39: An Economist's View*, Baltimore and London: John Hopkins University Press (1975), believes the irrationality of expectations, in their optimism to 1929, and their pessimism in 1930s, have been underestimated in explanations of the interwar economy.
47. Maizels, op. cit., ch. 8.
48. Drummond, op. cit., p. 428.
49. Maizels, op. cit., p. 207, f. 1.
50. League of Nations (1948), op. cit., p. 111.
51. D.K. Fieldhouse, *Unilever: Anatomy of a Multinational*, London: Croom Helm (1978), ch. 4.
52. J.S. Foreman-Peck, 'The American challenge of the twenties: US multinationals and the European motor industry,' *Journal of Economic History*, **42** (1982), pp. 865–81.
53. J.S. Foreman-Peck, *Economies of Scale and the Development of the British Motor Industry Before 1939*, unpublished University of London PhD thesis (1978), pp. 75–6.
54. A. Nevins and F. Hill, *Ford: Expansion and Challenge 1915–1933*, New York: Scribner (1957), Appendix I.
55. C.P. Kindleberger, *The World in Depression 1929–1939*, London: Allen Lane (1973), pp. 133–4.

56. Rowe, op. cit., p. 85.
57. J.S. Weiller, 'Long run tendencies in foreign trade', *Journal of Economic History*, **21** (1971), pp. 804–21.
58. H.K. Heusser, *Control of International Trade*. London: Routledge (1939).
59. C.A. Rodrigues, 'The non-equivalence of tariffs and quotas under retaliation', in Bhagwati (ed.) (1981), op. cit.
60. Heuser, op. cit., p. 43.
61. ibid., pp. 52, 128.
62. H. Liepmann, *Tariff Levels and the Economic Unity of Europe*, London: Allen & Unwin (1938), pp. 343–4.
63. J.H. Richardson, 'Tariffs, preferences and other forms of protection', in British Association for the Advancement of Science, *Britain in Recovery*, London: Pitman (1938), p. 129.
64. F. Capie, 'Shaping the British tariff structure in the 1930's', *Explorations in Economic History*, **18** (1981), pp. 155–73.
65. Liepmann, op. cit., 353–7.
66. Lewis, op. cit., p. 10.
67. P. Friedman, 'An econometric model of national income, commercial policy and the level of international trade', *Journal of Economic History*, **28** (1978), pp. 148–80.
68. Drummond, op. cit., pp. 25–6, 31.
69. ibid., pp. 286–7.
70. P. Svedberg, 'Colonial enforcement of foreign direct investment', *Manchester School*, **39** (1981), pp. 21–38.
71. The Runciman–Roca Agreement between Britain and Argentina in 1933 is discussed by R. Gravil and T. Rooth, 'A time of acute dependence: Argentina in the 1930's', *Journal of European Economic History*, **7** (1978), pp. 337–78. The allegation that the Agreement was particularly exploitative of Argentina is not born out by a comparison of the performance of that economy with similarly structured Australia, which had the advantage of being a party to the Ottawa Agreement. See Table 7.1.
72. L. Neal, 'The economics and finance of bilateral clearing arrangements: Germany 1934–8', *Economic History Review 2nd series*, **32** (1979), pp. 391–404. For an econometric model of the monopoly/monopsony approach, see P. Friedman, 'The welfare costs of bilateralism: German–Hungarian Trade 1933–35', *Explorations in Economic History*, **13** (1976), pp. 113–25.
73. A. Le Roy Bennett, *International Organizations*. Prentice-Hall 2nd edn (1980), ch. 2.
74. F.A. Hayek, *The Road to Serfdom*, London: Routledge & Kegan Paul (1962), p. 69, f. 1 (first published 1944).

# 8 The Disintegration of the Gold Standard

International monetary relations between the two world wars were profoundly influenced by the different budgetary policies pursued between 1914 and 1918, and by the intensity of national mobilisations. Relative national costs and prices were thereby altered, and international debts and assets redistributed, as they were also by the peace treaty. The social upheavals that came with the peace put additional pressures on fiscal and monetary policies, unprecedented before 1914. Despite a widespread desire to return to the 'normality' of the fixed exchange-rate gold standard immediately after the war, most former belligerents did not manage to do so and instead floated their exchange rates. The political problems, budget deficits and inflation that necessitated floating rates, form the subject matter of the first section of the chapter.

In Britain, the keystone of the pre-1914 system, the objective was not only to return to the gold standard, but also to resume the pre-war parity, despite the changes that had taken place during the war. The political and economic reasons for these decisions to return to floating rates and the success of the floating regimes in helping Britain return to gold are discussed in the following section. Towards the end of the 1920s most of the world had returned to a form of gold standard, but one in which, it has frequently been asserted, the exchange rates were inappropriate to prevailing costs and prices and where central banks pursued policies which prevented the working of the classic gold standard adjustment process, culminating in Britain's departure from the gold standard in 1931. These allegations form the third topic of the chapter.

The depression that began in 1929 was the severest that the world has seen before or since that date. Though the primary product exporters were clearly heading for a recession, the severity of the downturn depended on the US economic collapse. The role of the gold standard, and the changed conditions of the 1920s in transmitting this depression and its reverberations are analysed next.

The world economy which emerged in 1933 was divided into three monetary blocs; (i) a sterling area centred on the United Kingdom and (ii) a dollar area centred on the United States, both floating against the rest of the world, and (iii) the countries that remained on the gold standard, to a greater or lesser extent with the help of exchange controls and import quotas. These were the years of competitive depreciation and international monetary chaos according to the later architects of the Bretton Woods system. The final section attempts to assess the truth of the judgement.

## Floating exchange rates and post-war inflation

The belligerent states maintained the visible structure of the gold standard, but the foundations were cracked. Allied exchange rates were pegged at their pre-war gold standard parities by official purchases and sales of the currencies. The Russian economy had been least able among the belligerents to withstand the strains of war. Thus the Russian budgetary explosion and exchange rate collapse were among the earlier warnings to contemporaries of the dire consequences of the departure from fiscal rectitude (policy-makers' perceptions of the post-war inflations played a key role in the events of the later 1920s). As a proportion of total government expenditure, the Russian budget deficit rose rapidly during the war. In 1915 31 per cent, and in 1916 25 per cent of the deficit was financed by an increase in the money supply.[1] This rate of monetary expansion was inconsistent with stable prices. Prices increased by 20–30 per cent per annum in 1914 and 1915, while the annual monetary expansion was around 80–90 per cent. From 1916 prices began to increase faster than the money supply. A portion of this changed relationship is attributable to a decrease in the quantity of goods being placed on the market, but probably the major part was a consequence of an increased unwillingness to hold money which was declining in value so rapidly.

With a greater average income per head and more developed capital markets, the United Kingdom did not have the same budgetary problems as Russia. Even so the British government were so reluctant to impose additional taxes to cover the cost of the war that revenue covered only 27 per cent of expenditure in the financial year 1915/16.[2] Prices therefore rose substantially during the war, retail prices perhaps doubling by 1918 and during the immediate post-war monetary expansion until 1920, wholesale prices increased by about a third, and retail prices rose by approximately one quarter.

Even Japan, not engaged in the European hostilities, experienced inflation, transmitted from the industrial economies. Japanese foreign exchange balances, virtually all held as sterling in London, counted as part of the specie reserve against the note issue on the grounds that sterling was as good as gold. During the war the Bank of Japan greatly increased the note issue in exchange for the claims on foreign exchange accumulated from exports. Wholesale prices had more than tripled by 1920.[3]

Exchange rates could only remain unchanged with countries such as the United States which experienced a lesser rate of inflation if they were supported by governments or if there were restrictions on the international movement of goods and gold. The British government spent over 2 billion dollars supporting the dollar–sterling exchange rate after 1915.[4] Once peace was restored the even greater level of official intervention required to maintain 1914 parities was clearly impossible and the pound was allowed to find its own level on the foreign exchanges. It fell against the dollar, reaching a low of $3.378 in 1920.

The collapse of the German exchange rate as inflation soared was the most dramatic and influential immediate post-war monetary event. In contrast to Britain, there was no attempt to reduce the budget deficit after the war. A coalition between industrialists and workers maintained government expenditure in 1919.[5] Transfer payments to the wounded, to dependents of the dead, unemployment relief and payments from the Bismarkian social insurance institutions were all raised. Armaments orders were prolonged and compensation for assets lost through the treaty consumed large sums. Revenue remained low because of the arrangement inherited from the German empire whereby the states, rather than the Reich itself which had the greatest demands on its expenditure, controlled the most flexible taxes, direct taxes. The collection of taxes was in any case inefficient, because of the political disturbances, and public enterprises needed massive subsides because they charged prices insufficient to cover costs.

The official German position was that the unfavourable balance of payments was the cause of the inflation that accelerated during the early 1920s; the government budget deficit acted only as an intermediate variable. Certainly there was a vicious circle in which the exchange rate depreciated, internal prices rose, the note issue was increased and the exchange fell further.[6] Towards the end of October 1923, the special paper used for notes had to be made in thirty paper mills. On 25 October, notes to the total of 120 000 000 billion paper marks had been stamped ($12 \times 10^{16}$), but demand during the day had been for about a trillion ($10^{18}$). The adverse balance of payments on occasion was associated with the war reparations and hence the attraction of the official view of inflation. Unsound government financial policies always preceded depreciation however. During 1919 the deficit was financed by an increase in the floating (short-term) debt, and then the signing of the Treaty of Versailles marked the beginning of a sharp decline in the exchange rate until February 1920. From August 1921 depreciation of the mark again became rapid. The fall was generally held to be caused by the payment of reparations at the time, as the German authorities bought foreign exchange. The depreciation depressed the yield of taxation in gold marks, but expenditure in gold marks fell in parallel. Not even for the financial year 1921 was the budget deficit provoked by the depreciation as the official view had it. In the summer of 1922 there was a definite reaction of mark depreciation on the Reich budget for it had become increasingly difficult to obtain from taxes the necessary paper marks for the purchase of the foreign exchange required for the payment of reparations. But the burdens imposed upon Germany by the Treaty of Versailles were not the only or even the most important cause of the fall of the mark. The increase in the floating debt always exceeded the expenses under the Treaty by a factor of three to one on average between 1920 and 1923. In July 1922 reparations payments in foreign exchange were suspended, but depreciation continued.

Speculation probably did not destabilise the mark because of the dispersion of views about future changes in its value. In Germany, as in Russia earlier and France later, the normal demand for foreign exchange to make payments was supplemented by a demand for foreign exchange as a stable store of value for savings. Working in the other direction many foreigners, unable to believe the mark could permanently depreciate so much, bought the currency expecting it to rise in value. In the middle of 1922 foreigners held about 60 000 billion paper marks, on which they must have lost approximately 5000 billion gold marks, as the exchange rate fell, a sum triple that paid by Germany in foreign exchange for reparations.[7] After stabilisation in 1924 the German profit from the sale of marks between 1918 and 1924 was estimated at between 7.6 and 8.7 thousand billion gold marks. Against this profit has to be offset an unknown sum for the purchase of German assets such as houses by foreigners, under the stimulus of the low mark.

French budgetary policy and the course of the franc exchange rate can be explained by the French attitude to Germany – 'le Boche paiera' (Jerry will pay). The French political conflict could at first be disguised by running a massive budget deficit which was to be financed by the German reparations.[8] Only when these expectations became obviously unrealistic in the second half of 1922 was there unusual volatility of the franc exchange rate, apparently unjustified by considerations of relative purchasing power. It was especially the experience of the floating franc that bolstered the view that speculation was destabilising and, by implication, that fixed exchange rates would have been more satisfactory. During the winter of 1923–4 the franc lost nearly half of its dollar value in less than twenty weeks. A second speculative attack in the summer of 1926 resulted in a further decline of 20 per cent. Yet these movements may easily be interpreted as merely the reaction to new information by speculators about future equilibrium exchange rates, and an anticipation of the franc's inevitable move towards that new equilibrium.

From June 1922 France broke with Britain and her other former allies over the flexibility of the schedule for German reparations laid down at the London conference of May 1921. As the realisation dawned that reparations on the scale previously expected were no longer feasible, the prospects for sound French public finance diminished.

In 1923 the French occupied the Ruhr to enforce payment of reparations. The Germans responded with passive resistance financed by the government. The German hyperinflation that followed contributed to the depreciation of the franc by decreasing the likelihood that reparations payments could be successfully extracted from the Germans. The imposition of new taxes in March 1924 and a pledge on part of the Bank of France's gold reserves allowed the raising of a foreign loan which was used successfully to stablise the franc. Facing difficulties raising taxes to cover the budget deficit, the left-wing coalitions that governed from May 1924 to July 1926 proposed a capital levy which, together with the disclosure of subterfuge in the Bank of France's 1924 balance sheet, led to further downward pressure on the exchange rate, as French bond-holders sold for foreign currency.

During 1925 the easier course was followed of four times raising the limit on the Bank of France's advances to the government and three times increasing the note issue. The franc continued to fall. Eventually the moderate left-wing deputies concluded that the government-induced inflation was becoming harmful to their supporters, who could no longer be protected by fiscal benefits.[9] Only then were they prepared to cede power to a conservative-led coalition which required sacrifices in order to eliminate inflation and stabilize the exchange rate. However the moderate Left were able to use their remaining political influence to prevent any substantial revaluation of the franc. The relatively low value of the franc established in 1926 was a contributory factor to the international monetary crisis of the early 1930s, yet international considerations played no part in the choice of exchange rate. In view of the difficulty of achieving agreement on domestic issues within the French political system, such an outcome is perhaps not unexpected.

## Floating exchange rates and sterling's return to gold

Amidst this monetary disorder British policy-makers were determined to restore the sterling gold standard at the pre-war parity and in so doing, they hoped, restore Britain's former prosperity based upon international economic relations. The post-war inflations politically ruled out the maintenance of a managed currency with which they were associated.[10] In any case there were strong political pressures from the Dominions who at the Imperial Economic Conference of 1923 recommended the early return of Britain and the sterling area to an effective gold standard.[11] The southern Dominions objected to holding sterling for fear of depreciation, and were impatient to stabilise on gold. South Africa threatened to return independently.

In deciding when to return, as well as the appropriateness of the pre-war rate, purchasing power parity calculations then and subsequently played an important part. These calculations and the role of speculation have formed much of the basis of the condemnation of the floating rates of the 1920s, which allegedly failed to reduce the international disparities in prices and costs that had opened up during the war, and encouraged speculative capital flows which led to eventual stabilisation at rates that overvalued the pound and undervalued the franc, and to the collapse of the mark.[12]

Relative prices were certainly not an infallible guide to exchange rates in the post-war world although they offered a long-term indication. During the massive Russian inflation from 1919, the exchange rate did not match the fall in internal purchasing power.[13] By mid-1920 in Moscow, the rouble–sterling rate was about twice as high as warranted by the relative purchasing powers of the two currencies. From the end of 1920 the fall in the exchange rate exceeded the decline in the internal value of money until by the end of the following year, the purchasing power parity of pre-war had almost been achieved at £1 = 1.25 million roubles on 1 January 1922. This equalisation was the result of closer international monetary relations as fighting diminished, the relaxation of exchange controls and also because of falls in price levels in other countries.

Similarly the British–Japanese wholesale price indices of purchasing power parity indicated a fall in the sterling–yen exchange rate should have occurred between 1920 and 1922 and thereafter should have been stable. The fall in 1925 allowed the exchange rate to reach the level indicated by relative prices that would have been appropriate in 1922.[14] Inouye, a former Governor of the Bank of Japan and Minister of Finance, acknowledged the yen was over-valued in the early 1920s because of the government's ability to spend its sterling balances accumulated during the war. Once these balances were exhausted, as they were by the costs of reconstruction after the 1923 earthquake, the yen was bound to fall unless Japanese prices were reduced.

While war and the spending of sterling balances caused temporary divergences of the Russian and Japanese floating exchange rates from purchasing power parity, national budgetary policies, as already shown, mainly explained the deviation of the French franc and the German mark from levels implied by relative prices. When responsible domestic policies were pursued, floating rates generally followed movements in relative purchasing powers and did not fluctuate widely. Floating rates also permitted a degree of freedom for monetary policy. Finland maintained a fairly stable internal purchasing power, while abandoning any attempt to stabilise the exchange rate.[15] The wholesale prices index of Finland, unlike that of almost any other nation, remained unchanged throughout the 1920s.

The wholesale price indices used in purchasing power parity calculations are often said to be suspect because they measure the prices of internationally traded goods, whose prices in domestic currency will *reflect* changes in foreign exchange rates reasonably accurately.[16] But the prices of non-traded domestic goods are important for *determining* the equilibrium exchange rate, yet these are greatly understated in the wholesale price indices. Hence the test by Clements and Frenkel on the dollar–sterling exchange rate between February 1921 and May 1925 which includes real wages as a measure of non-traded prices, is particularly interesting.[17] Ninety six per cent of the variation of the exchange rate in the period studied could be explained by relative prices and wages, relative money stocks, incomes and interest rates. This evidence is consistent with causation running from relative prices to the exchange rate.

An earlier study of the floating pound similarly concluded that the exchange rate was not generally disturbed by non-economic circumstances. Only between October 1923 and July 1924 did the exchange rate depart from the level expected according to fundamental current economic factors.[18] During those months fears became widespread, with some justification, that the British government (the first Labour Government) would abandon the deflationary policy previously pursued, and the future exchange rate would fall. More pertinent to the usefulness of floating rates for British purposes in the 1920s is Aliber's finding evidence from the forward sterling rate that speculation that the British authorities were going to return to gold at the pre-war rate from autumn 1924 did cause floating sterling to become overvalued.[19] And Thomas, after his analysis of the Canadian, British, French, Dutch, Spanish and Swedish dollar exchange rates from monthly data in the twenties found that there was no destabilising speculation when reasonably stable domestic financial policies were followed, remarked that expectations of a return to former 1914 rates may have provided a stabilising element.[20]

Did speculative capital movements allow the sterling-dollar rate in 1925 to be fixed at an inappropriate rate? Overvaluation offers a convenient explanation for why British unemployment (and that of other countries in north western Europe) was so unusually high during the 1920s. The pre-1914 rate of $4.86, Keynes argued at the time, and later so also did Moggridge in more detail, overvalued sterling by at least 10 per cent.[21] Moggridge gives some quantitative backing to his claim by assuming elasticities of demand for British exports and imports (respectively $-1.5$ and $-0.5$), making some adjustments for supply side reactions, and then calculating the deterioration in the current account of the balance of payments (£80 million approximately) caused by a 10 per cent overvaluation of sterling. Assuming domestic economic policy had to be more deflationary than it otherwise would have been to offset this deterioration, he finds the reduction in income and employment necessary to lower imports in order to restore the current account, if the marginal propensity to import was 0.3. An £80 million reduction in imports, Moggridge calculates, lowered employment by about 1.44 million.[22]

This reduction seems excessive because between 1923 and 1929 total registered unemployment only exceeded 1.44 million in 1926, the year of the General Strike. If the assumed price elasticities are too high (in absolute value) the excessive unemployment figure Moggridge obtains can be explained; lower price elasticities mean a smaller improvement in the current account from a devaluation. Another possible reason for the figure (see footnote 22) is the relationship assumed between income and employment.

The overvaluation thesis adequately explains the unusually high

British unemployment centred in the export industries, but requires further support to explain why the effects of the overvaluation were not offset by a monetary contraction. The contraction necessary to support the exchange rate should also have reduced the domestic price level, restoring competitiveness to the export, and to import-competing, industries. British prices did in fact decline between 1925 and 1929; the consumers' expenditure average value index fell by almost 5 per cent. The decision to return at $4.86 was based on the assumption that prices in the rest of the world, in particular the United States, would rise, but they did not. Between 1925 and 1929 the US consumers' expenditure average value index fell very slightly, ensuring that if the sterling–dollar rate was not to be too high, British prices would have to fall substantially, and this fall could only be accomplished slowly.

As much an error as the choice of the sterling exchange rate, Pressnell suggests, was the resumption of sterling area arrangements against gold in 1925 at the pre-war rate.[23] A lower parity for the whole sterling area in 1925 would almost certainly have increased dollar earnings of the system as a whole, despite possible counter-depreciations elsewhere, because of the indirect nature of Britain's earnings from the outer sterling area. Sterling area raw material exporters often sold for dollars and spent in sterling. The southern Dominions currencies were supported by borrowing and were probably overvalued as well against sterling. By 1928 the trade and income of primary producers were deteriorating badly, and sterling countries contributed to the strain on sterling that preceded its collapse in 1931.

## The reconstructed gold standard

The reconstructed gold standard lasted only a short while and ushered in the world's greatest depression which it exacerbated. Although the late 1920s saw no repetition of the post-war inflations, in a number of countries, heavy unemployment persisted; the expected pre-1914 prosperity did not return with the pre-1914 monetary system. In this section we discuss whether the difference was due to central banks no longer following the gold standard 'rules of the game', to greater rigidities in the system that made it less responsive, or to the changed conditions brought about by the war to which the restored monetary regime was inappropriate.

### *The impact of the war on the monetary system*

The war had changed the United States from a major debtor to a major creditor, and the sale of overseas assets had greatly reduced the United Kingdom's international investments.[24] London's pre-eminence as a financial centre was reduced relative to New York and Paris, but neither of these two centres had the same stake in the health of international commerce, nor experience in international financial management. The uncertainty generated by the disturbances of the early 1920s, the restrictions on overseas investment from London (not necessarily ultimately British investment) and the lesser experience of New York in long-term foreign investment, left short-term securities as the main instrument of saving, in contrast to the position before the war. Perhaps £2 billion of these potentially volatile funds were free to cross national borders at short notice, greatly increasing national liquidity requirements. The exchange rates at which so many nations had hurriedly returned to gold were not necessarily appropriate, requiring rapid adjustment in a number of economies. One apparent difference between the pre-war and the restored gold standards was not a difference at all, the use of foreign exchange reserves instead of gold reserves. This so-called gold-exchange standard, recommended at the Genoa Conference in 1922 as a means of economising on gold, was in use as much as 1910 it was in 1924 and 1925, when measured by the ratio of foreign exchange reserves to gold reserves.[25] The real difference lay in the changed liquidity of sterling as a reserve currency. Sterling was no longer perhaps quite as good as gold.

## International debt

The redistribution of international debt during the war has frequently been alleged to have hampered the restored gold standard. The first world war left the allies with debts owing to each other totalling about $26.5 billion, mostly owed to the United States and the United Kingdom, with France as the main debtor. In addition the Reparations Commission in 1921 required Germany to pay $33 billion, mainly to France and Britain.[26] The attempted international transfer of these sums of money was the largest 'transfer problem' in economic history until then, and the reparations payment destablised Germany in various ways.

The basic elements of the transfer problem are that for a real resource transfer to take place, the donor nation must be able, voluntarily or under compulsion, to give them up, and the recipient nation must be willing to accept them. Germany was not willing to make the transfer, hence the inflation of 1923–4.[27] Keynes calculated that the Germans would have to pay 43 per cent of their national income in taxes, a proportion that could not be extracted by 'the whips and scorpions of any government' (though that level has been exceeded in many countries since then). Even with perfectly flexible prices and wages, and full employment, an apparently manageable transfer might prove impossible. If the size of the transfer is fixed on the basis of pre-transfer prices, the increased supply of exports from the donor country may force down their price so far that raising the requisite volume of foreign exchange is impossible. The recipient here is unwilling to accept.

With imperfectly flexible prices and wages the classical assumption that full employment would be maintained is incorrect. In the donor country real resources can be released for foreigners only by cutting domestic demand, but there is no reason to suppose there would be a corresponding increase in the foreign demand for these goods; imports are deflationary. If the recipient does not accept the imports, then the fall in aggregate demand in the donor country will react back, depressing demand further in the recipient country. In the international economy as a whole, planned savings increase the planned investment falls. As it turned out the transfer was not made and so these economic problems did not arise. Before 1924 we have seen that Germany received a transfer from foreign speculators in marks which offset the reparations paid, and after 1924, American capital flowed into Germany, balancing German transfers abroad. For Germany the main problem of the transfer was the constraint, discussed below, that it imposed on policy especially in 1931.

Similarly the economic impact of the transfers associated with inter-allied war debts were less significant than the political repercussions.[28] In 1931 U.S. net receipts from war debts were about 10 per cent of the value of her exports and 68 per cent of the positive balance of trade. For Britain the net liabilities were 2 per cent of import value and 4 per cent of the negative trade balance. For France the proportions were 7 per cent and 25 per cent respectively. Between 1918 and 1931, the United States received $2.6 billion from the allies, less than half the amount specified in the revised settlements of the 1920s.[29] France received in reparations $3\frac{1}{2}$ times what she paid in war debts to the United States and Britain. The United Kingdom ended up with a negative overall balance.

The British had suggested cancelling all war debts. When the United States turned this down, Balfour stated in 1922 that Britain had no choice but to collect the debts owed to her, but would do so only up to the limits of the British debt to the United States.[30] Consequently the war debts and reparation issue caused political instability and economic deflation throughout the 1920s, culminating in the German deflationary policies of the early 1930s that helped

Hitler to power, and perhaps contributed to the crucial failure in 1931 of the Austrian Creditanstalt Bank.

Private international transfers, lending, borrowing and debt service, in the 1920s also played a part in the difficulties of the gold standard from 1929, but it seems unlikely that these differed from the nineteenth century problems such as Barings' embarrassment in 1890. The new lenders did not learn from the mistakes of the old. Foreign lending by the United States at over $6 billion from 1924 to 1929 was about double that of Britain, but when the capital flows are considered net of war debt and reparation payments, the lending of the two countries was roughly equal.[31] Germany changed from being a creditor in 1924 to the most heavily indebted country in the world after Canada, in 1929. Other countries, Poland, Romania, Yugoslavia and Bulgaria, even after 1924 maintained such poor international credit ratings that their international borrowings were extremely limited. Australia was most successful at borrowing funds apart from Germany, followed at some distance by Argentina. Each of these countries began to experience balance of payments problems by 1929 when American foreign investment dried up, and the servicing of their foreign debt became impossible

## Price levels and price rigidities

Changes in relative prices during the war had still not been entirely reversed by 1928, and given the exchange rates adopted, inevitably created difficulties for the restored gold standard.

Table 8.1 gives an indication of the extent to which national prices relative to gold had diverged since 1914. The limitations of these indices must be borne in mind; some of them are of very restricted coverage, for example measuring only the prices of goods in the capital city, and including only a small number of commodities. In the absence of better data however they provide some indication of the difficulties the gold exchange system had to operate under. Some of the differences might be explained by taxes and tariffs, international investment, or changes in exchange rates, but not all. Britain had increased her prices relative to gold between 1914 and 1928 by more than France, (despite France's more rapid inflation, because the French had lowered the gold value of the franc by 80 per cent) but the franc–sterling exchange rate was very much lower than in 1914. Australia and India had maintained their pre-war parities with sterling but their prices measured in gold terms had increased by more than Britain's. Similarly Norway and Denmark maintained their pre-war exchange rates but had increased their prices by more than the United States.

**Table 8.1.** *Wholesale price levels in 1928 (gold indices 1913 or 14 = 100)*

| | | | | | |
|---|---|---|---|---|---|
| Australia | 165 | New Zealand | 147 | Bulgaria | 133 |
| British India | 163 | Finland | 145 | Austria | 130 |
| Norway | 161 | Switzerland | 145 | Latvia | 129 |
| Japan | 159 | Spain | 144 | France | 126 |
| Peru | 157 | Czechoslovakia | 143 | Belgium | 122 |
| China | 155 | UK | 140 | Estonia | 121 |
| Denmark | 153 | Germany | 140 | Egypt | 120 |
| Canada | 151 | USA | 140 | S. Africa | 120 |
| Dutch E. Indies | 149 | Hungary | 135 | Poland | 120 |
| Netherlands | 149 | Italy | 134 | Chile | 119 |
| Sweden | 148 | | | | |

*Source*: B. Ohlin, *The Course and Phases of the World Depression* (1931).

A belief in the flexibility of prices and wages prevented much consideration of relative prices in the choice of exchange rate, despite the emergence of apparently unprecedented unemployment in north-western Europe after the post-war boom of 1919–1920.[32] If this unemployment was caused by a new rigidity in prices and wages, the failure of the interwar gold standard to secure the necessary adjustment in domestic economies, and the severity of the Great Depression may also be attributable to this cause. During the 1930s unemployment rates in northern Europe were similar to those in the 1920s, whereas in the rest of the world rates were much higher; for France they were higher by a factor of fifteen for example. The Scandinavian countries and Britain returned to their pre-war exchange rates whereas most other European nations adopted a lower rate when they eventually stabilised. It is therefore tempting to attribute the unemployment of northern Europe to overvalued exchange rates.

A direct comparison of unemployment before and after 1914 is problematical because the coverage of the statistics was greatly increased after 1913 with the extension of unemployment benefits to more of the labour force. The level as well as the extent of these benefits have been used to explain the interwar British unemployment rates in terms of decreasing the willingness to search for jobs.[33] Possibly the payment of unemployment benefits may have reduced wage flexibility; eligibility for benefits did not require the applicant to accept lower wages or worse conditions than in his former job.[34] But in Britain money wages declined very markedly from 1920 to 1923, while unemployment benefits rose in both amount and scope. Furthermore, there is no evidence for a structural change in the working of the British labour market between the pre-war and interwar periods, as indicated by the Phillips relationship between employment and changes in money wages. Between 1860 and 1914 however there had been few falls in average money wages.

On the side of prices, increased market power may have given firms a greater opportunity for rigidity. There was a major merger boom during the 1920s in Britain, and in the United States Bell's study of interwar productivity growth concluded that unemployment emerged and persisted because of inappropriate pricing policies.[35] The absence of these suitable pricing policies might be attributed alternatively to changes in the cost structure of firms. Temin has suggested that around the time of the first world war there was a major shift of employment in the United States from family firms to large industrial enterprises.[36] In family firms labour was treated as a fixed cost, and could not be sacked when demand declined Instead prices were reduced and output was more or less maintained. The reverse was true of the impersonal capitalist firms that came to dominate the economy of the twenties. These firms reduced output and employment when demand fell off, rather than cutting prices.

The fundamental structural change in the industrial economies if it happened at all came during, not before, the 1920s, as shown by a comparison of the slump of 1920–2 and that after 1929. In the first slump all prices seem to have been very flexible, thanks to the use of paper currencies; slump-induced price declines were frequently reversed quickly, money wages fell by 30–40 per cent in two years, and the large drop in bond yields stimulated investment.[37]

By 1929 the price system was much more rigid. Because of the pervasiveness of tariffs and cartels protecting the domestic markets, prices in international trade declined very seriously while domestic prices were fairly inflexible. The prices of about half the industrial raw materials and semi-manufactured goods, as measured by the employment in supplying them, were controlled by cartels or producers associations in Germany. As a result the prices of German cartellised products fell from an index number of 104 to 103 between December 1928 and July 1930 while the non-cartellised prices fell from 103 to 79. Belgian prices showed a similar pattern, with 'stabilised' prices actually rising from an index number of 811 to 871 over the same period but other prices falling from 898 to 680. The primary product exporting economies, as has been seen in the previous chapter, increasingly during the 1920s attempted to 'stabilise' prices; that is, maintain them in the face of increased supply or falling demand. The consequences for the economy were that downturns in economic activity were more severe, and the adjustment of economies to overvalued exchange rates took longer and were accompanied by severe unemployment.

## Monetary policy

A third explanation, in an influential League of Nations Report, for the failure of the restored gold standard is that central banks no longer followed the 'rules' of the gold standard 'game'.[38] Divergences of national price levels were possible because central banks did not ensure that changes in gold reserves were accompanied by parallel or multiple changes in domestic credit in the same direction. Between the two world wars, gold and other international assets came to act as a buffer or cushion for disturbances originating abroad. The effects of gold on the credit base were increasingly sterilised, so the maintenance of fixed rates became difficult. But monetary policy alone, the report maintains, was insufficient to offset the multiplier effects of a large fall in foreign demand as in 1929–32. Sixty per cent of the annual observations on twenty-six countries between 1932 and 1938 were inconsistent with the rule that a loss of foreign exchange reserves and gold should be met by a policy of contracting domestic credit.[39] The report goes on to argue that the greater mobility of short-term funds tended to produce inverse movements of a central bank's international and domestic assets, if the bank followed the 'rules'. A loss of reserves countered by a higher discount rate attracted foreign assets. At the same time, domestic assets declined in response to open market purchases of securities intended to make the rate effective.

As was shown in Chapter 6, this central bank behaviour was not new, and therefore cannot account for the failure of the gold standard between the world wars. Before 1914 central banks were also concerned about domestic employment and income, as well as their gold reserves. The banks' behaviour depended on balancing the two objectives and on the relative phases of domestic and foreign economic activity. The examination below of American, French and British central bank policies shows little deviation from the pre-1913 pattern except that then there was no American central bank (the Federal Reserve System was set up in 1913). Friedman and Schwartz believe that this was a key difference, because American monetary policy between the wars was singularly inept, and the mistakes of American management were rapidly transmitted to the rest of the world. The slump of 1920/1 probably originated in the United States. Unprecedentedly high American discount rates attracted large gold exports from other countries who were similarly forced to raise interest rates to staunch the outflow.[40] The 1929 stock market boom which withdrew US capital abroad back just when many primary producers were beginning to experience a downturn and especially needed this capital for their balance of payments, was also the result of a policy error. In 1924 and 1927 domestic and international requirements coincided; lower interest rates were needed in the United States to prevent a recession, while they also encouraged short-term capital to move into sterling, reducing Britain's foreign exchange problems. In 1929 domestic and international requirements diverged, and domestic interests predominated.

Gold flowed into the United States in every year during the 1920s except 1927 and 1928. These flows were not allowed to expand American credit and raise prices and employment for two reasons: the gold imports were thought to be temporary and so sterilisation was a stabilisation policy; and a fear of inflation presuaded member banks of the Federal Reserve to use their newly-acquired gold to repay Federal Reserve credit, which therefore *declined* by the volume of gold imports.[41]

France also absorbed substantial amounts of gold but, as noted in Chapter 6, the extensive French use of gold was not a phenomenon that began in the 1920s. Rather the undervalued exchange rate was the more fundamental cause. The British Treasury economist, Hawtrey, likened the Bank of France to a boa constrictor swallowing a goat; once it started taking in gold it could not stop whether it wanted to or not.[42] France, with one-ninth the national income of the United States, needed one-half the amount of gold because of legislation governing the central bank, together with the desire of the French public to hold their money in the form of legal tender paper, rather than bank deposits. A much larger proportion of the purchasing power of the public in France therefore had to have a backing narrowly defined by the central bank statutes. The obligations of the Bank of France amounted to more than 100 billion francs; most of this sum had to be covered by gold or by foreign exchange. There was an upper limit to the amount of foreign exchange which the Bank of France felt could safely be held; once this was reached an increased demand for money by the French public had to be covered by equal gold imports.

Like the Bank of France, the Bank of England needed to accumulate gold, but did not deliberately neutralise all reserve movements much more than before 1914. Despite shortages of the appropriate assets for open market operations the Bank usually reinforced the effects of reserve losses. In view of the general weakness of sterling the Bank did however tend to offset reserve gains.[43] Possibly the restrictive policy was not restrictive enough because the growth of the money stock slightly exceeded the growth of domestic output, but then there were the effects on income and employment to consider. The Bank was so concerned to protect the money market and credit for industry and trade that in 1929 it was even prepared to seek an increase in the fiduciary issue to allow a gold loss without deflation.[44]

## Liquidity and the onset of the international depression

A consequence of central bank policies was that by 1928 the United States held 37.8 per cent of official monetary gold reserves and the gold bloc centred on France held 20.8 per cent.[45] Combined with the concentration of gold in a few countries, the slowing down of gold production after 1915 justified fears that supplies would provide insufficient international reserves and gave an impetus to the 1922 Genoa Conference at which the gold exchange standard was given official blessing. The experience of 'hot money' movements in 1930 and 1931 implied that reserves were nevertheless inadequate. The ratio of reserves to imports was probably higher in the late 1920s than in 1913, but conditions had changed between those years, invalidating the comparison.[46] International currency reserves are needed to meet any temporary balance of payments deficits which are not worth while correcting by exchange rate or expenditure changes. The abnormal capital movements of the 1930s were a major cause of such deficits. During the 1920s much gold was tied up as official reserves against notes and deposits so that it could not be used for international settlement, even though there was an increasing need for it.

The weakness of agricultural prices in the late 1920s meant that primary good exporters were having increasing difficulty in earning the foreign exchange to service their international debts. And the main international debtors were exporters of agricultural goods. New Zealand and Australia with net interest payments per head of over $27 in 1928 headed the list of debtors.[47] International balance of payments difficulties were compounded when the United States, a key country under the gold exchange standard, ceased to export capital in 1928, as the Federal Reserve reduced monetary growth in an attempt to control speculation on Wall Street. Germany, as the main recipient of American capital, was severely affected.

The slump in United States income in 1929 gave another twist to the contractionary forces in the international economy. New foreign lending by the United States to the non-European economies declined by $301 million in 1929, because of a decrease in portfolio investment, mainly to Latin America.[48] The importance of this is revealed by a comparison with the decline of South American exports revenues of $73.8 million. The flow of new capital from the US to the non-European economies had, by 1929, fallen below the payments on past American investment of amortisation, interest and dividends. Deficits were being financed by reductions in gold and foreign exchange reserves in attempts to cushion the impact of the American depression. Reserves in many countries proved insufficient to the task.

By the beginning of 1931 seven countries (Australia, New Zealand, Uruguay, Brazil, Bolivia, Venezuela and Argentina) had been forced to allow their currencies to be quoted at discounts below their gold parities. The gold reserves moved mainly to the United States and to France. US gold reserves increased by $845, million to June 1931, but France acquired $1 billion, a sum equivalent to the whole new gold production of the world. About one-third of the French increase represented the conversion of foreign assets into gold by the Bank of France.[49] The gold reserves of the British empire and the sterling bloc were relatively stable at first, with some tendency for those of the UK to increase after 1929.

## The second phase of the depression

The decline in foreign investment rendered the Central European economies vulnerable to the second phase of the Depression beginning in May 1931 with the failure of the Creditanstalt, the largest bank in Austria. The Austrian government guaranteed its liabilities and the bank's foreign creditors agreed to stop withdrawals. This meant however that the assets of the creditors lost liquidity. German banks were affected particularly and their creditors started to withdraw deposits in anticipation of further trouble. The loss of foreign reserves by Germany was so severe that currency controls were instituted in July. With the imposition of German controls, the pressure shifted to Britain.

The end of the gold exchange standard – effectively when Britain left gold on 20 September 1931 – came as a result of London's illiquidity as an international financial centre.[50] Although reserves were higher than in 1914, their level had not been determined by any analysis. The post-war target of £150 million grew out of a rough guess by Lord Cunliffe and was later justified as being about right because it roughly corresponded to the gold holdings of the Bank of England, the clearing banks and individuals (in the form of sovereigns in their pockets) in 1913.[51] Had London been able to rely on the pre-war bank rate mechanism to attract funds the reserves may have been adequate. But once London's changed net asset position became known the confidence necessary to make the old system work disappeared.

The Bank of England tried to maintain its former position as the world central banker by organising international credits that blunted the impact of the internal difficulties of the Central European countries. In the United Kingdom the Bank helped to ease the strain of the slump by bringing down bank rate. On 14 May 1931 the rate was dropped from 3 to $2\frac{1}{2}$ per cent. When figures on London's short-term liabilities were published in the Macmillan Report on 13 July, realisation of London's weakness and of the damage done to London by the Austrian and German crises became much more widespread.

An escape from the crisis and maintaining the gold standard depended on maintaining a high degree of confidence. The collapse of confidence was due, first, to acceptance of the overvaluation of the pound, especially by the Macmillan Committee, and, secondly, to the budget deficit, especially in August and September. Memories of the currency disorders of the early 1920s had not faded.[52] The Labour government could not agree to cuts in the unemployment benefit to satisfy the market, and broke up on 22–3 August. MacDonald formed a National government that introduced an Emergency Budget on the 10 September. The across-the-board pay cuts of all government employees were not well received by some naval personnel, whose objections were described in newspaper headlines as a mutiny. Britannia appeared to be about to cease to rule the waves and gold could be the next symbol to fall. Ministers seemed inclined to alleviate the hardship the cuts might cause. The Bank lost increasing amounts of reserves – on the 18 September, £$18\frac{3}{4}$ million. Late on Sunday, 20 September, the government announced the suspension of the gold standard.

By then the great fall in raw material prices had directly affected Britain more than most industrial countries because the primary producers were her major overseas markets and places of investment. British income from foreign investments provided sufficient to cover 60 per cent of the balance of trade deficit in 1929, but only 40 per cent in 1931 after the fall in primary prices had reduced income abroad.[53] But the international multiplier also affected the United States indirectly. Between 1929 and 1933 US imports declined by $3 billion, a fall of two-thirds, representing 13 per cent of the total decline of world imports. Imports of the non-European and non-

American economies in turn fell from $10 billion in 1929 to $7.9 billion in 1930, and to $3.4 billion in 1933.[54] Since a substantial proportion of these imports were US exports, American economic activity was accordingly reduced further by the international reverberations of the 1929 American downturn.

From mid-1931 to the end of 1932 most countries lost very large amounts of gold to France and other members of the gold bloc. The gold movements were on a scale unparalleled in monetary history. The pound rapidly fell by 30 per cent providing some boost to the British economy at the expense of competitors whose currencies remained linked to gold. Holders of dollars began to speculate against a similar movement of that currency. The United States lost $1 billion in gold in the second half of 1931 and the first half of 1932. In 1932 the central banks of the gold bloc countries converted the bulk of their remaining foreign assests into gold.

## America in the Depression

American policy differed both from the German and Austrian use of controls and the British policy of devaluation; the Federal Reserve raised interest rates enough to stem the outflow of funds. This deflationary pressure coming from the international collapse squashed recovery in the United States.[55] Prices and production fell as interest rates rose. A trough of the American depression was reached in the Summer of 1932, but recovery was again prevented by the presidential election compaign and the long 'lame duck' period between the election and Roosevelt's inauguration. Confidence in the American banking system finally collapsed altogether during this latter period and Roosevelt was inaugurated in the midst of a banking panic. He proclaimed a Bank Holiday and began the 'New Deal': between 1929 and 1933 United States real GNP had fallen 29 per cent. During 1932 most South American countries which had not already done so left the gold standard.[56] The United States left the gold standard on 20 April 1933 and by September the gold value of the dollar had fallen by a third, approaching the old parity with the pound. The depreciation must have been the result of capital transfers because the current account continued to be favourable to the US.

Reserves were clearly inadequate in volume to prevent the international transmission of Depression, but because holding reserves had an opportunity cost, and because of the scale of the contraction, it is implausible to place the greatest weight on reserves shortages in an explanation of the international depression. Ultimately the fault lay in American economic policy.

Kindleberger maintains that the solution would have been for America to accept the leadership of the international economy in three ways: by providing a market for the products of countries in balance of payments difficulties; by engaging in counter-cyclical overseas investment so that countries experiencing a decline in the American demand for imports would have received an offset from an increased inflow of foreign capital; and by acting as lender of last resort to countries with balance of payments problems.[57] Britain had performed these functions in the heyday of the gold standard, but was no longer able to do so in the interwar years. Because the United States was the largest economy in the world, no effort to make national policies mutually compatible and supporting would have been possible without American participation. This was clearly shown when President Roosevelt wrecked the World Economic Conference of 1933 by announcing that he was going to ensure the restoration of equilibrium in the domestic economy before worrying about the international economy.

Whether it is historically plausible to have expected the United States to have assumed the sort of leadership required is doubtful. The American economy was largely self-sufficient by the 1920s and had little reason to be concerned about the 'Old World' and the international bankers, except to make a world safe for American foreign investment. Hence the American concern to depoliticise the German reparations problem with the 1924 Dawes plan. Only the threat of a world dominated by an anti-capitalist ideology was to force the United States to assume the leadership of the international economy after the second world war. In any event the roots of the Depression lay in the inability to maintain economic activity in the American economy, a failing that augured ill for any American attempts to manage the international economy between the wars.

## Exchange rates and the Depression

Another explanation for the world-wide nature of the Depression was the gold exchange standard. In his 1925 Budget Speech, announcing Britain's return to the gold standard, Winston Churchill remarked felicitously that 'All the countries related to the gold standard will move together like ships in a harbour whose gangways are joined and who rise and fall together with the tide.'[58] From 1927 international economic activity was synchronised, and in 1929 nearly all the economies fell together.[59] France remained an exception until 1930 because her massive gold reserves allowed her to defer deflationary policies for a year. Floating exchange rates probably reduced the impact of the international depression of 1974–5 and the evidence suggests they may have done the same in 1929–32. For small European countries the Great Depression was an exogenous disturbance. Spain operated with a floating exchange rate over the years 1929-32 and avoided much of the deflationary impact. The peseta fell by more than 50 per cent against the US dollar between 1928 and 1932. The Spanish money supply remained stable, except in 1931 when there was a contraction because of the European banking crises which made customers withdraw bank deposits before the expected bank failures. Other small European countries on the fixed exchange rate gold standard experienced substantial monetary contractions. Belgium, Italy, Poland and Netherlands, all on the gold standard, had movements in their national outputs and price levels closely associated with those of the United States, whereas Spain did not.[60] Denmark, Finland and Norway represent intermediate cases, switching to floating rates in 1931. These economies began to recover from the Depression after 1931 as did Britain.

China reaped a similar benefit from remaining on the silver standard. At the beginning of the Great Depression the Chinese exchange rate fell as the decline in silver prices, which began in 1920, accelerated. But though wholesale prices continued to go up, the relative rise in Chinese prices was less than necessary to compensate for the decline in the exchange rate. Hence the effects of the Depression may have been partly offset. The value of Chinese exports in gold fell by one-third in 1930 compared with a fall in imports of one-quarter. Exports consisted mainly of raw materials for which prices had fallen more than for imports, so that it is difficult to discern whether the volume of exports fell by less than imports. Exports from Japan and the United States to China declined by the same proportion as to others, contrary to the insulation hypothesis, but exports from the United Kingdom declined by more. Indian exports were also probably more than usually affected because of the comparative ease with which domestic products could be substituted for these imports. The fortuitous benefits conferred by the silver standard ceased when the departure of the United Kingdom and the sterling area from the gold standard removed much of China's competitive advantage.[61]

Floating exchange rates are unlikely to have proved a satisfactory solution to the capital flights that affected Germany and the United Kingdom. Here a stronger international net asset position would have helped. In turn a more rapid recovery of the German economy, untrammelled by reparations and political repercussions, would have helped achieve this position, as probably would a different sterling exchange rate after 1925.

## The managed exchange rates of the 1930s

The international monetary system emerged from the great Depression with the gold exchange standard destroyed and the few remaining countries on the gold standard under increasing pressure. By the end of the 1930s most major countries operated a form of managed floating rate, with an exchange stabilisation fund, which often differed little from a pegged exchange rate. The pound sterling was a freely fluctuating currency only from September 1931 to the Spring of 1932. The sterling area currencies were pegged to sterling. The US dollar floated freely only from April 1933 to January 1934. France, having remained at its gold parity until the devaluation of September 1936, reverted to a floating franc from 30 June 1937 to 4 May 1938, although with some intervention. Some currencies of Central and Eastern Europe, notably the mark, were kept at the old parities with extensive exchange controls.[62]

Purchasing power parity calculations (Table 8.2), bearing in mind the usual caveats, suggest that by 1934 the Germany currency was the most overvalued currency in the world as a result of the continued link with gold. Where the figures are less than 100 in the table, the cost of the franc and/or sterling is less than it should be on the basis of price relations, if exchange rates were in equilibrium in 1929: in other words the currency is overvalued. The multiple exchange rate system and the bilateral clearing arrangements which were devised to maintain the overvaluation of the German mark has been described in the previous chapter. At the other extreme the yen was the most undervalued currency, but prices in Chile, India, Argentine, Australia and Spain also failed to adjust to the heavy fall in the external value of the currencies. These countries were all exporters of raw materials or foodstuffs, whose terms of trade were adversely affected by the price decline and so some of the 'under valuation' is spurious.

### Competitive depreciations

Countries that applied expansionary measures, either coupled with devaluation or floating, began recovery from the Depression earlier than those like France which maintained the old rates. Such exchange

**Table 8.2** *Cost of the French franc and sterling as a percentage of purchasing power parity cost in 1934 (1929 = 100)*

| End of year | Cost of franc (1934) | Cost of sterling (1934) |
|---|---|---|
| Germany | 74.3 | 62.6 |
| Hungary | 80.6 | 67.8 |
| Austria | 83.1 | 69.0 |
| Czechoslovakia | 86.0 | 72.8 |
| Switzerland | 87.0 | 71.3 |
| Italy | 98.0 | 82.5 |
| Poland | 98.7 | 83.0 |
| S. Africa | 99.2 | 83.0 |
| France | — | 84.2 |
| Netherlands | 101.1 | 85.1 |
| Belgium | 102.9 | 84.8 |
| Portugal | 103.3 | 87.0 |
| Bulgaria | 104.4 | 88.0 |
| Albania | 107.1 | 90.0 |
| Peru | 110.1 | 92.0 |
| United States | 114.3 | 90.2 |
| Yugoslavia | 115.3 | 97.2 |
| Finland | 115.9 | 97.5 |
| Greece | 116.0 | 97.7 |
| Sweden | 118.2 | 90.4 |
| Norway | 118.6 | 100.0 |
| United Kingdom | 118.7 | — |
| China | 110.0 | 100.2 |
| Canada | 122.4 | 103.1 |
| Denmark | 124.5 | 104.8 |
| New Zealand | 126.6 | 105.7 |
| Estonia | 127.1 | 107.2 |
| Spain | 137.6* | 107.5* |
| Australia | 141.6 | 108.0 |
| India | 145.1 | 122.3 |
| Chile | 150.2 | 126.6 |
| Argentine | 152.9 | 128.8 |
| Japan | 193.9 | 163.4 |

*Source*: League of Nations, *Commerical Banks 1929–34*, Geneva (1935).
*August

rate policies gave rise to charges of competitive depreciation, but at the time when currencies were depreciated or stabilised it was often impossible to know whether the change would entail a country 'exporting unemployment' or would restore equilibrium. The 16 per cent devaluation of the Czech crown in March 1935 was calculated on the basis of purchasing power parity with wholesale price indices, but in October 1936 another devaluation was necessary. On the other hand the Belgian devaluation of 28 per cent in 1935 was deliberately large to allow domestic expansion. Imports were rapidly drawn in and an import surplus emerged, so this did not constitute a 'beggar-my-neighbour' policy. Even so it did put deflationary pressures on France and the gold bloc by inducing speculative capital outflows.[63]

The competitive depreciation of the yen was among the clearest and successful examples. As Table 8.2 shows, the yen depreciated the most against the franc and sterling by 1934 and Japanese export expansion in the 1930s was very fast. But competitive depreciation was not necessarily desired by the government whose currency was falling. The 1931 depreciation of the pound in response to a capital outflow, undervalued the currency and helped economic activity increase. The depreciation of the dollar was perhaps the classic example of competitive depreciation, for there were no pressures on the current account, and gold reserves were immense. The dollar was devalued against gold on October 1933 by 59.06 per cent by fixing a gold price of $35 per fine ounce. Part ($2000 million) of the profits from the revaluation of the national gold stocks was used to establish an Exchange Stabilisation Fund. Gold flowed into the US because the dollar price of gold at the franc rate was less than the price for which it could be sold to the US Treasury. The gold-buying policy was intended to raise American commodity prices and, because the United States was neither a large international supplier nor international buyer of most commodities, it was fairly successful.[64]

The floating of the dollar in 1933 clearly reduced the undervaluation of the franc against the dollar in 1934. France and the gold bloc countries (Belgium, Netherlands and Switzerland) lost most of the advantages they had gained in the 1920s as other economies depreciated against them in the 1930s. Nevertheless they pledged themselves to stay at the existing parities at the World Economic Conference in 1933 and again at Geneva in 1934. As a result they remained depressed well after recovery had begun elsewhere. Between 1929 and 1937 hours worked in French industry fell by one-third, and more people were employed in French agriculture in 1939 than had been during the 1920s.

*Sterling in the 1930s*

The British float was managed by the Exchange Equalisation
Account (EEA) which originated in the Bank of England's secret
hoard of dollars, accumulated since 1925. By 1932 the profits and
losses on exchange intervention had become too great for a privately
owned bank, and the fund became officially financed, reaching £635
million in 1937.[65] The rules followed by the Account in stabilising
sterling would have been quite acceptable to the International
Monetary Fund of the later 1970s.[66] In its objective of preventing
the exchange rate from being influenced by non-rational speculation,
the EEA seems to have been successful. Only in December 1931,
before the EEA began operations, was there evidence of severe
speculative overshooting of the equilibrium value of the sterling–
dollar exchange rate.[67] The political crises of the period such as
the Belgian devaluation, the French changes of ministry in 1935 and
1936, and Hitler's march into the Rhineland in 1936, did not seem
to cause untoward movements in sterling. Although the activities
of the EEA had beneficial effects, the contribution towards the
stabilisation of month-to-month variations in the rate was only
modest. The very existence of the Account may have curbed
short-term variability in capital flows, and this would have been
valuable because controls on capital movements were incomplete
and probably had little impact.

The effective exchange rate of the pound, the trade weighted
average against all other currencies, gives a rather different impression of the behaviour of the sterling exchange rate during the
1930s from the sterling–dollar rate.[68] The benefits of freeing the
exchange, and the effects of increased competitiveness on British
economic recovery, persisted in the years 1934–6, when the effective
rate remained 4–5 per cent below the 1929–30 level, and 8 per cent
below the level of August 1931. The effective rate shows a steady
upward trend after the shock of devaluation had worked itself out
by late 1932, providing a motive for the EEA to hold the pound
down, as it was widely believed to be doing. Between 1931 and 1937
there was a steady capital inflow which tended to push the rate up,
a tendency the EEA may have wished to prevent in order to maintain
purchasing power parties. But the Account's resources were inadequate for that task, being merely sufficient to dampen trends.

The EEA pegged sterling closely to the dollar from late 1933 until
1938. A very large part of the trading world therefore enjoyed
stability, while suffering in so far as the stabilised rates were
inappropriate. In addition pegging meant that Britain shared in the

US recession of 1937–8. The pegging was in part a recognition that the United States would not tolerate a really cheap pound. It also helped maintain sterling's role in international trade, much of which was still invoiced in sterling and financed through London. Sterling balances held by other countries continued to provide Britain with a source of income. Some idea of the size of this income can be inferred from the balances of £598 million in 1938, and assuming (a) that the funds released were allowed to go into new foreign investment yielding 5 per cent; and (b) that the cost of the balances to the United Kingdom was the interest that had to be paid on Treasury bills, 0.611 per cent. These assumptions give a gross yield of £26.2 million (£598m × [0.05 − 0.00611]), a sum that amounted to 2.5 per cent of British export receipts in 1938, and 0.5 per cent of GNP.[69]

A more widely recognised milestone on the path to the acceptance that exchange rates were matters for multilateral agreement than the pegging of sterling against the dollar, was the Tripartite Agreement of 1936. Strictly speaking there was no agreement at all, only national declarations. The governments of Britain, France and the United States issued similar statements on 25 September 1936 accepting the devaluation of the franc, agreeing to minimise the associated exchange market disturbances, and agreeing to work for improved conditions for international trade. Drummond believes the Agreement provided only a shadow of co-operation not the substance. The French government had only nominally accepted the British phrase about the progressive relaxation of quotas and exchange controls. In October they suppressed one-third of their quotas, but these only covered one-tenth of the value of French imports, and the French reduced duties on the few goods without quotas. Having devalued, the French were almost as protectionist as before. For this reason the Agreement was not a bridge to the Bretton Woods system. In addition the British were already managing sterling before 1936 with an eye on American desires, in so far as they could understand them or learn about them, purely from a recognition of American economic power.[70] The events of the next decade were to force an even greater awareness of this strength.

## Summary and conclusion

The war brought a number of political and economic conflicts to a head which, in most of the former belligerent states, resulted in substantial post-war inflation and depreciating exchange rates. There is evidence to suggest that the floating exchange rate regimes of the 1920s did well their job of reflecting underlying economic conditions. They obtained their bad reputation by association with often misguided government policies, especially those that resulted in the overvaluation of the pound and the yen, the undervaluation of the franc and the collapse of the mark and the rouble.

The establishment of the fixed exchange rates of the gold exchange standard during the 1920s was seen as a return to 'normality' that would impose restraints on governments. The exchange standard, entailing the holding by central banks of currencies (usually sterling or dollars) which were convertible into gold instead of gold itself, was expected to enhance world supplies of liquidity at a time when the annual increase in gold output was small. A disadvantage of the system was that there was a greater mass of claims on the gold reserves of the key currencies which encouraged panic withdrawls, and therefore deflationary policies in key currency countries during the crisis of the early 1930s. A second disadvantage was that of all fixed exchange rate regimes – that when a depression came, countries in which depression tendencies were not primarily generated by the domestic economy, such as Japan and France in 1930 and the United Kingdom in 1929, were dragged into the general collapse.

The behaviour of central banks under the gold exchange standard in not following 'the rules of the game' has sometimes been blamed for the poor performance of the system. France and the United States showed a persistent tendency to acquire the greater part of the gold reserves of the world without any corresponding expansion of domestic prices and incomes. Before 1914 central banks had not followed the rules either. The difference between the world wars stemmed from new American monetary management and from the undervaluation of the franc. Other countries therefore had inadequate reserves to finance their balance of payments deficits during the early stages of the Depression and had to resort to deflationary policies.

Certain changes in the monetary system in the 1920s had made it more vulnerable to disturbances. Prices and wages seem to have become less flexible in many countries so that a decline in demand by the late 1920s would be met to a much greater extent than before by the contraction of output and employment, rather than by a reduction in prices. In addition, there was a much greater accumulation of debt, both private and public, between nations and within nations than ever before. The first world war had left behind a network of inter-allied war debts and reparations. Payments of these created problems of transferring the real resources in the face of the unwillingness of some donors to give them up, and of some recipients to receive them. The increase in debt payments due from primary producers at a time when primary prices were weakening resulted in bank collapses in agricultural areas within nations, and eventual exchange rate depreciation and deflationary policies among primary product exporters by the beginning of the thirties.

Had there been no depression in the United States it is unlikely that the rest of the world would have experienced anything like the slump it actually did, despite the tendencies in many primary commodity exporting countries and in Germany. Capital exports from the US normally increased in a boom and would have provided additional balance of payments finance for those countries in difficulty. American demand for imports, which fell off so rapidly in the Depression, would have supplied additional support. Kindleberger has blamed the Depression on the United States for not fulfilling these conditions in the way that Britain did during the nineteenth century, but for which she lacked the economic strength in the interwar years. Unable to prevent a fall of almost 30 per cent in her own national income between 1929 and 1933 it is not surprising the United States failed to operate constructive policies for the rest of the world.

A much reduced volume of world trade emerged from the Depression, with the gold exchange standard gone and most nations on floating exchange rates. The managed floats of the 1930s gave the international economy rather more stability than it had in the 1970s and almost as much as in the 1920s. Charges of competitive depreciation only have any substance when the effect of capital flights are considered, with the exception of the United States, and capital flights came to be mainly determined by political factors. Britain continued to receive earnings from providing the reserve currency for the sterling area, and in the Tripartite Agreement of 1936 there was a sign of international co-operation over exchange rates, although the importance of this Agreement has been over-estimated. The domestic unemployment in many countries persisted partly because the inflation of the 1920s had created a fear of reflating, and partly because the intellectual framework provided by J.M. Keynes in 1936 had not been widely accepted.

## Notes

1. S.S. Katzenellenbaum, *Russian Currency and Banking 1914–1924*, London. P.S. King (1925).
2. E.V. Morgan, *Studies in British Financial Policy 1916–1925*. London (1952).

3. J. Inouye, *Problems of Japanese Currency and Exchange 1914–26*, Glasgow (1931).
4. D.E. Moggridge, *British Monetary Policy 1924–1931: The Norman Conquest of $4.86*, Cambridge: Cambridge University Press (1972), p. 17.
5. T. Balderston, 'Inflation in Britain and Germany 1908–1923: a comparative study', mimeo, Department of History, University of Manchester.
6. C. Bresciani-Turoni, *The Economics of Inflation: A Study of Currency Depreciations in Post War Germany 1914–1923*, London: Allen & Unwin (1937). Bresciani-Turoni was a member of the Allied Reparations Commission in Germany during the period of inflation. See also F.D. Graham, *Exchange, Prices and Production in Hyperinflation: Germany 1920–23*, Princeton, N.J.: Princeton University Press (1930).
7. ibid., p. 252.
8. D.E. Moggridge, 'The gold standard and national financial policies 1919–1939', in *The Cambridge Economic History of Europe*, vol. VIII (forthcoming). R.Z. Aliber, 'Speculation in the foreign exchanges: the European experience 1919–1926', *Yale Economic Essays* vol. II, part I, Spring (1962), pp. 171–245. M. Wolfe, *The French Franc between the Wars, 1919–1939*, New York: Columbia University Press (1951). B. Eichengreen, 'Did speculation destabilize the French franc in the 1920s'. *Explorations in Economic History*, **19** (1982), pp. 71–100.
9. G.C. Schmid, 'The politics of currency stabilization: the French franc 1926', *Journal of European Economic History*, **3** (1974), pp. 359–77.
10. Moggridge (1972), op. cit., pp. 85–6.
11. L.S. Presnell, '1925: the burden of sterling', *Economic History Review*, **31** (1978), pp. 67–88.
12. R. Triffin, *Our International Monetary System*, New York: Random House (1968), ch. 2. D.H. Aldcroft also asserts international cooperation could have produced a better exchange rate regime. D.H. Aldcroft *From Versailles to Wall Street 1919–1929*, London: Allen Lane (1977). p. 95.
13. Katzenellenbaum, op. cit.
14. Inouye, op. cit.
15. B. Ohlin, *The Course and Phases of the World Depression*, Geneva: League of Nations (1931), p. 25.
16. For example Moggridge (1972) op. cit., p. 101.
17. K.W. Clements and J.A. Frenkel, 'Flexible exchange rates, money and relative prices: the dollar–pound in the 1920's', *Journal of International Economics*, May (1980), pp. 249–62.
18. J.S. Hodgson, 'An analysis of floating exchange rates: the dollar–sterling rate 1919–1925', *Southern Economic Journal*, **39** (1972), pp. 249–57.
19. Aliber, loc. cit. The forward exchange rate is the rate at which a currency can be bought or sold now for delivery or receipt at a particular future date. The forward rate therefore reflects expectations about the future changes in the 'spot', or current, exchange rate.

20. L.B. Thomas, 'Behaviour of flexible exchange rates: additional tests from the post-world war 1 episode', *Southern Economic Journal*, **40** (1973), pp. 167–82.
21. J.M. Keynes, *The Economic Consequences of Mr. Churchill*, London: Hogarth Press, (1925); Moggridge, op. cit. esp. Appendix 1.
22. The calculation of the impact effect of an 11 per cent appreciation of sterling between 1924 and 1925 assumes that export prices in foreign currency would rise by 7 per cent and on the import side prices in sterling would fall by 8 per cent. (If domestic and foreign supplies were perfectly elastic, sterling import prices would have fallen by 10 per cent and export prices in foreign currency would have risen by 11 per cent.) Given his assumptions, Moggridge found British export volume lower by 10.5 per cent ($1.5 \times 7$ per cent) and British import volume higher by 4.0 per cent ($0.5 \times 8$ per cent) as a result of overvaluation. The sterling earnings from exports were lower by the reduced volume times the assumed 4 per cent lower sterling price. 14.1 per cent ($100 - [100 - 4]\% \times [100 - 10.5]\%$) and sterling requirements to pay for imports fell by 4.3 per cent; the higher volume times the lower price ($100 - \{[100 - 8]\% \times 104\}\%$). Since 1924 exports of UK produce were £801 million and retained imports were £1137 million, the visible current account worsened by $0.141 \times £801\text{m} - 0.043 \times £1137\text{m} = £112.9\text{m} - £489\text{m} = £64\text{m}$. The invisible account Moggridge believes, deteriorated by at least £15 million, mainly because of the fall in the sterling value of British overseas equity earnings. Hence the overall deterioration on current account was £64m + £15m = £79m, compared with an actual surplus of £73 million.

The employment effects of an £80 million reduction of imports can be found, (i) by dividing the change in imports by the assumed marginal propensity to import (£80m/0.3) to obtain the necessary reduction in income (£266.67m); (ii) by taking the net national income per person employed of £185.6 and dividing the figure into the income reduction to find the cut in employment (1.44m). Another, perhaps less *ad hoc* second stage calculation requires (a) noting that the required income reduction is about 5.5 per cent of 1925 counter-factual income (1925 actual income $+ £266.67\text{m}$); and (b) assuming a short-run unit income elasticity of demand for labour. Since 5.5 per cent of the 1925 counterfactual labour force is 1.03 million, this is also the induced unemployment, a more plausible figure than Moggridge's.
23. Pressnell, loc. cit.
24. J.H. Jones, 'The gold standard', *Economic Journal*, **43** (1933), pp. 351–74.
25. P.H. Lindert, *Key Currencies and Gold 1900–1914*, Princeton: Princeton University Press (1969), p. 76.
26. D.H. Aldcroft, op. cit., p. 79.
27. J.M. Keynes, 'The German transfer problem', *Economic Journal*, **39** (1929), pp. 1–7. H.G. Johnson, 'The classical transfer problem: an alternative formulation', *Economica*, **42** (1975), pp. 20–31. J.M. Keynes, *A Revision of the Treaty*, London: Macmillan (1922). E.

Mantoux, *The Carthaginian Peace ; or the economic consequences of Mr Keynes*, London: G. Cumberledge (1946). D.C. McIntosh, 'Mantoux versus Keynes: A note on German income and the reparations controversy', *Economic Journal*, **87** (1977), pp. 765–7. T. Balogh and A. Graham, 'The transfer problem revisited', *Oxford Bulletin of Economics and Statistics*, **40** (1979), pp. 183–92.

28. G. Haberler, *Theory of International Trade*. London: Hodge (1936), ch. 8.
29. Aldcroft, op. cit., p. 95.
30. C.P. Kindleberger, *The World in Depression 1929–1939*, London: Allen Lane (1973), p. 41.
31. ibid., p. 56. Ohlin, op. cit.
32. I. Svennilson, *Growth and Stagnation in the European Economy*. Geneva: United Nations Economic Commission for Europe (1954), Table 3.
33. D.K. Benjamin and L.A. Kochin, 'Searching for an explanation of unemployment in interwar Britain', *Journal of Political Economy*, **87** (1979), pp. 441–78.
34. J.F. Wright, 'Britain's inter-war experience', *Oxford Economic Papers*, Supplement (1981), pp. 282–305.
35. L. Hannah and J. Kay, *Concentration in Modern Industry*, London: Macmillan (1977). S. Bell, *Productivity, Wages and National Income*, NBER (1940).
36. P. Temin, 'General equilibrium models in economic history', *Journal of Economic History*, **31** (1971), pp. 58–75.
37. B. Ohlin, op. cit., pp. 165–7, 289–90.
38. R. Nurkse, *International Currency Experience*, Princeton: League of Nations (1944), pp. 212–13.
40. M. Friedman and A. Schwartz, *A Monetary History of the United States*, Princeton: Princeton University Press (1963), p. 369 *et seq.*
41. Nurkse, op. cit., p. 74.
42. Royal Institute of International Affairs, *The International Gold Problem*. London: Oxford University Press (1931), p. 208.
43. D. Moggridge, loc. cit. See also, Nurske, op. cit., p. 76.
44. R.S. Sayers, *The Bank of England 1891–1944*, Cambridge: Cambridge University Press (1976), pp. 211, 223, 312.
45. League of Nations, *Commercial Banks 1929–34*, Geneva (1935) p. LXXXI.
46. Moggridge, loc. cit.
47. Ohlin, op. cit.
48. H. Flessig, 'The United States and the non-European periphery during the early years of the Great Depression', in H. van der Wee, *The Great Depression Revisited*, The Hague: M. Nijhoff (1972).
49. League of Nations, op. cit.
50. Sayers, op. cit., p. 389.
51. Moggridge, op. cit., pp. 18, p. 243.
52. Sayers, op. cit.

53. League of Nations, op. cit., p. LXIV.
54. Flessing, loc. cit.
   Ignoring for simplicity the price declines, the international impact of the fall in American income between 1929 and 1932 can be approximated by the international multiplier with foreign income repercussions ($F$). A fall in American spending lowered American imports which cut foreign incomes and indirectly reduced American exports, further lowering American income, and so on. The illustrative calculation below uses the multiplier formula (from P.H. Lindert and C.K. Kindleberger, *International Economics*, Homewood, Illinois: Irwin (1981) p. 310):

$$F = \frac{1 + mf/sf}{s + m + (mf \cdot s/sf)}$$

where $m$ and $mf$ are, respectively, the domestic and foreign marginal propensities to import, and $s$ and $sf$ are, respectively, the domestic and foreign marginal propensities to save (including the marginal tax rate). Assume $s = m = 0.1$, $mf = sf = 0.2$, then a \$10b fall in American spending ultimately lowered American income by \$66.6 billion, (US investment fell by almost \$10b in 1929–30). In the process, American imports, or the exports of the rest of world to the United States, fell by $m \times$ \$66.6b or \$6.66 billion. This decline in the rest of the world's exports to the United States that resulted from the \$10b fall in American spending caused an ultimate reduction of \$22.2b. in the rest of the world's income. American and British GNPs in 1929 were respectively about \$103 billion and \$22 billion.
55. P. Temin, *Did Monetary Factors Cause the Great Depression?*, New York: Norton (1976).
56. League of Nations, op. cit., Introduction.
57. Kindleberger, op. cit., ch. 14.
58. *Hansard*, House of Commons, v 183. 28 April 1925. p. 58.
59. Ohlin, op. cit., p. 110.
60. E.V. Choudri and L.A. Kochin, 'The exchange rate and the international transmission of business cycle disturbances: some evidence from the Great Depression', *Journal of Money Credit and Banking*, **12** (1980), pp. 565–74.
61. League of Nations, op. cit., Introduction.
62. Nurkse, op. cit., pp. 122–3.
63. G. Haberler, *The World Economy, Money and the Great Depression 1919–1939*, Washington DC: American Institute for Public Policy Research (1976), p. 35.
64. Moggridge, loc. cit.
65. Sayers, op. cit., pp. 487–8.
66. S. Howson, *Sterling's Managed Float: The Operation of the Exchange Accounts 1932–39*, Princeton: Princeton University Press (1980).
67. J.K. Whitaker and M.W. Hudgins, Jr 'The floating pound sterling of the 1930's', *Southern Economic Journal*. **43** (1977), pp. 1478–85.

68. J. Redmond, 'An indicator of the effective exchange rate of the pound in the nineteen thirties', *Economic History Review*, **33** (1980), pp. 83–91.
69. I. Drummond, *The Floating Pound and the Sterling Area 1931–1939*, Cambridge: Cambridge University Press (1981), pp. 248. 258–9.
70. ibid., pp. 220, 227. 248.

# 9 The Redirection of the International Economy, 1939–53

The second world war broke the mould of pre-war economic relations. This destruction allowed a conscious decision to be taken as to whether there should be a return to the state of affairs of the 1930s, or whether a new system should be introduced. In contrast to the period after the first world war a new set of economic relations was chosen. Greater control by governments over economic life during the war had demonstrated new possibilities, and achieving agreement was made easier by the enhanced bargaining power of the United States which emerged from the war as the pre-eminent world power, with the determination and the ability to create a new system based upon multilateral, non-discriminatory trade. The Russian challenge to American beliefs gave an added stimulus to the United States not to withdraw into isolation as she had done after Versailles.

The perceived 'lessons of history' greatly influenced the changes that were implemented. The planners in the American administration saw the 1930s as a period of economic nationalism and 'beggar-my-neighbour' policies, to be avoided by internationalist institutions to which all countries would belong. The western allies believed that recovery during the 1920s had been bedevilled by war debts and reparations, and they were concerned that this would not happen again. Those countries lacking the power to restructure international institutions sometimes adopted different interpretations of the past. Some newly-independent countries believed their economic development had been stunted by trade and foreign investment imposed upon them by the imperial powers. They preferred to opt for state-controlled economic development policies, in which the only trade necessary was imports for industrialisation. Other non-industrial countries saw the depressed inter-war trade in primary products as demonstrating the impossibility of developing through exporting raw materials and foodstuffs, and pursued similar policies.

## International economic relations during the war

In a variety of ways the transformation of international economic relations during the second world war influenced the pattern of the system after 1945. The most important change arose from the increased economic strength, both absolutely and relatively, that the United States attained during the war. While still a neutral, the United States' employment and income were boosted by the massive orders for armaments placed by the British and French in 1939. Subsequently, with the entry of America into the war, the inter-allied financial transfers furthered an international division of labour in the war effort by which American financial aid allowed Britain and the empire countries to maintain a larger proportion of their manpower in the armed forces than would otherwise have been possible.[1] The United States could do this and yet still commit a smaller proportion of its economy to the war than Britain. In 1944 22 per cent of the British labour force was in the armed forces and 33 per cent in war employment; for America the figures were $18\frac{1}{2}$ and $21\frac{1}{2}$ per cent respectively. Both because of the relatively enhanced American productive capacity and because a larger section of American industry was free to invest and expand, together with the absence of the direct effects of enemy action on the economy, the United States was bound to dominate the post-war world if she chose to do so. The Japanese attack on Pearl Harbour symbolised the inability of the United States to isolate herself from the rest of the world, and the necessity to exercise some influence over international relations.

Between 4 and 5 per cent of the national income of the United States was transferred to the British empire for lend-lease goods and services. Cash payments were not required for the munitions and combat equipment (65 per cent of lend-lease) or the other goods, such as concentrated foods sent from specially-built plants in the United States to Britain. Reciprocal aid from Britain and the empire countries paid for the upkeep of US forces in allied countries. If all aid financed by the United Kingdom is included, the share of British national income transferred to the United States was also 4 to 5 per cent. Australia and New Zealand respectively contributed nearly 7 and 10 per cent of their national incomes to the United States as reciprocal aid. After the German invasion of 1941, Russia also became a major lend-lease beneficiary. By early 1945, mutual aid supplies amounted to $5000 million per annum. Canada operated a system similar to lend-lease in supplying allied countries, and, where Britain was concerned, was equally generous after the end of the war.

In the Mutual Aid Agreement signed between Britain and America in 1942, Roosevelt was concerned that the financial costs should be divided so 'that no nation [would] grow rich from the war effort of its allies'. He wanted to avoid the problems of inter-allied war debts that had dragged on through the 1920s.[2] Churchill and Roosevelt similarly agreed that experience showed that large indemnities did not work. The settlement of December 1945 cancelled the whole of the mutual aid account between the US and the UK on which there was $22 000 million of lend-lease against £1200 million of reciprocal aid. Measured in financial terms, Britain was clearly the beneficiary to the tune of at least $16 000 million. The Mutual Aid Agreement and the cancellation were tied to an agreement on commercial policy by which Britain was committed to discussions on the elimination of Commonwealth Preferences established at Ottawa in 1932 (see Chapter 7). The meaning of this Agreement and the objective itself remained a sensitive point in British–American relations for a number of years after the war. Churchill had secured a declaration from Rossevelt that the UK was no more committed to the abolition of Commonwealth Preferences than the American government was committed to the abolition of their high protective tariff.[3]

The American dislike of Commonwealth Preferences was rooted in the belief that discrimination in international trade was a major source of political conflict and reduced welfare. Japanese expansion in the Far East, which was eventually to bring the United States into the war, owed much to Japan's exclusion from the great trade blocs of the 1930s. The Japanese concern for raw material, fuel supplies and for markets led to the establishment of the Manchurian Industrial Development Corporation as the instrument of economic development in the puppet state of Manchukuo in North China.[4] Korea and Taiwan for some time had been Japanese colonies which were developed so as to complement the Japanese economy. The weakness of the European colonial powers provided Japan with another opportunity to expand her economic sphere of influence. However in response to the Japanese occupation of the Saigon area in July 1941, the American government froze all Japanese assets and imposed an economic embargo. The Japanese decided to break the embargo by continued expansion and war. Once war with the western powers began, the difficulties of maintaining sea transport between the various states of the 'Co-prosperity Sphere' reduced the extent and effectiveness of economic relations within the Japanese empire. By the end of the war 88 per cent of Japan's 6.5 million ton merchant marine had been sunk.

The most important long-run effects of the 'Co-prosperity Sphere' were the political changes it precipitated. Japanese wartime expansion was pursued under the slogan of 'Asia for the Asians'. Nominally independent regimes were set up in conquered colonies: in Burma and the Philippines in 1943. and in Indo-China and Indonesia in 1945.[5] Britain, the United States and China committed themselves in 1943 to independence for the Japanese colony of Korea. The political forces unleashed encouraged the granting of independence soon after the end of hostilities to many Asian territories, both those formerly occupied by the Japanese, and others. In 1946, the Philippines[6] and in 1948 Burma, the Federation of Malaya and Ceylon were granted independence. Fighting continued in Malaya and in Indo-China.

India was not a battlefield and so was able to reap some economic advantage from the war. An export surplus allowed the accumulation of sterling balances which could be spent afterwards when sterling became convertible and peacetime production began in the sterling area. With a small technological base on which to build in comparison with the western powers, the economic advantages to be gained were correspondingly small – India actually experienced a decline in coal, pig iron and steel production after 1940.[7] Only in munitions, shipbuilding and engineering were there signs of growth adequate for industrialisation. What economic benefits there were from being on the periphery of the war were soon dissipated. In 1947 India was given independence and split into two countries, India and Pakistan, amidst fighting and forced migration. Pakistan was a producer of raw materials, especially jute and cotton, and food needed by India. India produced manufactures and coal needed by Pakistan. Because of trade barriers with Pakistan, Indian exchange reserves accumulated during the war were largely spent on importing food.[8]

One of the greatest international redirections of economic activity during the war occurred after the German invasion of France in 1940. Under the guise of occupation costs, payments extracted from France in 1943 amounted to perhaps 8–9 per cent of Germany's GNP.[9] This figure excludes the benefits derived from French workers in Germany and confiscations. The German gains from France were much greater than those from the German-occupied eastern territories, where a combination of a 'scorched earth' policy of the retreating troops, poverty and a bestially destructive occupation policy meant that, for example, coal production was usually inadequate even for the troops on the spot. The German chemical firm, IG Farben, used the occupation in the east as an opportunity to engage in 'multinational' production with slave labour.[10] Workers in IG Farben's camp could expect to live on average for three months; for the company, the supply price of this labour was virtually zero, and so there was no incentive to provide more food or less brutal treatment.

In contrast to the Slavs of the east, the Norwegians were believed by the occupying Nazis to be 'racially pure', and as a result were the beneficiaries of German plans for massive investment to take advantage of Norway's hydro-electric potential and for increased food production.[11] Although subsequent wartime shortages prevented much of this investment coming to fruition, one of the major new aluminum factories was finished and two of the power stations.

As with the Japanese occupations in Asia the longer-term significance of the German-imposed international economic relations in Europe arose from their indirect results. The liberation of the eastern territories allowed Russia to pull them into the communist, centrally-planned economic system and away from their relations with Western Europe of the interwar years. In Western Europe the German invasion of France for the third time within a century, instead of provoking the hostility and mistrust after the war as on previous occasions, eventually led to the formation of economic unions designed to prevent such wars ever occurring again.

The war served to ease the international economic relations of most Latin American countries which, during the 1930s, had faced the problems of trying to sell exports to Europe and buy imports from the United States. Enormous American purchases from Latin America during the war eliminated the dollar shortage and allowed the accumulation of dollar reserves.[12] The Latin American share of world exports rose from 7.8 per cent in 1938 to 13.4 per cent in 1946. With markets and supplies outside the continent largely cut off, trade increased between Latin American countries as a proportion of their total trade. Those countries like Chile importing mainly foodstuffs which could be supplied by other Latin American countries maintained the value of their trade. Economies dependent on European suppliers for imports of machinery, fuel and raw materials reduced their trade markedly; Argentina cut imports to one-third of the pre-war volume and one-half of the value.

Many African economies, especially the French territories heavily dependent on Europe as a market for their primary product exports, were damaged by the war; but others, like the Belgian Congo, south Africa and British East Africa, which exported materials of strategic significance, benefitted.[13] Both Canada and Australia made significant advances in industrialisation supplying the allied war effort. Manufacturing output in Canada at the end of the war was $2\frac{1}{2}$ times the average between 1935 and 1939, which had been, however, considerably less than full employment output. Overall the war did not produce import substitution on the same scale as the first world war had done for those not heavily involved in the fighting. Though it similarly provided protection from foreign competition, this alone was inadequate for mass production (outside textiles), which was by then necessary for industrial development.

## The post-war international system

As already noted, a preliminary agreement between Britain and America about the ultimate shape of the post-war international trading system had been reached in 1942. Planning for the new order in both countries began the same year. Not surprisingly the planners failed to foresee and allow for the magnitude of the post-war dollar gap stemming from the reconstruction needs of the devastated areas. What perhaps *was* surprising was that the intentions behind the system were eventually put into practice despite the difficulties of the late 1940s. In 1943 preparatory negotiations between British and American Treasury experts about the post-war monetary system were based on their plans, prepared respectively by J.M. Keynes and Harry Dexter White.[14] The common ground of the two plans lay in their opposition to floating exchange rates and to competitive trade restrictions, and their favouring the national right to control short-term capital movements. This agreement derived from a shared interpretation of the interwar years which owed much to the analysts of the League of Nations.[15]

The United States differed from Britain in the concern, described above, about the incidence and application of barriers to trade rather than about tariffs themselves. With a continental-size domestic market the United States could afford to assert the need for non-discrimination, and for the elimination of the British Common-Wealth Preference as it had in the interwar years. A second difference arose from the distrust by American officials of banking and 'big money' interests; the same attitude that had introduced the de-centralised American central banking system with twelve Federal Reserve Banks. Related to this attitude was a belief in the necessity for a written constitution for any new institutions. In addition the arrangements had to be acceptable to Congress which could nullify any agreement.[16]

To Britain, the national circumstances made it more obvious than to the United States that a relaxation of exchange controls and restrictions on trade would only be feasible if American aid and credit were very liberal. The British were especially concerned to maintain full employment and to be allowed to choose the exchange rate necessary to achieve that end.

The economic dominance of the United States ensured that the Bretton Woods Agreement of 1944, which set up the two new international monetary institutions of the post-war world, more closely resembled the American plan than the British. This was despite the view expressed in a verse allegedly salvaged from the first Anglo–American discussions during the second world war:

> In Washington Lord Halifax
> Once whispered to Lord Keynes:
> 'It's true *they* have the money bags
> But *we* have all the brains.'

The two institutions were the International Monetary Fund (IMF), for the maintenance of exchange stability and to deal with balance of payments problems, and the International Bank for Reconstruction and Development, to deal with long-term international investment. The IMF was to achieve its objectives by insisting that member countries establish a par value for their currencies in terms of gold or the US dollar.[17] These par values could be changed only to correct a 'fundamental disequilibrium' in the balance of payments. Reserves for the support of the fixed exchange rate could be supplemented by the Fund's resources. The resources were obtained from the quotas assigned to member countries. Quotas were assigned according to a country's national income, trade and international reserves. One quarter of the quotas had to be paid in gold or US dollars and the rest in the member's own currency. A member country could borrow up to the point where the Fund was holding currency equal to 200 per cent of the member's quota. The member supplied its own currency in exchange for the currency of a member country whose reserve position was relatively stronger. A member enjoyed automatic access to borrowings up to 25 per cent of its quota. Additional drawing rights were subject to increasingly restrictive conditions generally supporting a programme that would establish or maintain the stability of the member's currency at a 'realistic' rate of exchange.

The IMF thus acted as a bank making loans and receiving deposits and could increase the stock of international reserves. So, for example, if a borrower drew on its first credit tranche and received US dollars, its reserve position (the country's quota less the Fund's holdings of the country's currency) increased by that amount. At the same time the United States' reserve position increased by the same amount so that world reserves increased by double the amount originally drawn. However, no explicit allowance was made for a long-term growth in the stock of world international reserves to accommodate the growth in world trade.

The chaotic state of so many economies immediately after 1945 meant that in fact the IMF had little to do and its rules were largely ignored after the disastrous experience of Britain's attempt at restoring currency convertibility in 1947.

The International Bank for Reconstruction and Development, later better known as the World Bank, had a capitalisation of 2 per cent to be paid in gold or dollars, 18 per cent in the currencies of the member countries and usable for lending purposes only with the consent of the contributing country, and 80 per cent as a guarantee fund.[18] This capital structure sought to ensure that every country, rich and poor, would participate in providing the capital (the 2 per cent portion). It recognised that countries temporarily impoverished and in balance of payments difficulties would be able to contribute usable capital later (the 18 per cent) and it embodied the expectation that the mobilisation of capital from other sources would be much more important than the use of the Bank's own assets (the 80 per cent). Unlike the IMF the World Bank did make a significant though small contribution to the international economy by the end of the period of redirection, by lending first to war-torn Europe, and then to poor countries.

The plans for the new liberal order in international trade went even more awry than did those for international monetary arrangements. But the institution that emerged as a by-product to liberalise international trade was at first unexpectedly successful. In December 1945 the American government published proposals for an international trade organisation and invited various countries including the USSR to take part in negotiations for reductions in barriers to trade.[19] Out of the international deliberations in London, Geneva and Havana between 1946 and 1948 came the Havana Charter for setting up the International Trade Organisation (subject to ratification which never took place).

The discussions were marked by confrontation between Britain and America in which the British and then other countries successfully pressed for changes in the Charter allowing trade discrimination and quantitative restrictions under various circumstances. As these loopholes widened and increased, the Charter became less and less attractive to American multilateralists.[20] At the same time the success of the first GATT session in 1947 did much to reduce the urgency for an International Trade Organisation.

The General Agreement on Tariffs and Trade (GATT) originated in the recommendation of the Preparatory Committee for the Havana Conference at the London meeting of 1946 that negotiations for the reduction of trade barriers should be held under the sponsorship of the Committee.[21] The code of conduct incorporated in GATT involved two major principles: first a multilateral and non-discriminatory approach to international trade, and second, condemnation of quantitative trade restrictions. The first of these principles was implemented through the inclusions in the code of the most-favoured nation clause. Under this clause GATT prohibited any preferential trading agreement designed to favour one nation over another. Before negotiations started each member was to transmit to all others a preliminary list of tariff reduction concessions which it proposed to request. When negotiations began they were to present a corresponding list of concessions they were prepared to grant. Negotiations would then take place between two or more countries.

The procedure allowed participating countries to assess the value of concessions granted by other countries over and above the direct concessions negotiated. Negotiations began in April 1947. Twenty-three countries signed GATT on 30 October 1947. The first round of negotiations in 1947 between these countries resulted in 123 agreements and twenty schedules covering about 45000 tariff items relating to about one-half of world trade. In this and subsequent GATT rounds negotiations were threatened by a breakdown due to different interpretations in America and Britan of the rule concerning the elimination of preferences. The Commonwealth Preference system continued to irritate the United States at later GATT meetings and retarded tariff reduction.

In January 1952 the thirty-four contracting countries accounted for more than 80 per cent of world trade. By the mid-1950s it was estimated that a net reduction in United States duties of 50 per cent had been achieved since 1934 by tariff concessions alone, the greater part of which had been accomplished in the period after 1945.

## The dollar gap

The United States had the goods the rest of the world wanted to buy after the war, both for present consumption and for reconstruction, but the devastated areas did not have suitable goods and services to exchange. Only if they could borrow or run down their foreign exchange reserves could these countries import anything like the quantities of goods they needed. The alternative of exchange depreciation does not seem to have been considered a serious possibility until 1948.

The United States produced nearly one-half of the world's manufactured goods in the late 1940s. The wartime increase in American productive capacity meant that for the world as a whole industrial production by 1947 was 42 per cent above the 1938 level.[22] The lesser importance of the United States in world agricultural supplies, and the devastation in Europe and the Far East, resulted in world agricultural production in 1947/8 being 4 per cent below 1934/8 average levels. Practically all of Europe and Asia suffered a decline in food consumption in terms of calories and a deterioration in the quality of their diet.[23] In 1946/7 there was an average deficiency of 18 per cent in average calorie consumption per head in comparison to pre-war diets in deficiency areas (excluding China and the USSR). As a result of poor harvests, the availability of food supplies worsened in Europe in 1947/8. Similarly there were deficiencies in coal supplies; European coal consumption fell by 12 per cent between 1937 and 1947. Even allowing for compensation from other energy sources, coal supplies in 1947 were inadequate in most European importing countries to meet requirements in industry, transport and domestic use.

In 1947 merchandise imports of the devastated areas were $20.2 billion while exports and other current receipts amounted to $13.1 billion, leaving a deficit of $7.1 billion.[24] Because the currencies in which exports were valued were inconvertible, they could not all be used to buy the desired imports, so the problem was larger than the dollar value of the deficit indicated. The net deficit had been reduced to $1.6 billion by capital account transactions and by the United Nations Relief and Rehabilitation Administration, but UNRRA operations in Europe ended on 30 June 1947 and therefore no more finance could be hoped for from that direction.

The convertibility of sterling from 15 July 1947 had reduced Britain's ability to import by depleting her dollar reserves. As part of the American Loan Agreement at the end of lend-lease Britain was required to make sterling freely convertible into other currencies within two years.[25] Lend-lease terminated on VJ day, at 12:01 am on 2 September 1945, but the need for transfers from the United States did not simultaneously end. The British had not expected the war against Japan to end so soon and had planned on receiving aid until mid-1946. Britain had a large trading deficit with America and many countries had accumulated sterling balances during the war because they had supplied Britain goods without taking any goods or services in exchange. These countries wanted American products and converted their sterling into dollars which the British authorities were obliged to supply at the fixed exchange rate of $4.03 = £1. By the 20 August 1947 dollar reserves were nearly exhausted and sterling returned to inconvertibility.

These difficulties reduced European foreign trade in 1948 to a level lower than it had been ten years earlier. Had it not been for the remarkable British export performance (by the last quarter of 1948 export volume was 147 per cent of the pre-war level), the European export trade would have been even lower than the 18 per cent below the 1938 level that it was.[26] The reduction of European imports by 14 per cent over the same period was mainly due to reduced British and German imports. These were lower for different reasons. British production was higher than the 1938 level because some import substitution had been induced by controls, whereas German imports were low because of the failure of the economy to recover from the war; German production was still only 64 per cent of pre-war level.

Apart from the problem of the European deficit with the United States, and of Germany, European recovery proceeded well. Unlike the period after the first world war there was no mass unemployment. Improved supplies of raw materials imported from abroad and the restoration of incentives following monetary reforms pushed output for fifteen European countries approximately back to pre-war levels by 1948, when Marshall Aid began flowing (see below). Price and wage inflation was reduced to the 2–5 per cent range in 1948 as against a range of 10–20 per cent the previous year, with the exceptions of France and Greece.

In Eastern Europe (excluding USSR and East Germany) trade with Western Europe had reached the pre-war level in real terms by 1948.[27] Before the war the USSR had almost no ties with the nations of Eastern Europe; Gemany had been the main focus of East European trade before 1945. The collapse of Germany gave these countries little choice but to trade with each other and the Soviet Union if they wished to trade at all. The former enemy countries of East Germany, Hungary, Romania and Bulgaria were in any case occupied by the Russians, collecting maintenance payments for their troops, removing German and Italian plant and equipment, and establishing and running jointly-owned enterprises. Unlike the British and Americans, the Russians did impose substantial reparations on their defeated enemies. Nominal reparations of

$500 million were imposed on Romania and Hungary, but these payments were valued in goods at pre-war prices fixed arbitrarily in Russia's favour. Reparations therefore served as a means of appropriating a substantial portion of a satellite countries' output.[28] An American estimate of the transfers from Hungary was that they amounted to 35 per cent of Hungary's national income. A six-year contract for Romania to supply 1.7 million tons of petrol a year valued the petrol at one-half of the world price. Even liberated countries suffered; coal exported from Poland to Russia was valued at 10 per cent of the world market price, and the tariff of the joint Yugoslav–Soviet navigation company provided that the rate for Yugoslav use should be double the Soviet rate. In East Germany the means of transferring goods and services to Russia was more direct. By 1946 one-quarter of total industrial production was run by Soviet-controlled companies, including the whole of iron and steel and motor vehicle production.

Japan was in the worst economic position with two-thirds of the large cotton textile capacity destroyed, and with food and raw materials supplied only through the allied occupation forces and financed mainly by the United States.[29] About 6 million Japanese were returned to Japan from overseas territories only partly offset by the return of 1 million of other nationalities, especially Koreans from Japan. Between October 1945 and October 1948 2.2 million Koreans moved into South Korea. Wartime devastation, as in Europe, had reduced the ability of the Asian economies to export. Asia's trade with the United States, which had been in balance before the war, was now in deficit.[30] Because of quotas and exchange controls, so also was the trade balance with the rest of the world, formerly in surplus.

In contrast to the devastated areas, Latin America did not suffer from a dollar shortage in the immediate post-war years, but a return to the pre-war pattern of trade with Europe was difficult because of the scarcity of convertible currencies. Consequently Bolivian tin exports went to the United States instead of to Europe.[31] American policy was in any case directed to replacing Asia as a source of strategic materials such as rubber and tin, and Latin America was an obvious substitute supplier. Argentina and Brazil had believed in the continuance of the pre-war importance of Europe in Latin American trade because they had extended credit to their traditional buyers. Although this was the type of policy necessary to solve the dollar gap problem of the post-war world, the scale of the credits needed to have a significant impact on the problem was such that they could only be provided by the United States.

## The Marshall Plan and West European reconstruction

American planners, meeting in a high level State-Navy-War Co-ordinating Committee foresaw in early 1947 that the world would be unable to continue to buy US exports at the 1946–7 rate for more than another 12–18 months.[32] Foreign currency reserves of the dollar gap countries would soon be exhausted, there was little international credit and UNRRA relief was ending. The committee warned that the substantial decline in the US export surplus would have a depressing effect on business activity and employment in the US. A major US aid programme to finance a continued high level of US exports was the solution proposed by the Committee. This was the embryonic form of the plan revealed in Secretary of State Marshall's Harvard speech in June 1947. The Marshall Plan also neutralised the forces moving Western Europe permanently away from multilateral trade; the strength of the European left-wing parties, the relative weaknesses of the European economies, and the pull of the Soviet Union. Without the intensification of the Cold War, it would have been impossible even to contemplate sending such a massive aid programme to Congress.

The ground had been prepared by the enunciation of the Truman Doctrine in March 1947, pledging the United States to supply economic aid to uncommitted countries. From 1948 to 1952 about $13 150 million was made available under the Marshall Plan to Europe where the major recipients were France ($2706m), Britain ($3176m), West Germany ($1389m), The Netherlands ($1079m), Italy ($1474m), Greece and Austria (each $700m).[33] This distribution of aid shows that the fear of Communism was not the sole inspiration of the programme (although a necessary one as far as Congress was concerned) because Britain, the largest recipient, was relatively safe from Communism. After June 1951 Europe received a further $2600 million in Marshall Aid mainly in the period up to mid-1953. The aid offered under the programme took the form of grants of commodities produced predominantly in the United States. Inevitably there were pressures from interested American parties influencing the programme. More agricultural products were offered than requested and instead of scrap and semi-finished iron and steel for which Europe had asked, more finished iron and steel than was wanted was sent.[34]

Compared with European reconstruction after the first world war, economic recovery during the Marshall Plan period was rapid, although no attempt has yet been made to distinguish the impact of the plan from other influences on recovery.[35] The most enthusiastic advocates of the programme thought that it would act as a catalyst, raising income by possibly five times the amount of the aid, by removing serious bottlenecks, by making dollars available in order to prevent a collapse of international trade, and by providing a weapon for making the European countries pursue responsible fiscal and monetary policies, and making them co-operate with each other. The European Recovery Programme had the desired effect on US exports, halting the decline in 1948 that had begun in the third quarter of 1947.

The American ERP administration adopted a positive role in restructuring European economic relations as an aid to recovery. The Organisation for European Economic Cooperation (as a committee) was formed to draft the request for American aid in the first place. In order to stimulate intra-European trade the OEEC member governments in 1949 started to liberalise their trade and in 1950 they accepted a Code of Liberalisation, the aim of which was the gradual freeing of up to 75 per cent (later 90 per cent) of their mutual trade from the network of quantitative restrictions which had resulted from the balance of payments difficulties after the war.[36] The liberalisation was not automatically extended to GATT members outside the OEEC and was thus a deviation from the general GATT rule of non-discrimination in the application of quantitative restrictions. The United States and others felt this would speed up the return to more normal conditions in trade and payments and for that reason did not object.

The European Payments Union (EPU) was another mechanism by which the ERP administrators planned the economic integration of Europe. The EPU was to revive intra-European trade by creating a multilateral payments mechanism within Europe. A network of more than 200 bilateral trade agreements had been negotiated by the European countries by 1947.[37] They temporarily removed some of the pressure for strict barter in the absence of convertible currencies, but since the credit margins in the trade agreements were small, their effects were short-lived. The bilateral agreements tended towards closed bilateral balancing and were both restrictive and distorting.

Nine months after the 1949 devaluations (see below) the new EPU was agreed. Once a month the central bank of each Union member, including its associated monetary area if any, reported to the Bank for International Settlements, the EPU agent, the net surpluses or deficits of its current transactions with each of the other members. The BIS then offset each country's total net surpluses and total net deficits and arrived at a single net figure for each member *vis à vis*

all other members. The net balance for each member was accumulated month by month. This was then set off against a quota assigned
to each country at approximately 15 per cent of each member's total
intra-European visible and invisible trade in 1949. Accumulated
balances were settled partly in gold and partly in credit on a sliding
scale. The Code of Trade Liberalisation which became effective when
the EPU was signed attempted to reduce quotas which GATT did
not touch. The EPU proved temporary, as intended, rather than
permanent because the participants avoided inflationary policies and
because those countries which had to pay the highest price for the
continuation of the scheme, the United Kingdom, Germany and the
Benelux countries, were among the more economically and politically
powerful.

In the long term one of the most significant American contributions to European economic relations was the support for the
formation of the European Coal and Steel Community, despite its
discriminatory implications and its violation of the principles of
GATT. The common market in iron and steel began with a speech
by the French Foreign Minister Robert Schumann in May 1950
proposing the entire French–German production of coal and steel
be placed under a common authority in an organization which other
European countries would be free to join.[38] The motivation was to
draw France and West Germany together, making a future war
impossible. The treaty was signed in 1951 and included the Benelux
countries and Italy. Great Britain declined the invitation to take
part in preparatory work when France indicated that participation
meant acceptance of the goals of a supra-national authority and,
ultimately, of political unity. The treaty went further than a customs
union in aiming at an integration of production but less far in only
covering a proportion of trade.

### The Cold War and the reconstruction of Eastern Europe

The war had inevitably reduced economic relations between Eastern
Europe and the West, and Russia in 1945 was necessarily the major
market and source of supply. But in the immediate post-war years,
helped by the payment of $1.1 million by UNRRA to the Russian
satellite states, trade with the West increased and the importance
of Russia declined.[39] Between 1945 and 1948 Polish imports from
Russia fell from 90 per cent of the total to less than 25 per cent.
The UK and the USSR had concluded a trade agreement which
foresaw expanding trade.[40] The Marshall Plan promised to break
the East–West tension caused by Soviet aggressive tactics in

Romania, Bulgaria and Poland. The USSR was included in the offer of financial assistance for the reconstruction of Europe. They accepted an invitation from France and Britain to discuss procedures in Paris in June 1947. The conference failed because the Russians would only accept unconditional aid and the Americans were concerned that this would be used to strengthen communist governments. When the Russians withdrew they forced the Czechs to withdraw their acceptance and prevented the participation of the other East European nations. The communist *coup* in Prague occurred in February 1948 and a few months later the Russians sealed off Berlin. The US began constructing its economic warfare apparatus against the Communists, culminating in the Export Control Act of 1949. Nato was formed in 1949 and hostilities in Korea began in June 1950, resulting in a complete US embargo on trade with China.

Table 9.1 shows that East–West trade both before and after the war had been much less important to the West than to the East, and that although the war and occupation had reduced the trade's significance, the additional fall between 1948 and 1953 as a result of the Cold War was very severe.

The greater part of the reduction in trade was due to western, rather than eastern, controls. The USSR continued to ship chrome and manganese ores to the United States throughout the period of most intense economic warfare. Tension was eventually reduced by the end of the Korean War and the death of Stalin in 1953, together with the armistice in Indo-China the following year.

The Marshall Plan foiled the influence of the communist parties in Western Europe. Russia therefore tightened its control on Eastern Europe and began to develop East European resources by industrialisation. Reparations were reduced and eliminated completely for

**Table 9.1**   *East–West trade as percentages of the trade of the developed West and of the East, 1938–53.*

| Year | West | East |
|------|------|------|
| 1938 | 9.5  | 73.8 |
| 1948 | 4.1  | 41.6 |
| 1953 | 2.1  | 14.0 |

*Source*: J. Wilczynski *The Economics and Politics of East–West Trade*, New York: Praeger (1969), p. 54.

Hungary, Romania and East Germany in 1952, 1953 and 1954, respectively. However, together with troop maintenance payments, reparations remained sufficiently heavy to require Russian tanks to quell the East German riots of 1953. Equipment removed from East Germany and Romania to Russia was brought back. The first international organisation of the Eastern nations, the Council for Mutual Economic Assistance, was established on 25 January 1949. The CMEA in part was a rebuff to Yugoslavia which had broken with the USSR the previous year, and in part a response to the Marshall Plan and the formation of the OEEC. The Council did little to facilitate trade in the early years but intra-bloc trade rapidly came to dominate the trade of members, accounting for 80 per cent of the total trade by 1953.[41] Before the formation of CMEA intra-member trade was about 15 per cent of total member trade. The great shift in trading patterns undoubtedly imposed large economic losses from trade diversion on all participants including the USSR. All nations would have been better off if they could have continued or begun trading with the West. The losses were greater for the smaller countries, more dependent on trade. These sacrifices emphasise the political nature of CMEA, though once the Cold War had begun in earnest there was little alternative.

The industrialisation of the dependent countries of Eastern Eurupe solved one of the Soviet planners' problems of how to gain foreign currency to buy goods, especially copper, rubber, tin and wool in which the Soviet bloc was deficient. So long as they maintained a surplus in their trade with Western Europe, the satellite countries supplying Romanian oil, and Czech and Polish timber, could earn this currency. This ability to earn was enhanced by economic integration, prevented by the nationalism of the interwar years. The transmission of electricity and the supply of steel-rolled products across national borders were amongst the most common of the trans-national projects, inevitably supervised and standardised by Soviet administrators.[42]

The industrialisation effort of the Soviet Union was concentrated in five designated zones accounting for 7 per cent of the land area of the USSR. The dependent countries formed a sixth area complementary to the western regions of Russia. Iron ore was abundant in these western regions but most of the increase in Russian coal output since 1940 had occurred in the Urals or further east. The dependent countries had substantial coal mining sectors to which the west Russian iron ore could be shipped.[43]

Yugoslavia was the one communist European country not to become integrated into the Soviet system, and suffered accordingly. Between 1948 and 1953 the Russians gradually escalated towards a total economic blockade of Yugoslavia because it was unwilling to become an obedient satellite. Western assistance reduced the damage and though the blockade harmed the Yugoslav economy, it did not achieve the desired political effect.

## The pattern of trade and finance

As has been seen, government aid capital flows were crucial for financing the West European balances of payments in the recovery period. By the end of the 1940s with diminished volume they became a major support for the international payments of many less developed countries, assuming some of the role of private investment during the period before 1914. These non-industrial areas received $2000 million per annum in official grants and loans on average between 1953 and 1957.[44] The greater part was government-to-government aid, but the World Bank also made a significant contribution. By 30 June 1952 the Bank had made sixty-eight loans totalling the equivalent of $1.4 billion.[45] More than 35 per cent of the loan total was accounted for by the four European reconstruction loans of 1947, for France, Netherlands, Denmark and Luxemberg.

Under its Articles of Agreement the Bank was expected to finance only those productive projects for which other financing was not available on reasonable terms. The management thought private capital would be most readily available to the low income countries for the development of export products and was opposed to financing government-owned industry. The Bank also eschewed financing sanitation, education and health facilities because of their less measurable contribution to production and the associated problem of Wall Street's view of the soundness of the Bank's management. (Initially the Bank's securities were sold mainly on the American market.) The Bank came to concentrate on investment in power plants, railways, roads and similar physical facilities in part because such projects were large enough to justify review and appraisal by a global agency. The selection was the result of circumstances, but led the Bank to argue for public utility investment, financial stability and the encouragement of private investment as the best means of economic development.

Official funds often tended to flow to areas and industries neglected by past private investors, and they increased the volume of capital flowing to non-industrial countries over the previous peak of the late 1920s. Net private investment of all industrial countries in the non-industrial areas in the years 1952–7 returned to the classic nineteenth-century pattern where most funds went to Latin America or the regions recently settled by Europeans. The one change was that India ceased attracting long-term private funds on balance as a result of the new economic policies pursued after independence. The widespread governmental restrictions on international capital movements in the early 1950s were reflected in the altered relation between world exports and foreign investment; world exports had tripled since 1928 but private foreign investment had only attained its 1928 level.

The non-industrial areas remained dependent on the industrial economies[46] not only for capital imports but also as a source of demand for their exports. The United States recession of 1948/9 caused primary product prices to fall by about 10 per cent.[47] Only the uninterrupted prosperity of Western Europe offset similar repercussions from the American recession of 1953/4. Although the volume of trade quickly recovered from the war and exceeded the levels of the 1930s, the growth of production was still more rapid, so that economies were proportionately less open in the mid-1950s than they had been in the late 1920s. The composition of trade had also changed. Exports of manufactures from major suppliers rose by one-quarter between 1937 and 1950 and by three-quarters between 1937 and 1955.[48]

Under the stimulus of a government export drive to earn the currency to repay foreign loans, benefitting from the collapse of the Japanese and German economies, and helped by the devaluation in 1949 (see below), Britain increased competitiveness in international markets for manufactures between 1937 and 1950 for the only period in the twentieth century (see Table 9.2). Half of the increase in world exports of manufactures came from Britain and the other half from the United States between 1937 and 1950. The size of that increase corresponded with the decline in Japanese and German exports of manufactures over the same period.

Primary product trade increased much less strongly. Exports from non-industrial countries in the period 1937–55 rose by little more than one quarter (Table 9.3). Increased agricultural protectionism in industrial countries resulted in a substantial fall in trade in non-tropical foodstuffs. Oil exporters benefitted most from prevailing technological trends and income effects on demand, which were a continuation of those of the interwar years. The volume and value of oil and oil products rose from 10 per cent of exports of non-industrial areas in 1937/8 to 20 per cent in 1955.[49] Trade in manufactures was affected by the same trends: machinery and transport equipment for recovery, industrialisation, and for consumption became much more important, and the share of textiles

**Table 9.2** *Changes in volume of exports of manufactures, 1937–50 ($ billion at 1955 constant prices)*

|  | United Kingdom | France | Germany | Other Western Europe | Canada | United States | India | Japan | Total |
|---|---|---|---|---|---|---|---|---|---|
| 1937 exports | 4.03 | 1.15 | 3.24 | 3.87 | 1.16 | 4.08 | 0.48 | 1.89 | 19.90 |
| Change to 1950 attributable to: |  |  |  |  |  |  |  |  |  |
| market growth | +1.00 | +0.29 | +0.80 | +0.96 | +0.29 | +1.00 | +0.12 | +0.47 | +4.92 |
| diversification | −0.09 | −0.08 | +0.16 | −0.26 | 0 | +0.91 | −0.20 | −0.43 | — |
| competitiveness | +1.58 | +1.11 | −2.39 | −0.12 | +0.04 | +0.74 | +0.15 | −1.12 | — |
| Total | +2.49 | +1.32 | −1.43 | +0.58 | +0.32 | +2.65 | +0.06 | −1.07 | +4.92 |

*Source*: A. Maizels, *Industrial Growth and World Trade* (1963).

**Table 9.3** *World trade, 1937–55 (volume and unit values, 1928 = 100) (value, $000 million fob)*

|  | Exports from non-industrial countries | | | Exports from industrial countries | | | World exports | | |
|---|---|---|---|---|---|---|---|---|---|
|  | Value | Vol. | Unit value | Value | Vol. | Unit value | Value | Vol. | Unit value |
| 1937–8 | 7.80 | 108.5 | 69 | 15.11 | 85 | 83 | 22.91 | 93 | 78 |
| 1955 | 28.22 | 138 | 197 | 53.44 | 139 | 180 | 81.66 | 139 | 185 |

*Source*: GATT, *Trends in International Trade* (1958).

in manufactures trade declined as former importing areas developed their own textile industries.[50] The prices at which goods were traded were considerably higher than before the war because of wartime and post-war inflation, a response to political and social pressues.

The Korean War boom of 1951–2 radically altered relative prices. Before then foodstuffs were expensive because of the disruption of agriculture, and raw materials were relatively cheap because the industrial demand for them had not recovered. Thus Chile as an exporter of minerals and an importer of food in the immediate post-war period suffered a deterioration in the terms of trade, whereas Brazil, as an exporter of coffee and an importer of raw materials and machinery, experienced a favourable shift in the terms of trade. With the emergency stockpiling and direct demands of the war, raw material prices increased massively: the price of rubber in the London market quadrupled in 1950 and wool prices tripled.[51] Fears of a new Malthusian crisis emerged in which world manufacturing capacity would outstrip the supply of raw materials, threatening mass unemployment.[52] As the world's largest consumer of practically all raw materials, the United States was at the centre of these fears. The President appointed a Materials Policy Commission, and in January 1951 an International Materials Conference was convened to introduce rationing schemes. By 1952 most of the more farfetched Malthusian concerns had disappeared, although raw material prices remained above their pre-Korean War levels. Large-scale investment in primary production, having been neglected throughout the depressed 1930s, began after the outbreak of the Korean War. The American government at the same time gave lavish financial assistance for the exploitation of new deposits and the expansion of existing sources of supply within its territory. These stimuli soon had the intended result.

Despite the hopes of the American planners, discrimination remained an important determinant of the pattern of trade and finance throughout the period of redirection, and afterwards. Countries belonging to the overseas sterling area and the associated territories of Western Europe, together with Cuba, increased their exports by 227 per cent between 1928 and 1955, whereas 'unsheltered' countries, with no privileged access to markets, increased their exports by half that proportion over the same period.[53] The sterling area had only become legally discriminatory from 1939 when sterling was made inconvertible outside the group of countries that used sterling as a normal means of international settlement. This meant member governments strictly controlled payments out of the area while payments within the area were relatively unrestricted.[54]

Members sold their hard foreign currency earnings, especially dollars and gold, to the United Kingdom Treasury in exchange for sterling and agreed to limit their drawings on this 'dollar pool' to amounts needed for certain purposes; generally to buy items unattainable or very expensive within the area. Thus non-sterling area less developed or industrial economies had difficulties selling to sterling area countries until the area was abolished. In 1952 Britain and other members of the area began a new drive to make the pound convertible, not altogether successfully, but not as disastrously as the 1947 attempt. Not until 1961 did Britain assume full responsibility for the external convertibility of sterling as the IMF agreement required.

Not only the sterling area violated IMF principles, but the greater part of the international economy ignored them. Despite the considerable international payment difficulties for some time after 1947, the Fund's currency transactions over the first five years of its operations amounted to only $851 million of which $606 million was drawn in the first year of the Fund's existence.[55] The Fund's activities were limited partly because members were expected to rely largely on exchange controls during the transitional period. In addition, when Marshall Aid began, the Fund adopted the policy of refusing recipient countries access to its resources, so that in 1950 there were no drawings at all.[56] (Under Marshall Aid the country receiving assistance from the IMF had aid reduced by the amount of the assistance.)

The one area in which the IMF might be held to have had some discreet success was over the 1949 devaluations. In 1948 the IMF thought that European exchange rates needed changing because of the dollar gap and discussed the matter confidentially with member governments.[57] The Fund's Managing Director was privately informed in advance the following year of Britain's intention to devalue the pound by 30.5 per cent, because of a growing loss of gold from the reserves. British officials also notified Governors of other sterling area countries to arrange a simultaneous devaluation. The board of the IMF provided a means of keeping governments informed of the views and plans of other member governments. Each country's proposal was submitted to the criticism of other Directors so that the decisions reached were more acceptable to world opinion than those taken after 1931 and did not provoke retaliatory action. Although some non-sterling area countries also devalued at the same time they did so by a smaller proportion – West Germany by 20.7 per cent, France by 5.6–22.2 per cent (because of the multiple exchange rates which had earlier incurred IMF disapproval),

Belgium and Luxemburg by 12.3 per cent, Canada 9.3 per cent and Italy 8.1 per cent. One of the two countries which rapidly bit into Britain's export market share after 1950, Japan, did not devalue at all, while the other, Germany, also owed its export success more to recovery than to altered price relations. The short-run effects of devaluation did increase British competitiveness and reduce exchange losses as would be expected if the foreign demand for British goods and the British demand for foreign goods were elastic. The longer-run effects are more consistent with the monetary theory of the balance of payments. Price increases in the United Kingdom following the 1949 devaluation were insufficient to wipe out the effects on the relative prices of British and American exports, but big enough to offset much of the advantage by 1954.[58] Compared to other devaluing countries, British export price behaviour was about average in 1950 and 1951, but from 1952–4 these prices fell less than those of other European devaluing countries. From a comparison of domestic price increases, Britain was one of the more inflationary countries in Europe.

## Summary and conclusion

International economic relations by 1953 could not be said to have adopted the pattern of the American wartime planners. Yet the greater part of these relations were moving in the direction of freer trade with convertible currencies, the movement made easier by the rapid expansion of national incomes in Western Europe, which also owed much to the easing of trade restrictions. In some respects the new order towards which much of the international economy was changing resembled that of the classic free-trade era of 1850–75 in its internationalist orientation. The major difference, however, was the much greater role of government even in the market economies and their commitments to maintain full employment.

In honouring this commitment governments were successful, especially by contrast with the period after the first world war. This success was due in part to Keynesian economics that provided a justification for expansionary fiscal and monetary policies, but more importantly, to most countries not allowing again the subordination of domestic policies to international considerations. It was for this latter reason that the dismantling of controls took so long. Military spending played an important part in reaching and maintaining full employment in the United States. The causes of this spending, first the second world war and then the Cold War, accounted for one of the major structural changes of the international economy; the dragging of Eastern Europe into the economic orbit of Russia, away from the central European bloc of the 1930s centred on Germany. China also became a major Soviet economic satellite, closed to economic relations with the non-communist world.

The second world war triggered nationalist movements in the colonial territories of Asia, encouraged by the Japanese invasions. These played a part in securing independence for some territories, which allowed the pursuit of independent trade policies. After Indian independence, which owed little to the war, India was the most important example of state planning for economic development involving limitations on imports to protect infant industries and the rigorous control of private foreign capital. In the early GATT negotiations the Indian representative argued for exemptions from multilateralist principles for developing countries. This marked the beginning of the creation of the third system of post-1945 international economic relations; in addition to the western liberal and the Soviet systems, the state-controlled developing country system.

These less developed countries benefitted from another prominent change that occurred in this period: the rise of official international capital flows. At first these flows were between wartime allies (lend lease and mutual aid) or to finance the dollar gap created by the devastation of war (Marshall Aid). Subsequently these flows, though diminished in volume, were redirected towards less developed countries and allowed them to run an import surplus, in contrast to the pre-war period when their trade was balanced. Private foreign investment returned to peak interwar levels but remained low in relation to production.

A further benefit to some less developed countries was the Korean War boom in raw material prices. The lack of investment in supplying these commodities throughout the 1930s and 1940s, combined with the stockpiling of the Korean War and the recovery of industrial Europe, rapidly pushed up material prices and the shortages encouraged fears of a new Malthusian crisis. As new investment took place and increased supplies, prices fell relative to other goods during the 1950s and 1960s; the pattern became reminiscent of the nineteenth-century cycle in investment.

The volume of manufacturing trade expanded more rapidly than trade in primary products because of the recovery of industrial Europe and the greater scope for technical progress in manufactures production. In relation to the much higher production and national incomes of the early 1950s compared with 1937/8, trade remained low because of the persistence of a large number of restrictions. Some of these the American planners of the post-war economic system had hoped to eliminate; inconvertible currencies, multiple exchange rates and floating exchange rates were outlawed by the International Monetary Fund; discriminatory tariffs and quantitative restrictions were condemned by the General Agreement on Tariffs and Trade. The sterling area and Commonwealth Preferences were therefore a major source of friction between America and Britain, and the United States attempted to abolish them, for example, by tying the post-war British loan in 1945 to sterling convertibility within two years. The attitude of the United States changed somewhat with the intensification of the Cold War in the late 1940s. The discriminatory trade practices of Europe in the form of the Payments Union and the ECSC were supported as means of accelerating European recovery as a bulwark against Communism.

The IMF throughout this process remained ineffective except perhaps in the devaluations of 1949 when it may have helped avoid retaliatory action that could have reduced world trade and employment. The other institution of the Bretton Woods Agreement, the World Bank, was more important although it only provided a small proportion of the capital flowing to less developed countries.

## Notes

1. R.G.D. Allen, 'Mutual aid between the United States and the British empire 1941–45', *Journal of the Royal Statistical Society*, **110**, part III (1946), pp. 243–71.
2. K. Kock, *International Trade Policy and the Gatt 1947–1967*, Stockholm: Almiquist & Wiksell (1969), p. 24. W. Churchill, *The Second World War: Closing the Ring*, Boston: Houghton Mifflin (1951), p. 400.
3. Kock, op. cit., p. 25.
4. A.S. Milward, *War Economy and Society 1939–1945*, London: Allen Lane (1977), p. 166.
5. United Nations, Department of Economic Affairs, *Economic Survey of Asia and the Far East 1948*, New York: UN (1949), p. 32.
6. In 1933 the US Congress had voted that the Phillipines should become independent in ten years.
7. Milward, op. cit., pp. 349, 353–4.
8. United Nations, op. cit., p. 35.
9. Milward, op. cit., pp. 137–44.
10. J. Borkin, *The Crime and Punishment of I.G. Farben*, London: Andre Deutsch (1979), pp. 111–27.
11. A.S. Milward, *The Fascist Economy in Norway*, Oxford: Clarendon Press (1972), p. 177.
12. United Nations, Department of Economic Affairs, *Economic Survey of Latin America 1948*, New York: UN (1949), pp. 231–4.

13. Milward (1977), op. cit., p. 356.
14. F.L. Block, *The Origins of International Economic Disorder: A Study of United States International Monetary Policy from World War II to the Present*, Berkeley: University of California Press (1977), ch. 3. R.N. Gardner, *Sterling-Dollar Diplomacy in Current Perspective*, New York: Columbia University Press (1980) chs 5, 7, 13. Kock, op. cit., ch. 1. J.K. Horsefield, *The International Monetary Fund 1945–1965*, vol. 1, Washington DC: IMF (1969), chs 1–4.
15. In particular, League of Nations, *International Currency Experience* (1944), by R. Nurske.
16. W.M. Scammell, *The International Economy Since 1945*, London: Macmillan (1980).
17. V. Argy, *The Postwar International Money Crisis: an Analysis*, London: Allen & Unwin (1981), ch. 2. Horsefield, op. cit., pp. 110–13.
18. E.S. Mason and R.E. Asher, *The World Bank Since Bretton Woods*, Washington DC: The Brookings Institution (1973), ch. 5.
19. Kock, op. cit., p. 62.
20. Block, op. cit., pp. 75–6, 84. Gardner, op. cit., chs 14, 17.
21. Kock, op. cit., p. 62.
22. United Nations, Economic and Social Council, *Economic Survey of Europe in 1948*, Washington: US Government Printing Office (1949), p. 149.
23. United Nations, Department of Economic Affairs, *Postwar Shortages of Food and Coal*, New York: UN (1948).
24. United Nations, Department of Economic Affairs, *The Foreign Exchange Position of the Devastated Countries*, New York (1948).
25. Block, op. cit., ch. 3. Gardner, op. cit., ch. 16.
26. United Nations, *Economic Survey of Europe*, (1948), pp. 35–6.
27. F. Holzman, *International Trade Under Communism*. London: Macmillan (1976), ch. 3.
28. A. Zauberman, *Economic Imperialism: the Lessons of Eastern Europe*. London: Ampersand (1955), p. 11.
29. United Nations, *Economic Survey of Asia 1948*, pp. 27, 34.
30. ibid., ch. 12.
31. United Nations, *Economic Survey of Latin America* (1948), pp. 209, 247.
32. Block, op. cit., p. 82.
33. H.B. Price, *The Marshall Plan and Its Meaning*. Ithaca, New York: Cornell University Press (1955), pp. 88–90.
34. S.E. Harris, *The European Recovery Program*, Cambridge, Mass.: Harvard University Press (1948), p. 12.
35. S.M. Hartmann, *The Marshall Plan*, Columbus, Ohio: C.E. Merrill (1968), p. 63.
36. Kock, op. cit., p. 115.
37. G. Patterson, *Discrimination in International Trade: The Policy Issues 1945–1965*, Princeton, NJ: Princeton University Press (1966), pp. 75–119.

38. D. Swann, *The Economics of the Common Market*, Harmondsworth: Penguin, 2nd edn (1972), pp. 19–21.
39. Zauberman, op. cit., pp. 21–2.
40. Holtzman, op. cit., pp. 132–3.
41. J. Wilczynski, *The Economics and Politics of East–West Trade*, New York: Praeger (1969), pp. 48–9. Holtzman, op. cit., p. 40.
42. Zauberman, op. cit., pp. 39–54.
43. A. Zauberman, *Industrial Progress in Poland, Czechoslovakia and East Germany 1937–1962*, London: Oxford University Press (1964), pp. 156, 217.
44. GATT, *Trends in International Trade*, Geneva (1958), pp. 32–43.
45. Mason and Asher, op. cit., ch. 6.
46. GATT, op. cit., pp. 32 – 43.
47. ibid., p. 17.
48. A. Maizels, *Industrial Growth and World Trade*, Cambridge: Cambridge University Press (1963), ch. 8.
49. GATT, op. cit., p. 21.
50. I. Svennilson, *Growth and Stagnation in the European Economy*, Geneva (1954), ch. 9. Maizels, op. cit., ch. 8.
51. United Nations, Department of Economic Affairs, *Commodity Trade and Economic Development*, New York: UN (1953), p. 7.
52. Royal Institute of International Affairs, *World Production of Raw Materials*, London (1953), pp. 1, 13, 16–19.
53. GATT, op. cit., p. 26. P.W. Bell, *The Sterling Area in the Postwar World: Internal Mechanism and Cohesion 1946–1952*, Oxford: Clarendon Press (1956).
54. Patterson, op. cit., pp. 67–75.
55. J.K. Horsefield (ed.), *The International Monetary Fund*, Washington (1969), vol. II, p. 397.
56. S. Horie, *The International Monetary Fund*, New York: St Martins Press (1964), pp. 138–9.
57. Horsefield, vol. I, op. cit., pp. 234–42.
58. M. June Flanders, 'The effects of devaluation on exports, a case study; the United Kingdom 1949–54', *Bulletin of the Oxford University Institute of Statistics*, **25** (1963), pp. 165–98.

# 10 The New Liberal Trade Order

In the two decades after 1953 international economic contacts expanded at unprecedented rates within the framework provided by the institutions of the new order. At the same time national incomes rose faster than they ever had before. The General Agreement on Tariffs and Trade, and Cold War competition, in particular encouraged great cuts in restrictions on trade in manufactures between industrialized countries, although there was much less success with primary product trade. Governments maintained high levels of aggregate demand which induced investment and massive outlays by firms on research and development, generating a large number of inventions and innovations that fuelled the engine of international economic growth.

These new technologies influenced the pattern of the world economy both by the channels through which they were transmitted between economies and in their impacts upon the receiving society. In the developed countries the main effect was to accelerate economic growth. In the poor countries, although standards of living also usually rose, the new ideas and techniques indirectly led to a population explosion. Measures such as chemical spraying to eliminate malaria-carrying mosquitos, suddenly and radically reduced death rates, yet fertility remained high.[1] From an annual rate of population increase in the second quarter of the century of 1.5 per cent, the southern group of countries in Latin America, Africa, South Asia and Oceania raised their population growth to 2.4 per cent per annum between 1950 and 1975.[2] Prosperity raised birth rates in the northern group in North America, Europe, USSR and East Asia, but their population growth increased from 0.6 per cent to only 1.3 per cent over the same period.

Given the importance of the advances in industrial knowledge, the first section of the chapter describes the generation and international transfer of technology, going on to consider the influence on economic growth and the pattern of trade. This pattern was radically changed by the commercial policies of both industrial market economies and non-industrial countries as well, the subject of the following two sections. Less obvious forces also need to be invoked if actual trade flows are to be explained and we therefore go on to consider the role of spheres of influence. Policy in non-industrial countries was particularly concerned to avoid being trapped by declining relative prices of primary goods. For this reason the terms of trade between manufactures and primary product are discussed next. Operating a different foreign trade regime, the centrally-planned economies described in the sixth section were not so radically affected by the international price explosion of the early 1970s, but they experienced different problems. In contrast to the less developed countries and the industrial market economies, productivity growth decelerated in the 1960s. By the 1970s Eastern Europe was urgently trying to import western technology to support flagging growth rates.[3] Yet another difference between East and West in international economic relations arose in migration policy, explored in the next section. The extent to which international relations contributed to the overall growth performance of the world economy, and a discussion of the value of that growth, concludes the subject matter of the chapter.

## The new technology: generation and international transfer

Technology was transferred mainly from a few highly industrialised countries. The most advanced western industrial countries accounted for the bulk of major product and process innovations. Of one hundred major innovations between 1945 and the late 1960s about 60 per cent were introduced by US companies, 14 per cent by UK companies and 11 per cent by West German companies.[4]

American technological leadership necessitated a ratio of research and development (R & D) expenditures to gross domestic product significantly higher than that of other countries until the early 1960s. In addition, a much larger GDP than any other country enabled the United States to undertake by far the greatest amount of R & D. As the highest income country in the world with the most productive industry, the United States could rarely copy technology from other countries, and therefore had to invest more in achieving a given rate of technical progress. Second among the major OECD (industrial) countries in both total R & D, and in the ratio of R & D to GDP, was the United Kingdom. High government spending on defence, nuclear and space research and development accounted for much of the higher than average R & D ratios of both countries in the early 1960s, and during that decade the gap in non-defence R & D ratios between OECD countries narrowed rapidly.[5] By 1975 the non-defence ratios in Germany, Japan and Netherlands exceeded those of the US and the UK.

Typically, about 60 per cent of the R & D of OECD countries was performed in manufacturing industries. In the same countries, particularly France, Germany, Sweden, Britain and America, government-financed programmes accounted for a considerable part of total industrial R & D. About three-quarters of the private industry-financed R & D was concentrated in electrical and electronics, chemicals, machinery and other transport (excluding aerospace).[6] Government-financed expenditures were directed to the same sectors except that governments excluded other transport and included aerospace.

The effect of research and development was clearly to raise economic growth (although it is unlikely that 'spin-offs' from defence R & D raised the productivity of that expenditure to the level of non-defence R & D). Rapid productivity growth industries or sectors either were high R & D spenders, such as chemicals, or bought equipment from big R & D spending sectors, such as air transport. Even in such a traditional industry as textiles, research and development began to have a major impact. In the years after 1960 textile production in OECD countries was transformed from a labour-intensive to a capital-intensive industry.[7] Textile machinery incorporated progress in materials science, fibre technology, hydrodynamics, aerodynamics and, later, in electronics. From 1970 numerical control spread rapidly in the machine-tool industry. Most dramatic of all the industrial transformation was perhaps the 'micro-electronic revolution' beginning in the second half of the 1970s. The capabilities of one of the first electronic computers, ENIAC, built in the 1940s for several millions of dollars, could be reproduced in 1978 for less than $100 in a microcomputer which calculated 20 times faster, was 10 000 times more reliable, required 56 000 times less power and 300 000 times less space. Such radical innovations were bound to have pervasive effects in many sectors. On the other hand innovations in some other science-based sectors slowed down in the 1970s, especially in pharmaceuticals and in pesticides because of more stringent safety and environmental standards.

The new technology was transferred from the producing countries in a variety of ways. In the non-communist world multinational companies played a major role; a large proportion of international payments for technology were between parent and subsidiary companies. It was to encourage such flows that Japan slightly eased restrictions on foreign direct investment in the 1960s.[8] Countries such as the USSR that excluded this investment handicapped themselves, although there may have been offsetting political advantages.

Official aid flows played a part in transferring technologies from the advanced industrial countries to the less developed economies. The appropriateness of some of the technologies imported by LDCs both through official channels and multinationals has however been questionable. The costs of redesigning equipment to use efficiently the resource endowments of less developed countries may have been excessive, or the decision to buy particular technologies may have been economically irrational. A statistical study of 1484 US multinational enterprises in Europe and in less developed countries in 1970 nevertheless concluded that in 9 out of 11 industries the chosen production process was *run* more labour-intensively in the less developed countries because of the cheaper labour relative to capital in developed countries, although there was no significant difference between the *installed* techniques of developed and less developed country affiliates in 5 of the 11 industries.[9] At least some of the production methods used in LDCs were a consequence of government regulations. The transportation industry employed identical methods in the two groups of countries, but 40 per cent more capital per man was used in LDCs than in DCs. In Latin America, at least, this was attributable to regulations requiring specific proportions of motor vehicles be manufactured domestically, regardless of the small size of the market. The emphasis on technologies using oil, instead of traditional indigenous energy sources, or using less energy-intensive techniques, raised the total demand for energy in Latin America almost fivefold between 1939 and 1973. Motor transport and urban motorways were energy-intensive choices compared with mass transit facilities. Rural electrification displaced wood as an energy source. For Brazil and Argentina by the seventies oil was accounting for 25 per cent of available foreign exchange, even though oil prices tended to fall until 1970.

## Technology imports and economic performance

Despite the possible transfer of inappropriate technology in some instances technology imports boosted the growth rates of most of the recipient countries. The greater willingness and ability of all industrial countries to take advantage of new techniques compared with the interwar years was based on the strength of demand. High demand pressure reduced the risks inherent in utilising new techniques by lowering the probability that the new products or processes would be unprofitable.[10] The governmental commitment to full employment (variously defined), and the widespread belief that Keynesian economics allowed governments to fulfill this obligation, were mainly responsible for the great strength of demand in the two decades after 1950. Because fiscal and monetary expansion were not at first expected to raise prices by very much, but instead were expected mainly to increase output and employment, their inflationary impact was initially low. Only towards the end of the 1960s and the early 1970s when these policies were increased in intensity did expectations of future inflation begin to nullify their beneficial effects. Wage-earners began to anticipate higher prices in their money wage demands and in so doing raised unemployment by pricing the marginal workers out of the market.[11]

Differences in growth rates between industrial countries cannot adequately be explained by differences in demand pressure, however. Rather the major determinants were the extent of the technological lag and the size of the ratio of investment to GNP, reflecting entrepreneurial vigour in innovating and borrowing technology, flexibility of the labour force in accepting new production tasks, work rules and equipment, and a willingness to move to new jobs and areas. Surplus labour from the agricultural sector, where the growth of labour productivity usually outstripped the growth of demand for agricultural produce, fuelled the growth of many economies, but it was not an essential contribution.[12] Labour could be made available from other sectors if required.

Growth rates decelerated in the 1970s not because of the exhaustion of labour supplies, but because of the technological catching up of the other OECD countries with the United States and because these countries had low income elasticities of demand for manufactures (the manufacturing sector had the greatest scope for productivity increases). The oil price rise towards the end of 1973 (discussed in Chapter 11), which reduced demand in industrial countries, combined with restrictive monetary policies in the face of rising inflation, also contributed to declining growth rates through the effect on the generation and importing of new technology; 1974 was the first year since 1945 that the combined growth rates of the OECD countries failed to increase, and 1975 was the first year in which aggregate income actually declined.

By contrast with many western industrial countries the communist bloc countries required increasing imports of western technology in order to prevent growth rates declining. Soviet total factor productivity growth decelerated from the high levels of the early 1950s, becoming negative between 1967 and 1973. The central planning system seemed to be inadequate for the development and application of new technology except in the high priority areas of the military and aerospace industries. Consequently in an effort to remedy this deficiency Russian imports of western machinery rose rapidly between 1955 and 1978, as a proportion of Soviet equipment investment from around 2 per cent to about $5\frac{1}{2}$ per cent.[13] The importation of technology remained small by comparison with that of the Japanese. Soviet licence purchases in 1970 were about one-eighth of the value of Japan's (although this statistic conceals the high import dependence of some Soviet sectors such as chemicals, shipping in the late 1950s and early 1960s and, by the 1970s, the motor industry).

The overall effect of imported western technology was probably to raise Soviet industrial growth by between 0.2 and 0.4 per cent per annum. In Poland, where the share of western machinery in industrial equipment investment reached as high as 30 per cent in the mid-1970s, the effects were considerably greater, at least temporarily, though the subsequent crisis suggested an inability of the central planning system to absorb new technology on this scale.

## Trade patterns and new technology

The rapid technological change outlined above inevitably affected the pattern of international trade. In the three decades after the Korean War trade in manufactures between industrial countries grew remarkably. Mainly for this reason by far the largest market for industrial areas exports was the industrial world itself (see Table 10.1). Communist bloc countries were the most rapidly growing market between 1963 and 1978, but remained a small proportion of total trade, in the last year amounting to only 7 per cent of the industrial area's exports to itself. The developing areas increased their importance as markets for the industrial countries but in 1978 were only one-third as important as the industrial economies for themselves.

Between 1963 and 1978 exports from developing countries to the industrial countries rose by almost ten times, and within the developing area increased by more than ten times. Throughout the period the industrial countries remained the main market for developing country exports, taking three times as much as the

**Table 10.1** *The network of world trade, 1963–78 ($m, fob)*

| | Destination Year | Industrial Areas | Developing Areas | Eastern Trading Area |
|---|---|---|---|---|
| *Origin* | | | | |
| Industrial Areas | 1963 | 69 285 | 21 900 | 3 495 |
| | 1973 | 288 915 | 68 740 | 18 160 |
| | 1978 | 578 760 | 199 570 | 41 955 |
| Developing Areas | 1963 | 22 140 | 6 685 | 1 670 |
| | 1973 | 79 475 | 22 540 | 5 290 |
| | 1978 | 215 120 | 68 765 | 12 855 |
| Eastern Trading | 1963 | 3 505 | 2 465 | 12 375 |
| Area | 1973 | 15 370 | 6 545 | 32 390 |
| | 1978 | 33 445 | 18 410 | 69 400 |

*Source*: GATT *International Trade 1981/82*, Geneva (1982).
*Note*: Australia, New Zealand, South Africa are excluded.

developing countries themselves. The communist bloc economies were considerably less dependent on trade outside their area, but this dependency increased over the period, the greatest trade increase being in exports to industrial areas, which by 1978 were almost half of intra-bloc exports. Exports to less developed countries also rose markedly, amounting to almost one-quarter of intra-bloc exports.

The product composition of the trade of industrial and oil importing developing countries (see Figure 10.1) shows how wrong it is to identify industrial countries solely as exporters of manufactures and as primary product importers. During the 1970s the proportion of non-fuel primary products in total imports of the two groups was fairly similar. Although non-fuel primary products were a smaller proportion of industrial than of developing country exports, the value of these goods exported by industrial countries was much greater than those exported by developing countries.

Manufactures increased their share of the exports of both groups, but the rise was much more rapid for the developing countries. The composition of the latter group of manufactures exports were more heavily weighted towards textiles and clothing, whereas industrial countries' exports were biased more towards engineering products (although the industrial country proportion of imports accounted for by engineering products was much lower than for developing countries). This emphasis on textile exports had important consequences for the average tariff faced by developing country exports, discussed below.

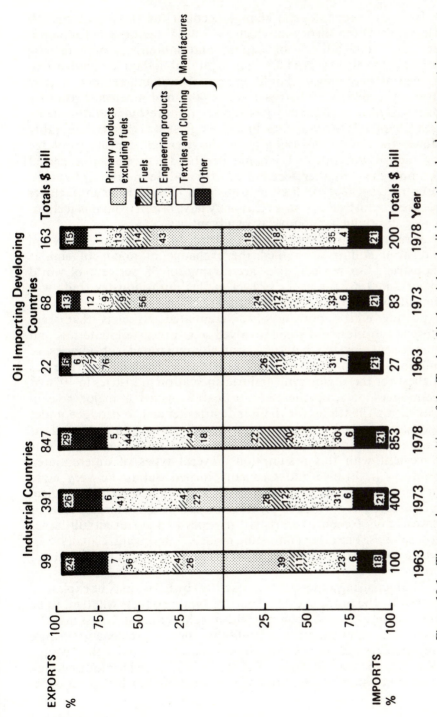

**Figure 10.1** The product composition of the Trade of industrial and oil-importing developing countries

*Source:* G.A.T.T. International Trade 1978/9

*Note:* Percentage do not sum of 100 because of exclusions and rounding errors.

How can technological change account for these patterns? A Hecksher–Ohlin theory in which the crucial factors of production are land and labour, or capital and labour, is of little use because the theory predicts that capital-abundant or land-scarce industrial economies should export manufactures and import primary products. Whereas trade in the mid-nineteenth century seems to have been mainly based on natural resource endowments (see Chapter 2) the rate of technical progress was then considerably slower than in the third quarter of the twentieth century (to judge by the growth rates of income per head). In the later period technologies were therefore more likely to differ markedly between countries because of lags in diffusions. Trade in manufactures between industrial countries then may have arisen from this techno-logy gap producing comparative advantages.

A very substantial portion of the trade in manufactures between industrial countries entailed the exchange of goods of similar industries. For ten countries accounting for 58 per cent of world exports in 1967 the average level of this intra-industry trade was almost two-thirds of their total trade.[14] Some of the trade was the exporting and importing of differentiated products that were close substitutes, and some involved semi-processed materials and components passed between vertically-integrated subsidiaries of multinational companies – intra-firm trade. Intra-industry trade was highest for the engineering and transportation industries in 1976.[15] Economies of scale therefore probably played a major role in generating the trade, for these industries tended to produce under such conditions. Furthermore the disappearance of many small car manufactures in Europe since 1958 with the creation of the EEC is consistent with this assumption. Several types of differentiated products in France and Germany turned out to be very close substitutes for each other once tariffs were reduced. Whichever firm producing one of these competing models had the largest runs or lowest costs (or both) increased its sales and achieved still larger cost savings. The other competing models – Borgwald, Lloyd, NSU, Simca and Citroën, either went bankrupt or were absorbed by larger firms.

The increasing export of manufactures by LDCs may be explained in part by the product cycle theory.[16] New products will tend to be manufactured first in a country with a high income and mass market, because the opportunities for profitable sales are greater and because entrepreneurs need to be close to the consumers to judge their wants. When the product has been successfully introduced for long enough it becomes standardised and the production can be relocated to areas that have lower labour costs, but still provide a substantial market, so that advantages can be taken of scale economies. The high income country exports the new products and the lower income country exports the standardised products.

If a country maintains a comparative advantage in innovating and continually develops new products and processes, then the Hecksher–Ohlin theory can be modified to take this into account. The United States in the post-war years, at least until 1971, maintained and increased an advantage in innovating, that is, an advantage in research-intensive products.[17] A study by Leontief of US trade in 1947 showed, apparently contrary to the Hecksher–Ohlin theory, that America exported labour-intensive products and imported capital-intensive products,[18] exactly the opposite result expected for a relatively capital-abundant economy. However in this and other instances of the 'Leontief paradox' discovered for other countries, the introduction of human capital as a factor of production in the form of skilled labour resolves the paradox. Rich countries tend to be relatively abundantly endowed with skilled labour and therefore export those products intensive in this factor. Thus in the period of rapid US export growth, between 1960 and 1970, US comparative advantage shifted further towards research and development intensive commodities (Table 10.2) which were not so subject to import substitution as the fairly standard manufactures mainly exported between 1953 and 1960.

If the United States was a technological leader, her exports reflecting the continuous generation of new products and processes, then Japan was a technological follower economy during the 1950s

**Table 10.2**  *US net exports* $(X - M)$ *of manufactures by production characteristics, 1960–70 ($m, fob)*

|  | 1960 | 1970 |
|---|---|---|
| R & D intensive, high wages | 1800 | 4096 |
| R & D intensive, high wages, capital intensive | 1537 | 4392 |
| Capital intensive, high wages | 716 | − 1334 |
| Capital intensive | 285 | − 424 |
| Residual (mainly labour intensive) | 1170 | − 2145 |
| All manufactures | 5508 | 4585 |

*Source*: GATT, *Trends in United States Merchandise Trade 1953–1970*, Geneva (1972), p. 24.

and 1960s. In 1955 Japanese payments for foreign licences and patents rose from $20 million in 1955 to nearly $350 million in 1969. These were payments that allowed Japan to utilise foreign R & D, although Japanese research and development expenditure grew at the same time, as Japan diminished the technological gap.[19]

At least part of the composition of trade is attributable to the commercial policies of the governments of both industrial and developing groups which resisted the market forces tending towards changing and increased international specialisation. Even so, the volume of trade in manufactures greatly exceeded trade in non-fuel primary products and this was unusual by historical criteria. Much of the expansion of the trade was explicable by the easing of trade restriction, especially on manufactures, during the 1960s, together with the growth of national incomes. Only in the late 1970s did the world trade/GNP ratios reach 1913 levels.[20]

## Trade policy of the industrial world

After the early tariff reduction success of GATT the item-by-item approach to negotiation began to run out of steam. The nature of these negotiations was to pursue the path of least resistance, allowing each negotiator to select himself those items on which he was prepared to give concessions. Countries with low tariffs had little to offer in exchange for a reduction in their partner's high tariffs; and the US Reciprocal Trade Agreement Act only gave the US administration power to cut tariffs by 5 per cent per annum. The inability of GATT to deal with the European tariff problems encouraged a move to complete trade integration among the six countries that eventually formed the European Economic Community with a common external tariff.[21] The Treaty of Rome laying down the rules for the Common Market was signed in 1957. The American and the British were therefore faced with the prospect of tariff discrimination in important export markets. Britain then attempted to create a European-wide free trade area within the OEEC. French industry and agriculture objected strongly to the international competition implied by this proposal, and the French government thus apparently unilaterally announced in November 1958 that the free trade area was not possible.[22]

As a temporary measure Britain created the European Free Trade Association for those countries remaining outside the EEC. The Americans set about obtaining a reduction in the proposed common external tariff of the EEC. The Dillon Round of multilateral negotiations within the GATT framework was the result of their initiative. Although this was clearly inadequate for what was intended of it, the EEC used the Round to help the US administration obtain more negotiating freedom from Congress. A linear cut of 20 per cent in the Community's external tariff was to become operative if and when Congress gave the US administration power to reciprocate. The new administration of President Kennedy took the opportunity to promote a 'Grand Design' for Atlantic partnership with the US Trade Expansion Act of 1962, intended to push Britain into the Common Market.[23] The Act proposed a 50 per cent linear tariff cut and the complete elimination of duties on those products in which the EEC and the US accounted for more than 80 per cent of free world exports.

General de Gaulle was unwilling to allow Britain to join the EEC because of the possible challenge to French political influence in the Community. He therefore vetoed Britain's application in 1963. As a consequence of this failure to enlarge the EEC, nothing came of the proposal to eliminate duties on goods mainly supplied by the United States and the EEC, because this category was now small. Nevertheless the Act was even more successful than the Anglo-French treaty of 1860, the major step in spreading free trade in the first liberal era (see Chapter 2). The industrialised countries participating in the Kennedy Round made tariff reductions on 70 per cent of their dutiable imports (excluding cereals, meat and dairy products). Moreover, two-thirds of these cuts were of 50 per cent or more. Trade in temperate zone agricultural products however was relatively untouched. Other achievements of the Kennedy Round included the discussion of non-tariff barriers to trade, and a protocol by which a planned increase of imports in communist countries was to be considered equivalent to a tariff concession on the part of a market economy. The Tokyo Round ending in 1979, by contrast, achieved little beyond a code of practice on subsidies and government buying.

Almost all the major reductions in tariffs took place between 1959 and 1971. The most important cuts, apart from the Kennedy Round, were those of the Dillon Round, the Canadian–United States Automotive Agreement and those associated with the formation of the European Economic Community and the European Free Trade Area. The changes in the area and commodity pattern of trade show the effect of these reductions. More than half the trade increase between the United States and Canada was accounted for by transport equipment resulting from the 1965 free trade agreement, and over the period 1959–72 total manufactures trade between the two countries increased at $12\frac{1}{2}$ per cent per annum.[24] The growth in EFTA manufactures trade was slightly higher at 13 per cent per annum, but because of slow British economic growth, the rate was well below the expansion of EEC intra-trade in manufactures of nearly 18 per cent per annum in dollar value. Some of this increase in EEC trade was the diversion of trade from lower opportunity cost non-EEC suppliers to higher opportunity cost EEC suppliers because of the common external tariff.[25] But the trade creation effect, stemming from improved resource use as internal tariffs were eliminated, is generally thought to have outweighed the diversion, and was probably about 25–35 per cent of trade in the absence of the EEC. The EFTA effect was smaller; probably EFTA imports were about 10–15 per cent higher because of trade creation. A lower-bound estimate of the effects of the US–Canada Agreement is that it accounted for two-thirds of the 'additional' Canadian imports in 1967, and around 30 per cent of the 'additional' US imports. The Dillon Round could have created 10–15 per cent 'additional' US imports. The Kennedy Round led to the biggest cuts in duties of 50 per cent falling on machinery and vehicles. It is likely that American and British imports were affected most strongly by these reductions; in the British case the upper-bound effects were probably to raise imports by 15 per cent, and the United States' imports were raised more than this. These estimates of the effects of tariff cuts together with changes in price competitiveness explain most industrial countries' rising propensity to import. But for the United States, the United Kingdom and Germany between one-third and a half of 'additional' imports remain unaccounted for; apparently all three countries had autonomously rising import propensities.

A constant market share analysis of trade in manufactures (Table 10.3) between 1963 and 1967 shows many similarities to the interwar years pattern and earlier, in particular in the massive increase in Japanese competitiveness. Germany as well as the United States by now had overtaken Britain in the size of their manufactures exports, but they both also showed a loss of market shares. The much greater decline in British competitiveness was corrected by the 1967 devaluation although the decline continued at a slower rate. The arrival of Italy as a major exporter and the increase in Italian competitiveness were new features of the post-war era. The commodity composition of trade had a significantly unfavourable effect on Japan, Belgium–Luxemburg and Canada. Differential rates of growth by market area were more important. Britain's trade was unfavourably affected, as it had been through most of the century, by the high proportion of its exports still going to markets outside

**Table 10.3** Changes in the volume of exports of manufactures attributable to changes in the size of the world market, the pattern of world trade, and market shares, 1963–7 ($m, 1963 prices)

| 1963–7 exports | Base year exports | World market growth | Commodity pattern | Area pattern | Market share (current weighted) | Actual change |
|---|---|---|---|---|---|---|
| United States | 13 503 | 5 500 | 127 | 606 | −710 | 5 523 |
| United Kingdom | 9 984 | 4 578 | 71 | −217 | −3 299 | 1 133 |
| Japan | 4 949 | 2 275 | −149 | 253 | 2 692 | 5 071 |
| EEC Six | 29 168 | 13 554 | −58 | −462 | 712 | 13 746 |
| France | 5 841 | 2 637 | 8 | −278 | −382 | 1 985 |
| Germany | 12 910 | 6 029 | 193 | −39 | −197 | 5 986 |
| Italy | 3 877 | 1 870 | −71 | −64 | 1253 | 2 988 |
| Belgium–Luxemburg | 3 830 | 1 769 | −180 | −58 | −96 | 1 435 |
| Netherlands | 2 710 | 1 249 | −8 | −23 | 134 | 1 352 |
| Canada | 2 830 | 1 265 | −100 | 607 | 946 | 2 718 |
| Sweden | 2 195 | 1 026 | −22 | 16 | −56 | 964 |
| Switzerland | 2 196 | 1 030 | −13 | 14 | −289 | 742 |

*Source*: R. Batchelor *et al.*, *Industrialization and the Basis for Trade*, Cambridge: Cambridge University Press (1980).

the industrial areas, especially the semi-industrial countries. Unlike Japan, Britain had no compensation in the form of an unusually high dependence on the US market with its rising import propensity.

## Primary product trade policy

Trade in temperate zone agricultural products showed nothing like the same expansion as trade in manufactures because the developed countries tended to become more protective of their agricultural sectors, rather than less, just as the developing countries became more protective of their industrial sectors. The fundamental difference was that the developed countries were sufficiently rich to use resources in this fashion without dire consequences for themselves. The industrialised or high income countries are located in the temperate zone and were the main consuming countries for temperate zone products (grains, meat, dairy products, sugar beet). This meant production could be, and was, expanded in countries which had been traditional importers. Temperate zone products at the beginning of the 1970s accounted for about 30 per cent of world agricultural exports, or about 10 per cent of total world trade.[26]

Although apparently contrary to the General Agreement on Tariff and Trade, the United States maintained import controls on cotton, wheat and wheat flour under the Agricultural Adjustment Act.[27] After 1951 American butter imports were virtually eliminated by controls. On the other hand, because exports of agricultural products were the single most important export trade of the United States, America had an interest in expanding world markets for temperate zone primary produce. In 1956 60 per cent of total US wheat shipments abroad and 80 per cent of cotton were non-commercial:[28] disaster relief, economic aid and surplus disposal agreements were the main means of disposing of US agricultural produce that would otherwise force down domestic prices. In the late 1960s, about one-quarter of total US agricultural exports were dealt with like this.

The introduction of the EEC Common Agricultural Policy in 1962 greatly increased agricultural protectionism. The EEC operated a variable levy to raise foreign prices to domestic price levels, similar to Britain's corn laws that had been abolished in 1846. In 1962 Germany's 'threshold price' of wheat set by the EEC was 106 per cent above the landed price. A refund system to EEC exporters of cereals of the same size as the levy allowed them to sell below world prices.[29] The cost of agricultural protection to the consumer or taxpayer in the six EEC countries and Britain in 1961 has been estimated at $3.75 billion.[30] The benefits included those derived from strengthening and maintaining the peasantry. Where the peasantry was an important electoral force, these benefits were obviously likely to be reflected in policy, but for a country such as Britain from which the peasantry had long disappeared such an explanation will not do. Here the effects of wartime expansion of domestic food supplies must have played an important role. The agricultural sector suffered from a limited demand for its products. The sector also experienced a rapid growth of supply capacity, which meant that people had to leave the land in large numbers, if market forces were not restrained, as they were. Even so, agricultural sectors continued to shed labour in advanced economies. The high income levels, and high calorie consumption, of the developed countries implied that market growth would be mainly from population growth although there were changes in the composition of demand; a decline in cereal consumption and a rise in meat, milk and sugar consumption since the war. Technological advance in some countries was extremely fast: gross output per man hour in US agriculture more than tripled between 1950/52 and the mid 1960s. World production of temperate zone products since the war increased by very much less; about 50 per cent for feed grains, mutton and lamb to about 100 per cent for sugar beet.

The level of protection for a range of commodities and countries varied from 20 to 40 per cent when calculated by valuing output at prices received by farmers and at import prices for the same year, and expressing the excess as a percentage of the value of output at national prices.[31] D. Gale Johnson estimated the reduced exports from LDCs consequent upon this protection at more than $3.5–4.5 billion.[32]

For individual countries, exports of particular products such as Canadian or Australian wheat or New Zealand meat and dairy products sometimes exceeded.75 per cent of national production. These countries showed only moderate increases in their exports in contrast to the major proportionate and absolute rise in exports by the protected agricultural sectors of the USA and the EEC.

The difficulties caused by the increased temperate zone agricultural protectionism since the war were felt most acutely perhaps by New Zealand. Agriculture dominated New Zealand's GNP and accounted for 92 per cent of her exports.[33] Moreover industrial growth was limited both by the country's resource base and her small population (2.6 million). The economy was therefore extremely vulnerable to external influences on its agricultural trade. Traditionally New Zealand had been dependent on the British market for about half of her exports. Increasing British and other countries self-sufficiency, culminating in Britain's entry to the Common Market which limited New Zealand agricultural exports, accentuated New Zealand's balance of payments problems and required the continuation of the import licensing first adopted in 1938. Efforts to develop alternative markets in Japan and the US met with considerable success, but both markets pursued protectionist policies. New Zealand therefore had to try to diversify her economy into secondary industries including textiles, forest products, basic iron, steel and aluminum smelting, a policy apparently similar to the import-substituting industrialisation of LDCs (see below).

The industrial countries were less unwilling to accept the changing pattern of comparative advantage when adjustment was required in their industrial structures although even here the market was not allowed free play. Japan during the 1950s in particular, pursued a policy similar to the import-substituting industrialisation of developing countries.[34] Nevertheless opportunities were provided for exports from other countries. A long-term arrangement on cotton textiles from 1962 was negotiated under the auspices of GATT contrary to two fundamental principles of GATT – non-discrimination and the freeing of trade from quantitative restrictions. Cotton textile industries in industrial countries were allowed to decline, but at a slower rate than market forces dictated. Total output of woven cotton piece goods in the UK halved between 1951 and 1965 and textile employment fell 5 per cent per annum.[35] Diversification in the textile centre of Lancashire proceeded rapidly; whereas 11 per cent were employed in textiles in 1959, by 1964 the proportion had fallen to 8 per cent. Perhaps three-quarters of the cotton mills closed between 1951 and 1964 were reoccupied for other purposes.

Similarly, in response to oil imports, the coal output of the EEC declined from 1956, and in the UK from 1958. European OECD hard coal production fell 12 per cent between 1958 and 1965. The increase of consumption of oil in competitive uses was one-half of total coal production in 1965. New imports of oil rose 15 per cent per annum, and coal employment in Belgium, France, Britain and West Germany fell by 6 per cent per annum. Even so, oil was not allowed to compete freely; oil usage was heavily taxed and financial assistance was given to displaced miners.

The remarkable dependence of the United States on oil imports by 1973, which dominated international relations in the 1970s, came about quite contrary to the professed intentions of trade policy. Imports of crude oil into the United States were limited by a quota system in 1959.[36] The quotas were allegedly intended to provide an incentive for making America independent of crude oil imports in times of emergencies. Higher oil prices induced by the quotas were expected to encourage a more intensive search for domestic oil. But oil prices did not rise. In January 1969 the price of oil relative to other wholesale products was 10 per cent lower than it had been eleven years earlier.[37] The fall in the domestic real price of oil and a high growth rate of the economy during the 1960s were the most important reasons for the rapid growth in the demand for oil in the US and elsewhere. The rapid increase in American imports during the early 1970s was caused by the curtailment of natural gas supplies by regulations, the unexpectedly low rate of growth of nuclear power and a variety of environmental restrictions on the strip mining and burning of coal, and on the development of domestic oil supplies. America's indigenous oil supplies nevertheless meant that American oil imports in 1972 at 4.74 million barrels a day were similar to the Japanese, and small by comparison with Western Europe's 14.06 million barrels, even though Western European oil consumption was less than that of the United States.[38]

## Trade policy of non-industrial countries

The quadrupling of oil prices in 1973 is perhaps the best known example of trade policy of the non-industrial countries. Oil however differs from most other non-industrial country commodity exports by virtue of being imported, instead of exported, by most less developed economies. The wresting of control over the oil trade from western multinational companies by LDC governments also distinguishes oil from most other commodity exports. The oil companies pursued restrictive practices in selling to LDCs longer than in other markets. Until the mid-1960s the West African Supply Agreement for supplying the small markets of West Africa eliminated all competition and kept prices high.[39] Only when some West African countries begin to refine their own oil did the arrangement end. Similarly, the price rigging of oil supplies to the Indian market only ended when in 1960 the Indian government was offered cheaper oil from the USSR and formed a national oil company able to handle imports independently. LDCs attempted to reduce dependence and oil import costs by building refineries even where the market was smaller than the 2 million tons per annum minimum efficient size. Generally speaking, the larger countries were successful and the smaller were not.

The exploitation by the oil companies turned out to be nothing in comparison to the exploitation by the Organisation of Petroleum

Exporting Countries (OPEC). Oil companies took $1–2 a barrel at the most, whereas from 1973 the oil-producing countries took $10 or more on 10–30 cent production costs. Consequently the foreign exchange reserves were not available to pay for this increase. The ability of OPEC to raise oil export prices so dramatically in 1973 stemmed from the breakdown of the 'working relationship' of the eight major oil companies with the entry of independent oil companies to the Middle East oil fields, and from the increase in the ability of the oil-exporting countries to collect and interpret information that affected their negotiating position.[40] Libya, for example, learned how to use Occidental, an independent oil company, to put pressure on the 'majors'. A common desire of the main oil-producing countries to defeat Israel and the ability of some. especially Saudi Arabia, to cut their oil production if necessary, were the trigger of the price increase in October 1973.

The success of non-industrial countries in raising oil prices encouraged the United Nations Conference on Trade and Development (UNCTAD) to press harder for schemes of commodity price management which they had always advocated. The developing countries in the United Nations formed UNCTAD in 1964 to advance their particular concerns about international economic relations. The only major international commodity price stabilisation scheme that operated through the past-war period did not justify UNCTAD's enthusiasm. The International Tin Agreement (ITA) since 1956 set up a buffer stock and a management that was to buy or sell tin on the world market to keep the price within an agreed range for most of the time. Unfortunately, the buffer stock was not large enough to maintain the price within the desired limits; producer countries did not want to bear the costs of financing an adequate stock.[41] The ability of ITA to hold the tin price above the agreement floor in most years required the buffer stock operation to be supplemented by tin export quotas. The agreement only slightly reduced the instability of tin prices and producer incomes.

Before the oil price rise of 1973 the lack of concrete achievement by successive UNCTAD conferences prompted the disrespectful to spell out the acronym as 'Under No Circumstances Take Any Decision'. The most constructive change brought about by UNCTAD was the Generalised System of Preferences (GSP), whereby manufactured exports from poor countries received non-reciprocal tariff preferences in developed country markets. The impact of these preferences on LDC exports was probably small because developed countries usually excluded the crucial textile sector (see above) and were also liable to implement quotas.[42]

It was much easier to pursue national policies to combat export instability than to try to secure international agreement on what should be done. Import-substituting industrialisation (ISI) was the most common national response to export instability, for this policy also promised to solve the other problems of non-industrial countries' exports; the tariff discrimination and other restrictions on their manufactured exports to developed countries, and the limited scope for economic growth based on the expansion of markets for (non-oil) primary products (which not being competitive with developed countries were therefore not discriminated against). As Table 10.4 shows, developed countries taxed manufactured imports from poor countries more heavily than others. This was because of the heavy concentration in textiles and clothing, industries losing competitiveness in the West, that therefore clamoured for protection. The tariff reductions of the Kennedy Round, though benefitting LDCs did not alter this discrimination.

The effective rate of protection was even higher than the nominal rate. The effective rate is an attempt to measure the extent to which a domestic manufacturer can increase his processing costs (or value-added) as compared with a foreign competitor without exceeding the price of the imported product. Employing certain restrictive assumptions, the effective rate takes account of the effects of tariffs on the prices of (importable) inputs, as well as output. The protective effect of a tariff on domestic manufacturing is therefore larger the lower is the duty on the (importable) raw materials used in the manufacturing process. The higher effective than nominal rates in Table 10.3 can be generated then by nominal rates on final goods generally exceeding those on intermediate goods.[43] Tariffs and quotas in foreign markets nevertheless did not prevent the small open economies of South–East Asia from achieving remarkable

**Table 10.4**  *Rates of protection of manufactured imports*

| | *Nominal rate of protection* | | *Effective rate of protection* | |
|---|---|---|---|---|
| | *developed country total imports* | *imports from less developed countries* | *developed country total imports* | *imports from less developed countries* |
| Pre-Kennedy Round | 10.9 | 17.1 | 19.2 | 33.4 |
| Post-Kennedy Round | 6.5 | 11.8 | 11.2 | 22.6 |

*Source*: Little *et al.*, op. cit., Table 8.1.

performances in increasing manufactured exports. Hong Kong, South Korea and Taiwan, whose combined manufactured exports rose from under $500 million in 1959 to at least $20 billion by 1976, were especially successful.[44]

Another reason for supposing import-substituting industrialisation policies were not essential is that fluctuations in exports were not necessarily as harmful as has been thought. The implications for export instability of the permanent income hypothesis of consumption and saving suggests this instability might actually be beneficial for economic development.[45] Transitory changes in income contribute more to saving and less to consumption according to this hypothesis, than 'permanent' or long-run and predictable changes. An economy with substantial unpredictable variations in export earning will therefore save more than an economy with stable earnings, other things being equal. If the financial system is efficient enough to channel those additional savings into investment, the first economy might reasonably be expected to experience a higher rate of economic growth. An empirical test for thirty-eight countries between 1949 and 1967 supports this theory. Consistent with the conclusion for the nineteenth century (see Chapter 4) export instability is unlikely to have offered an insurmountable obstacle to economic development, because in the new liberal trade era, although a lack of diversification in exports was a cause of instability, it was less significant for LDCs than for developed countries.[46]

The instruments for promoting ISI policies included the heavy taxation of primary produce exportables and the use of the revenues so obtained to subsidise domestically produced manufactures. Tariffs and quotas on manufactured imports were also applied to induce the same effect: a shift of domestic prices against the agricultural sector in favour of manufactures. Protection of domestic manufactures by tariffs and quotas on imports in pursuit of ISI was often carried to extreme lengths. The 118 per cent average rate of effective protection in Brazil ranged from 41 per cent on machinery products to 8480 per cent on perfumes and soap.[47] The domestic farmers were hurt by the higher prices they had to pay for manufactures and by the lower prices they received for their own produce. In Pakistan for much of the 1950s and 1960s the prices of manufactures in relation to farm prices were twice as high as the world market average prices. Incentives to produce food and even to stay in the countryside were therefore greatly reduced. The result was often food shortages and accelerated migration to urban areas. Indian agricultural production failed to increase in the fifteen years after 1950 despite the populaton explosion and the average growth of GDP per head at 1.5 per cent per annum. The ISI policy against the agricultural sector in LDCs meant that before the quadrupling of oil prices in 1973/4, LDC imports of food were increasing at almost twice the rate of exports of food.[48] Fifteen per cent of all LDC imports were foodstuffs in the early 1970s and 30 per cent were primary products.

The diversion of resources from agriculture to manufactures not only increased food imports but also reduced exports, both of primary products and of manufactures. LDCs lost market shares in the 1950s and 1960s in three-quarters of their primary product exports, exclusive of fuel, in which substitute or competitive commodities were produced in developed countries (grains, fruits, vegetables, and oils and oil seeds).[49] But about one-third of the non-oil exporter LDCs for which statistics are readily available achieved export growth rates in excess of 6 per cent per annum during these decades. The first thirteen had higher export growth rates than the industrial countries as a whole. All of these were small countries. Successful exporters also tended to have more rapid growth in real incomes. This may have been the result either of world markets or of supply conditions, whether spontaneous or brought about by policies, the opposite of ISI, favourable to trade. If supply conditions were the explanation, successful exporters must have increased their relative shares in traditional exports and diversified the commodity composition of their exports. GATT computed world market growth, diversification and competitiveness factors for LDC export performance 1959/61–1964/5 classifying the countries into three groups by export performance. The successful performers were distinguished from the less successful primarily by increases in their shares of world markets for their traditional exports, rather than by a rapidly expanding world demand for their particular exports. The successful exporters tended also to have gained more exports by diversification, although the margins of superiority here were much smaller. As has been seen in previous chapters, India's manufactured exports tended to increase in competitiveness during the twentieth century, but with the pursuit of ISI policies on independence, from being a leading exporter of manufactures in 1953, India lost 18 per cent of total exports in 1965 through failing to maintain her shares in world exports. The system of import and investment licensing gave virtually every firm a monopolistic position and severed the critical link between profitability and economic performance.[50]

### Trade patterns and spheres of influence

The trade policies of the industrial and non-industrial countries, together with a three or four factor Hecksher–Ohlin model, can explain much of the pattern of trade during the two booming decades after the Korean War, but not all. Apart from the formation of regional customs unions, commercial policies under GATT were not supposed to discriminate between countries. It was true that British Commonwealth tariff preferences persisted until the entry of Britain to the EEC in 1973, but by 1948 the preference rate for British goods averaged only 7 per cent (although since then and the early 1960s, changes in the area and commodity pattern of Commonwealth trade tended to raise the margin).[51] The sterling area controls during the early 1950s also tended to create discriminatory trading pattern. The US–Canadian Automotive Trade Agreement of 1965 worked in the same direction, as did a number of other administrative controls and conventions. The net effect of these forces, historical and cultural ties between traders, the tying of aid, the establishment of multinational subsidiaries, preferential tariffs, as well as transport costs all tended to bias the manufactures goods trade flows from the industrial countries of the world in a way which would not be expected from Hecksher–Ohlin theory.

Industrial countries tended to market their weakest sectors of manufactures disproportionately in areas which could be thought of as 'spheres of influence,' a pattern which cannot be explained solely by physical distance between traders.[52] For instance, in ships, furniture, domestic electrical appliances and iron and steel, the United States in 1971 had at least seven times the market share in Canada that it had internationally for those sectors. The US had a world market share in each of these sectors less than half of its world market share in manufactures as a whole. These results cannot be explained by H–O theory; in every area market a given country was competing with the same adversaries and their relative factor endowments, although varying for different trade sectors, remained unchanged for the same sector between market areas. Neither can multinational subsidiaries account for the phenomenon because, for countries other than the US, intra-firm trade in manufactures was a small fraction of total trade in manufactures (for Japan about 5 per cent). For the United States, eliminating intra-firm trade did not alter the relationship. For most countries other than Britain and the British Commonwealth, sphere of influence and economic distance were correlated, but transport costs were a small proportion of output value and therefore could not account for the trading patterns. An exporter's strong sector commanded about the same market share in all areas. On one interpretation the importers were a captive market. On another the trade may have been less imperfect than trade between arbitrary pairs of countries because channels of communication and information were more highly developed. It was cheaper and less risky for importers to buy a known product than to pay the costs necessary to compare products of various exporters.

The captive market interpretation is usually most favoured in accounting for the dominance of the imperial power in colonial trade. Hence the granting of independence to European colonies in the 1950s and 1960s, by freeing the markets, must have lost the former imperial powers trade. In the period after independence the imports of former colonies did grow much more slowly than those of other less developed areas.[53] Thus it seems likely that had colonial rule persisted, the imports of the colonies would have been greater and the colonising power's share higher than they actually were after independence. Kleiman argues on this basis that the export loss of the UK in 1972 from decolonisation was 8.5 per cent of UK exports and that the French loss was 13.1 per cent of French exports.[54] The gains of Britain and France in 1960 from not having decolonised earlier were 8.2 and 16.2 per cent respectively of their exports, though the magnitude of the export loss varies significantly with the choice of control group. In the above case imports of former colonies are assumed to have grown at the same rate as world imports as a whole in the absence of independence. If instead import growth into other less developed areas are chosen as the control, then the losses to Britain and France are radically reduced. There is a problem in applying a common import substitution factor to all ex-colonies despite differing sizes of domestic markets, stages of industrial development, and economic structures.[55] Furthermore many of the factors 'distorting' trade under colonialism were part of a process which continued under independence; comparative advantage and market forces are not easily abolished by a change of political regime. The Associated State Status of some former colonial African countries giving them privileged access to the EEC market was another continuing distortion, although only the small low income Commonwealth nations were allowed this status when Britain joined the Common Market in 1973.

The effects of colonial status on economic structure and international trade in the 1950s and 1960s are fairly well agreed, at least in qualitative terms. Colonial status appeared to raise the ratio of trade to output among the least developed countries, to depress the share of manufactured goods in total exports and of chemicals and capital goods in imports.[56] Achievement of independence more than reversed this effect on the composition of exports but did not seem to change the relationship between total trade and output, although a weakening of trading links with the former colonial power followed the weakening or severance of political links.

There is evidence of a difference in experience between colonial powers. Between 1960–2 and 1968–70, the decline in the British share in former dependencies could for the most part be explained by Britain's generally reduced role in the trade of the world's less developed areas.[57] By contrast the French share in the trade of former dependencies declined no less rapidly, despite the considerable increase in France's share in the trade of other less developed areas. The greater effect of decolonisation on the French group is consistent with the conclusion based on the situation in 1960–2 that the degree to which the share of the imperial power in the colonies' trade can be ascribed to colonial role was inversely related to the importance of the colonial power in world trade, as the account of colonisation in the last two decades of the nineteenth century in Chapter 4 also suggests.

If colonisation had the effect of raising the share of the colonial power in the colonies' trade, decolonisation cannot be attributed to a declining significance of this trade, because the importance of the dependencies in the trade of their imperial countries incresased in the three decades before their independence began to be considered. In any case, relative to the domestic product of the imperial countries, any potential gain from colonial trade could only have been of limited significance for them. The colonial territories on the other hand, with a combination of high imperial trade shares and a high ratio of trade to GDP, were very vulnerable to the behaviour and development of their imperial powers, as had been demonstrated in the interwar years (see Chapter 7). Before and after decolonisation, the industrial countries influenced these territories through the terms of trade between primary and manufactured products, among other ways.

### The terms of trade between primary and manufactured products

The investment in primary products triggered by the Korean War boom proved sufficient to expand supply so that the terms of trade of primary products with manufactures declined gently from 1952 until the end of the 1960s despite the massive growth in the production of, and trade in, manufactures.[58] Nevertheless, primary product prices in money terms had risen. At the end of 1971 market prices in sterling for staple commodities other than oil were between three and four times as high as in 1939.[59] By the Spring of 1974 they had tripled again. Most of this rise was concentrated in the 18 months from the Autumn of 1972, over which period the rise was half as great as in the preceding century. The increase in oil prices, after a gradual recovery from the low levels of 1969–70, was more violent, raising import costs fourfold within a year. Other commodities – zinc, wool, and sugar, for example – matched the rise in oil prices, but lacked the economic importance of oil and did not provide comparable gains to their producers. The price increases did little more than to restore the price relations with manufactures of the early 1950s. Taking British import and export unit values as an imperfect measure of these relations, the shift in relative prices was about 22 per cent in favour of British exports between 1953–5 and autumn 1972, and 27 per cent against British exports over the next year-and-a-half. Fuel imports costs in 1972 were no higher in sterling terms than fifteen years earlier, whereas manufactures were selling at much higher prices.

Apart from the OPEC's actions, there were three main explanations for the price explosion; the 17 per cent expansion of world production between 1971–3 as all industrial countries reflated their economies together, delays in the development of new primary product sources of supply and a speculative boom, touched off by international monetary uncertainties, that made the holding of commodities preferable to currency. The consequence of these price increases was to raise the value of imports in the first quarter of 1974 for Italy by 92 per cent, for Japan by 85 per cent (Feburary to April) and for the UK by 60 per cent (February to April). This created a transfer problem comparable to the German reparations problem of the 1920s (see Chapter 8). In the British case, even allowing for a 20 per cent rise in exports prices, the implied transfer of resources to the countries from which the imports came was equivalent to 8 per cent of GDP, or a 10 per cent drop in consumption. In order to make the transfer, exports would have had to increase by nearly 50 per cent in volume within a year. Where some of the oil exporters were concerned, the transfer was complicated by the inability of the recipients to spend all their new income on oil importers exports, or on anything else, because their new earnings were so large.

By mid-1974 commodity prices (excluding food) were falling, adding to the difficulties of the oil-importing developing countries.

Speculative activity had declined and world industrial production growth decelerated.

## Communist system trade policy

Not being dependent on free markets, the communists bloc economies were less affected by these massive swings in prices. In the centrally planned economies supplies and demands were balanced instead by physical controls. Prices remained fixed for long periods of time (in Russia, from 1955 to 1967) and did not reflect relative scarcities or consumers' wants. Inflation was therefore suppressed and was measured by shortages of goods, rather than by price rises.[60]

The absence of a rational internal pricing system required intrabloc trade through the Council for Mutual Economic Assistance (CMEA) to be based on historical world prices. Raw materials were thereby obviously underpriced, and a form of bilateralism therefore tended to be introduced; the exchange of raw materials for other raw materials, and similarly for manufactures. The USSR, for example, being primarily a raw material exporter to CMEA, lost from that trade. In 1980, at the prevailing rouble–dollar exchange rate, the Polish import price for Soviet crude oil was 52 per cent below the average import price from the West.[61] Irrational prices made difficult the securing of gains from trade and the communist countries consequently had much lower trade/GNP ratios than the West; in 1967 the communist ratio was 11.3 per cent whereas the West's ratio was 69.3 per cent. In some respect trade within the communist bloc (CMEA), encountered difficulties similar to those of market economies unwilling to accept the specialisation imposed by market forces; Romania for instance resented the demands of the more advanced CMEA countries that she should concentrate on low technology production. But unlike the trade of western economies intra-bloc trade was clearly motivated by political objectives. Russia would have benefitted from exporting its energy and raw materials to the West and buying manufactures there, rather than conducting this trade with Eastern Europe. The trade subsidies the Soviet Union granted Eastern Europe averaged $5.8 billion between 1976 and 1978, rising to $10.4 billion in 1979 and $21.7 billion in 1980. These payments can only be regarded as a means of obtaining important military, strategic and political benefits associated with the control of Eastern Europe. The subsidies are unlikely to have compensated fully for the loss of economic sovereignty. But such full compensation was unnecessary because of the high cost of a popular rebellion to Eastern Europe as was demonstrated in Hungary in 1956, in Czechoslovakia in 1968 and, with the introduction of martial law, in Poland in 1981. Moreover a restructuring of internal and external economic relations, which the removal of Russian domination would have allowed, would almost certainly have raised the low productivity of the Eastern European economies by many times more than necessary to offset the hypothetical loss of the trade subsidy.

The absence of prices reflecting opportunity costs and the use of quantity planning created a number of difficulties in communist trade with the West. Tariffs in centrally-planned economies did not protect because they did not affect prices or the availability of goods. Hence tariffs were usely solely as bargaining devices in negotiations with the West for most favoured nation treatment. Dumping, the selling of goods in foreign markets at prices below the domestic costs of production, could not be defined for a communist bloc economy, yet from the viewpoint of western producers in import-competing industries such sales could be extremely harmful. As Table 10.1 shows, East–West trade was a rapidly expanding, though small, proportion of world trade.

Economic interest sometimes transcended ideology; Poland was admitted to the Kennedy Round negotiations in 1965, and Romania and Hungary joined GATT in 1971 and 1973. Romania was the most dissident of the satellite states in expanding trade with Western Europe. Between 1959 and 1968 such trade as a proportion of the Romanian total rose from 20 to 45 per cent. Politics was however always liable to take priority in East–West trade, as in intra-bloc trade, as was demonstrated by the US–USSR Trade Agreement approved by Congress in 1974. The following year the Agreement was annulled by the USSR because the revaluation of gold and oil so improved the Russian foreign exchange position that the Russians felt the concession of allowing Jewish emigration with which the Agreement was linked was no longer necessary.

## International labour mobility

As the above example shows, communist countries differed from the western economies in their attitudes to international migration. Whereas the centrally-planned bloc attempted to stop people leaving, the market economies were concerned to prevent new arrivals settling. Despite the greater sense of national exclusiveness exemplified by immigration controls, the return of international full employment in the 1950s allowed migration largely to resume the nineteenth-century pattern; a movement from the populous lands of Europe to the regions of recent European settlement; and within Europe, from agricultural regions to the rapidly developing industrial regions. There were important differences though. Indians and Chinese migration ceased to follow the nineteenth-century pattern, but in greatly reduced volume some migration from Asia (and Africa) now went to Europe. Latin America which had formerly been a net receiver of migrants now lost population on balance as relative prosperity diminished, and the United States became a destination for Latin American, especially Mexican and Caribbean, migrants. Immigration no longer major contribution to the population growth of the United States, but continued to do so in Australia, Canada and New Zealand. Fifty-nine per cent of Australia's population growth between 1947 and 1973 was due to immigration.[62] Immigration to Canada accounted for up to 35 per cent of Canadian population increase in years of high immigration.[63] The precise contribution of immigration to the US population is masked by the unknown number of illegal immigrants. By the 1970s between 2 and 12 per cent of the US labour force came into this category, and of these one half to three-quarters were Mexicans, mainly working in south-western agriculture.[64]

A slow down of European migration overseas was accompanied by an intensification of international migration within Europe, and by the emergence of new migration into Europe from other areas, notably from Northern Africa and Turkey, and from some previously colonial countries overseas. By contrast with previous history Europe as a whole had an outward migratory balance of fewer than 3 million during 1950 to 1960, and fewer than 400 000 during 1960 to 1970.[65] West Germany became a destination, as it had been before the first world war, and France took even more immigrants (see Table 10.5). By 1973 there were around $11\frac{1}{2}$ million legal and illegal foreign workers in Western Europe.[66]

Encouraged by the integration policies of the EEC and EFTA, the countries of the Mediterranean, first Italy then Greece, Spain and Portugal and later Turkey and Yugoslavia, became a reservoir of manpower for the industrial nations. Until 1950 the majority of Italian emigrants left Europe but subsequently, with the European boom, most stayed on the continent.[67] Switzerland took almost half of Italian European migration. As the Italian domestic demand for labour expanded rapidly during the 1960s Italian migration went into decline. A similar pattern but later in timing, is shown by Greek emigration. Until 1960 Greek emigrants went mainly to America and Australia, then the majority were drawn into West German industry, and after 1968 with the growth of Greek industry and the

**Table 10.5** *Approximate net international migration, 1960–70 (m)*

| Destinations | | Origins | |
|---|---|---|---|
| US | 3.9 | Latin America | 1.9 |
| Australia | 0.9 | N. Africa | 0.6* |
| Canada | 0.7 | Portugal | 1.3 |
| France | 2.2 | Italy | 0.8 |
| W. Germany | 2.1 | Yugoslavia | 0.7 |
| Switzerland | 0.3 | E. Germany | 0.6 |
| Sweden | 0.2 | Spain | 0.5 |
| Belgium | 0.15 | Greece | 0.45 |
| | | Poland | 0.3 |
| | | UK | 0.15 |

Source: UN, *The World Population Situation in 1970–1975* New York (1974), p. 23.
* Excluding the million or so French settlers who returned to France after Algerian independence.

slowing of West European growth rates, Greek emigration in total declined.

In addition to migration inspired by pecuniary motives, the post-war decades saw other major population movements. Ten million refugees left Bangladesh for India during the fighting of 1971 and subsequently returned. The following year the Asians of Uganda were expelled. Indo-China, the Middle East, Algeria Hungary, Cuba and Czechoslovakia all supplied migrants for political reasons who did not return.

By redistributing labour from lower productivity economies to higher productivity economies, commercially-motivated inter-national migration should have raised total world production, and both economies should usually have gained a share of this increased output. Concern about the economic costs of migration both to the host and the donor countries often originated in the operation of national fiscal systems. A donor country could be concerned at the emigration of skilled manpower educated at the expense of the taxpayer, and a host country could be worried about unskilled immigration becoming a net drain upon the social services. Britain received a net inflow of largely unskilled New Commonwealth (coloured) immigrants, which reached a peak between 1960 and 1966 before being restricted by law to avoid racial disturbances such as had occurred in Notting Hill in 1958. The New Commonwealth immigrants were sometimes accused of being a drain on the social services which more than offset their work contribution. In fact, their demands on the social services were less than those of the indigenous population and indigenous living standards probably did not suffer because of the migrants capital needs.[68] The immigrants bore the weight of deflationary fluctuations, suffering greater than average unemployment during slumps, although when general unemployment was low, immigrant employment rates did not differ significantly from general unemployment.

Nevertheless antagonism to foreign labour led Switzerland to attempt to 'stabilise' its migrant labour force in the Spring of 1971 and then to introduce measures to reduce it in July 1973. In 1972 and 1973 France, Holland and West Germany introduced restrictions on new entrants, culminating at the end of 1973 in a ban by the latter two countries on the entry of non-EEC workers. The oil crisis was probably merely a trigger for a decision that had already been reached.

The tightening of immigration controls tended to alter the international division of labour. Controls tended to eliminate the manufacture of those goods whose production demanded a high proportion of immigrant-type labour and to replace them by imports, and to mechanise the production of non-traded goods such as construction, where the proportion of foreign workers in Europe was highest. Countries supplying manpower might 'inherit' activities abandoned by the countries of immigration either through direct investment or through loans financed on the international capital markets. The use of immigrant workers to manufacture in West Germany either delayed the transfer of that activity to other countries or more likely delayed increasing mechanisation of immigrant-intensive industries such as car production.[69]

A favourable view of the impact of migration on a land-abundant economy underlay the very accommodating Australian immigration policy that lasted until the late 1960s. But more important were strategic considerations. Near-invasion by Japan during the second world war seemed to prove the vulnerability of the vast and relatively empty Australian continent to the overcrowded countries of Asia. In order to ensure enough people to provide troops and to support an economy capable of providing advanced armaments, it was estimated that a population of 25 million was required, yet the 1945 population was only 7.3 million.[70] Even in 1970 national security was used to justify official immigration policies. The practical consequence of this policy was that more than 60 per cent of new arrivals had government financial assistance. Between 1945 and 1976 about 3.3 million settlers went to Australia. A little under half of all immigrants were British. The 'White Australia' immigration policy became an increasing embarrassment as Australian relations with Asia developed. Between 1970/1 and 1975/6 the proportion of immigrants from Asia in the total rose from 5 to 14 per cent as a result of modifications to this policy.

The effects of migration on an indigenous population can be analysed with an elementary 'sources of growth' model. The contribution of factor inputs to the growth of the output of the economy is assessed by weighting the actual growth rate of the inputs by the share of the respective factor payments in national income.[71] The implications of a hypothetical elimination of immigration can be derived by cutting the growth rate of the labour force. Applying this approach to the study of skilled migration into Canada between 1950 and 1962, Canadian GNP would have grown at 3.3 per cent per annum instead of 3.8 per cent per annum, and GNP per head would have grown faster, at 2 instead of 1.8 per cent per annum.[72] Such a calculation has to be modified to take into consideration the capital that immigrants brought with them and the capital and technical progress induced by migration. The immigrants to Canada were more skilled on average than the indigenous population; they added disproportionally to the stock of human capital. In 1967 the average stock of education of the labour force was 3 per cent higher than it would have been without immigration. However the immigrants' needs for physical capital may have offset the beneficial impact on the indigenous population of the human capital they brought, although this seems unlikely.

More often the donor country is thought to suffer from skilled migration, and the host country to benefit. Such a reflection probably contributed to the change in immigration regulations in a number of major recipient countries during the mid and late 1960s. The United States, Australia, Canada and the UK reduced discrimination by country of origin and promoted immigration of skilled manpower. As a result there was an increase in professional and technically-trained manpower emigrating to the United States from LDCs. The evidence for the UK and Canada is however mixed, perhaps because of diversion of this manpower to the United States.[73] The LDCs will have suffered from this 'brain drain', unless their skilled manpower was underemployed, and emigration acted as a 'safety valve'.

Any evaluation of unskilled migration must take into consideration that aspirations and wants are often changed by migration. Particularly, this is true of the second generation who becomes dissatisfied with accepting their parents' lot at the bottom of the wage and status scale. Puerto Rican migration, concentrated in the 1940s and 1950s, exemplifies the process. New York by the 1970s had a second generation Puerto Rican community, the youth of which generally refused low-wage menial jobs and showed second generation rebellion symptoms of rioting and unemployment.[74] The riots in the English conurbations during 1981 can be attributed in part to the same phenomenon at work in the West Indian communities. In such cases the host country had a problem that the liberal doctines of free trade and factor mobility, with unchanging or exogenous preferences, did not predict.

Some beneficial effects of the migrant workers on the donor countries were as obvious as they were for nineteenth-century Ireland (see Chapter 1). For Turkey, repatriated earnings amounted to 57 per cent of the import bill and about 7 per cent of GNP in 1973, when just over 5 per cent of the active population was working abroad.[75] On the other hand, savings and remittances out of earnings abroad were mainly spent on consumption, not on agricultural or industrial investment. Few returned migrants learned new skills abroad and those who did so tended not to use them on their return. Because the poorest did not migrate from Turkey and because land purchase was the most common use for the savings of returned migrants, the distribution of income was made more unequal.

## Welfare and economic growth

If migration to new environments changed preferences and thereby made the evaluation of that migration problematic, economic growth created similar difficulties. Rapid economic development changed environments in ways that were not always chosen, and perhaps also altered tastes, causing doubts to be expressed towards the end of this unprecedented economic expansion as to its benefits. Even though national income per head increased, it was argued, people were not necessarily better off in view of the stress, overcrowding and pollution of the modern economy. A further reason for doubting the benefits of rising incomes was the confusion of means with ends in national income accounts, such as the inclusion of the costs of the journey to work as an item of final consumption, instead of as an intermediate good.[76] However the use of social indicators of well-being, such as the suicide rate, protein consumption per head, doctors per head of population, and students as a proportion of the population, suggests that between 1951 and 1969 for twenty advanced industrial countries there was a positive association between economic growth and welfare indices computed from seventeen social indicators (although the strength of the association diminished over time).[77] The association of welfare with national income was not exact when countries were compared. A social well-being index ranked the United States below the Scandinavian countries and Canada in 1969. On the basis of income per head the USA should have been ranked above these countries.

The social indicator approach does not show that people judged themselves to be happier in the 1970s than in the 1950s even if they were, by 'objective' standards, better-off. According to Scitovsky, the psychology of consumption implies that it is novelty which gives gratification and therefore to maintain a given level of 'utility' a constant *increase* in consumption is required;[78] the television sets, motor cars and central heating that spread through the industrial world may not have permanently raised welfare. Hence any inability of the national economies to maintain a constant growth rate and thereby to continue to supply new consumption experiences, would be liable to cause industrial unrest and wage-push inflation, such as happened in the 1970s.

There are a number of processes by which the international economy could have contributed to this economic growth. The two gap theory, discussed in Chapter 11, focuses on the relaxation of the import constraint by foreign capital but can be extended to show how a larger share of exports in national product also can remove the constraint and promote economic growth. Where output is constrained by inadequate domestic investment the opposite relationship holds: a lower ratio of exports of national product allows a large investment component and therefore larger output. This latter relationship seemed to hold for Western Europe excluding the UK in the 1969s.[79].

Figure 10.2 shows the direct contribution of exports and other components of total expenditure to overall growth in the 1960s. Exports made major contributions to output only in Western Europe, Oceania and Africa, although in no case did trade growth account for more than about a third of output growth, and the comparatively high trade contributions stemmed from differing circumstances. Exports from Africa during the 1960s increased slowly but accounted for an exceptionally high proportion of total demand, whereas in Western Europe and Oceania they increased rapidly. For the advanced countries generally exports appeared to be equally significant with investment as an explanation of differences in growth performance. This was true also for LDCs where, probably because of foreign exchange constraints, capital imports

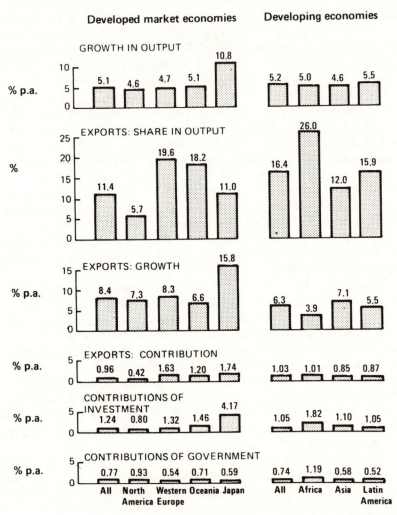

**Figure 10.2** Direct contribution of exports and other factors to economic growth, 1960–70 (Note: "Direct Contribution" of aggregate demand component to growth is share of output x growth of component)

*Source:* R. Batchelor et al, *Industrialization and the Basis for Trade*. Cambridge: Cambridge University Press (1980)

were strongly correlated with export receipts. In the bigger semi-industrial countries investment emerged as the more important factor, but in the smaller, it was exports, in particular manufactured exports.

Figure 10.2 also shows divergences in growth rates of which the most extreme is that of Japan. A comparison of developed market economies with developing economies shows very similar growth rates for the 1960s, despite their different rates of population growth. Because of the faster growth of population in less developed countries, this similarity meant a lower growth of income per head on average for developing countries. Within the LDC group the divergent growth experiences of the oil countries and the newly-industrialising countries of East Asia, Brazil and Mexico, on the one hand, and on the other, remaining LDCs, were wider than the discrepancies in mean growth rates for the total developed and developing groups. Technology gap theories of growth imply that the growth of income per head in poor countries should have been higher instead of lower than in the rich countries, other things being equal. The discussion of economic policy showed that other things, were *not* equal, and that policies between countries differed in a way that had significant impacts on their economic performance. In addition the experience of the OPEC economies showed that national resource endowments remained an important ingredient of economic growth, even if less so than in the nineteenth century.

## Summary and conclusions

Judged by the increase in trade and incomes, the new liberal trade order was an enormous success, more so than the original liberal achievement of the nineteenth century despite the failure to eliminate or even reduce international income inequality. The economic experience of the 1950s and 1960s cannot however be attributed solely to international economic relations. The United States, by virtue of its size and technological leadership, was largely independent of these relations, although most other economies were greatly influenced by the American economy. Even large countries with a low ratio of trade to national income probably benefitted substantially more than their 'openness' suggested from the international flow of new technologies which was not completely mirrored in the international exchange of goods and services. All types of economies were subject to this process, advanced market economies, less developed countries and the communist states, although the means by which technology was transferred varied; multinational companies, official development assistance, licensing, exports of capital equipment and the interchange of ideas all played a part in varying degrees. The extent to which different economies took advantage of the new technologies depended primarily on their economic system, their investment rates and the size of their technological lag behind the United States.

Trade patterns reflected the new technological dynamism, with research and development and human capital becoming major determinants of trade in manufactures between industrial countries. Manufactures trade between these countries was boosted by widespread tariff cuts implemented in particular by the Kennedy Round. This liberal commercial policy led by the United States gave a further lease of life to the long post-war boom. America's acceptance of international economic leadership already noted in the redirection of the world economy in the immediate post-war period, contrasted strongly with US policy in the interwar years. Then there was no obvious external enemy against whom the market economies of the world had to be unified, whereas Russian expansion after 1945 and the ideological competition between the two super-powers showed there was in the later period. Nevertheless the United States was not uniquely responsible for the burgeoning of western economic relations. The demand management policies of western governments were probably more important in encouraging the investment and innovation that underlay the expansion of the world economy, although by embedding inflation into the system they also eventually brought the era to an end. Even where commercial relations were concerned, the new order of the 1940s developed its own momentum independent of the United States. Western European co-operation in iron and steel flowered into the Common Market as a means of reducing tariff barriers, once GATT seemed to have become ineffective.

The Common Market introduced the greatest western divergence from free trade in the form of the Common Agricultural Policy. The United States also pursued extreme agricultural protection in contrast to her liberal trade policy in manufactures. Though expensive to domestic consumer and potential foreign suppliers of temperate zone primary products, these policies may have had some justification in slowing the rate at which people had to make the transition from rural to urban life, for despite protection, technical progress in western agriculture was sufficiently fast to reduce the farm population while farm output increased.

Less developed countries typically pursued the opposite policy of taxing domestic agriculture to support urban manufacturing industries, on the grounds that their economies' former pattern of exporting agricultural produce or raw materials offered no prospect for long-term economic development. The policy was usually unsuccessful, resulting in the necessity for increasing food imports, while at the same time the subsidised manufacturing sector did not increase competitiveness on the world market. Independence from colonial rule allowed an increasing number of less developed countries to adopt these policies and reduce their dependence on traditional manufactured imports from the colonial powers. The removal of the colonial restraint on their policies was not because these countries were of diminishing economic significance to the imperial power. On the contrary political forces were fundamental because the colonial share in the trade of the imperial powers had been increasing before independence.

After the Korean War throughout the 1950s and 1960s the declining terms of trade of primary products relative to manufactures gave some substance to the claims of less developed countries that the export of primary products was not a viable road to economic development. The simultaneous expansion of the industrial economies in 1972, and the use of the oil weapon by OPEC the following year, ended this trend, bringing price relations back to Korean War levels, and appearing to end the post-war boom.

The communist economies were subject to different though related problems both in intra-bloc trade and investment, and in relations with market economies. The central-planning system had difficulties encouraging innovation across all sectors, and therefore the communist economies became more dependent on western technology imports. Lacking a rational pricing system, communist countries attained much lower trade/GNP ratios than western economies, and engaged in the heavy subsidisation of trade. Some subsidisation, in particular that by USSR of Eastern Europe, was intentional in return for political advantages.

Outside the communist economies a resumption of international factor mobility accompanied the increase in world trade, even though the two processes are usually thought to be substitutes for each other. Tight controls limited labour migration once the boom of the 1960s came to an end (and even earlier in some cases) for fear of friction between immigrants and the indigenous population. The pattern of migration showed the effects of strong Western European economic growth, which by the 1960s substantially eliminated net emigration by providing an alternative demand for labour to that of the regions of recent European settlement. Nevertheless, the latter areas continued to take considerable numbers of Europeans and others with a new bias towards encouraging skilled manpower regardless of origins, as befitted the new direction of the international economy.

Overall, the period was one of remarkable economic progress. Even though there were offsets, often associated with urban conditions, surveys of the urban poor showed they usually thought their conditions better than in the countryside from which they had come, and where they were so much less noticeable.[80]

## Notes

1. S.H. Preston, 'Causes and consequences of mortality declines in less developed countries during the twentieth century', in R.A. Easterlin (ed.), *Population and Economic Change in Developing Countries*, Chicago and London: University of Chicago Press (1980). At the end of 1964 1.935 billion persons lived in areas that were originally malarious. Of these, 41 per cent were living in areas from which malaria had been eradicated, and only 19 per cent lived where no specific anti-malarial measures had been taken.

2. United Nations, *The World Population Situation in 1970–1975*, New York: UN Department of Economic and Social Affairs (1974), p. 65.

3. F.D. Holzman, *International Trade Under Communism: Politics and Economics*, London: Macmillan (1976). J. Wilczynski, *Technology in Comecon*, London: Macmillan (1974), ch. 1.

4. OECD, *Gaps in Technology: Comparisons Between Member Countries*, Paris (1970).

5. OECD, *Technical Change and Economic Policy*, Paris (1980).

6. ibid., p. 30.

7. ibid., p. 51.

8. P. Hanson, *Trade and Technology in Soviet-Western Relations*, London: Macmillan (1981).

9. W.H. Courtney and D.M. Leipziger, 'Multinational corporations in LDCs: the choice of technology', *Oxford Bulletin of Economics and Statistics*, **37** (1975), pp. 297–304. R.O. Jenkins, *Dependent Industrialization in Latin America: The Automotive Industry in Argentina, Chile and Mexico*, New York: Praeger (1977), ch. 5. P.R. Odell, 'Oil', in C. Payer (ed.), *The Commodity Trade of the Third World*, London: Macmillan (1975).

10. For example, J. Cornwall, *Modern Capitalism*, London: Martin Robertson (1977).

11. This phenomenon was identified by M. Friedman, 'The role of monetary policy', *American Economic Review*, **58** (1968), pp. 1–15.

12. On surplus labour, see N. Kaldor, *Causes of the Slow Rate of Economic Growth of the United Kingdom*, Cambridge: Cambridge University Press (1966); C.P. Kindleberger, *Europe's Postwar Growth: The Role*

*of Labour Supply*, London: Oxford University Press (1967); and T.F. Cripps and R.J. Tarling, *Growth in Advanced Capitalist Economies 1950–1970*, Cambridge: Cambridge University Press (1973).

13. Hanson, op. cit., chs. 8, 9.
14. H.G. Grubel and P.J. Lloyd, *Intra-Industry Trade*, London: Macmillan, (1975), p. 36, ch. 6.
15. United Nations Industrial Development Organisation, *World Industry in 1980*, New York: United Nations. For a formalisation of intra-industry stemming from product differentiation and economies of scale, see A. Dixit and V. Norman, *Theory of International Trade*, Welwyn, Herts: Nisbet and Cambridge University Press (1980), pp. 281–95. These authors conclude from their model that there are not necessarily gains from trade. Possibly trade may increase biases in product selection and encourage the establishment of too many firms.
16. On technology gap trade theories and product cycle, see M.V. Posner, 'International trade and technical change', *Oxford Economic Papers*, **13** (1961); R. Vernon, 'International investment and international trade in the product in the product cycle', *Quarterly Journal of Economics*, **80** (1966); and L.T. Wells (ed.), *The Product Life Cycle and Internation Trade*, Boston: Harvard Business School (1972). A useful brief survey of the effects of technological change on trade is P.H. Lindert and C.P. Kindleberger, *International Economics*, Homewood, Ill.: Irwin, 7th edn, ch. 5.
17. B. Balassa, 'Revealed comparative advantage revisited: an analysis of relative export shares of industrial countries 1953–1971', *Manchester School*, **45** (1977), pp. 327–44.
18. W. Leontieff, 'Domestic production and foreign trade: the American position re-examined', in J.N. Bhagwati (ed.), *International Trade: Selected Readings*, Baltimore: Penguin (1969).
19. GATT, *Japan's Economic Expansion and Foreign Trade 1955 to 1970*, Geneva (1971), p. 8.
20. S. Grassman, 'Long-term trends in openness of national economies', *Oxford Economic Papers*, **32** (1980), pp. 123–33.
21. G. and V. Curzon, 'Options after the Kennedy Round', in H.G. Johnson (ed.), *New Trade Strategy for the World Economy*, Toronto and Buffalo: University of Toronto Press (1969). G. Curzon, *Multilateral Commercial Diplomacy*, New York: Praeger (1965), pp. 87–107.
22. M. Camps, *The Free Trade Area Negotiations*, London: PEP (1959).
23. A.M. Schlesinger, Jr, *A Thousand Days: John F. Kennedy in the White House*, Boston: Houghton Mifflin (1965), pp. 842–844.
24. R.A. Batchelor, R.L. Major and A.D. Morgan, *Industrialisation and the Basis for Trade*, Cambridge: Cambridge University Press (1980), ch. 4.
25. On the trade creation and trade diversion effects of a Customs Union, see P. Robson, *The Economics of International Integration*, London: Allen & Unwin (1980), chs 2–4.

26. F.O. Grogan, *International Trade in Temperate Zone Products*, Edinburgh: Oliver & Boyd (1972). J.C. Nagle, *Agricultural Trade Policies*, Farnborough: Saxon House (1976).
27. K. Kock, *International Trade Policy and the Gatt 1947–1967*, Stockholm: Almquist & Wiksell (1969), ch. 7.
28. Curzon, op. cit., p. 175.
29. ibid., p. 202.
30. Grogan, op. cit.
31. GATT (1971), op. cit.
32. D. Gale Johnson, 'Agriculture and foreign economic policy', *Journal of Farm Economics* 46 (1964), pp. 915–29. Johnson assumes the lowest elasticities of supply and demand likely are respectively 0.15 and 0.2 in absolute value.
33. Grogan, op. cit., p. 59.
34. GATT (1971), op. cit.
35. I.M.D. Little, T. Scitovsky and M. Fg. Scott, *Industry and Trade in Some Developing Countries*, London: Oxford University Press (1970).
36. GATT, *Trends in United States Merchandise Trade 1953–1970*.
37. J.W. McKie, 'The United States', in R. Vernon (ed.), *The Oil Crisis*, New York: W.W. Norton (1976), pp. 73–4.
38. J. Dornstadter and H.H. Landsberg, 'The Economic Background', in Vernon, op. cit., p. 21.
39. Odell, loc. cit.
40. R. Vernon, 'An Interpretation', in Vernon, op. cit., pp. 7–8; and A. Sampson, *The Seven Sisters*, New York: Viking Press (1975), ch. 7. For an economic analysis of the OPEC cartel, see Lindert and Kindleberger, op. cit., ch. 10.
41. M. Desai, 'An Econometric model of the world tin economy 1948–1961', *Econometrica*, 34 (1966), pp. 105–34. G.W. Smith and G.R. Schink, 'The international tin agreement: a reassessment', *Economic Journal*, 86 (1976), pp. 715–28. On commodity schemes in general, see C.P. Brown, *The Political and Social Economy of Commodity Control*, London: Macmillan (1980).
42. R.E. Baldwin and T. Murray, 'MFN tariff reductions and developing country benefits under the GSP', *Economic Journal*, 87 (1977), pp. 30–46.
43. The effective rate of protection can be represented by the expression

$$e = \frac{n - mi}{v}$$

where $e$ = effective rate, $n$ = nominal rate on the final good, $m$ = nominal rate on the input good, $i$ = coefficient of material input, $v$ = proportion of final output accounted for by value added. Suppose the nominal duty on steel was 20 per cent, and steel was 40 per cent of manufacturing costs of cars, on which there was 10 per cent duty. Then $n = 0.1$, $m = 0.2$, $i = 0.4$, $v = 0.6$ and $e = 3.33$ per cent on cars. The formula assumes perfect substitutability between imports and domestic products, all goods are traded at fixed world prices and no changes in the input–output coefficients.

44. Batchelor *et al.*, op. cit., p. 25.
45. P.A. Yotopoulos and J.B. Nugent, *Economics of Development: Empirical Investigations*, New York: Harper & Row (1976), pp. 328–40. The survey by L. Stein, 'Export instability and development: a review of some recent findings', *Banca Nazionale Del Lavoro Quarterly Review*, **30** (1977), pp. 277–90, concludes that the relationship between export instability and growth could be in either direction, depending on particular national circumstances, although the relationship is a weak one in either case.
46. Batchelor *et al.*, op. cit., p. 222.
47. Little *et al.*, op. cit.
48. ibid., pp. 102–3.
49. I. Kravis, 'Trade as a handmaiden of growth: similarities between the nineteenth and twentieth centuries', *Economic Journal*, **80** (1970), pp. 850–72.
50. A.O. Krueger, *The Benefits and Costs of Import Substitution in India: A Microeconomic Study*, Minneapolis: University of Minnesota Press (1975), p. 108.
51. D. MacDougall and R. Hutt, 'Imperial preference: a quantitative analysis', *Economic Journal* (1954), pp. 233–57; 'Commonwealth Preference: tariff duties and preferences on United Kingdom exports', *Board of Trade Journal*, 11 June (1965); 'Commonwealth Preferences: United Kingdom customs duties', *Board of Trade Journal*, 31 December (1965).
52. J. Roemer, 'The effect of sphere of influence and economic distance on the commodity composition of trade in manufactures', *Review of Economics and Statistics*, **56** (1976), pp. 318–27.
53. E. Kleiman, 'Trade and the decline of colonialism', *Economic Journal*, **86** (1976), pp. 459–80.
54. E. Kleiman, 'Metropolitan exports lost through decolonization', *Bulletin of the Oxford University Institute of Economic and Statistics* (1978), pp. 273–8.
55. I. Livingstone, 'Metropolitan exports lost through decolonization – a Comment', *Bulletin of the Oxford University Institute of Economics and Statistics* (1978), pp. 279–80.
56. Batchelor *et al.*, op. cit.
57. Kleiman (1976), loc. cit.
58. J. Spraos, 'The statistical debate on the net barter terms of trade between primary commodities and manufactures', *Economic Journal*, **90** (1980), pp. 107–28.
59. A. Cairncross, 'The world commodity boom and its implications', *London and Cambridge Economic Bulletin, Times*, 8 July (1974).
60. Holzman, op. cit.
61. J. Vanous and M. Marrese, 'Soviet subsidies to eastern economies', *Wall Street Journal*, 15 January (1982), excerpt from forthcoming

book to be published by University of California Press, Berkeley.

62. R.L. Smith, 'Australian immigration 1945–1975', in P.J. Brain, R.L. Smith and G.P. Schuyers, *Population, Immigration and the Australian Economy*, London: Croom Helm (1979).

63. A Scott, 'Translantic and North American International Migration', in C.P. Kindleberger and A. Shonfield, *North American and Western European Economic Policies*, London: Macmillan (1971).

64. M. Piore, *Birds of Passage*, Cambridge: Cambridge University Press (1979).

65. United Nations, *The World Population Situation in 1970–75*, New York (1974).

66. S. Paine, *Exporting Workers: the Turkish Case*, Cambridge: Cambridge University Press (1974), p. 1.

67. H. Rieben, 'Intra-European migration of labour and the migration of high level manpower from Europe to North America', in Kindleberger and Shonfield, op. cit.

68. K. Jones and A.D. Smith, *The Economic Impact of Commonwealth Immigration*, Cambridge: Cambridge University Press (1970), pp. 159–61.

70. R.L. Smith, loc. cit.

71. If the economy was perfectly competitive and had constant returns to scale, then the share of wages in national product would measure the elasticity of output to the labour input. This type of measurement was popularised by E.F. Denison, *The Sources of Economic Growth in the United States and the Alternatives Before US*, New York: Committee for Economic Development (1962).

72. Scott, loc. cit.

73. J. Bhagwati (ed.), *The Brain Drain and Taxation*, Amsterdam: North Holland (1976), pp. 6–7.

74. Piore, op. cit., p. 165.

75. Paine, op. cit., ch. 3.

76. One of the most published exponents of this view was E.J. Mishan, see his *The Economic Growth Debate: An Assessment*, London: Allen & Unwin (1977).

77. M.A. King, 'Economic growth and social development: a statistical investigation', *Review of Income and Wealth*, **20** (1974), pp. 251–72.

78. T. Scitovsky, *The Joyless Economy*, London: Oxford University Press (1976).

79. Batchelor *et al.*, op. cit., pp. 202–4.

80. United Nations, op. cit., p. 35.

# 11 The Bretton Woods System and its Transformation

Twinned with the new liberal trading order was a fixed exchange rate international monetary regime. The regime formally differed from the earlier gold exchange standard mainly by allowing the possibility of changing exchange parities. Actual international monetary practice, even when the IMF began operating as intended from the mid-1950s, deviated substantially from the rules of the system. And the fixed exchange rates among the major trading powers lasted a remarkably short time by historical standards. Yet the distinctive characteristic of the system – consultation between the largest economies that recognised their interdependence – allowed change and flexibility in response to the crisis of the 1970s, preventing a repetition of the 1931 international collapse. This co-operation continued throughout the period despite the changing relative strengths of the nations involved, which nevertheless influenced the outcome of negotiations.

During the 1950s and 1960s the greatest efforts in international economic relations were directed to enhancing world liquidity. This chapter therefore first explains the pressures to raise international reserves and liquidity, the necessity for these increases and the means by which the increases were implemented. While the 'adjustable peg' exchange rate system lasted, greater liquidity was not intended to remove the necessity for nations eventually to adjust their economies to balance of payments disequilibria. The pattern of such adjustment under the Bretton Woods system is discussed next. The end of the Bretton Woods exchange rate system came in the early 1970s but the transition to floating rates described in the next section was soon overshadowed by the disruptions of the oil price increases of 1973/4. The recession that began that year was the severest the international economy had experienced since 1929. A comparison between the two slumps, attempted next, illuminates why, nevertheless, the later recession was not as deep as the earlier. The increasing unification of world capital markets contributed to the environment in which the old monetary system was no longer viable. Hence the new institutions and forms of short- and long-term private investment, and their consequences, are considered next. Private capital flows to the less developed countries were substantially supplemented by official flows, raising different questions, discussed in the following section. Finally, the problems created by the accumulation of foreign debt are described and analysed.

## The growth of international reserves and liquidity

As a creditor nation with a balance of payments surplus and with little dependence on foreign trade, the United States at Bretton Woods had been little concerned with international reserves, instead focusing on the necessity to ensure the rapid adjustment of deficit nations to keep them within their incomes. Keynes, representing the British as a deficit nation, had argued strongly in favour of a more liberal reserves and adjustment policy, but had been overridden. As described in Chapter 9, the American position was soon modified in the face of the state of Europe and the Cold War. With the change in the US balance of payments, the American view on international reserves began to move round to the British position during the 1960s, so that reserve and credit facilities were enlarged and a new form of international reserves, Special Drawing Rights, was eventually created.

At the end of 1958 Western European currencies became fully convertible into dollars on current account as required by the IMF. The willingness of the rest of the world to hold US dollars as a reserve currency, as an international store of value and medium of exchange, meant that the balance of payments deficit was not then a problem for the United States. In any case US total dollar liquid liabilities in 1958 were only 80 per cent of US gold reserves.[1] From the viewpoint of the rest of the world there was however a *potential* problem – the shortage of reserves and credits. Sudden calls on the IMF in the wake of the Suez crisis towards the end of the 1956 caused the fund's holdings of the US dollars to fall by nearly a third.[2] An emergency solution had to be found by selling IMF gold to the US Treasury. The fear was not that a lack of liquidity would oblige the Fund to suspend operations, but that a general economic recession might ensue without a continuous injection of dollars. The problem was to decide what determined the size of the injection of dollar reserves that was needed to avoid a slump, or, what determined the demand for reserves.

## *The demand for international reserves*

The demand by governments for reserves must be distinguished from the need or desire of governments for reserves. The availability of reserves affected governments' policies by changing the perceived relative costs of different means of responding to balance of payments disturbances, primarily financing, as against adjustment of balance of payments disequilibrium.[3] If the objective was to avoid unemployment, as it was in the 1950s and 1960s, an increase in the growth of liquidity was required so that financing was preferred to deflating demand to reduce imports. If the objective was to restrain demand and inflation, as it was from the mid-1970s, a contraction of the rate of the growth of liquidity was called for, but the result of this contraction could have been instead increased resort to devaluations or import restrictions.

The demand for reserves was necessarily more unstable than a national demand for money because there were only 133 members of the IMF by 1978, and the two largest reserve holders alone accounted for about 25 per cent of world reserves. Consequently there was substantial variability in the relationship between payment imbalances and the level of world trade. Nevertheless, a reasonably stable demand relationship for gross reserves (unadjusted for foreign liabilities) did seem to exist both for the fixed exchange rate years and the floating exchange rate period from 1973, in which demand depended on the average propensity of an economy to import, the size of the country's imports and the variability of imports.[4] The more open the economy, the greater the demand for reserves because the more susceptible was the country to foreign disturbances. But if the average propensity to import was highly correlated with the marginal propensity to import, the opposite relationship with reserves would have obtained. The higher the marginal propensity to import, the smaller would have been the fall in income necessary to bring about a given fall in imports to eliminate a balance of payments deficit, and therefore the lower would have been the real cost of adjustment. The costs of holding reserves generally did not seem to have a statistically significant effect on the demand. Higher imports were associated with a higher demand for reserves. Greater variability in the balance of payments created greater uncertainty and increased the demand for reserves. With precise measurements of the influence of these variables it was possible to say what demand would be for different variable values.

## *Shifts in the composition of reserves*

The composition of reserves changed with the differing elasticities of supply of reserves as the demand expanded. Table 11.1 clearly

**Table 11.1**  *Percentage composition of international reserves, 1956–73*

| Year | Gold | Foreign exchange | Reserves in IMF | Special drawing rights |
|------|------|------------------|-----------------|------------------------|
| 1956 | 64.2 | 31.7 | 4.1 | — |
| 1965 | 59.3 | 33.0 | 6.7 | — |
| 1970 | 40.2 | 48.2 | 8.3 | 3.3 |
| 1973 | 23.7 | 66.4 | 4.1 | 5.8 |

*Source*: IMF, *International Financial Statistics.*

shows that the American insistence on maintaining a fixed dollar price of gold throughout the 1950s and 1960s reduced the role of gold in international monetary relations. The artificially low price reduced production and stimulated commercial use, while the United States' currency became the international medium of exchange. Had the price of gold been determined in the free markets, or had the IMF provided a suitable substitute reserve asset in the appropriate volume, the dollar would not have been the dominant reserve currency for so long. However, the United States obtained substantial benefits from the reserve currency role of the dollar and therefore resisted any change that might supersede it. Nevertheless, like sterling in the years before 1914, the reserve currency role of the dollar contained the seeds of its own destruction in the declining foreign confidence in the exchange value of the currency.[5] The confidence problem stemmed from the large and persistent US balance of payments deficit, which raised the ratio of US dollar liabilities to gold reserves as other countries held more dollar reserves. An attempt by foreigners to convert all their dollars into gold by 1967 when external US liabilities were three times gold reserves, and official US liabilities were $1\frac{1}{2}$ times gold reserves, would have required a devaluation of the dollar against gold. A more suitable reserve asset in which there was more international confidence may have allowed the Bretton Woods system to survive longer. As it was, the value of American gold reserves were held down by the fixed gold price, while dollar liabilities rose.

Holding a fixed gold price proved increasingly difficult. Between 1954 and 1960 the gold price in the London market kept within the limits prescribed by the Fund, the dollar price fixed in 1934. Upward pressure on the price of gold was countered in 1961 by the formation of the London Gold Pool. Britain, the Common Market and

Switzerland agreed to provide half the gold necessary to maintain a market price of $35 per ounce, and the United States agreed to provide the other half.[6] This arrangement was ended in 1968 after the long awaited devaluation of sterling shifted speculative pressure to the dollar as the next most likely currency to change its exchange rate. Speculation took the form of selling dollars for gold and driving the gold price of dollars upwards. The London gold market was forced to close temporarily in March 1968 to stop the drain on official monetary reserves.[7] Unable to maintain the Gold Pool, the central banks instead established a two tier price system with gold exchanging between themselves at $35 per ounce, but trading elsewhere at the free market rate. Henceforth, speculation could only be against the exchange rate of the dollar with other currencies, and foreign central banks could be expected to bear the cost of countering such speculation.

There were savings to the world as a whole from the increasing use of a fiat money, such as the dollar, which cost little to produce rather than a commodity money, such as gold, which cost a lot. The resource cost of a gold standard has been estimated at $2–5 billion for the 1960s.[8] The seignorage benefits to the United States arising from other nations' willingness to hold dollars solely because of their usefulness as international media of exchange have been calculated at $420 million in 1963, and $1.8 billion in 1961 by different authors and methods. The reserve currency use of sterling in the 1960s may have earned the United Kingdom £100–165 million, but whereas the international use of the dollar rarely constrained American economic policy, British policy was severely restricted by sterling balances (non-British holdings of sterling), and by speculation about the sterling exchange rate caused by these balances.

Although there were real resource savings from fiat reserve currency, they accrued to the reserve currency countries as seignorage. By contrast a revaluation of gold would have conferred benefits on the gold producers, of which the largest were South Africa and USSR, and on gold hoarders, especially France, which was determined to reduce the international role of the dollar. In 1967 General de Gaulle converted all the French dollar reserves into gold with severe repercussions on the world gold market. An additional benefit to the United States but not to the rest of the world from the reserve currency role of the dollar was that the United States need not bother about its own balance of payments. Instead America could require the rest of the world to adjust their balance of payments.[9] From the mid-1960s until the end of the fixed rate system in the early 1970s, this enabled America to pursue expansionary economic policies, and thereby to export inflation to some countries through higher import and export prices and low interest rates.

*Measures to increase international reserves*

During the earlier period of the Bretton Woods system it was probable that the American deficit was mainly demand determined; the rest of the world's demand for a larger supply of reserves required them to hold dollars in view of the lack of a suitable alternative. Although the IMF quotas were increased in 1959, this enhancement of international liquidity quickly proved inadequate for an adjustable peg regime in a world of increasing capital mobility. This regime provided those who had to make large and frequent international payments, or who merely had a desire to make or avoid losing money from foreign exchange transactions, with a one-way bet. Either a government would fulfill its obligation to maintain its exchange rate, or it would be unable to resist pressures for a change, which in any period would always be in one direction.[10] The Basle Agreement, the General Arrangements to Borrow, and the introduction of Special Drawing Rights were all ways of trying to provide suitable supplementary reserves to dollars in order to resist speculative pressures to change exchange rates.

In the late 1950s and early 1960s it was obvious that the growing relative strength of the German economy was increasing the probability of a revaluation of the mark. Speculators therefore bought marks knowing they could not lose and might well gain, and thereby created more pressure for a revaluation. The revaluation of the mark in March 1961 shifted speculative pressure to sterling. At Basle in 1961 the central banks of the richest industrial countries had agreed to provide automatic short-term support for any currency whose exchange rate was threatened by foreign exchange market pressures.[11] They would do this either by accumulating sterling (if that was the threatened currency) and holding it for at least three months, or they would recycle the hot money inflows by depositing in the central bank of the country of origin an equivalent sum in the refugee currency. Under this agreement $900 million was supplied to Britain between March and July, but Britain still had to draw $1500 million from the IMF in August. This drawing practically exhausted the Fund's resources and obliged the IMF to sell $500 million of its gold holdings.

The Group of Ten industrial nations (independently of the IMF) in December 1961 made public their agreement, the General

Arrangements to Borrow, to create a fund of $6 billion for members of the Group from October 1961.[12] The General Arrangements to Borrow, first used in 1964 by Britain, was thought inadequate to the growing demands for liquidity, at least by the United States, and this led to the creation of Special Drawing Rights, a new reserve asset. In 1969 a $3.5 billion issue was agreed for the first year and $3 billion for each of two subsequent years.[13] The IMF had concluded that reserve needs were $4–5 billion on the basis of reserves/imports and reserves/imbalance ratios, and that other reserve growth would amount to $1.5 billion.

In contrast to a reserve currency, the SDR seignorage accrued to the SDR participants not the issuer of the reserve currency. Interest initially at $1\frac{1}{2}$ per cent was paid by holders of SDRs. When a participant decided to use SDRs to finance a balance of payments deficit, the IMF then had to designate another participant who would accept these SDRs and provide foreign exchange in return. A participant who had used some of its SDR allocation continued to pay charges at $1\frac{1}{2}$ per cent on its original allocation, but received interest on its depleted holdings. Conversely, the SDR recipient received interest on its now larger holdings of SDRs and paid charges only on its original allocation. The acquisition of SDRs had no initial impact on the money supply, appearing as a balance sheet adjustment of the national monetary authorities, though SDRs may have allowed the creation of domestic money.

In the event of crises in the gold and foreign exchange markets national governments and central banks reactedly promptly, whereas when faced with the need to adapt international institutions, such as the introduction of the SDR, change was much slower.[14] The creation of SDRs took place only because of the policy reversal of the United States resulting from her changed balance of payments position, and because of the persistence of negotiating officials who thought that, in ways not then clear, SDRs would alleviate the frequent monetary crises. The slow pace of reform was also attributable to the changing political and economic environment of the period of negotiations and the technicalities involved.

As it turned out, by the time the SDR reforms were implemented they were unnecessary, for balance of payments disequilibria were endogenously generating increases in reserves; in particular, expansionary American monetary policy in the late 1960s and early 1970s, by worsening the US balance of payments, increased world reserves by more than was desirable. Apart from the special position of the United States, the growth of international capital markets allowed other countries to increase reserves also. A price increase for an

**Table 11.2** *Growth in world reserves and world trade, 1950–76[a] (% pa)*

|        | Reserves   | Exports |
|--------|------------|---------|
| 1950–4 | 3.1        | 6.2     |
| 1955–9 | 1.6        | 6.1     |
| 1960–4 | 3.7        | 8.6     |
| 1965–9 | 2.5        | 9.8     |
| 1970–3[b] | 29.7    | 16.5    |
| 1973–6[c] | 9.7(3.6[d]) | 23.7 |

*Source*: D. Crockett, 'Control over international reserves', *IMF Staff Papers*, **25** (1978) pp. 1–24.
[a] In SDRs
[b] Through the first quarter of 1973.
[c] Beginning with the second quarter of 1973.
[d] World reserves less those of OPEC.

important traded commodity, altering current account flows, may have led the surplus country to place newly-acquired reserves as short-term deposits in a Eurobank (that accepted deposits denominated in foreign currencies), rather than change the exchange rate. These deposits counted as an increase in reserves. If the deficit country did not wish to see a decline in its reserves it could borrow the funds deposited by the surplus countries. These borrowings were not counted as offsets to reserves. Gold and SDRs could not be increased however, but national currencies were substitutes for them. Hence the IMF could not control the supply of international liquidity, as shown by the erratic relationship between reserves and export growth, especially the explosion of reserve growth in the primary commodity boom period of 1970–3 (Table 11.2).

## Balance of payments adjustment under Bretton Woods

Under the fixed exchange rate Bretton Woods system countries inevitably had to adjust to balance of payments disequilibria eventually whatever the availability of reserves. Imbalances occurred because of differing income elasticities of demand for imports and export growth, especially the explosion of reserve growth in slow growing markets, because of shifts in the term of trade or recessions, or because of monetary expansion different from that of the rest of the world, unwarranted by differential productivity growth. The cost and availability of reserves and the cost of adjusting determined the optimum pace of adjustment back to a balance of payments equilibrium. Either output had to be increased or domestic expenditure had to be reduced so that more goods were made available to foreigners. Expenditure-reducing policies consisted primarily of monetary and fiscal policy. Expenditure-switching policies, designed to switch foreign expenditure to domestic goods and domestic expenditure from foreign goods by altering the price of domestic to foreign output, by devaluation or tariff imposition or multiple exchange rates, might have been adequate where there were unemployed resources, but not in conditions of full employment.

The monetary approach saw the adjustments as coming about through an elimination of the excess supply of money. A contraction of the supply of money (which includes foreign exchange reserves), or an increase in the demand for money, was required to eliminate a balance of payments deficit. A devaluation raised domestic prices, increased the demand for money, and thereby improved the balance of payments.[15] A study of eighteen independent devaluations by less developed countries, small open economies unable to influence world prices, between 1959 and 1970 showed that devaluations were quite successful in improving their payments position, although the effects were reduced by the usually simultaneous trade liberalisation.[16] A moderate decline in the rate of growth of credit was sufficient to ensure the success of the devaluations.

Until the mid-1960s, Bernstein, a former Research Director of the IMF, thought that the adjustment process had been working well. When an effort had been made to restore the balance of payments either through a change in parity or through domestic policies, it had been successful.[17] France in 1958–9, Italy in 1963–4 and Germany in 1965–6 had all achieved a prompt turnabout from payments deficit to a surplus. The United States had a remarkable increase in its trade balance between 1960 and 1964, although this was offset by the enormous rise in US foreign investment. The failure of the adjustment process was a development of the later 1960s, seen in the large and persistent deficits of the United States, in the payments difficulties of France, in the enormous surplus of Germany and Japan on goods and services account, and in the recurrent exchange crises. This was also the period when the dollar began to dominate international reserves, these reserves began to grow rapidly, and international inflation started to rise.

The 1967 devaluation of sterling was one of the most important balance of payments adjustments under the Bretton Woods system, and the way the process worked is vital to an assessment of the fixed rate regime. In the year following the devaluation, British import prices in sterling increased almost proportionately to the change in the exchange rate, by 14.3 per cent against the dollar.[18] The case for a devaluation rests to a large extent on the hypothesis that hourly labour earnings in money terms will be adjusted significantly less than by the full amount of the change in the exchange rate. This will improve the international competitiveness of domestic firms. In the British case the rise in hourly labour earnings caused by the devaluation was slow to appear and was significantly smaller than the increase in the price of foreign exchange. Primarily this was because food, rent and public service components of the cost of living index were not sharply increased by the devaluation. The incomes policy introduced in March 1968 also delayed the adjustment of labour earnings to the cost of living.

The increases in hourly earnings in manufacturing, adjusted for overtime, were abnormally low in 1968/9 considering the rise in retail prices and the level of employment. In 1970, real earnings more than caught up with the rate of increase in output per man hour, when the period of wage restraint ended and the devaluation effect took place. Feedbacks of the 1967 devaluation on export prices of British manufactures were large. By 1971 they accounted for an increase in export prices of British semi-finished and finished manufactures of 6.5 and 9 per cent, respectively. Prices of British finished manufactures competing with imports rose by only about 1 per cent because of devaluation, and by 5.9 per cent because of higher labour earnings by 1971.

High price elasticities of demand make it more likely that a devaluation will succeed because the large initial switch in demand away from foreign traded goods and services and away from traded goods and services will start the adjustment process on the right path. For finished manufactures the British long-run import price elasticity was $-1$ and for semi-finished manufactures, $-3.4$ according to Artus. Even for food and beverages, the Cambridge Growth Project found an elasticity of $-0.3$. For British exports of semi-finished and finished manufactures respectively, Artus found long-run price demand elasticities of $-2.5$ and $-1.4$. Previous work that had found trade flows unresponsive to relative price changes had been marred by biases in aggregating different commodities with different price changes and elasticities. The impact of the devaluation on the current balance of payments is shown in Table 11.3.

The improvement in the full employment current balance by 1971 was almost £1300 million. Such calculations assume that a sufficient

**Table 11.3**  *The effect of the 1967 devaluation on the British balance of payments (£m)*

|  | 1968 | | 1969 | | 1970 | 1971 | Final effect at the scale of flows in 1971 |
|---|---|---|---|---|---|---|---|
|  | I | II | I | II |  |  |  |
| Trade balance | − 134 | 140 | 354 | 533 | 726 | 940 | 709 |
| Current balance (includes services plus other variables) | | 77 | 360 | 592 | 795 | 1036 | 1271 | 996 |

*Source*: J. Artus, 'The 1967 devaluation of the pound sterling', *IMF Staff Papers* **22** (1975).

resource transfer into the balance of payments can take place without additional inflation because real domestic absorption is cut by the improvement in the current balance plus the terms of trade effects; about 3 per cent of GNP in 1971.

Just before devaluation the government had expanded rather than contracted demand. When added to the 'J curve effect' (the initial tendency of the balance to deteriorate because of the immediate impact of higher import prices and the delayed impact of lower export prices), the trade balance worsened so much that there was another speculative attack on sterling. Thereafter domestic demand was reduced nearly to a standstill until mid-1971 when an actual surplus on current balance of £1093 million was obtained, compared with a deficit of £316 million in 1967.

Successful adjustment then required only the pursuit of appropriate domestic policies which raised unemployment. As it happened, much of this adjustment was vitiated by the international monetary changes of 1971, when the pound was repegged at a higher parity with the dollar. In June the next year sterling was forced to float.[19]

## The IMF and national adjustment policies

IMF surveillance policies were usually responsible for seeing that appropriate domestic policies were pursued, that credit growth was restrained, that trade was liberalised, and often that devaluation took place. The Fund took over many of the functions of the nineteenth-century gold standard in ensuring international monetary discipline and incurred much opprobrium thereby in countries where social cohesion was weak. Some accused the IMF of deliberately frustrating the very type of financial discipline and production adjustments that were most badly needed in less developed countries, by maintaining these countries' openness to international money. The Brazilian slide from democracy to military dictatorship in the early 1960s, for instance, has been quoted as an instance of the insidious influence of the Fund.[20]

In 1958 a $300 million loan from the United States to Brazil was made contingent on an agreement with the IMF on stabilisation measures. The President of the Bank of Brazil refused to acquiesce in a credit squeeze that threatened to depress the private sector. Coffee growers protested when the coffee purchase programme was cut back, and radical nationlists accused the Brazilian President, Kubitschek of selling the country to the United States and the IMF. Negotiations were broken off and finance was instead obtained from high cost private foreign sources, the repayment problem being left to the next Brazilian President, Quadros. Quadros immediately came to terms with the IMF, reformed the exchange system, abolishing exchange auctions and substituting instead a dual exchange rate which effectively devalued the currency by 50 per cent for the rate at which 'necessaries' were imported. The other exchange rate was handled on the free market. Credits were obtained, but inflation continued and Quadros resigned after only eight months. Under his more left-wing successor, Goulart, economic growth levelled off in 1962. The last serious attempt at stabilisation under the democratic system was made in 1963, designed with the hope of securing IMF approval, so that the foreign debt burden would not take 45 per cent of Brazil's export earnings as it threatened to do. An agreement for $398.5 million was signed with the United States conditional upon Brazil pursuing an agreed stabilisation programme. The contemplation of a 70 per cent pay rise for civilian and military government employees signalled the departure from this programme and aid was suspended. Inflation reached 100 per cent and the laws about the remittance of profits by multinationals were made more restrictive.

In early 1964 negotiations with the IMF and European creditors were again begun, but Goulart also announced that in response to peasant agitation large tracts of private land would be expropriated and redistributed, and that all private oil refineries would be nationalised. The military deposed Goulart and formed their own government which quickly obtained new IMF credits, the rescheduling of foreign debts and large sums of American aid – $1.6 billion between 1964 and 1968. In return the military abolished import subsidies on wheat and petrol. Industrial production fell by 7 per cent in 1965 and living costs increased by 45–60 per cent. The right to strike was virtually abolished, trade union leaders were imprisoned and the income distribution became more unequal. Nevertheless, even if Brazil had been a closed economy quite independent of the IMF or the United States, the same political pressures and their manifestation in the form of high rates of inflation would almost certainly still have been present. International institutions and foreign powers merely provided a convenient scapegoat for domestic difficulties.

Not only less developed countries objected to IMF loan conditions. France's drawings of 1958 were conditional, whereas Britain's in 1957 and 1958 were not, encouraging beliefs that the Fund was run primarily for the benefit of Britain and America.[21] Latin American countries typically were subject to a much more detailed list of conditions. In ensuring these conditions were met the Fund was increasingly concerned from 1959 not to give overt offence to debtor governments, while keeping its power as a creditor. The use of objective performance criteria, such as domestic credit expansion by members with standby arrangements, were one means of achieving this end. These standbys provided the right to draw on the Fund for an agreed amount over an agreed period, subject to the pursuit of agreed policies. The conciliatory stance of the IMF in the 1960s made it easier for Britain among others to seek such conditional assistance. The Chancellor of the Exchequer wrote Letters of Intent specifying the policies he intended to pursue in 1964 and 1965, when Britain drew $1 billion and $1.4 billion.

*Biases in Adjustment*

In addition to IMF surveillance and the constraint imposed upon national economic policies, the Bretton Woods system was criticised for forcing deflation and devaluation on to reserve-losing countries without providing a corresponding incentive to revalue and reflate for reserve-gaining countries. A delay in devaluing leads to a rapid loss of competitive strength, but a postponement of revaluation benefits export industries which often have the ear of governments, so it was argued.[22]

Most parity changes by Fund members were by LDCs which resisted the decision to devalue because of the political impact of higher import prices, instead opting for overvalued exchange rates and exchange controls. Hence a devaluation bias can best be sought among industrial countries. Between 1960 and mid-1971 there were among the industrial countries four decisions to devalue (Canada in 1962, Britain and Denmark in 1967, and France in 1969) and five to revalue (Germany and the Netherlands in 1961, Germany in 1969, and Austria and Switzerland in 1971). In addition the Canadian authorities in 1970 and the German and Dutch governments in May 1971 allowed their currencies to float upwards. The devaluations ranged between 8 and 14 per cent and the revaluations between 5 and 9 per cent.

This experience can be summarised by weighting the parity change by the share of exports of the industrial countries supplied by the country whose parity was altered. Largely because of the heavy weight given to the two German revaluations by this method, there was a near balance between devaluations: the net weighted change to mid-1971, excluding the floats from 1970, was − 0.65 per cent.[23] This negative sum was reduced by the inclusion of the post-1970 floats and increased by the inclusion of the French devaluations of 1957–8.

The near balance in exchange rate decisions between devaluation and appreciation contradicts the devaluation bias hypothesis. An explanation may be found in the increased access to official credits available to deficit countries during the 1960s. The continuing use of such finance nevertheless proved a costly strategy by which government policies were tightly constained as a condition of access to funds. The British decision to devalue in 1967 after borrowing for three years to resist the change in part was taken for fear of the conditions that might be attached to further loans.

The Fund could exercise much less influence over surplus countries. Revaluation undoubtedly reflected a desire to avoid imported inflation, especially by Germany which twice already in the twentieth century had had its currency destroyed by inflation. Japan reacted differently, however, being more concerned with export competitiveness.

For much of the Bretton Woods period, from 1950 to 1962, and again from 1970, Canada was distinguished from other developed countries by operating a floating instead of a fixed exchange rate regime and thereby being spared some of the adjustment problems of other countries. Canada needed such a regime, the government stated, because of her close connections with the massive American economy and the necessity to maintain some independence of economic policy. Later Trudeau, the Canadian Prime Minister, compared Canada's problem to sharing a bed with an elephant; however good relations were, even a slight movement of the partner could cause a disaster.[24] Canada could adopt floating rates and yet remain a member of the IMF because of her special political relation with the United States.[25] The regime was very successful. When subjected to temporary disturbances, short-term private capital flows played a role analogous to changes in foreign exchange reserves, but the Canadian government did not have to hold these funds or make judgements about the equilibrium exchange rate.[26] The floating rate in fact operated much like a fixed rate, with a depreciation of the exchange rate causing a net capital inflow, thereby tending to stimulate an offsetting movement of the rate.

### The end of the fixed exchange rate regime

Despite, or perhaps because of, the variety of measures undertaken to enhance international liquidity, the international monetary system partly broke down in 1971. The proportion of reserves held as foreign exchange and the level of these reserves both increased greatly from the mid-1960s as the United States balance of payments deficits showed the signs of the financing of the Vietnam War and the Great Society social programmes substantially by monetary growth. The second half of the 1960s was also the period when the balance of payments adjustment process ceased to work well, and inflation began to rise, suggesting perhaps that the supply of reserves was excessive, although only Germany at the time adopted this position. The creation of SDRs probably was in a form calculated to raise inflation rather than to enhance liquidity, because the interest rate payable on SDR holdings was less than on dollars, offering an incentive to sell these reserves rather than to hold them.[27] Johnson asserts that the low interest rates on SDRs were fixed specifically to prevent these assets becoming a substitute for dollars and thereby reducing American seignorage. The IMF view was that the SDRs were unlikely to increase significantly the imbalances of countries in deficit and that stabilisation measures in these countries might otherwise be frustrated by the defensive measures of other countries if no SDRs were created.[28]

The failure of the United States to take measures to adjust to her deficit in the Spring of 1971 caused a flow of dollars to Germany and the Germans allowed the mark to float upwards.[29] The Japanese however resisted the speculative pressure to appreciate the yen against the dollar to avoid reducing the competitiveness of Japanese exports. In a bid to force the rest of the world to revalue, and thereby reduce the American deficit, President Nixon announced in August the closing of the official gold window and the levying of a 10 per cent import surcharge, producing an atmosphere of crisis in monetary relations. The problem was ultimately that the United States was going· to have to adjust to her deficit and, as an indication of a willingness to do this, Nixon also imposed price and wage controls.

The Smithsonian Agreement of December 1971 settled new exchange rates and a 10 per cent devaluation of the gold price of the dollar, an official gold price of $38 per ounce. These changes did not solve the basic problems of the fixed rate regime, partly because the basic US deficit remained. US policy-making was little concerned with international monetary relations, as shown by the following Presidential response to the currency disorders of 1972:

*Haldeman* (*H*): Did you get the report that the British floated the pound?
  *President* (*P*): No, I don't think so.
    *H*: They did.
    *P*: That's devaluation?
    *H*: Yeah, Flanigan's got a report on it here.
    *P*: I don't care about it. Nothing we can do about it.
    *H*: You want a run-down?
    *P*: No, I don't.
    *H*: He argues it shows the wisdom of our refusal to consider convertibility until we get a new monetary system.
    *P*: Good, I think he's right. It's too complicated for me to get into. [unintelligible] I understand.
    *H*: Burns expects a 5-day per cent [sic] devaluation against the dollar.
    *P*: Yeah. Okay. Fine.
    *H*: Burns is concerned about speculation about the lira.
    *P*: Well, I don't give a [expletive deleted] about the lira.[30]

Early in 1973 higher US inflation with the removal of the price and wage controls caused a new run on the dollar and then a 10 per cent devaluation against gold.[31] The three major currencies that were already floating, the pound sterling, the Canadian dollar and the Swiss franc, continued to do so and were joined by the yen and the lira.

From 2–19 March the major European central banks and the Bank of Japan closed their official foreign exchange markets in the face of the dollar glut. The EEC decided to float jointly against the dollar, limiting the fluctuations between their currencies to 2.25 per cent. Currencies in the European narrow margins arrangement, or closely associated with those currencies, appreciated against the US dollar by 9–18 per cent from early May to mid-July 1973.[32]

The December oil price rises led to a rapid appreciation of the dollar under the influence of expectations that most of the surplus oil money would be invested in the United States. The removal of capital controls and re-evaluation of the oil funds position pulled down the dollar between January and May of 1974. The effective exchange rate for the dollar in June 1974 was about the same as in April 1973 before the oil shock. Effective rates for sterling, the franc, the lire and the yen showed depreciation, and for the mark, appreciation.

Large countries whose economies were more diverse and whose dependence on foreign trade was less were most inclined to floating. Conversely, smaller countries usually opted to peg their currencies. Eleven currencies, accounting for 46.6 per cent of the trade of fund members in 1975, were floating independently out of 122.[33] Seven currencies, the European groups, accounting for 23.2 per cent of trade, floated jointly. All floating currencies were subject to some official intervention between 1973 and 1975, and for this reason among others the IMF guidelines on floating of 1974 were necessary to define and avoid competitive exchange alteration. The legal problem was that under the Bretton Woods Agreement countries were obliged to maintain par exchange rates. The 1976 Jamaica Agreement, by removing this obligation, acknowledged officially the demise of the adjustable peg system.

Exchange rates were very volatile from 1973 because of the new uncertainties of the economic environment. In June and July 1973 some European currencies appreciated against the US dollar by 4 per cent a day, and by 10 per cent in little more than a week. Changes in the current balance were normally small in relation to potential changes in capital flows, which consequently exercised the most influence on exchange rate movements in the short run. Because of delays in the adjustment of trade flows changes in the current balance did not provide much resistance to exchange rate changes resulting from capital movements. The relative yields on assets held in different countries, and expectations about future exchange rate movements, were the main influence on capital flows.

Movements in the effective rates of the US dollar and the mark were generally in the same direction as movements in their market rates against each other, but the amplitude of their swings was only about half as great.[34] This reflected each country trading substantially with other countries whose currencies were linked to their own or that followed an independent course. A greater stability of effective than market rates was also characteristic of other currencies, whose market rates generally changed less than the dollar–mark rate.

The most important systematic factor in the longer-run trends in

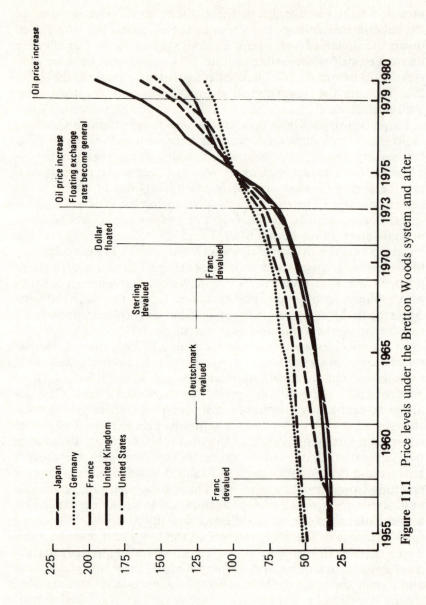

**Figure 11.1**  Price levels under the Bretton Woods system and after

exchange rates was the rate of price inflation in different economies. Between 1973 and 1975, Italy, the UK and Japan experienced price increases faster than the average for industrial countries. Germany had a markedly lower rate, and the United States, France and Canada were clustered more closely about the average (see Figure 11.1). These differential price movements were associated with changes in exchange rates. The two countries with the fastest inflation, Japan and Italy, experienced a substantial depreciation of their exchange rates which seemed more than sufficient to compensate for price trends.

Despite their earlier opposition to floating rates, the IMF concluded optimistically from the 1973–5 experience that exchange rate flexibility appeared to have enabled the world economy to surmount a succession of disturbing events and to accommodate divergent trends in national costs and prices with less disruption of trade and payments than a system of par values would have been able to do. On the other hand, rate fluctuations had been in some cases much greater than could be justified on the basis of changes in underlying economic conditions. For example the Swiss–United States exchange rate between 1973 and 1979 overshot the longer-term equilibrium rate in response to a monetary change by a factor of about two, taking two to three years to settle at the purchasing power parity rate.[35]

Developing countries experienced new problems arising from pegging to one currency, but these uncertainties were probably no greater than those that would have been involved under a par value system. Traders between developed countries at least could protect themselves against the exchange risk of any particular transaction by using the forward exchange markets. But forward rates were subject to much the same volatility as spot rates, and therefore such use did not reduce the variability of a firm's receipts. Hence there must have been some discouragement of trade. However, since uncertainty was part of the economic environment, fixed rates arguably would have led to more international trade than ideal. There is no reason why foreign trade should have been subsidised by the governments' bearing the costs of holding exchange reserves when domestic trade was not similarly subsidised.

## The Crash of 1974

The great adjustment that economies had to make to the depression of 1974–5 and the preceding commodity price rises was eased by floating exchange rates. The only other time in the post-war period when both Western Europe and the United States were simultaneously depressed was in 1958 and for much of Western Europe this recession meant a decline in growth rates rather than a fall in their real national incomes. Fixed exchange rates – hedged with controls – were therefore not much of a handicap then. In explaining this pattern of fluctuations it is difficult to distinguish the role of general economic conditions from the effects of Keynesian demand managment policies before 1974. However, the higher instability of the United States in the 1950s is suggestive; military expenditures especially were responsible for cyclical reversals.[36] By contrast, in other countries, especially Britain, Japan, the Netherlands, Denmark and Italy, policy changes can to a large extent be explained by balance of payments problems. In the UK where restrictive actions were mainly directed at government expenditure, fixed investment and durable good purchases, this policy may have restrained supply growth, as well as demand growth. Denmark experienced problems similar to Britain's until 1957, but thereafter with a rapid rise of industrial exports, Denmark's economic performance improved. Similarly, the better performance of the Dutch economy, compared with the British economy, may be attributable to the rapidly and continuously expanding Dutch exports. In France, persistent foreign exchange problems were up to 1958 not dealt with by restricting domestic demand as in Britain, Denmark and the Netherlands, but by import restrictions and devaluations, and so did not constrain demand and supply in the same way as those in Britain.

The balance of payments difficulties themselves should not be regarded as exogenous influences on policy, but rather a consequence of the pursuit of policies which generated an inflation that was only kept in check because of the need periodically to balance foreign payments. When floating exchange rates removed these constraints, inflation could and did accelerate initially. Thereafter the depression of 1974–5 owed much to the simultaneous and severe contractionary policies pursued by the governments of the industrial world to bring inflation down again. Even more was this true of the depression following the 1979 oil price-rise.

Although the depression of 1974 was the worst since the one that began in 1929, it did not have anything like the same duration or severity. A major difference between the two depressions in the key country, the United States, was the course of prices which rose between 1973 and 1975 but fell between 1929 and 1931 (see Table 11.4). The real money stock declined in the later depression, but rose in the earlier one. Stock prices fell greatly in both

**Table 11.4**  *Percentage changes for the United States' economy in some macroeconomic variables, 1929–31 and 1973–5*

|  | 1929–30 | 1930–1 | 1973–4 | 1974–5 |
|---|---|---|---|---|
| GNP deflator | − 3 | − 9 | + 10 | + 9 |
| Real M1 | − 1 | + 3 | − 4 | − 4 |
| Real M2 | + 1 | + 3 | − 1 | − 1 |
| Real stock prices | − 16 | − 26 | − 36 | − 7 |
| Real residential construction, 1958 prices | − 39 | − 19 | − 27 | − 22 |
| Real consumption expenditures, 1958 prices | − 7 | − 4 | − 2 | + 1 |
| Real GNP, 1958 prices | − 10 | − 8 | − 2 | − 3 |

*Source*: P. Temin, 'Lessons for the present from the Great Depression', *American Economic Review, Papers and Proceedings*, **66** (1976), pp. 40–5.

depressions as did residential construction.[37] The instability of foreign exchange markets, the difficulties associated with large capital movements, and the problems of countries experiencing sharp changes in the terms of trade, were all important in the 1930s and present in the 1970s. But the floating exchange rate regime seemed less vulnerable than the fixed rate gold exchange standard and the strength of autonomous consumers' expenditure steadied the economy in the 1970s so that GNP then fell by much less than in the 1930s. Temin suggests the collapse of consumer expenditure in the first period may have been attributable to the stock market crash which reduced household wealth and raised the ratio of their debts to their assets. In 1974 debt had not accumulated to the same extent and inflation reduced the real value of debt. The bank failures of the 1930s were not repeated because a lesson of the 1930s had been learned. The Federal Deposit Insurance Corporation was able to contain the failures of the United States National Bank of San Diego in 1973 and the Franklin National Bank of New York in 1974.

Balance of payments adjustment to the oil price increases, to the economic recession and to the partial recovery, worked rather slowly because of the enormous volume of financing available through the private markets. From 1974 to 1976 foreign borrowing undertaken by OECD deficit countries and non-oil developing countries amounted to over $175 billion.[38] Private banks recycled almost $100 billion of this sum to deficit countries. In any case the OECD area's oil import bill rose in 1974 by $65–70 billion, but the deterioration in the current balance was little more than half this amount because of increased OPEC imports and the widening deficit of the non-oil rest of the world. The recession of 1975 reduced OECD imports and combined with big increases in exports to OPEC, the deficit nearly disappeared, only to reappear again with the beginning of recovery in 1976.

The most advanced industrial countries had little to fear from the balance of payments effects of the oil price increases because their highly developed financial institutions ensured that they would receive most of the unspent oil money back in the form of savings. Of the 1974 OPEC financial surplus, 20 per cent was invested directly in the United States, another 13 per cent in the United Kingdom and over 40 per cent in Eurocurrency markets. Direct OPEC investments in the UK exceeded additional oil payments and British foreign exchange reserves rose marginally in 1974.[39] Most major countries borrowed on international capital markets to ease their balance of payments. So also did non-oil LDCs which supplemented these funds with additional aid, commercial credit and some official borrowing. The external debt of these countries rose from 13 per cent of GNP in 1973/4 to 18 per cent in 1977/8. Another boost to foreign indebtedness occurred when the Iranian crisis helped increase oil prices by a further 50 per cent in 1979. Between 1974 and 1978 the OPEC current account surplus fell from $60 billion to about $10 billion as a result of a 20 per cent fall in their terms of trade, the growth of OPEC imports and the decline in oil imports from OPEC by the industrial countries with the development of non-OPEC oil supplies in the North Sea, Mexico and Alaska.

The fall in economic activity was worldwide from 1974. Argy shows that the principle factor in the collapse of economic activity was the sharp decline in the rate of growth of real money balances (monetary growth less the inflation rate). In part this was due to a deliberate anti-inflation policy slowing monetary growth particularly severely in Australia, Japan and Britain. The lagged effect on inflation of earlier monetary growth, together with the oil price rise acting directly on the price level, both reduced the growth of real money balances relative to nominal monetary growth. The oil price increase also directly reduced demand by a significant amount in all countries except Australia and Canada. Total expenditure was switched from home demand to imports to pay for the oil, and there was a less than offsetting increase in the demand for domestic goods for export to OPEC countries. Fiscal policy, unlike monetary policy, contributed little to the downturn, except in Britain. In Australia, Canada, France, Germany and Japan the downturn was accompanied by more expansionary fiscal policies as Keynes might have prescribed.

Because monetary policy did not accommodate the rise in wages to cover the higher prices, unemployment grew as the real value of wages was pushed up faster than productivity. Among the OECD countries only the United States and Sweden were free of this wage–productivity gap in 1975. Although unemployment after 1976 was higher than at any other time in the post-1945 period, fiscal policy was not used to reduce it, and monetary policy was switched towards the announcement of monetary targets which gave little room for any significant reduction in unemployment. The main fear had become inflation.

## International private capital mobility

The international mobility of private capital had proved a two-edged sword for the Bretton Woods system. It had helped destroy the adjustable peg exchange rate regime but had also assisted the adjustment of the modified system to the events of 1973 to 1975. During the 1950s and 1960s banks extended their international operations in parallel with the largest companies of the industrial world. In so doing they contributed to the emergence of the Eurodollar market (a market in dollar deposits held in banks outside the United States) which was among the most efficient vehicles of greater capital mobility. The origins of the market can be traced to the attempt of the British government of 1957 to restrict the use of sterling to finance foreign third party trade. The British banks therefore began to use dollars instead.[40] There were advantages from not repatriating these dollars stemming from an interest rate differential between the United States and Western Europe. Federal Reserve Regulation Q, designed to prevent stock market speculation like that of 1929, limited interest payable on deposits in member banks of the Federal Reserve system below what could usually be earned in Europe.

The Eurocurrency system expanded in response to American capital controls of the early 1960s, especially the Interest Equalisation Tax of 1963 (a tariff on new securities), which in turn were an attempt to stop the United States balance of payments deficit enhancing world liquidity. The rapid growth of this market continued into the 1970s helped by the desire of the Russian and OPEC governments to hold dollars where they would not be confiscated or measured. American and foreign borrowers demanded Eurodollars more as a result of restrictions on transfer of funds by Americans to Euromarkets. In 1968 and 1969, when United States' financial conditions became tight, American banks borrowed heavily from their foreign branches operating in the Eurodollar market, and thereby partly neutralised the contractionary monetary policy.[41]

The capacity of the Eurodollar market for creating liquidity was very limited, unlike a domestic banking system, because the proceeds of loans by Eurobanks were rarely redeposited in another Eurobank.[42] The existence of the Eurodollar market facilitated the financing of deficits and so, effectively, increased the availability of reserves. This probably more than offset the effects on the balance of payments of any increase in capital mobility allowed by the market, but it reduced the effectiveness of monetary policy by limiting control over domestic interest rates as a policy instrument; sterilisation became less feasible.

It was the mobility of long-term American capital that stimulated French concern about the United States balance of payments after 1960, as much as the belief that the burden of adjustment was forced onto the rest of the world. The balance of American private long-term capital was massively negative, a little over $3 billion in 1960, $4.2 billion ten years later, and after the depression of 1974–5, $8.5 billion in 1977.[43] Most of the stock of American foreign direct investment (73.7 per cent in 1976) was in developed countries, and in particular in Europe (40.7 per cent in 1976). The French were worried that American multinationals were coming to dominate all the advanced technology sectors of European industry.[44] Because of their enormous home market these firms had economies of scale, and in addition received the benefit of the large research and development outlays of the United States government on armaments and aerospace. The size of the firm was thought crucial to the ability to innovate and therefore to grow. This was the 'American Challenge'. With the benefit of hindsight, the growth of large firms had no relation to firm size during the 1960s (although the variability of growth did).[45] Hence, on this account, there was no reason to expect American capital to take over Europe, and American multinational investment in Western Europe indeed turned out to have been no greater in the 1960s than European investment in the United States.

For the OECD countries as a whole the capital balance with the rest of the world in 1960 was small ( − $398 million) by contrast with the capital export and import of the OECD countries, consistent with most investment being in developed countries. For small, open developed economies, foreign investment could be of considerable importance. Between 1949 and 1964 the flow of overseas capital to Australia, 90 per cent of which was direct investment, amounted to about 10 per cent of total savings.[46] Foreign owned enterprises in Norway in the 1960s accounted for one-third of all corporations. In Canada, capital imports financed 15 per cent of total imports between 1955 and 1960.

## The political impact

However it was in less developed countries that hosting foreign direct investment was most controversial. As in the nineteenth century, foreign investment combined with a belief by the investing country that important national security issues were at stake could prove a dangerous mixture for host countries. Those who felt foreign direct investment jeopardised national objectives were vindicated by the role of the United Fruit Company in Guatemala in the early 1950s. The United Fruit Company was the largest landowner in the country and objected to President Arbenz's expropriation of the Company's uncultivated land as part of a land reform programme. By playing on fears about Soviet threats to free enterprise in Guatemala, the company persuaded the United States to intervene and overthrow Arbenz in 1954.[47] The 1951 national-isation of BP's oil interests in Iran also ultimately led to a coup assisted by the American Central Intelligence Agency (CIA) in 1953, but the connection here was less direct because BP was a British Company half-owned by British government.[48]

The political activities of ITT in Chile, though apparently less successful than those of United Fruit in influencing the American government, appeared to be equally effective. ITT by the 1960s employed 6000 people in their Chilean telephone company with assets valued (by ITT) at $150 million.[49] In 1970, ITT plotted to stop the election of the Marxist Allende to the Chilean presidency on the grounds that the election would jeopardise the safety of their assets; the company had offered to contribute a dollar sum of up to seven figures to the White House to stop Allende.[50] Allende nevertheless became President in 1970. Thereafter ITT regularly dealt with the CIA to try to create economic chaos in Chile and to encourage a military *coup*. In September 1973 this was achieved, and Allende was killed. No visible evidence connected the *coup* with the CIA or ITT, but the circumstantial evidence was compelling.

Shortly afterwards, bombs exploded in the ITT offices in Zurich, Rome and New York.

## Long term economic effects

In addition to political interference, potential LDC recipients of foreign capital were fearful of some economic effects, the problem of finding sufficient foreign exchange to pay the interest and dividends on the capital, for instance. Foreign investment in exploiting natural resources for export was sometimes thought to be less beneficial than in manufacturing because the resources were not renewable. In other investment projects the foreign entrepreneurial input was greatest during the early stages. Subsequently, the payment of profits abroad tended to rise, while the necessity for foreign entrepreneurial talents diminished. For this reason many LDCs preferred to aim for a minimum foreign equity stake in a project consistent with obtaining the benefits of a multinational's technology.

Donor countries were not very favourably inclined to foreign investment either. After 1960, United States' balance of payments difficulties forced a reappraisal of the former policy of active encouragement of overseas investment. Similarly, the United Kingdom controlled overseas investment for most of the post-war period, although the extent of control varied with the balance of payments position. There was also a longer-term concern that even if the private marginal return on overseas investment was higher than at home, the loss of tax revenues, the possible deterioration in the terms of trade, and the retardation of growth at home because of the diversion of capital overseas, might outweigh the benefits of higher profits.[52] The Reddaway Report of 1967 concluded that, for Britain, there was no evidence of any great resource misallocation from investment overseas, and that the expected gains from extending the international division of labour were therefore being obtained.[53]

The distinctive post-war pattern of foreign direct investment (FDI) provides clues as to the reasons it occurred and therefore also offers suggestions as to the long-term economic impact. Most FDI took place between developed capital-abundant countries and therefore could not be interpreted as a process of equalising factor returns in the same way as labour migration, which flowed to relatively labour-scarce countries. Furthermore, FDI could take place without any international transfer of capital, if the multinational took over an indigenous firm using capital raised in the host country's capital market, or otherwise borrowed in the host country using the subsidiary's assets as collateral. The possibility of nationalisation of the multinational's assets gave an added incentive for firms to hedge in this fashion. If a change of regime brought expropriation, the head office of the company could tell their host country creditors to collect their repayments from their own nationalising government.

In Chapter 10 it was suggested that FDI transferred technology, and the concentration of FDI in manufacturing industry where new technology would be most important confirms this view: in Brazil foreign firms controlled 22 per cent of manufacturing output in 1972, but only 7 per cent of primary output and 2 per cent of the service sector.[54] Even so, the question remains as to why multinational firms did not more often license foreign firms to use their technology for an appropriate payment and avoid the problems of learning to compete in a different economic, legal and cultural environment. One answer is the difficulties of agreeing a price for the technology. If the buyer knows the market value of the technology and therefore knows the fair purchase price, the chances are that he will also know what the technology is, and therefore will not have to buy it. The seller, on the other hand, knows the value of the technology and will be unwilling to lower the sale price to the level acceptable to the (ignorant) buyer. Another answer is that the existence of national boundaries with different tax and tariff regimes confers an advantage on a firm which can straddle the frontiers. Such a company can transfer intermediate goods between subsidiaries at national 'transfer prices' which minimise the firm's tax burden, whereas enterprises exporting to other firms at market prices across the same frontier pay higher taxes or tariffs, and are less competitive therefore than the multinational. These two answers have different implications for the dispensability of FDI. The first suggests FDI was probably the most efficient means of transferring technology, whereas the second implies FDI was primarily a device for tax avoidance.

## International official capital flows

As noted in Chapter 9, the early 1950s effectively saw the rise of a new component of international capital flows, official aid. Though a small proportion of total flows in the ensuing two decades, for the less developed countries, receipts of foreign official development assistance in 1976 amounted to one-third of total net investment receipts. Because these flows were non-commercial, issues arise concerning their causes and consequences, quite different from commercial flows.

An early rationale for aid was that the structure of LDCs made foreign aid particularly valuable in raising their growth rates. The two gap theory attempts to give an account of growth constrained by the availability of foreign capital, and in particular official aid.[55] According to this theory there is a minimum necessary additional amount of imports required to support a given increase in national output. Exports are not related to internal factors, but are determined by external demand which increases at some given rate. For some projected future level of national output, imports may exceed exports, and this gap must be financed by foreign aid if the projected level of output is to be attained. At that level of output, the amount that people would be prepared to save may exceed the amount required to finance the investment needed to sustain the projected rate of growth, after subtracting the contribution of foreign aid to this financing. Hence aid is required, not as a supplement to domestic savings, but as a supplement to foreign exchange earnings. The 'trade gap' (the excess of imports over exports) dominates the savings gap (the excess of savings over investment). Increased savings will not increase investment because they will not raise exports and permit more imports to be bought, a prerequisite of a higher output. A cut in aid, therefore, reduces output by a multiple of its value.

The theory implicitly assumes inflexible domestic policies; that there should or can be no substitution of domestic for imported goods or of exports for domestic supplies to eliminate the current account deficit.[56] It is therefore a rationalisation for, and a support of, the post-war policies pursued by a majority of LDCs which in many cases have had unfortunate consequences. For this reason, and others, some have doubted that aid flows made any positive contribution to LDC development in the 1950s and 1960s. These other reasons include the possibility that aid flows acted merely as a supplement to consumption. Even though often tied to investment projects, foreign aid may have released funds that would otherwise have been allocated to these projects for spending on projects more correctly defined as consumption projects, albeit government consumption. Instances of such consumption were state airlines in some developing countries.

Even if the consumption benefits did filter through to the population, the undesirable consequence can only have been to encourage permanent international dependency. If aid had the desired effect of supplementing investment, the results may still not have been worth while: donors typically required large and visible projects, like the Aswan Dam in Egypt, to minimise the administrative costs and maximise prestige. Such motivation is likely to have reduced the productivity of investment by its emphasis on providing infrastructure. If domestic savings were also reduced, because the savings were now being made by foreigners, then together with reduced productivity of capital, the overall beneficial impact of the aid could have been extremely small.

The effect of foreign capital inflows in less developed countries cannot be settled by *a priori* arguments of this nature. It is possible to identify particular cases where aid probably did reduce domestic savings: in Korea in the mid-1950s, and in India and Pakistan. The supply of United States surplus agricultural stocks probably encouraged the neglect of domestic agriculture.[57] But overall, statistical evidence suggests aid was an important beneficial influence. During the 1950s and 1960s countries with higher investment, private foreign, official aid and domestic savings, had significantly higher growth rates. A 1 per cent higher ratio of aid to national income between countries on average was associated with a 0.39 per cent higher growth rate. There was no evidence of reverse causation, of higher growth rates encouraging donors, in these results. The strongest impact of aid flows was found in the Asian and Mediterranean countries.

## The pattern of official capital flows

The distribution of aid was inequitable, with moderately prosperous developing countries receiving 20–100 times as much aid per head in 1970 as a number of other extremely poor countries. The OECD noted a marked tendency for small countries to receive more aid per head than large ones.[58] Hence the desire to redistribute world income equitably does not apparently explain distribution of aid. One study assumed that donors expected to get something in return, such as political support or markets and sources of supply, which depended in part upon the size of the original flow of foreign aid to the recipient.[59] Auxiliary variables in the model included political ties, defined as former colonial status, exports from donor to recipient, and a bandwagon effect whereby the donor residents evaluated the impact of this aid more highly the greater the aid given by the rest of the world to the recipient in question.

The results suggested that the degree of distortion due to the division of the world's poor into countries of different size population was small (with the exception of French aid). The negative correlations of aid per head with country population was the consequence of the negative correlation between population on the one hand, and exports, aid from the rest of the world and political links, on the other. Political and economic links were very important determinants, but bandwagon effects were less significant.

Inspection of the largest recipients of British aid in 1974 confirms the importance of political and economic links in a more impressionistic fashion (Table 11.5). Ten of the eleven recipients were Commonwealth countries, which as expected from the sphere of influence analysis, had the strongest, non-oil trade and investment links with Britain of all LDCs. The inclusion of Indonesia in the group might be explained as an attempt to secure reliable oil supplies.

Official bilateral development assistance as a proportion of GNP of all industrial countries declined from 0.52 in 1960 to 0.34 in 1970. In an attempt to reverse this trend the Pearson Commission, set up by World Bank President, Robert McNamara, in 1969 called for a commitment to a 0.7 per cent aid/GNP ratio from the developed countries, but to no avail.[60] Similarly, the Brandt Commission (also first proposed by McNamara in 1977) repeated the need to reach this target by 1985 and to reach 1 per cent by the end of the century, but

**Table 11.5**   *The main recipients of British aid, 1974*

| Country | Gross disbursements 1974 (£000) | Population (m) | National income per head (£) | UK exports to aid recipients (£m) |
|---------|--------------------------------|----------------|------------------------------|-----------------------------------|
| Bangladesh | 6 437 | 71.61 | 30 | 11.6 |
| India | 75 445 | 574.22 | 50 | 126.8 |
| Malaysia | 5 452 | 11.28 | 210 | 113.3 |
| Singapore | 4 470 | 2.69 | 690 | 153.5 |
| Indonesia | 8 866 | 124.60 | 40 | 46.8 |
| Nigeria | 5 966 | 59.61 | 70 | 222.2 |
| Botswana | 4 047 | 0.65 | 100 | 1.3 |
| Kenya | 16 435 | 12.48 | 80 | 79.3 |
| Malawi | 8 071 | 4.79 | 50 | 10.5 |
| Zambia | 8 397 | 4.64 | 170 | 63.7 |
| Jamaica | 4 788 | 1.98 | 370 | 50.1 |

*Source*:   *British Aid Statistics 1970–74*, HMSO; OECD, *Development Cooperation 1974 Review and Annual Statement of Overseas Trade of the United Kingdom for the year 1974, vol.* IV.

received an identical reaction. By 1980 the ratio achieved was only 0.38 per cent falling to 0.35 per cent the following year.[61]

Multilateral aid through the World Bank did little to correct the 'distortion' of bilateral official capital flows, and in any event contributed little more than 10 per cent of official flows. None of the top ten recipients of World Bank loans per head of population had a population as large as 5 million.[62] So for whatever reason, the poor of large countries received less of both types of aid than the poor of small countries.

Like foreign private direct investment there could be political consequences from accepting World Bank loans. The Bank's perception of the development process influenced the conditions of its loans and those of the aid consortia organised by the Bank. The Bank managed to persuade the Indian government to change some balance of payments policies and reduce direct economic controls in the mid 1960s in order to get foreign aid.[63] The Bank's recognition of the importance of agriculture, shown by the increase in the proportion of World Bank lending for agriculture from 9 per cent in 1960 to 18 per cent in 1971, also began to act as a partial antidote in some cases to indigenous policies of import-substituting industrialisation.

## International debt

Institutions that had to raise money in commercial markets, the commercial banks and the World Bank, had to monitor closely the ability of their clients to repay. The rising burden of debt caused increasing problems in this respect. Between 1955 and 1962 the external debt of LDCs rose at 15 per cent per annum. In the mid 1950s debt service averaged 6 per cent of export earnings, rising to 12 per cent ten years later. Unable to service the foreign debt Argentina rescheduled four times in eight years, and Indonesia rescheduled three times in three years.

The world recession of 1974–5 markedly increased the foreign borrowing of LDC governments. Less important was the quadrupling of oil prices and the demands of development finance. The private banking system provided the greater part of the debt build-up of the 1970s. As the risk of default increased with debt accumulation in 1975, the banks increased the rates they charged on loans to LDCs.[64]

Three-quarters of the world's deficits between 1974 and 1976 had been financed by the banks.[65] Unlike the IMF, they could not impose conditions on borrowing country governments to ensure they were repaid. These governments' policies and prospects had to be taken as given in assessing the risk of lending in the first place. Country risk assessment was difficult and hence there could be a tendency for the herd instinct to predominate. Once a country had borrowed substantial sums from international banks or institutions, the banks could be forced to lend more in order to avoid a default, a worthy subject for fiction:

'Interest on present loans, my good President, plus the salaries of our civil service, account for a hundred and eleven per cent of the Kush national budget.'
Elloloû's heart sank at the statistic.
But Ezana said, 'Not to worry, These debits are in fact credits for they persuade the capital-holding countries to hold us upright. Meanwhile all capital drifts to the oil-exporting nations. From there however it drifts back to the countries that produce machinery and luxury goods. Praise Allah, we need no longer, in a sense, concern ourselves with money at all, for it exists above us in a fluid aurosphere, that mixes with the atmosphere, the stratosphere and the ionosphere, blanketing us all with its invisible circulations.'[66]

So anxious were banks and officials to avoid a default as the volume of debt accumulated that rescheduling became increasingly common as a means of debt relief (see Map 11.1). Between 1975 and the end of 1980 there were sixteen official debt negotiations for $9 billion, whereas in the previous eighteen years there had been thirty, for debts of $7 billion.[67] The most surprising rescheduling, as well as the largest, was of Poland's $4.9 billion debt in 1981. Western capital, instead of driving a wedge between Poland and her Russian master, pulling Poland towards the market economies, had given the Solidarity Union a taste for freedom that almost brought down the tottering economy, and had joined the interests of Western banks with Poland's martial law administrators.

Nevertheless the performance of the private banks through the market seemed to be consistent with efficient lending behaviour. As the cost of borrowing increased, the amount of lending declined. Brazil, Taiwan, Indonesia and others undertook internal adjustment programmes because they found it increasingly costly and difficult to finance their external deficits.[68] Furthermore, the variety of alternative sources of finance gave countries more freedom of manoeuvre than if they were reliant solely on the IMF.

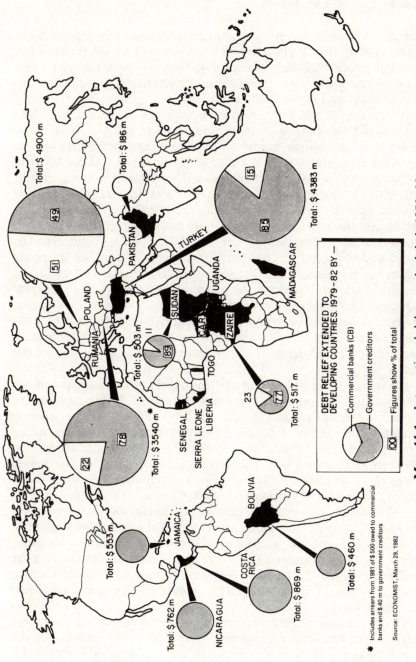

**Map 11.1**   International debts rescheduled, 1979–82

Total: $ 4900 m

Total: $ 186 m

PAKISTAN

TURKEY

POLAND

RUMANIA

SUDAN

UGANDA

MADAGASCAR

CAR

ZAIRE

TOGO

LIBERIA

SIERRA LEONE

SENEGAL

Total: $ 503 m

Total: $ 4383 m

Total: $ 517 m

Total: $ 3540 m

DEBT RELIEF EXTENDED TO
DEVELOPING COUNTRIES, 1979–82 BY –

Commercial banks (CB)

Government creditors

◯◯ — Figures show % of total

JAMAICA

BOLIVIA

COSTA
RICA

NICARAGUA

Total: $ 553 m

Total: $ 762 m

Total: $ 869 m

Total: $ 460 m

✱  Includes arrears from 1981 of $ 500 owed to commercial
   banks and $ 40 m to government creditors

Source: ECONOMIST, March 29, 1982

## Summary and conclusion

The international monetary system after 1945 clearly differed from all preceding systems in the much greater role of governments in forming, modifying and operating it. Together with the overriding goals of the great majority of these governments to minimise unemployment and boost living standards, this greater governmental participation drove up the international price level as well as encouraged economic growth. Analogously to the mainly sterling-based gold exchange standard of the years before 1914, international exchange became based on the dollar, which ceased to be exchangeable for gold at a fixed price from 1968. The fundamental difference between these two systems was that the nineteenth-century liberal doctrines of the balanced budget had been abandoned and therefore the world rapidly came to experience a dollar glut by the late 1960s. Because the rest of the world was concerned to avoid a slump, and the United States did not want to adjust its balance of payments deficit, negotiations to enhance world reserves and international liquidity took place throughout the 1960s, despite rising prices. An increase in the price of gold as a means of increasing reserves (a decrease in the gold price of the dollar) was ruled out by the United States. In part this may be explained by the benefits America obtained from the increasing international role of the dollar.

However as the dollar glut continued, the international trading community lost some of its former confidence in the purchasing power of the dollar, and in the viability of many fixed exchange rates. Speculative crises therefore dominated the last few years of the fixed rate system, which may be said to have ended sometime between 1971 and 1973. The floating rate regime for the major industrial countries that followed it was remarkably successful in dealing with the oil price rise of 1973 and the consequent redistribution of international income and saving because, recognising their interdependence, countries did not attempt to engage in competitive exchange rate depreciation to export their unemployment. The depression of 1973–4 was in any case less severe than the collapse of 1929–32 because despite a stock exchange crash of a similar order of magnitude, the American economy remained relatively buoyant.

Under the fixed rate regime, emerging balance of payments deficits had required adjustments of the economy (except for the United States) to remove them, unless the disequilibria proved temporary and the international reserves were available to finance it.

Inadequate international reserves could lead countries to deflate unnecessarily and to spread the resulting unemployment worldwide through a reduction in their demand for foreign goods. A devaluation of the exchange rate could also have this effect by reducing the demand for imports and increasing the competitiveness of exports, and it was for this reason that IMF surveillance of exchange rate policies was introduced in the Bretton Wood system. As a lender of international reserves, the IMF had considerable power over government policies when a nation was in deficit and needed to borrow, although this was not true of surplus or reserve currency nations. The IMF often incurred opprobrium for the imposition of the restrictive policies, but these policies were effective in correcting deficits at a cost. The relatively low rates of inflation, so long as the fixed exchange rate regime persisted among the industrialised countries, suggests that the discipline so exercised worked. The causal chain could operate in the opposite direction as noted in earlier chapters; the fixed rates may only have worked as long as countries preferred relatively low rates of inflation.

Capital mobility appears to have played an important role in the breakdown of the fixed rate regime. The adjustable peg system of the 1960s was less capable of generating stabilising speculation than the fixed rates of the 1900s once capital controls were removed. Capital mobility also reduced the control that national monetary authorities could exercise over their own economies by influencing interest rates.

The greatest source of capital movements arose from the massive transfer of income from oil consumers to oil producers from 1973. The inability of some of the richest oil producers to spend all their newly-acquired income meant that 'petrodollars' began to flow into the financial centres of the industrial world as short-term investments. The net effect for most of the West was largely to offset the detrimental effects of higher oil prices on the balance of payments, but for poor oil importing countries there was no such compensation and their balance of payments deteriorated under the combined influence of the recession and the cost of oil imports. Their foreign debt increased, an increasing proportion of it held by private banks which did not and could not exercise the same surveillance over these debtors to ensure repayment as the IMF or the World Bank. Rescheduling of debt payments to avoid default therefore increased in the second half of the 1970s.

Longer-term capital movements in many instances were as controversial as they had been in the nineteenth century. Bilateral official aid flows tended to reinforce national spheres of influence.

Multinational investment sometimes had political consequences and, where it did not, its benefits were frequently questioned by both donor and recipient countries. Some statistical analysis does however suggest that both official and private flows benefitted recipient LDC growth rates in the 1950s and 1960s.

The failure of many governments to continue to combine low inflation and low unemployment was the greatest monetary problem from the seventies but this was not a problem of international relations. It had consequence for these relations though. The severity and duration of the world depression after 1974 was largely induced by restrictive policies which placed a greater value on lower inflation than on higher employment.

## Notes

1. V. Argy, *The Postwar International Money Crisis: An Analysis*, London: Allen & Unwin (1981), p. 34.
2. S. Strange, *International Monetary Relations*, vol. 2, *International Economic Relations of the Western World 1959–71*, ed. A. Shonfield, London: Oxford University Press (1976), p. 196.
3. A.D. Crockett, 'Control over international reserves', *International Monetary Fund Staff Papers*, **25** (1978), pp. 1–24.
4. H.R. Heller and M.S. Khan, 'The demand for international reserves under fixed and floating exchange rates', *IMF Staff Papers*, **25** (1978), pp. 1–24. Floating is generally assumed to reduce the demand for reserves although if under fixed exchange rates a peg acts as a focus for stabilising speculation, this will not be true. Currencies pegged to a single floating currency (as many Latin American exchange rates remained fixed to the US dollar) might actually have needed more reserves because of the added variability in payments balances caused by exchange rate movements between third countries and the intervention currency.
5. R. Triffin, *Gold and the Dollar Crisis*, Yale (1960) was the first to draw attention to this problem.
6. J.K. Horsefield (ed.), *The IMF 1945–65: Twenty Years of International Monetary Cooperation*, vol I, (1969), pp. 484–5. Strange, op. cit., ch. 3, pp. 77–9.
7. M.G. de Vries, *The IMF 1966–71: The System Under Stress*, Washington: IMF (1976), pp. 403–4.
8. J. Williamson, 'International liquidity: a survey', *Economic Journal*, **83** (1973) pp. 685–746.
9. Giscard d'Estaing, at the time French Finance Minister and later Prime Minister, compared the United States and Italian deficits of 1963 and 1964. The United States, deficit began earlier, but it was Italy that had to reduce employment, trade and growth to return to

equilibrium, he asserted, in R.A. Mundell and A. Swoboda (ed), *Monetary Problems of the International Economy*, Chicago: Chicago University Press (1969).

10. See J. Williamson, *The Failure of World Monetary Reform*, Sunbury-on-Thames, Middlesex: Nelson (1977), pp. 44–6, on the incompatibility of the discrete changes of the adjustable peg system with any probable process of formation of speculators' expectations, in a world of high capital mobility.

11. Horsefield, op. cit., pp. 483–7. Strange, op. cit., pp. 83–9.

12. Horsefield, op. cit., pp. 511–15.

13. Argy, op. cit., p. 55.

14. de Vries, op. cit., p. 188. Strange, op. cit., p. 255.

15. This was true of most consistent models in the long run. The early monetarist models e.g. in H.G. Johnson and J.A. Frenkel (eds), *The Monetary Approach to the Balance of Payments*, London: Allen & Unwin (1976), were distinguished by their prediction of very rapid adjustment. Later monetarist models postulated only that the balance on capital account depended on the excess demand for money. See the Stockholm Conference papers in *Scandinavian Journal of Economics* (1976).

16. M. Connolly and D. Taylor, 'Testing the monetary approach to devaluation in developing countries', *Journal of Political Economy*, **84** (1976), pp. 849–59.

17. E.M. Bernstein, 'The evolution of the International Monetary Fund', in A.L.K. Acheson, J.F. Chant and M.J.F. Prachowny, *Bretton Woods Revisited*, Toronto: University of Toronto Press (1973).

18. J.R. Artus, 'The 1967 devaluation of the pound sterling', *IMF Staff Papers*, **22** (1975).

19. J.H.B. Tew, 'Policies directed towards the balance of payments', in F.T. Blackaby (ed.), *British Economic Policy 1960–74*, Cambridge: Cambridge University Press (1978), p. 315.

20. C. Payer, *The Debt Trap: the IMF and the Third World*, New York and London: Monthly Review Press (1974), p. 210, ch. 7.

21. Strange, op. cit., p. 54.

22. For example, L.B. Yeager, *International Monetary Relations: Theory, History and Policy*, New York: Harper & Row (1976), p. 104.

23. S.I. Katz, 'Devaluation bias and the Bretton Woods system', *Banca Nazionale Del Lavoro Quarterly Review*, **25** (1972), pp. 178–98.

24. M.J. Drouin and H.B. Malmgren, 'Canada, the United States and the world economy', *Foreign Affairs*, **60** (1981), pp. 393–413.

25. Strange, op. cit., pp. 45–6.

26. J. Helliwell, 'Adjustment under fixed and flexible exchange rates', in P.B. Kenen (ed.), *International Trade and Finance*, Cambridge: Cambridge University Press (1975).

27. H.G. Johnson, 'A General Commentary', in A.L.K. Acheson *et al.*, op. cit.

28. de Vries, op. cit., p. 221.

29. Strange, op. cit., pp. 334–44. de Vries, op. cit., pp. 520, 531–3.
30. Watergate Tapes, 23 June 1972, quoted in J. Williamson, *The Failure of World Monetary Reform* (1977) Sunbury-on-Thames, Middlesex: Nelson, pp. 9, 175, fn. 9.
31. International Monetary Fund, *Annual Report 1973*, Washington, pp. 2–6.
32. International Monetary Fund, *Annual Report 1974*, p. 16.
33. International Monetary Fund, *Annual Report 1975*, p. 23.
34. ibid., pp. 29–30.
35. R.A. Driskill 'Exchange rate dynamics: an empirical investigation', *Journal of Political Economy*, **89** (1981), pp. 357–71.
36. E. Lundberg, *Instability and Economic Growth*, New Haven and London: Yale University Press (1968), pp. 26, 128, 133–6. See also Table 5 in A. Maddison, 'Phases of capitalist development', *Banca Nazionale del Lavoro Quarterly Review*, **39** (1977), pp. 103–38 which shows the remarkable absence of international recessions after 1945 compared with the period from 1870 to that date.
37. P. Temin, 'Lessons for the present from the Great Depression', *American Economic Review, Papers and Proceedings*, **66** (1976), pp. 40–5.
38. OECD, 'The Adjustment process since the oil crisis', *Economic Outlook*, **21** (1977), pp. 86–97.
39. Argy, op. cit., pp. 195–207.
40. G. Bell, *The Eurodollar Market and the International Financial System*, London: Macmillan (1973), pp. 8–12.
41. ibid., p. 54.
42. Argy, op. cit., ch. 7.
43. OECD, *Balance of Payments of OECD Countries 1960–1977*, Paris (1979).
44. Esp. J.J. Servan-Schreiber, *The American Challenge*, New York: Athenaeum (1968).
45. R. Rowthorne, *International Big Business 1957–1967: A Study of Comparative Growth*, Cambridge: Cambridge University Press (1971).
46. J. Dunning, *Studies in International Investment*, London: Allen & Unwin (1970), p. 35.
47. S. Schlesinger and S. Kinzer, *Bitter Fruit*, New York: Doubleday (1982).
48. A. Sampson, *The Seven Sisters: the Great Oil Companies and the World They Made*, New York: Viking Press (1975), ch. 6.
49. A. Sampson, *The Sovereign State of ITT*, New York: Stein & Day (1973).
50. Kissinger, then Secretary of State, reports that he politely declined ITT's offer because he considered that sort of activity inappropriate for private enterprise. H. Kissinger, *Years of Upheaval*, Boston: Little, Brown (1982), p. 389.
51. Dunning, op. cit., p. 44.

52. M. Casson, *Alternatives to the Multinational Enterprise*, New York: Holmes & Meier (1979).
53. W.B. Reddaway, S.J. Potter and C.T. Taylor, *Effects of UK Direct Investment Overseas*, Cambridge: Cambridge University Press (1967 and 1968).
54. Casson, op. cit., pp. 9–11.
55. H.B. Chenery and A.M. Strout, 'Foreign assistance and economic development', *American Economic Review*, **56** (1966). This model exercised a great influence over US aid policies in the 1960s.
56. K. Griffin, 'Foreign capital, domestic savings and economic development', *Bulletin of the Oxford University Institute of Economics and Statistics*, **32** (1970), pp. 99–112. P. Bauer, *Dissent on Development*, London: Weidenfeld & Nicolson (1971), offers a number of other more wide-ranging criticisms of aid.
57. G. Papanek, 'Aid, foreign private investment, savings and growth in less developed countries', *Journal of Political Economy*, **81** (1973), pp. 120–30.
58. OECD, *Development Assistance: 1969 Review*, Paris (1969).
59. L. Dudley and C. Montmarquette, 'A model of the supply of bilateral foreign aid', *American Economic Review*, **66** (1976), pp. 132–42.
60. C. Prout, 'Finance for developing countries: an essay', vol. 2, A. Shonfield (ed.), *International Economic Relations of the Western World 1959–71*, London: Oxford University Press (1976).
61. Report of the Independent Commission on International Development Issue, *North–South: A Programme for Survival*, London: Pan Books (1980).
62. E.S. Mason and R.E. Asher, *The World Bank Since Bretton Woods*, Washington DC: Brookings Institution (1973), p. 198.
63. C.P. Bhambi, *The World Bank and India*, New Delhi: Vikas Publishing House (1980).
64. W.H.B. Brittain, 'Developing countries' external debt and the private banks', *Banca Nazionale del Lavoro Quarterly Review*, **30** (1977), pp. 365–80.
65. A. Sampson, *The Money Lenders: Bankers and a World in Turmoil*, New York: Viking Press (1982), p. 299.
66. J. Updike, *The Coup*, New York: Alfred Knopf (1978), pp. 87–8.
67. 'Survey of international banking', *The Economist*, 20 March (1982).
68. R.D. Erb, 'International resource transfers: the international financial system and foreign aid', in R.C. Amacher, G. Haberler and T.D. Willett, *Challenges to a Liberal International Economic Order*, Washington DC: American Enterprise Institute (1979), p. 393.

# 12 The International Economic Order of the 1970s: A Historical Perspective and Prospect

The assertion of economic power by non-industrial states, and the onset of an era of high energy prices in 1974, seemed to mark the end of the old order. Despite the necessity for most of the non-oil, less developed countries to pay massively higher import bills as a result of OPEC's actions, the notion of shared historical injustices and the belief that they now had the power to remedy these wrongs at first maintained the solidarity of LDCs in demanding a new international economic order.

This concluding chapter has two objectives: to consider what light this study of the world economy from 1850 sheds on LDCs' claims, and to draw some inferences about the future shape of international economic relations. First the basis and nature of the demands for the new order are outlined, and the extent to which these demands were met in the 1970s is described. Consideration is then given to the justice of the claims and accusations about the international economy, before some speculations about the future end the book.

## The new order

At the end of 1974, the General Assembly of the United Nations approved a Charter of Economic Rights and Duties of States, consisting of the main proposals for a New International Economic Order (NIEC). Together with the resolution on 'Development and International Economic Cooperation' of 1975, these proposals, and two others of the previous year, were intended to alter both the rules of operation of the economic system, and the pattern that resulted

370

from its working.[1] In the words of the Brandt Commission which aimed at similar objectives in 1980:

Most people know that the existing system of international institutions was established at the end of the Second World War, and that the South [the less developed countries] – mostly as latecomers on the international scene – faces numerous disadvantages which need fundamental correction. Hence the demand for a new international economic order.[2]

Lewis maintains that there are four major elements of the relationship between developing and developed countries that the developed countries wanted to correct;[3] (i) the division of the world into exporters of primary products and exporters of manufactures; (ii) the adverse factoral terms of trade for the products of the developing countries; (iii) the dependence of the developing countries on the developed ones for finance; and (iv) the dependence of the developing countries on the developed for their engine of growth. The proposals of the UN Charter intended to achieve this alteration included:

(1) An international primary commodity policy, asserting the 'right' of primary product producers to associate in producer's cartels, and other countries' 'duty' to refrain from efforts to break these cartels, the adoption of an 'integrated' approach to price supports for an entire group of commodity exports of less developed countries, the indexation of LDC export prices to tie them to the rising prices of developed countries' manufactured exports, and the development of an international food programme.
(2) An international industrial policy affirming each state's 'fully permanent sovereignty' over its natural resources and economic activities, specifically intended to include the right to nationalise foreign property without regard to existing international laws, the negotiated 'redeployment' of the industries of some developed countries to LDC's, the establishment of mechanisms for the transfer of technology to LDCs separate from direct capital investment, and the preferential lowering of tariffs on exports of manufactures from LDCs.
(3) Increased resource transfer to LDCs, including the boosting of official development assistance to reach the target of 0.7 per cent of GNP of developed countries, and the linkage of development aid with the creation of Special Drawing Rights (SDRs) by the International Monetary Fund.

(4) A fairer international monetary system, by altering the rules o.
the IMF and the World Bank to favour less developed countries.

*Changes in the international economic order during the 1970s.*

The 1970s did see some developments along these lines. In primary
commodities, the STABEX mechanisms of the 1975 Lomé
Convention between the European Community and the forty-six
associated states in Africa, the Caribbean and the Pacific was the
most striking institutional innovation.[4] The mechanism was intended to stabilise the product earnings of twelve major exports of
the associated states by providing interest-free loans.

No group of primary product producers could completely
emulate OPEC as proponents of the new order hoped, but the
International Bauxite Association came close to it.[5] Jamaica began
the bauxite offensive in March 1974, successfully tying its income to
the prices of aluminium ingots, and raising its tax revenues from $25
million to $170 million. Over the following months, all four other
Caribbean producers and Gúinea instituted similar taxation methods. Of the main bauxite producers only Australia failed to follow
suit.

LDCs gained concessions in the reform of the International
Monetary Fund. Although the LDC share of world trade had fallen
during the 1970s, their share in IMF quotas was raised. Under the
original Bretton Woods formula, LDCs would have had a 17.6 per
cent share, whereas they achieved roughly half as much again.[6] In
addition the so-called Wittveen facilities of 1977 mainly benefitted
the LDCs.[7] This facility was created because IMF resources were
considered inadequate to cope with the very large imbalances
associated with the oil crisis and the depression. A number of
governments therefore agreed to establish a special $10 billion
supplementary financing facility.

On other, perhaps more important fronts there was little progress,
even regression. Particularly this was true of the liberalisation of
industrialised country trade. The Multi-Fibre Agreement (MFA),
for example, which began in 1977 and expired in January 1982,
promised a 6 per cent annual growth rate in the textile trade.[8] Hong
Kong, South Korea, Taiwan and India all had their exports slowed
over this period by unilateral cuts under the MFA's 'market
disruption' clause. If imports caused or threatened serious economic
disruption, the importing country could take temporary action that
did not discriminate against imports by country of origin. What in

fact happened was that some exporters were bullied into cutting back because they were more vulnerable to economic retaliation, while others were allowed to maintain their sales. The market disruption clause was invoked almost 800 times during the life of this agreement, usually with little or none of the prior consultation required by the MFA.

Not only LDCs were affected by creeping protectionism. In 1980 and 1981, domestic political pressure from American car manufacturers and workers in the face of Japanese imports resulted in the negotiation of the 'voluntary limitation' of these car exports to the United States. More Japanese car imports meant less consumption spending allocated to domestically-produced goods, and in particular to buying American cars. Fewer American car sales meant fewer jobs and lower profits. However, a study by Chase Econometrics indicated Japan's voluntary limits on car exports to the US would push car prices up, and improve Detroit's cash flow, but would not do much for sales or employment. Because of the projected changes in US prices US car manufacturers were likely to recoup only 45 000 of the 300 000 sales lost by the Japanese in the first year the restriction took effect. Hence there would be a negligible effect on US car employment. Even so it was primarily the fear of job losses that explained the lack of progress when the Geneva GATT talks ended in 1982.

In other areas, especially industrial policy, new technologies and expanding economic activity created new problems about which there was little international agreement. In the nineteenth century the expansion of economic activity into new geographical areas lacking an appropriate administrative and legal framework was met by European colonisation, which implanted these facilities in the successor states. Where undersea mining outside territorial waters in the 1970s was concerned, such unilateral solutions were no longer acceptable.

The problem originated only in the 1960s, when technology advanced sufficiently to make economically viable the mining of minerals, in a form known as nodules, lying on the ocean floors.[9] At the consumption levels of the end of the 1970s, there may have been enough economically accessible nickel to supply total world demand for 2000 years, enough copper for 140 years, manganese for 1600 years and cobalt for 500 years. Since most nodules lie in the deep ocean outside the limits of national jurisdiction, the 'freedom of the high seas' principle embodied in international law gave ownership to whoever could gather the nodules. However mining required very

substantial technical knowledge and capital. Those currently producing minerals found in nodules could expect to become worse off
as the new sources of supply depressed prices. Typically, LDCs,
therefore, would be made worse off. In 1967 the UN set up an *ad hoc*
Sea Bed Committee to investigate the issues, and in 1970 the UN
General Assembly unanimously adopted the 'common heritage
principle' for these minerals. But there was no agreement on the
appropriate regime for exploiting the resources. Industrial countries
could expect to gain from lower metal prices, and world income
would be redistributed towards them and away from LDCs. None of
the law of the sea regimes proposed during the 1970s satisfied the
common heritage principle; those that entailed a fairer distribution
also entailed a reduction in size of total net benefits.

The atmosphere of confrontation in international discussions was
not conducive to reaching a satisfactory agreement on the law of the
sea, or on most of the other issues raised by demands for a NIEO,
and by the end of the decade few of the proposals had been
implemented. In any case, according to Lewis's analysis, based upon
historical experience (Chapter 4), many of the proposals were
largely irrelevant or harmful to the LDC's development objectives.
The economic advancement of poorer countries did not depend
upon a transfer of wealth from richer to poorer nations, but upon a
technological revolution in the production of tropical food that
would raise the productivity of the LDC's large agricultural sectors
to the level of agricultural sectors in the rich countries.[10] As long as
half the labour force of LDCs was employed in low productivity
food production, the domestic market for manufactures and
services was limited, the propensity to import was kept too high,
taxable capacity and savings were held down, and goods and
services were exported on unfavourable terms. International trade
had been beneficial but was no substitute for technical change of the
appropriate type. Judging by Western European experience, that
depended upon the right sort of institutional conditions.[11]

## Justice and the international economic order

Having outlined the main demands for a new international economic order and the extent to which these demands were met, it now
remains to consider the justification for these demands, for which we
need a theory of justice. In Rawls' theory of justice he imagines
rational, mutually disinterested individuals meeting under a veil of
ignorance as to their place in society and their natural abilities to
decide the principles of justice.[12] He asserts they would choose two

principles, the first requiring equality in the assignment of basic rights and duties, the second asserting that inequalities of wealth and authority are just only if they result in compensating benefits for everyone and, in particular, for the least advantaged members of society. This second is the 'difference principle' which requires that participants under the veil of ignorance be averse to risk: Rawls believes contractees would not gamble with such fundamental matters, even though they might gamble for small stakes.[13]

Natural talents and abilities, according to Rawls, should be treated as collective assets, because the distribution of these abilities is arbitrary from a moral point of view; there is no moral reason why they should be that way. In short, Rawls argues for a particular 'end-state' theory of justice, which he thinks would arise from the need to distribute the fruits of social co-operation. End-state theories of justice are based not on the rules by which a distribution is generated, but on the structural characteristics of the distribution. Rawls' notion of co-operative venture for mutual advantage must encompass relations between the inhabitants of different states engaged in commercial relations. The original position then has to be extended. The contractees would agree to apply the difference principle as if the world comprised a single society, or to apply something like it, such as the treatment of natural resources as natural talents.[14] They would agree to permit inequalities only when necessary to maximise the expectations of those worst off in the entire world. This principle does not specify what a just distribution looks like, but it does allow an affluent state that is just internally still to be unjust relative to other nations. Justice then may require a substantial international redistribution of wealth. This conclusion does not depend upon any assumptions about how existing inequalities have arisen historically and how they are sustained. To demonstrate that redistribution is required under the difference principle, one only need show that it would improve the long-term expectations of the poor.

Rawls also discusses how to deal with injustice. His hypothetical contractees would agree to establish a 'natural duty of justice' which demands that every person support just institutions where they exist and work to establish them where they do not exist, at least wherever he can do so without great cost to himself. If the existing international order fails to satisfy the principles of justice then the inhabitants of the poor countries are justified in working to effect an international redistribution, preferably, but not necessarily, non-violently. Analogously, the rich have a duty to create a more egalitarian international order.

Transfers between nations cannot be justified on these Rawlsian grounds unless there is strong evidence that the resources involved in fact will serve the purposes of supporting the basic needs of life and self-improvement. A country that invokes the principle of total non-interference in their national affairs (see item 2 of the NIEO demands above) even while it is calling for international resource transfers to it, tends to rule out this verification.

The central question to be asked of an international economic order on Rawlsian principles then is 'Are the existing inequalities between nations necessary to make the worse-off nations as well off as possible?' Here historical experience is essential to deal with the implied counterfactual about how things might be otherwise. In what ways have the rich countries made the poor countries better (or worse) off, and are additional transfers of wealth from rich to poor likely to reduce that ability? When the industrialised countries grew fastest, after 1945, so did the less developed countries. Between 1950 and 1972 the growth rates of product per head of less developed countries as a whole grew at 2.6 per cent annum.[15] When the industrial world fell into depression in the 1930s and pursued autarkic policies, the LDCs stagnated. During the nineteenth century, LDC trade grew rapidy, though most rapidly when the most open economies, especially Britain, were growing fastest. The depression of the industrial world in the 1970s hit LDCs especially hard.

More transfers almost certainly mean more taxes which possibly will generate more social conflict in most DCs and less growth for both developed and less developed countries. So, for example, in the late 1960s, taxes in Britain (in this instance to finance domestic social programmes) bit into the average wage sufficiently to prevent any rise in take-home pay, despite rising productivity.[16] By the end of the decade the result was increasing industrial conflict, rising prices and a stagnating economy.

The belief in the efficacy of massive international transfers of wealth to make the recipients permanently better off is sometimes based on a misreading of the impact of Marshall Aid (see Chapter 9). The analogy of such transfer with Marshall Aid confuses recovery of developed economies from war damage with the institutional change and accumulation of human capital needed by poor countries. As argued in preceding chapters, only for small countries has the international flow of goods and capital played a major part in economic development. The affluence that comes from self-sustaining growth stems primarily not from international wealth transfers but from indigenous efforts at economic transformation, and a willingness to learn from other countries. On Rawlsian grounds, of course, it does not matter whether transfers make the recipients permanently better off as long as they do not reduce the capacity of the donor countries to make the poor countries better off. So much the worse for the international application of Rawls' difference principle, it might be said.

If the difference principle is judged unsatisfactory, Rawls can still offer his treatment of natural talents, as collective assets, transmuted at the international level to natural resources as a principle of justice. The treatment of natural resources as the common heritage of mankind is not open to the same objections as is Rawls' treatment of personal talents. Talents are a part of a person, and Rawls' formulation leads to regarding people as means to others' welfare, rather then as ends in themselves, which seems unsatisfactory. The geological contingencies that deposit oil, gold, coal or uranium in some parts of the world and not in others are not intrinsic parts of nation states. Furthermore, the transfer between governments of unearned rents on natural resources would have a minimal effect on an economy compared with the taxation of individual economic agents for purposes of an international transfer. However it is unlikely that nations would agree to this principle, except where deep ocean mining is concerned, and international fisheries perhaps, judging by the way, for example, the North Sea oil and gas rights were carved up between nations with coastlines on the North Sea.

If the difference principle and moral arbitrariness are not regarded as suitable principles for judging the justice of an international economic order, there is one further element of Rawls' theory that may be relevant. Rawls asserts the 'natural duty of mutual aid' which requires us to 'help another when he is in jeopardy, provided that one can do so without excessive risk or loss to oneself.' An international application of this principle would require substantial assistance from rich countries to poor in cases of drought, famine or other natural and man-made disasters. Though here again, judging by Sen's recent analysis of famines, the principle may require interference with national sovereignty, contrary to the demands of LDCs, because famines often take place when there is moderate to good food availability without any significant decline of food supply per head.[17] What matters is people's ability to command food though the legal means available in the society, such as production possibilities, trade opportunities and state entitlements. International food aid therefore needs to be properly directed if famine is to be relieved.

## Entitlement theories of justice

Although Rawls' theory of justice provides a conceptual framework for evaluating international economic orders with which many would agree, many would not. Nozick contrasts theories of justice based on end-states such as Rawls' with those based on entitlements.[18] Entitlement theories are historical in the sense that whether a given distribution of relevant things (or set of holdings, as Nozick prefers) is just, depends upon whether as a matter of historical fact just principles first for the acquisition of those holdings, and secondly for the transfer of these holdings, have been followed. The third and final principle of entitlement theories is the necessity for restitution for injustice as defined by the first two principles. Thus the legitimacy of the rules of the international economic system and the adherence to these rules guarantees that international income difference are just.

Like a constitution in the political sphere, an international economic order protects member states from the abuses of unrestrained Darwinism. Unlike a constitution, the coalescence of the monetary order into the late nineteenth-century gold standard was never codified in international law (and in being codified, by implication was agreed as just). The Genoa Conference of 1922 where countries agreed to use each others' currencies as reserves, thus ratifying the existing gold exchange standard, was the closest approach to an agreement about the order before 1944. The Bretton Woods monetary order was therefore unique in being based upon formal international agreement and, Mundell maintains, in not having been established, to serve the interests of an empire.[19] Although it did serve America's interests, the intention was to serve the interests of all other countries as well, but this was not the only reason why international agreement proved possible. As the passage of the 1974 UN Charter indicates, the formal constitutions of the international organisations have to be taken into account, and the United States was powerful enough to determine the Bretton Woods 'constitution' in 1944. In the United Nations each nation had one vote, regardless of population size, national income or importance in international trade. The Economic Charter was passed over the vigorous opposition of the major western trading nations by a vote of 86 to 10.[20] In the International Monetary Fund a weighted voting system, based on economic variables, was used, leaving the less developed countries as a whole in the minority, the obverse of the UN case. Consequently LDCs had less success in influencing IMF decisions. The other side of the coin is that the developed countries largely ignored UN economic resolutions like the Charter, but did generally accept the IMF rules – which during the 1970s were increasingly bent to favour LDCs.

Nevertheless, for the Brandt Commission and many LDCs the small participation of LDCs in formulating the rules of the system meant the system and its outcome must necessarily be inequitable. This does not follow. As argued in Chapter 10 the national economic sovereignty of many LDCs in the post-war era allowed them to pursue policies less advantageous to themselves than those in many instances formerly pursued on their behalf by the imperial powers. The central-planning policies adopted on independence were based in large part upon a misreading of Russian economic history between the world wars in which rapid industrialisation was equated with growth in welfare, and immunity from the depression that engulfed the United States in the 1930s distracted from the persistent lag of centrally-planned behind market economies in all but a few sectors after 1945.

In Chapter 1 some principles were laid down to judge the fairness of the operation of the international economy, regardless of who formulated them; that the exchanges had to be voluntary and that there had to be a number of alternative, independent, non-collusive sources of supply and demand. These conditions correspond to what nineteenth-century liberals like J.S. Mill required for a just economic order. If trade was voluntary, both parties must have gained from it or they would not otherwise have participated. Of course, one party may have gained more than the other because of the absence of alternative sources of supply, or because of the differential strengths of the demands of the two parties for each others' products. A form of exploitation (neo-classical) may be said to occur if the price paid in a transaction diverges from what it would have been had there been many buyers and many sellers. Historical experience suggests that the persistence for many years of such exploitation on a large scale was rare. More akin to the Marxian notion is the doctrine of Chapter 1 that exploitation occurs if some of the claims over traded goods and services have been obtained by theft; that is, the rules for just acquisition have been broken.

If the rules of past international economic systems have been unjust or have not been adhered to, then entitlement theories of justice prescribe restitution. Even given a workable definition of exploitation such as this, there remain awkward questions as to how far back in history to go in assessing the need for rectification, and for distant past wrongs, questions of who should make the payments, and who is entitled to receive them. The West African slave trade may give rise to claims for rectification by American blacks on contemporary West African countries, where the descendants of those powerful tribal chieftains who enslaved others, and received payment for them, still reside. Or perhaps to claims on the descendants of the consumers of cotton textiles in Western Europe, North America and India who paid lower prices than they would otherwise as a consequence of the enslavements.[21]

## Restitution and natural resource depletion

In assessing such claims the analyst is inevitably faced with the counterfactual 'What would things have been like if the wrong had not been done?', an extremely difficult question to answer even when agreement can be reached on what things were wrong. A simple, but incorrect, answer is to assume international economic life is a zero-sum game, so that what one party gains the other party necessarily loses (and therefore requires restitution). The belief that there is only a fixed quantity of essential natural resources on the planet and so more consumption now means less in the future, and more consumption by the rich means less by the poor, often underlies this erroneous view of the international economy. In Chapter 2 we noted Jevons' concern about the exhaustion of British coal reserves in the nineteenth century, a fear that proved groundless because of new coal discoveries, new technologies, (especially oil) and, during the 1970s, new oil discoveries that for example made Britain self-sufficient in oil by the end of that decade. The oil and rubber price rises of the 1920s which caused such distrust between the United States and Britain, described in Chapter 7, similarly did not check economic development as had been feared, and soon declined as the new investment stimulated by the high prices came to fruition. Chapter 9 described a similar phenomenon and panic at the time of the Korean War, and the raw materials boom of 1971–3 repeated it. Despite this cyclical pattern to raw material prices, the long-term trend in prices of such commodities as coal, oil and electricity has been downwards relative to wages with the exception of the break of the early 1970s.[22] The reasons were new discoveries, technical progress and the high degree of substitutability between various commodities.

Similarly the production of food has not been, and is not, constrained by the fixed land surface of this planet. The opening up of new areas to food production in the nineteenth century by the railway and the steamship, the use of fertilisers, first organic such as guano, and subsequently inorganic, the spread of the use of the tractor in the interwar years, and the use of high-yield variety grains in less developed countries from the 1960s, have all tended to improve on trend the balance between food and population, despite the growth of population.[23] In the last quarter of the nineteenth century, perhaps 20–5 million died in famines, whereas in the entire twentieth century probably about 12–15 million died from a larger population, and, as Sen has noted, such deaths were not mainly due to serious crop failures.

The world depression of 1974 underlined the nature of the demand of industrialised countries for raw materials. Many Indonesians who took to the streets only eight months earlier to protest about Japanese exploitation of their natural resources, began to complain they were not being exploited enough. The Japanese cut back their timber purchases by 40 per cent because of home recession, and Indonesian lumber prices consequently dropped by three-fifths.[24] Restitution, therefore, seems quite inappropriate solely on the basis of natural resource use.

## Restitution and colonisation

Contrary to the position that the industrialised countries, by consuming the world's natural resources, have made the LDCs poorer, it is quite possible and in many cases quite likely, that close contact with the colonial powers left the former dependencies better off than they would be otherwise have been.[25] The opening of Japan and China to foreign trade in the mid-nineteenth century, the European scramble for Africa in the late nineteenth century, and the imposition of relatively free trade on the colonies by the imperial powers arguably contributed fundamentally to the economic growth those countries experienced subsequently, growth which would not have occurred without the intimidation that then took place. In Japan, China and Africa there was substantial internal dissension, some groups such as the Taipings favouring western-style modernisation – not all groups were averse to their rulers being intimidated. On both counts, the forcible opening of these countries does not necessarily give rise to valid rectification claims.

The existing poverty in Africa, Asia, and Latin America should not obscure the virtually universal poverty in these areas before the European powers established themselves overseas. The introduction of modern legal and commercial systems, of capital, and of modern technology has helped a number of these countries to rise above the grinding poverty of the past. In those instances where living standards seem to have declined, it is usually due to rapid population growth worsening the position of subsistence agriculture by increasing the relative scarcity of land. The population growth in turn was due in part to improved health, sanitation and transport systems, introduced by, or with the help of, the European powers. Reparations could not reasonably be claimed for such actions.

### Restitution and monopoly power

There is little evidence of neo-classical economic exploitation in the form of above-normal profits. The British East India Company had persistent financial difficulties and the Dutch East Indies ceased yielding a financial surplus in 1874. Most imperial powers spent more on their colonies than was justified by taxes or trade (Chapter 4). British colonial investment generally yielded the same as, or even less than, domestic investment in the late nineteenth century. Foreign investment by American firms in Europe during the 1950s and early 1960s showed very high profitability, but subsequently rates declined to those on domestic investment. American investment in developing countries has not recorded high rates of profitability except in petroleum extraction, and this has been a consequence of accounting conventions and tax liabilities. Multinationals showed an overall rate of profit somewhat higher than non-multinationals, but the line of causation is as likely to have run from profits to foreign investment as from foreign investments to profits.

The focusing of attention on the need for additional resource transfers, for whatever reasons, diverts attention from those areas where mutual gain to both developed and developing countries is possibly through international co-operation. A prerequisite is recognising that man is pitted against nature in a positive-sum game, not solely man against man. Changes in western commercial policies, improved western demand management policies, closer co-operation on the management of collective resources, such as the ocean's mineral nodules and the world's fish stocks, and efforts to improve the food–population balance in LDCs – by technology transfer, financial assistance, general health care and family planning information – all offer means for both parties to gain from the international economic order.[26]

### The prospect

Barring a nuclear holocaust, what happens to the world economic order in the future depends in part upon whether such co-operation is forthcoming. Views formed about the history of international economic relations influence the possibility of co-operation as they have influenced so many other key issues in the past discussed in this and earlier chapters. Partly because people insist on learning lessons, albeit often the wrong ones, from history, and partly because some historical conditions necessarily cannot recur, much of the history of international economic relations is unique. The spread of formal colonies as trade grew during the nineteenth century, and the decolonisation movement after the second world war, the political and economic power of Britain in the mid-nineteenth century and of the United States in the mid-twentieth century, all depended on temporary imbalances in economic development between nations, combined with the operation of international economic relations and concern with security. These can form no part of the prospect.

The nineteenth-century pattern of boom and slump, culminating in the World Depression of 1931, promises not to repeat itself since most governments have learnt the importance of preventing the collapse of their financial systems. Only if international financial co-operation breaks down will the debt problems of the 1980s cause a similar crisis. That is not to say there will be no recessions, once expectations of future price and wage inflation, built up during the two decades of rapid expansion before 1973, are eliminated by persistent high unemployment. Investment and price adjustment are unlikely to occur smoothly in the future any more than in the past, although the cycle of economic activity will probably continue to be dominated by government policy, as it has been since 1945. And the recessions should be less traumatic than a hundred or even fifty years ago. The growth rates in the western world will be closer to those of the earlier periods though, so long as the memories of inflation are retained. Among less developed countries the transfer of technology offers the prospect of continuing high growth rates if social and political systems can cope. Oil price instability which so shocked the world economy of the 1970s, is unlikely to disappear entirely during the 1980s, but OPEC at last, after surprising economists by its longevity, looks as if its power is waning.

A return to a fixed, or par value, exchange rate regime is improbable unless there is a radical change in the western international economic order that restricts the movement of capital or co-ordinates economic policies. Otherwise the size of the reserves necessary to defend exchange rates where changes of government, or of policy, can radically affect economic performance, will almost certainly make such a regime too expensive. The difficulties experienced by the European Monetary System, formed in 1979 as a successor to the joint floating arrangement, are proof of this proposition. Though capital may be allowed continued free movement between countries, governments are unlikely to permit a resumption of the great intercontinental migrations of the nine-teenth century. Those migrations were acceptable, even desired, then because of the technological jump that lowered transport costs and improved agricultural methods, and coincided with the rapid growth of industrial European populations that demanded the products of the temperate zone lands recently settled by Europeans. That was a unique historical phase, and future migration is primarily going to involve people transferring human capital and new technologies between economies. Perhaps the major exception to this generalisation may be the EEC, where economic integration encourages migration. The EEC potentially allows the return of Western Europe to its late nineteenth century political and economic eminence before it was eclipsed by war and the empire-states of Russia and the United States.

One lesson of history should always be borne in mind when considering the future, that human being and their societies can innovate, and particular innovations by definition cannot be predicted.

## Summary and conclusion

For less developed countries their dependent position in the international economy over the preceding century or more seemed to be removed by the commodity price boom of the early 1970s culminating in the OPEC price rise and embargo. The confidence engendered by the apparently new vulnerability of the developed countries encouraged LDCs to push for a more just and, to them, a more favourable international economic order. Most of their proposals were antithetical to the principles both of the late ninetenth-century order and of the new liberal order of the post-second world war years. These policies were based upon the belief that the liberal order had not worked for the less developed countries. Neither the beliefs nor the proposals had much substance, and distracted attention from the increasingly protectionist stance adopted by the developed countries, contrary to the interest of the LDCs. Both DC actions and LDC proposals threated to contract the international economy and make it a source of political conflict as it had become in the 1930s, a period when LDCs had been particularly economically depressed. By contrast, the period after 1945 has seen the highest ever sustained growth rates in income per head of LDCs as a whole, when DCs have also been prosperous. Dependence did not mean being sentenced to perpetual poverty.

The justice of LDC demands for a new international economic

order can be assessed using some of the principles of Rawls' theory. The difference principle in this context asserts that inequalities between national incomes per head are justifiable only in so far as they are necessary to make the worst-off nations better off. The practical implications of this principle turn on whether increased resource transfers from rich nations to poor could be extracted from the taxpayers of developed countries without causing them to react in such a way that the DC economy deteriorated and that this deterioration affected LDCs adversely by, for example, reducing the demand for LDC exports. A second modified Rawlsian principle, the treatment of the world's natural resources as a common heritage, is not open to the same objection, but national governments would not concede this point except in special cases. A third Rawlsian principle of relevance to international economic relations is that of emergency aid. International famine relief clearly falls under this heading, yet since most famines are not caused by a food shortage but by a maldistribution of food, such relief to be effective would require interference in the famine-stricken country's national affairs, contrary to the insistence on complete national sovereignty by LDC proponents of a new order.

The theories of justice that have influenced defenders of the international economy's working over the last century or more have been entitlement theories. Such theories maintain that if the rules of the international economy are just, and that if they have been adhered to, then whatever the resulting distribution of income and wealth, it is just. If the rules have been unjust, as some LDCs argued, or they were not followed, then in principle restitution in the form of international resource transfers is due. Though many maintain otherwise, international history does not obviously imply that such restitution should be paid by developed to less developed countries. But concentration on international transfers diverts attention from both the sources of mutual gain in the international economy and from the springs of economic growth in less developed and developed countries.

## Notes

1. K.P. Sauvant, 'Towards the new international economic order', in K.P. Sauvant and H. Hasenpflug (eds), *The New International Economic Order*, Boulder, Col.: Westview Press (1977), p. 6.
2. Report of the Independent Commission on International Development Issues *North-South: A Programme for Survival*, London: Pan Books (1980), p. 11,

3. W.A. Lewis, *The Evolution of the International Economic Order*, Princeton, NJ: Princeton University Press (1978), p. 3.
4. H. Hasenpflug, 'The stabilization of export earnings in the Lomé Convention', in K.P. Sauvant and H. Hasenpflug (eds), op. cit.
5. C. Fred Bergsten, 'A new OPEC in bauxite', *Challenge* July/August (1976), pp. 12–20.
6. T.D. Willett, 'Major challenges to the international economic system', in R.C. Amacher, G. Haberler and T.D. Willett (eds), *Challenges to a Liberal International Economic Order*, Washington, DC: American Enterprise Institute (1979), pp. 38–9.
7. R.D. Erb, 'International resource transfers: the international financial system and foreign aid, in Amacher *et al.*, op. cit., pp. 398–9.
8. 'An accelerating drift towards protectionism', *Business Week*, 27 July (1981), pp. 22–5; and *The Economist*, 3 October 1981, p. 95.
9. D.E. Logue and R.J. Sweeney, *The Economics of the Law of the Sea Negotiations*. Los Angeles: International Institute for Economic Research (1977). I.G. Bulkley, *Who Gains from Deep Ocean Mining?*, Berkeley: Institute of International Studies, University of California, Berkeley (1979).
10. Lewis, op. cit., p. 37.
11. See, for example, D.S. Landes, *The Unbound Prometheus: Technological Change and Industrial Development in Western Europe from 1750 to Present*, London: Cambridge University Press (1969); and D.C. North and R.P. Thomas, *The Rise of the Western World*, Cambridge: Cambridge University Press (1973).
12. How much the meaning of 'liberal' has changed since 1850 is shown by the 'liberal' label attached to Rawls' theory'. B. Barry, *The Liberal Theory of Justice: A Critical Examination of the Principal Doctrines in A Theory of Justice by John Rawls*, Oxford: Claredon Press (1973).
13. J. Rawls, *A Theory of Justice*, Cambridge, Mass.: The Belknap Press of Harvard University Press (1971).
14. R. Amdur, 'Rawls theory of justice: domestic and international perspectives, *World Politics*, **29** (1977), pp. 438–61.
15. S. Kuznets, 'Aspects of post-world war II growth in less developed countries', in A.M. Tang, E.M. Westfield and J.E. Worley (eds), *Evolution, Welfare and Time in Economics: Essays in Honor of Nicholas Georgescu-Roegen*, Lexington, Mass.: Lexington (1976).
16. H.A. Turner, D. Jackson and F. Wilkinson, *Do Trade Unions Cause Inflation?* Cambridge: Cambridge University Press, 2nd edn (1975). This empirical argument, that the existing structure of rewards may be justified by their consequences is not to be confused with arguments about the justice of the rewards in entitlement theories of justice (discussed below), as A. Sen points out, 'Ethical issues in income distribution: national and international', in S. Grassman and E. Lundberg (eds), *The World Economic Order: Past and Prospects*. New York: St Martins Press (1981), p. 476.

17. A. Sen, 'Ingredients of famine analyses: availability and entitlements', *Quarterly Journal of Economics*, **96** (1981), pp. 433–64.
18. R. Nozick, *Anarchy, State and Utopia*, New York: Basic Books (1974), ch. 7.
19. R.A. Mundell, in A.L.K. Acheson, J.F. Chant and M.F.J. Prachowny (eds), *Bretton Woods Revisited*, Toronto: University of Toronto Press (1972).
20. D.B.H. Denoon, 'Facing the new international economic order', in D.H.B. Denoon (ed.), *The New International Economic Order: A U.S. Response*, New York: New York University Press (1979), p. 16.
21. R.N. Cooper, 'A new international order for mutual gain', *Foreign Policy*, Spring, **26** (1977), pp. 66–120. Much of the subsequent argument is taken from this paper.
22. C. Freeman and M. Jahoda (eds), *World Futures: The Great Debate*, London: Martin Robertson (1978). J.L. Simon, *The Ultimate Resource*, Princeton University Press (1981).
23. ibid., p. 61.
24. ibid., p. 153.
25. Cooper, loc. cit.
26. R. Jolly, 'Mutual interest and the implications for reform of the international economic order', in Grassman and Lundberg, op. cit., provides a more detailed analysis of the scope for co-operation in expanding the mutual benefits from the international economy.

# Index